FOOD IN HISTORY

REAY TANNAHILL

FOOD IN HISTORY

NEW, FULLY REVISED AND UPDATED EDITION

Crown Publishers, Inc.
New York

I should also, perhaps, remind readers that this is a history book, not a cookery book, and urge them not to experiment with the foods described herein. Anyone who chooses to eat unusual and unfamiliar foods may suffer harmful effects.

Published in the United States in 1989 by Crown Publishers, Inc.,
225 Park Avenue South,
New York, New York 10003.

Originally published in Great Britain by the Penguin Group.

CROWN is a trademark of Crown Publishers, Inc.

Manufactured in the United States of America

Library of Congress Cataloging-in-Publication Data
Tannahill, Reay.
  Food in history / Reay Tannahill.—New and rev. ed.
     p.   cm.
  Bibliography: p.
  Includes index.
  1. Food—History.   2. Dinners and dining.   I. Title.
GT2850.T34   1989
641.3'009—dc19   89-671
                                                                    CIP

ISBN 0-517-57186-2

2   4   6   8   10   9   7   5   3   1
First American Edition

For Shirley and John Curley

CONTENTS

PREFACE

When the idea of *Food in History* first occurred to me, I was mystified by the fact that no one had already written such a book. No one had written a world history of food across half a million years; no one had studied the question of how, over that same period, food and the search for it had influenced both human and historical development; no one had tried to correlate the information turned up by all the twentieth-century 'ologies' – archaeology and anthropology, biology, ecology, technology and zoology among them. During the next seven years I discovered why. It was not the kind of book anyone with a grain of sense or sanity would have embarked on (and in pre-word-processing days, too).

When it was published, however, it was received with the greatest generosity by reviewers and readers alike, and the sequel (if sequel it was) has been interesting. The *New York Times Book Review* said, 'Here at last is what may serve as the first textbook for what should become a new sub-discipline; call it Alimentary History I.' And it came to pass. Since 1973 there has been unprecedented academic interest in the subject and a spate of books on different aspects of it.

It may all be coincidence – and I suspect it is – but in view of the amount of illuminating new material that has become available over the last fifteen years, the time seemed right for a fully revised and updated edition of *Food in History*. From an authorial viewpoint it has been satisfying to find that some of the new material has provided factual back-up for conclusions that, in the first edition, were the product of a complex process of reasoning. Further, a number of books have appeared that fulfil the valuable function of bringing together information not normally accessible to Western historians. Two outstanding examples are Chang's *Food in Chinese Culture*, and *Bread and Salt: A social and economic history of food and drink in Russia*, by Smith and Christian. In this new edition of my own book I have been deeply indebted to both of them.

I have to emphasize, however, that *Food in History* remains what it was always intended to be – a panoramic survey designed for readers with a general, civilized interest in food. It is not for the dedicated gourmet, unless he (it is usually a he) recognizes the need to brush up on his sense of proportion; nor is it for the academic historian, except in so far as it supplies an overall context for his own more detailed perspectives.

It need scarcely be said that compressing half a million years of world food history into 400 pages has required ruthless discrimination and frequent resort to generalization. I have chosen to deal briefly with matters that I take most readers to be acquainted with, or that are satisfactorily documented elsewhere. Britain's diet until the 1960s, for example, is dealt with in exemplary fashion in Drummond and Wilbraham's *The Englishman's Food* and Burnett's *Plenty and Want*, while the growth of the American cuisine in its social context is elegantly covered in Furnas's history of *The Americans*, and there is a comprehensive (and somewhat chauvinistic) general history of food in Gottschalk's *Histoire de l'Alimentation*. I have also dealt briefly with subjects marginal to the main theme (the evolution of restaurants, for example), and others such as religious food taboos, the unifying influence of the family meal and the political nuances of hospitality, which, in the last analysis, are all more closely related to social psychology than to food.

If any reader should be disappointed to find that something of particular interest is missing from the pages that follow, I can only suggest recourse to the bibliography, adding a mild reminder that *Food in History* makes no claim to be other than a one-volume overview of a vast and fascinating field of study.

I should also, perhaps, remind readers that this is a history book, not a cookery book, and that I take no responsibility for the recipes quoted herein. Anyone who chooses to experiment with, for example, zamia bread, witchetty grubs or the rotten corn of the Maoris does so entirely at his or her own risk.

It would be impossible for me to list all the people who have answered my questions on food, history, anthropology, nutrition, ecology and a great variety of other subjects over the past years, and invidious to name only a few of them. But I must thank the many readers who wrote to me when *Food in History* first came out, giving me their own comments and recollections. To some of these – for reasons quite beyond my control – I was unable to reply personally; if they should happen to see this new edition, I hope they will accept my apologies and belated thanks.

I and my publishers are grateful to the following for permission to quote extracts from copyright works:

George Allen and Unwin Ltd for Arthur Waley's translations of *The Analects of Confucius* and *The Book of Songs* [*Shih ching*]; Clarendon Press for 'The Summons of the Soul' in David Hawkes' translation of the *Ch'u T'zu: The Songs of the South*; Mrs Anna Evans for Professor A. J. Arberry's 'A Baghdad Cookery-Book'; Miss Elizabeth Rosenbaum for *The Roman Cookery Book* by Barbara Flower and Elizabeth Rosenbaum, published by George G. Harrap and Co. Ltd; Rupert Hart-Davis Ltd for *Tibetan Marches* by André Migot; Loeb Classical Library (Harvard University Press: William Heinemann) for *The Deipnosophists* of Athenaeus and the *Natural History* of Pliny the Elder; Methuen and Co. Ltd and Random House Inc. for *My Voyage Around the World* by Francesco Carletti; Penguin Books Ltd for E. R. A. Sewter's translation of *The Alexiad of Anna Comnena*, Aubrey de Selincourt's translation of *The Histories of Herodotus*, E. V. Rieu's translation of *The Iliad* of Homer, and Ronald Latham's translation of *The Travels of Marco Polo*.

PROLOGUE

It is an obvious truth, all too often forgotten, that food is not only inseparable from the history of the human race, but basic to it. Without food there would be no human race, and no history.

For 50,000 years and more, humanity's quest for food has helped to shape the development of society. It has profoundly influenced population growth and urban expansion, dictated economic and political theory, expanded the horizons of commerce, inspired wars of dominion and precipitated the discovery of new worlds.

Food has played a part in religion, helping to define the separateness of one creed from another by means of dietary taboos; in science, where the prehistoric cook's observations laid the foundations of early chemistry; in technology, where the water wheel first used for milling grain became a tool of the industrial revolution; in medicine, which was based largely on dietary principles until well into the eighteenth century and is becoming so again today; in war, where battles were postponed until the harvest was gathered in, and well-fed armies usually defeated hungry ones; in class distinctions, where a man's quality and status were judged by the food on his table; and even in relations between peoples, where for 12,000 years there has been a steady undercurrent of antagonism between vegetarians and meat-eaters.

All this is undeniable, and yet . . .

In the late twentieth century, after more than 50,000 years of fully human intellectual and technological development – when chips of mineral from the earth have been taught to do the work of the human brain, when cruising in space and blowing up the world are among the commonplaces of international discussion – it is still possible for an estimated two million people in Africa to die in a few months from lack of food; possible for the entire economy of Europe to be distorted by the farm price of butter; for Thailand to be impoverished by a feedstuffs war between cassava root and barley; for wheat farmers in Australia to be driven bankrupt by subsidies paid to their competitors on the other side of the world; even for the Great American Hamburger to come under threat because the Russian harvest fails.

Food remains as essential – and as divisive – as it has ever been, and the comfortable belief that the world's diet is no longer at the mercy of nature and human ignorance is not as solidly founded as it might seem. History shows that, despite all the long millennia of human development, it is only the social context that has changed . . .

— PART ONE —

THE PREHISTORIC WORLD

Until 12,000 years ago Homo and Femina sapiens were little more than successful predators who lived according to the law of the wild and survived because they were well adapted to it. Although they knew how to fight, how to make tools and clothing, how to paint pictures on the walls of their caves, even how to cook, they had no more influence on the rest of the world than the lion, wolf or jackal. What self-preservation and the quest for food had done during millions of years of evolution had been to transform a particular family of apes into two-legged super-animals. What the next 7,000 years were to do – the years of the Neolithic Revolution, when the new super-animals learned how to cultivate plants and tame their fellow animals – was set them off on an independent course that was to change the face of the earth and the life of almost everything upon it.

— I —

IN THE BEGINNING

In the very earliest times nature was in charge and the problem of the food supply was a good deal simpler than it is now – although perhaps it would be wiser to say 'must have been simpler', since there are as many theories about prehistory and the pattern of human evolution as there are theoreticians. Most, however, agree that the search for food was, at every stage, a crucial factor.

The currently held view is that the ape-into-man transmutation began somewhere between 10 and 4 million years ago, after a shifting of the earth's plates brought about a change in climate. Tropical zones became temperate, jungles thinned out, and vegetation became seasonal. Tree-dwelling apes, deprived of their year-round supply of fruits and nuts, gradually ventured out into the grasslands, where they found not only roots and seeds, but lizards and porcupines, tortoises, ground squirrels, moles, insects and grubs.

And so human history began, in the pursuit of food that was to fuel so much subsequent development.

As time passed the ground-dwelling apes made specific adjustments to suit their new environment. They learned to kill or stun what they hunted by throwing stones at it, a technique that encouraged them to move on three, and then two, legs instead of four. Their wits became sharper and their brains larger as they competed with the lion, hyena and sabre-toothed cat that shared their hunting grounds. Their teeth, no longer a primary weapon, changed shape, which ultimately led to the development of human speech. And their forefeet adapted into hands capable of making and using tools. By somewhere around 2 million years ago (or possibly earlier) the first hominids, more ape than man, had developed into *Homo erectus*, more man than ape.

The best-known specimen of *Homo erectus* – and the first real personality in history – was Peking Man, who lived about half a million years ago. Fragmentary relics of other human ancestors, reputedly dating from much earlier periods (7.5 million years earlier in the case of one skull found in Yunnan), have been dug up in recent years in Africa and Asia, but all of them – even the half-skeleton folksily known as Lucy[1] – exist in a kind of anthropological vacuum. The fragments show that they lived, but not how they lived.

Peking Man, however, was a hunter and cave dweller and recognizably human. Only five feet tall, he still looked very much like an ape, though an ape that had developed the broad nose and high cheekbones that have characterized the Mongoloid and northern Chinese races ever since. The residues found in his caves showed that 70 per cent of his diet consisted of venison (*Sinomegaceros pachyosteus*, to be exact) and the other 30 per cent of whatever he was able to hunt or trap – otter, boar and wild sheep, buffalo, rhinoceros, even tiger.

But Peking Man's greatest claim to fame is that – although a number of antecedents have been mooted, some of them dating (arguably) from as much as a million years earlier – he is still the first member of the almost-human race who is *known* to have made use of fire. No more than 'made use of', however; there is no proof that he knew how to light it, and it is unlikely that he had learned how to cook. If he had, he would not have had to crack the bones of his food animals to get at the marrow, which, hot, could have been scooped out with relative ease.[2]

Knowledge of how to control fire came some time later – no one can be sure when – but the light and warmth it provided must have had a powerful effect on the humanizing process. There were other benefits, too. When the earth's orbital geometry changed and the ice sheets advanced, as they sometimes did, as far south as present-day London, New York and Kiev, the new breed of humans did not have to flee before them, but were able to stay on the fringes, adjusting their diet and their hunting techniques to suit the conditions. Preying on huge, cold-resistant animals like the woolly mammoth was a fresh challenge, necessitating a close cooperation on the hunt that must have reinforced the social links forged in the sanctuary of the cave.

New conditions continued to breed new kinds of people until, at the beginning of another cold spell in about 75,000 BC, there appeared on the prehistoric scene a group of *Homo sapiens* (the larger-brained successor of *Homo erectus*) known as Neanderthals, familiar today less for their anthropological interest than because they have become a twentieth-century cartoon cliché.

Were the Neanderthals true ancestors of modern man or an evolutionary dead end? It is a fertile source of disagreement among experts. But whether their clumsy figures represented physiological adaptation to climate or were a sign that they suffered either from the vitamin-D deficiency disease of rickets or from some congenital venereal affliction,[3] they had become skilled hunters, evolved their own rites and rituals, perfected a primitive surgical technique and begun to care for the sick and aged. Even so, like their predecessors at Peking, they were prepared to dine on their fellow humans when other meat was scarce.

Much of the mystery of evolution vanishes with the arrival of the more advanced peoples who supplanted the Neanderthals in about 30,000 BC. From that point on, the academic debate shifts from the minutiae of human biology to the problem of changes in the environment and how men and women adjusted to them. From that point, also, it becomes possible to build up a theoretical, if largely unverifiable, picture of what life and food were like in the 20,000 years that preceded the series of world-changing developments collectively known as the Neolithic Revolution.

2

FOOD AND COOKING BEFORE 10,000 BC

Whether or not life in prehistoric times was nasty and brutish, it was certainly short.* It is estimated that, prey to extreme cold, vitamin deficiencies, seasonal malnutrition and food poisoning, as well as all the other hazards of a primitive and predatory existence, nineteen out of twenty Neanderthals were dead by the time they were 40; ten of them by the age of 20.[1]

Even the Neanderthals' better fed and more comfortably placed successors lived very little longer. Nor did they have much choice in the matter of what they ate, although in many areas there was a kind of notional variety in the diet – meat from hunting; fish from the rivers and, later, the sea coasts; 'vegetables' in the form of wild plants. Where the weather or the terrain was inhospitable, however, the clans had to reconcile themselves to dependence on a single animal; in prehistoric France it was the reindeer. (Much later, in the grasslands of North and South America, the migrations of the bison and guanaco were to shape the calendar of the hunter's year; while some of the Eskimo in modern times have ordered their lives according to the habits of the caribou.)

The hunting-fishing-gathering groups led a marginally more settled existence than those forced to follow the herds, though even they needed two bases – a home cave on low-lying ground for the winter and a summer camp site in the uplands, where the lush new pastures attracted wild deer, sheep and goats.† There seems little doubt that the mixed-diet groups preferred meat when they could get it, if only

---

* As it has been through most of human history. Not until AD 1800 could the average woman expect to live beyond 50; men who escaped or survived war usually outlived their womenfolk by two or three years.

† *Plus ça change* . . . In Victorian times, crofting wives and daughters in the Scottish Highlands were still setting off annually with the community's cows, sheep and goats (tamed by now) for a three-months' sojourn in the upland pastures. The same custom persisted until even more recently in Norway, Switzerland and other mountainous countries.

because the average wild animal provided more sustenance for more people than any other kind of food.

HUNTING

Though extreme youth or old age may have been no great obstacle when it came to fishing or plant collecting, only the strongest and most active members of the community qualified as hunters, especially when the climate was harsh or game scarce. Most hunters were

Prehistoric hunters knew many tricks. One may have been to disguise themselves in skins, as nineteenth-century Amerindians did.

probably men, because although in theory a young and healthy woman should have been able to hunt just as successfully as a young and healthy man, it was woman the child-bearer who suffered most in prehistoric conditions. Young she might be, but healthy she was not. Modern research has also discovered that man's generally superior ability in judging distance and throwing accurately is genetically sex-linked in a way that suggests it must have conferred an advantage that worked primarily through the male.[2] Woman had different talents that were put to different food-gathering uses.

The skills needed for hunting were formidable. Sending a flint-tipped spear through the quarry's eye into its brain, homing a missile on the vital spot on its skull, crippling it with a slash through the heel tendons – these were techniques that demanded swift reactions and absolute coordination of hand and eye. A talent for stealth was needed, too, to avoid alerting the quarry to danger. It is even possible that the late prehistoric hunter, expert on animals as he was, may have learned from experience what science was later to confirm, that an animal placid at the moment of slaughter provides sweeter meat than one that is nervous or exhausted.*

It is interesting to speculate on how much game the hunters would have had to bring home to keep a group of, say, forty people alive in an icy climate when other food was scarce. At least two pounds of boneless meat per adult per day must have been needed, and by that reckoning a mature modern bull – weighing something like three-quarters of a ton on the hoof – would have supplied enough to feed the group for about ten days. His wild ancestor, very much smaller and bonier, may have provided enough for only three or four days.

The mammoth, the musk-ox and the bison were more substantial, so substantial that transporting them back to the cave would have presented as much of a problem as killing them in the first place. One mammoth carcass, after boning, represented more than a ton of meat – something like a month's food supply. What the hunters did, there-fore, was drag the carcasses to a secluded spot nearby, the 'kill-site', and carve them up there and then, discarding most of the bones and waste material and reducing the rest to manageable proportions.

This helps to explain the otherwise inexplicable results of a number of archaeological digs. In the Zagros Mountains of Iran, for example, a study of seventeen 'residential' sites covering a period of 30,000 years came up with no more than 6,000 identifiable bones from the smaller food animals. Granted, the human population was thin at the time (averaging out at one person to every thirty-one square miles,[3] but, even so, 6,000 bones would represent just one mutton cutlet

---

* The muscular tissue of animals contains a small amount of glycogen that breaks down at death into other substances, including a preservative, lactic acid. But physical or nervous tension before death uses up much of the glycogen and so reduces the amount of lactic acid that can be produced.

shared between the entire population every five years. A great many more bones must still remain scattered and buried at countless undiscovered kill-sites.

There is no way of knowing when people first began to notice that raw meat became tenderer and tastier if it were kept for a period of three or four weeks after slaughter (until, in today's phrase, it was 'well hung'), but considering the cold, the kill-sites and mammoth meat by the ton, conditions during the glacial eras were certainly propitious.

They were propitious, too, to the discovery of freezing, even if any such discovery was forgotten again as the climate improved. Hunters who delayed in returning to the kill-site for a second load of mammoth meat would find it frozen or, at the very least, well chilled. It would also be in better condition than meat kept in the warmth of the cave (unless, as was perfectly possible, smoking had been discovered), and the likelihood of the hunters recognizing the connection – even if they put it down to beneficence on the part of the ice god – should not be ruled out. Even freeze-drying may have been known during the 10,000 years between 30,000 and 20,000 BC, when harsh, flaying winds swept over much of the northern hemisphere.

'May have ... could have ... perhaps ... possibly ...' It is all highly speculative. But it is a mistake to dismiss such possibilities on the assumption that the first humans were, *ipso facto*, not very bright. The brain of early *Homo sapiens* was just as large, if not as experienced, as that of modern man. A surprising number of modern inventions and discoveries, especially those to do with survival and everyday living, can be traced back unequivocally to the earliest days of recorded history, and the development of others was frustrated only by lack of technology. In some cases, all that the nineteenth and twentieth centuries have done is identify the scientific factors that enable ancient ideas and techniques to be successfully translated into practice – not just sometimes, but always.

FISHING

When they were near a river, post-Ice-Age humans took a club or spear to basking monsters like the pike, and trapped smaller fish by damming the water with upright stakes or laced branches. On the coasts they made use of easily collected molluscs and shellfish.

It may have been the hunters' habit of laying bait that suggested the idea of fishing with a lure. Thorns made the earliest hooks, but in the

Dordogne by 25,000 BC the 'fish gorge' had been invented, a short, baited toggle with a line attached. When the fish took the bait, the fisherman pulled the line taut and the gorge became wedged at an angle in its jaws. A more familiar fishhook, tough and flexible, was developed during the following millennia as techniques of working with bone and horn improved.

By about 12,000 BC harpoons had been added to the fisherman's armoury in France and Spain, and soon afterwards the introduction into Europe of the bow and arrow (invented either in Central Asia around 13,000 BC or in Africa as early as 46,000 BC[4]) gave fishermen as well as hunters an invaluable new weapon. The power and range of the bow and the number of arrows that could be carried (solving the marksman's problem of risking the loss of harpoon or spear on a difficult shot) made it as revolutionary in its way as gunpowder was to be in medieval times.

Fishing for large catches round the coasts had to wait until humanity felt able to venture into rough waters with a reasonable expectation of surviving. The dugout canoe and reed raft of prehistoric times were of limited reliability, and those settlers, for example, who landed in Australia as early as 28,000 BC must have counted themselves lucky to arrive. Having crossed at least twenty-five miles of sea to get there, they would have no certainty of being able to get back again.

During the Neolithic era, however, oars were perfected. Inshore fishing had begun by about 8000 BC, and fishing nets made from twisted fibre, hair, or thongs had been invented.

GATHERING

While the men and boys went hunting, and the elders of the tribe occupied themselves with making tools, brewing medicinal potions, and instructing the infants, it was the women's task to collect such other foodstuffs as were to be found – snails, small turtles, edible roots, greens, acorns, nuts and berries – according to season and the region in which the clan lived.

Gathering did not depend, as hunting did, on distance assessment or marksmanship but on other talents more common among women than men. Research shows that women see better in dim light and have sharper hearing,[5] faculties that would be useful when searching for desirable plants in shady corners or tracking small game through the undergrowth.

Hunting was a flamboyant business – the drama of the chase and the return in triumph are still enshrined today in the ceremonial of many primitive tribes – whereas gathering depended on quiet patience and the kind of perseverance that was continuous rather than (as with hunting) sporadic. But though there might be little excitement in the task, the foodstuffs women collected were more than just supplementary to meat. When the hunting was poor, they were what everyone depended on.

This was particularly true in the Americas, where, over a period of 10,000 years, the combined depredations of nature and the first humans to arrive on the continent left only a handful of food animals. Human colonization there may well have taken place in two waves* – with the first wave reaching Brazil 30,000 years ago.[6] The second, much larger wave arrived during the millennia following 14,000 BC, by which time the hunter's weapons were of advanced design. His spirited pursuit of game – from Siberia to Alaska, and then southwards – led to the extermination of several indigenous species; the mammoth was wiped out, and the horse and, by 9000 BC, the giant sloth. Changes in climate did the rest when, 2,000 years later, the retreat of the glaciers opened up a north–south corridor over the country and exposed land formerly protected by the ice mountains to a wind direct from the Arctic. In the prairie provinces the giant bison, the mastodon and the camel fell victim to the sudden drop in temperature.

As a result of all this, the descendants of the first Americans had little choice but to rely on the primitive forerunners of vegetables like the potato, the cush-cush yam and the sweet varieties of manioc, which, protected by the soil, survived even the Arctic winds. It is impossible to know when human beings first began to dig for their food as well as gathering surface plants, but in Europe the wild ancestors of turnips, onions and radishes were used in prehistoric times, and what we now think of as flower bulbs may also have played a part in the diet. In the 5,000 years of recorded history the rhizomes of the Canna lily and the roots of the lotus, asphodel and Solomon's Seal have all been eaten with evident relish.

Other vegetables with a history stretching back into the most distant past include several members of the cabbage family, and prehistoric gatherers are believed also to have collected willow and birch shoots, young nettles, ferns, and waterweeds, and possibly mushrooms and

* Academic debate about how early the first Americans arrived has been going on for over a century.

other fungi.* There is sound evidence for the claim that beans, lentils and chick-peas in various wild forms were gathered in the Near East and parts of Europe, as well as in Central America, where there were maize and squash also.

Naturally enough, women also scooped up any small animal life that came their way. When the men's hunting was successful, they may have turned a blind eye to such dubious delights as snails – unjustified, as yet, by the invention of garlic butter – but things began to change in the Near East somewhere around 20,000 BC.

Anthropologists, taking as evidence the fact that the tribes began trapping or gathering a much wider variety of foods than before – river crabs, fresh-water mussels, partridges and migratory water fowl among them – believe that there was a sudden increase in the human population that began to put pressure on food resources. Perhaps there was, but it may simply have been that humans were acquiring more adventurous tastes and the knowledge of how to satisfy them.

One of the recurring hazards of trying to illuminate corners of the past about which little is known is that it is easy to over-value the little that *is* known, and the human menu is a shifting foundation on which to base any but the most general theories. Later history, in fact, shows that in times of shortage people are often inclined to become more, rather than less conservative about their diet, and that a willingness to try unfamiliar food is as likely to be a sign of plenty as of scarcity.

THE EARLY DEVELOPMENT OF COOKING

For hundreds of thousands of years the evolving human race had eaten its food raw, but at some time between the first deliberate use of fire – in Africa in 1,400,000 BC or Asia in 500,000 BC (depending on which theory happens to be flavour of the month)– and the appearance of the Neanderthals on the prehistoric scene, cooking was discovered.

Whether or not it came as a gastronomic revelation can only be guessed at, but since heat helps to release protein and carbohydrate as well as break down fibre, cooking increases the nutritive value of many foods and makes edible some that would otherwise be inedible.

* In later history it was not unknown for mushrooms to be almost a staple food – in nineteenth-century Russia, for example, and also in Tierra del Fuego. Charles Darwin remarked of the latter that, 'with the exception of a few berries, chiefly of the dwarf arbutus, the natives eat no vegetable food beside this fungus.'[7]

Improved health must certainly have been one result of the discovery of cooking, and it has even been argued, by the late Carleton Coon, that cooking was 'the decisive factor in leading man from a primarily animal existence into one that was more fully human'.*⁸

Whatever the case, by all the laws of probability roasting must have been the first method used, its discovery accidental. The concept of roast meat could scarcely have existed without knowledge of cooking, nor the concept of cooking without knowledge of roast meat.

Charles Lamb's imaginary tale of the discovery of roast pork is not, perhaps, too far off the mark. A litter of Chinese piglets, some stray sparks from the fire, a dwelling reduced to ashes, an unfamiliar but interesting smell, a crisp and delectable assault on the taste buds . . .

Taken back a few millennia and relocated in Europe this would translate into a piece of mammoth, venison or something of the sort falling in the campfire and having to be left there until the flames died down. But however palatable a sizzling steak in ice-age conditions, the shrinkage that results from direct roasting would scarcely recommend itself to the hard-worked hunter, so that a natural next step, for tough roots as for meat, would be slower cooking in the embers or on a flat stone by the side of the fire.

And what then? Did development stop dead at this stage until cooking pots were invented? Archaeology suggests that it did. There are, however, several ways of cooking – all of them attested from later times – that would leave few, if any, distinctive archaeological traces.

The ancestor of the modern chicken brick could have suggested itself when people discovered that a piglet that had been rolling in the mud, as piglets do, made a more succulent roast than its cleaner kin. Where vegetation was lush, a wrapping of large leaves may have been used to protect meat from the flames; it is a technique still practised in tribal areas today.† And spit-roasting was probably discovered by hungry, spear-carrying hunters, far from home, who knew that cut-up meat cooked faster than the same meat in one piece.

* While this is a tempting proposition for the food historian, it is based on the premise that humans could not get down to developing a culture until they were released from the need to spend hours every day chewing tough meat – whereas any deskbound sandwich-eater today knows that working and chewing tough meat are by no means mutually exclusive occupations.
† Not only in New Guinea, but in Paris, London and New York. The tribes of *cuisine minceur* have even elevated leaf-wrapping into a cult, although the leaves – vine, spinach or cabbage – are designed to hold a stuffing together rather than protect it from direct heat.

It is possible, too, that there were ovens (of a kind) as early as 25,000 BC. During excavations at Dolní Věstonice in Moravia some years ago what was unquestionably an oven was found containing, not food (or any evidence of it) but over 2,000 lumps of fire-baked clay – tiny models of animal heads, bodies and feet.[9] In the Ukraine, however, several small pits of roughly the shape and size of a cylindrical beanpot have been found dug in the earth surrounding the hearth, and these are believed to have been specifically food ovens.[10] The assumption is that leaf-wrapped food was put to cook in them on a bed of hot embers; it would emerge more steamed than baked.*

Although the accidental discovery of roasting would have been perfectly feasible in the primitive world, boiling was a more sophisticated proposition.

According to conventional wisdom, prehistoric man went to a good deal of trouble for his boiled dinner. First he dug a large pit in the ground and lined it with flat, overlapping stones to prevent seepage. Then he poured in large quantities of water, presumably transported in skin bags. Other stones were heated in the campfire and man-handled by some unspecified means (possibly on the bat-and-ball principle) into the water to bring it to a simmer. The food was then added and, while it was cooking, more hot stones were tipped in from time to time to keep the water at the desired temperature.

It is possible. There is no law that says things have to be done the easy way, and the method is still used by modern tribals.† But, in terms of discovery, it makes sense only if the idea evolved, imitatively, in some isolated part or parts of the world blessed with hot springs – as in New Zealand's North Island. Hot water being a rare natural phenomenon, both idea and method would subsequently have to be disseminated by migrating tribes – which could explain why there is no indication of the technique being used before 5000 BC.

One reason for the anthropological popularity of the pit-boiling theory is the belief that until the advent of pottery, cooking potential was severely restricted; that, lacking containers that were both heat-proof and waterproof, boiling was impossible except by the pit method. But this is not the case. Several perfectly viable alternative

---

* This technique still survives – on a somewhat larger scale and utilizing seaweed rather than leaves – in the clambake.

† However, despite anthropologists' claims to the contrary, the fact that modern 'Stone Age tribals' use it is no proof at all that it was used in the real Stone Age.

containers had been available for thousands of years, and the *idea* of boiling could well have been suggested by the fact that when meat or vegetables with a high water content were crammed into one of these containers over the fire, they sweated out an appetizing liquid.

In many parts of the world large mollusc or reptile shells were used for cooking in, as they still were on the Amazon in the nineteenth century, when the naturalist Henry Walter Bates sampled a dish made from the entrails of the turtle, 'chopped up and made into a delicious soup called *sarapatel*, which is generally boiled in the concave upper shell of the animal'.[11]

In Asia the versatile bamboo supplied hollow sections of stem that could be stoppered with clay at one end, filled with chopped-up raw ingredients and a little liquid, then stoppered again at the other. The method is still used in Indonesia today.

In the Tehuacan Valley of Central America, in about 7000 BC, the people who lived in rock shelters and gathered wild maize for their food had already begun to use stone cooking pots. These, once made, were sited in the centre of the hearth and, too heavy to move, left there permanently.

And long before the advent of pottery and bronze there was one kind of container that was widely distributed, naturally waterproof, and heatproof enough to be hung over, if not in, the fire. This was an animal stomach.

Hunters in Palaeolithic times seem to have regarded the highly perishable parts of their quarry (heart, liver, brains, the fat behind the eyeballs, and some of the soft internal organs) as their own special prize, and may also have relished the partially digested stomach contents,* as the aborigines of southern China did during the T'ang period, and Eskimos until almost the present day.[12]

With the advent of cooking, the notion of simmering the contents of the stomach in the stomach-bag itself would emerge quite naturally, and the same container ultimately came to be used for less esoteric foods.

There are occasional references to it in the later literature of many countries. In the fifth century BC, according to Herodotus, the nomad Scythians 'put all the flesh into an animal's paunch, mix water with it,

---

* In cud-chewing animals, digestion begins in the rumen, the largest of four stomachs – honeycombed with muscle and familiar in the kitchen as 'tripe' – where partial fermentation takes place (giving a certain piquancy to the contents).

and boil it like that over the bone-fire. The bones burn very well, and the paunch easily contains all the meat once it has been stripped off.* In this way an ox, or any other sacrificial beast, is ingeniously made to boil itself.'[13]

In the eighteenth century AD the system still had its uses. The American explorer Samuel Hearne found that a dish called beatee was 'handy to make'. This was 'a kind of haggis† made with blood, a good quantity of fat shred small, some of the tenderest of the flesh, together with the heart and lungs of the animal, cut or torn into small slivers, all of which is put into the stomach and roasted by being suspended before the fire with a string . . . It is a most delicious morsel, even without pepper, salt or any seasoning.'[15] He added that it was important not to overfill the paunch, otherwise it might burst during cooking.

By about 13,000 BC leatherworking techniques had improved so much that skins had come to replace many of the older containers. After skins came pottery, which was succeeded by bronze and then iron, from which most cooking pots continued to be made until the twentieth century.

THE MATERIALS OF REVOLUTION

Over the first few million years food had played its part in the making of the human race. Now it was to make history, and never more decisively than in the 7,000 years between 10,000 and 3000 BC, the gestation period of modern civilization.

Climatic changes were again the catalyst. In about 11,000 BC the ice began to shrink towards the north for the last time (so far). Cold-climate animals like the reindeer – and the peoples who depended on them – drifted after it, following the mosses and ferns that grew around its fringes. Others remained behind, the smaller ones flourishing on the margins of the forests that began to spring up. Under the influence of warm winds the vegetational pattern of the temperate zones began to change.

Most of this had happened before, and more than once, during the

---

* The rumen of a twentieth-century cow has a capacity of 30 to 40 gallons.
† The modern haggis is a slightly different beast, the sheep's-stomach container substituting less for a cooking pot than a dumpling cloth. Attitudes to the Scots version vary widely. One Inverness take-away packs it with curry and chips, whereas a five-star Singapore hotel prices it, at just under £11 a serving, second only to Russian caviar and king prawns.[14]

course of human evolution. But this time it was decisive, because this time the right people were in the right place, and at the right stage of intellectual development. Not only had all the basic human skills been mastered, but women had learned much of what they needed to know about plants, and men about animals.

There is little doubt that, from the millennia of gathering vegetables and fruits, women had discovered that it was sometimes possible to exert an active influence on plant growth. Given the right time of year and a modicum of good luck, an undersized turnip or radish put back into the ground would continue to swell; a single clove of garlic or a shallot would multiply into a cluster.

More important in the light of what was to come, the annual routine of moving from lowland caves in winter to upland pastures in summer must have taught them that some kinds of plant sprang from seed. In the hills the luxuriant growth sprouting from the previous year's refuse piles – which were, in effect, natural compost heaps – would be very apparent, and the discovery of a few stray plantlets with the casings still clinging to their seed-leaves would tell its own story. At first, the refuse heap itself may have been regarded as possessing magical properties (which, in a way, it did) and early experiments in agriculture may have been restricted to raising the more valued healing herbs. The likelihood is that wide, rippling fields of grain were beyond the scope of the Palaeolithic imagination; grass seeds, after all, were still used only as seasonings. But the knowledge of plant cultivation must have been there, waiting for the particular combination of conditions that would spark off the world's first agricultural revolution.

Man, like woman, also possessed much hard-won knowledge and had already embarked on the animal-taming process that was to lead to the second major development of the Neolithic era.

Even before the glaciers retreated from Europe, he had begun to come to terms with the reindeer. Feeding on the mosses and ferns that flourished on land watered by melting ice, the reindeer suffered from salt deficiency and instinctively compensated for it by making periodic excursions either to the seashore or to inland salt licks; even a sprinkling of human urine helped to satisfy its need.[16] Men, using this readily available substance as bait, began to entice the reindeer to the vicinity of their caves and even began building up the interdependence that was to play such a vital role in the subsequent domestication of animals.

Ultimately, the reindeer – like the gazelle in regions further east –

proved resistant to full domestication, but man's experience with it suggested the possibility of exerting a measure of control over the prey he was in the habit of hunting.

There was one animal that had already become a trusted companion in the millennia before the Neolithic period. Being a meat eater (even a man eater when opportunity offered), the small Asiatic wolf must at first have been seen as a competitor and therefore an enemy, but the cub is a gregarious little beast during its first six weeks of life and readily responds to human control. Domestication of the animal that became known to later history as the dog seems to have taken place as early as 11,000 BC.

Though his wild ancestors had served humanity as food animals (and though his tamed successors were to do so, too), the dog was more useful to prehistoric man alive than dead. His speed, hearing, sense of smell and hunting instinct supplemented his master's skills and incalculably increased his efficiency. And, certainly, without the aid of the first sheepdog, man's early experiments in the herding of other animals might well have proved abortive.

3

CHANGING THE FACE OF THE EARTH

The Neolithic 'Revolution'– no revolution in the violent sense, but a period of gradual change from a hunting-fishing-gathering existence to that of settled farmer and stockbreeder – took place at different times in different parts of the world, but until the improbable day when the entire surface of the earth has been excavated no one will ever be sure where or when it really began; perhaps not even then. As one expert in the prehistory of rice cultivation feelingly puts it, 'Uncertainties or deficiencies in history, archaeology, biogeography, anthropology, philology and biosystematics obscure the date and place.'[1]

It used to be held that there were two clearly defined heartland regions – one to the west and south-west of the Caspian Sea, the other in Central America – but this view has come increasingly under attack in recent years as new sites have been excavated in areas such as Thailand, which were formerly thought of as backwaters. Not all of the new sites are early, although some of them (notably in Iran and Syria) may overlie evidence of earlier periods, and some of the early sites are not necessarily as early as, in the first flush of enthusiasm, they are claimed to be. It is not unusual, in the publicity given to new discoveries, for dates to be mentioned that prove (after rather less well publicized laboratory tests) to be out by as much as 2,000 or 3,000 years.

In effect, a century of intensive field research has produced a large number of undisputed facts and almost as many disputable theories masquerading as facts. It is helpful sometimes to be reminded that archaeology, anthropology, palaeontology and palaeobotany are no more exact sciences than history itself, and that the experts are human and fallible just like the rest of us. As with theories about the origins of the human race, theories about the origins and progress of the Neolithic come and go, and none of them is gospel.

What follows in this chapter, therefore, like much of what has gone before, is an amalgam of ascertainable fact, human probability and deductions drawn from the wider historical context. The reader who has no patience with what is known in the groves of academe as 'informed speculation' is recommended to move on to the next chapter without delay.

THE BEGINNINGS OF AGRICULTURE

Despite growing doubts about its primary role, the Near East remains the most intensively studied area in the Neolithic world, and it is reasonable to suppose that the overall pattern may not have been very different elsewhere, even if the dates in south-east Asia ultimately prove to have been earlier.*

There are three frequently canvassed theories about the origins of the Neolithic in the Near East. One holds that it developed almost imperceptibly as a natural sequel to (unspecified) social and cultural changes at the end of the Palaeolithic era. The second, that an increase in the food supply became urgent because of an (unverifiable) population explosion. The third, that changing climatic conditions were the catalyst.

It is the third theory, relevant throughout the northern hemisphere, that best stands up to examination. The argument goes like this.

The mellowing climate after about 12,000 BC (by which time the glaciers were well on the retreat) resulted in conditions that favoured fast-growing plants. In winter cool moist air from the Mediterranean helped to stimulate early growth, while summer brought hot, dry, parching winds from Eurasia and Arabia. Grassy plants that could grow, mature and seed themselves before the arrival of the hot weather flourished at the expense of slow developers, so that fields of wild wheat and barley came into being on favourable land.[2]

The archaeologist J. R. Harlan was able to find fields of wild grain as dense as cultivated ones even in the mid-1960s, when, with a flint-bladed sickle, he set out to discover what an early Neolithic family in Turkey might have expected to harvest if they had worked hard at it. In an hour he gathered enough to produce over two pounds of cleaned grain, which was, incidentally, twice as rich in protein as the domesticated variety. He estimated that in a three-week harvesting period

* The question of who was first is of only marginal importance in prehistoric terms, since epoch-making discoveries did not, as now, become the property of the whole world in a matter of hours. In regions where the topography permitted, discoveries were disseminated by word of mouth. Elsewhere, they emerged independently.

a family of six could have reaped enough wild wheat to provide them with just under a pound of grain per head per day for a whole year.[3]

It used to be thought that the scattered early Neolithic peoples did not begin to congregate in villages until they learned that cultivating grain, as distinct from merely gathering the wild variety, needed a large labour force. Harlan's experiment, however, suggests otherwise. One of the characteristics of wild grains is that as soon as the plant reaches maturity, the ear shatters and sprays its seeds out to burrow in the soil for protection until the next growing season. Sometimes, if the weather is hotter than usual, a field of mature grain can turn to a field of barren stalks in as little as a week.

If all this free food was to be gathered, therefore, people had to be on the spot at the right time, which meant when the ears ripened; sooner, probably, but on no account later. Settlements, at first just open-air camps, are thought to have grown up around the fields in readiness for the moment of harvest.

But the harvest, even when successfully gathered, was not the end of the story. First, the mountains of stalks cut by Harlan's imaginary family of six would have to be reduced to manageable proportions by threshing and winnowing, a time-consuming task that would tie them to the camp for weeks. Then, in an era before the draught animal or the wheel, the cleaned grain had to be transported – well over a ton of it – to the home cave, which might be as much as fifty miles away. Ice age hunters had solved the same kind of problem by making several journeys, leaving what they were unable to carry in some temporary private cache, but private caches must have been at a premium when the Near East began to fill up with humanity.

In the end, instead of moving the food to their dwellings, the early Neolithic tribes began to move their dwellings to the food. By 9000 BC at such places as Mallaha in northern Israel there were settled villages sustained by a combination of hunting and intensive gathering.

Over the next 2,000 years, by almost imperceptible stages, gathering developed into cultivating. The villagers discovered after a while that if they were too efficient at harvesting the wild grain, the following year's crop would be drastically reduced. Then they learned to leave some of the ears on the stalks, with better but patchy results. When they took the next logical step and began to scatter some of their carefully collected seeds evenly, by hand, over the soil, they ceased to be gatherers and became farmers.

Early Grain Usage

Humanity's sudden and extensive dependence on grain, whether from wild or cultivated fields, raises several interesting questions, among them – what did they do with it all? Certainly, they did not eat it raw; in this form it would not only be difficult to swallow but would satisfy hunger only at the cost of acute inner discomfort, raw grain and the human digestive system being incompatible.

Some of it may conceivably have been used in germinated form. By Neolithic times people must have known from experience that grain that had begun to sprout did not have the same ill effects as dry grain,* and they may, to begin with, have considered the new fields as not much more than a source of material for the wild wheat or barley equivalents of beansprouts.

But sprouts as a supplementary food are one thing; as the mainstay of the diet they would be quite another. On a purely practical basis, germinating seeds entails keeping them moist and evenly spread to inhibit the formation of moulds, so that, if they are to be grown in quantity, a good deal of space and a large number of containers are needed. For this reason, if no other, sprouted grain could scarcely be considered a viable proposition, either as a basic foodstuff or in the wider context of bread and beer making, until containers became more easily available with the advent of pottery.†

If dry seeds and crunchy grainsprouts were not important enough to move home for, the peoples of the early Neolithic period must have evolved some other means of dealing with their desirable but intractable material, a means that involved cooking. Porridge/gruel and pit-boiling, say the archaeologists. And only after careful – indeed, extremely irksome – preparation.

The desirable part of wheat and barley consists of an embryo (the nutritionally valuable 'germ') embedded in a starchy mass called the endosperm, to which is attached a thin, tough coat of bran. This

---

* In the process of germination the starch content of the seed – indigestible in raw grain – is converted into digestible malt sugar. Some of the carbohydrate is converted into valuable quantities of vitamins B and C, and smaller amounts of A, E and K, and proteins are broken down into their constituent amino acids.

† One anthropologist has recently suggested that the primary Neolithic interest in grain was as a source of beer rather than food – an enticing hypothesis, except for this same problem of containers.[4]

whole seed unit is encased in a harsh outer sheath, the chaff, and tufts of the sheathed seeds, protected by further shells of chaff, make up the ear of grain.

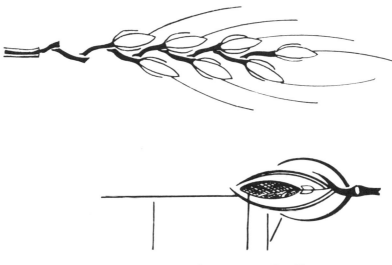

Awn, or Beard   Grain Chaff

Primitive wheat. As cultivation techniques improved, the ear became shorter and more compact, and in some cases the awn disappeared entirely.

The first thing that had to be done when clean grain was needed was separate the edible part of the grain from the husks surrounding it. In the case of wild types the seed and chaff are reluctant to be parted, and it was therefore necessary to toast ('parch') the ears to make the chaff brittle enough to be loosened. At places like Mureybat, in Syria, the system was to line the floor of a pit with flat stones, light a fire on them, allow it to burn and then rake it out, leaving a heat-retaining surface on which the grain could be threshed.[5]

Even after threshing and winnowing, some of the husks remained and had to be removed by rubbing the grain back and forth between two stones. This both split the inner chaff and helped to scrape off some of the bran from the seed itself. At Kom Ombo in Egypt, in the Sahaba aggradation of the Upper Nile, at Mallaha in the Jordan Valley and at Zawi Chemi Shanidar in Iraq very early rubbing stones have been found that were probably used for the purpose.[6]

Whether the result of these labours was whole, clean wheat or a spiky mix of groats, chaff and bran depended on the skill and patience of the grinder; the state of prehistoric teeth suggests that the skilful grinder was the exception rather than the rule.

Only after all this, say the archaeologists, was the grain fit for cooking. And since loose seeds (or rough flour) could not be cooked directly on the fire or on the less-than-spacious hot hearthstone, the people of the early Neolithic era must have used the pit-boiling method to make them into a kind of porridge.

This, of course, presupposes something very like canteen catering, and indeed, most eating was a communal affair until quite recent times. In theory, porridge could well have been the easiest way to feed a number of people; easier, certainly, than reducing the grain to flour, mixing it with water and baking bread-cakes on the hearthstone. But since the pit-boiling of meat is not attested until about 5000 BC, it seems unlikely that grain should have been cooked by the same method 4,000 years earlier, especially in a region where there were no hot springs.

Yet, somehow, it had to be cooked. One answer is perhaps to be found in the old Celtic technique of 'graddaning', which abbreviated the theoretical sequence of parching, cleaning and cooking. Three hundred years ago a traveller in Scotland described how it was done. 'A woman, sitting down, takes a handful of corn, holding it by the stalks in her left hand, and then sets fire to the ears which are presently in a flame; she has a stick in her right hand . . . beating off the grain at the very instant when the husk is quite burnt . . . The corn may be so dressed, winnowed, ground and baked within an hour after reaping from the ground.'[7]

The people of the Neolithic age may well have had the same general idea, on a larger scale. Although residues of roasted grain have been found on some threshing floors, archaeologists usually attribute them to unintentional overheating, in which they may be doing the Neolithic people an injustice. If they had been entirely incompetent, there might never have been a Neolithic Revolution at all.

Deliberate toasting of the grain as well as the chaff would make it instantly digestible, bypass the whole problem of containers and demand none of the intensive labour entailed in the production of pit-boiled porridge. After toasting, the grain would simply be rubbed clean in the usual way and then pounded into coarse flour or groats. The addition of a little water would convert these into a doughy substance that could be baked in a flat cake on the hearthstone, or eaten just as it was – in which form it would have been the forerunner of the Greek *maza* and Roman *puls* that were to be standard fare in later times. Forerunner, too, of the *tsampa* still consumed in twentieth-century Tibet.

André Migot, doctor and traveller, described in vivid terms how Tibetans prepare the dish, using toasted barley flour (*tsampa*) and tea, which is drunk thick and black in Tibet, flavoured with salt, and enriched with a lump of potent yak butter.

'You leave a little buttered tea in the bottom of your bowl,' he said, 'and put a big dollop of *tsampa* on top of it. You stir gently with the forefinger, then knead with the hand, meanwhile twisting your bowl round and round until you finish up with a large, dumpling-like object which you proceed to ingest, washing it down with more tea. The whole operation demands a high degree of manual dexterity, and you need a certain amount of practical experience before you can judge correctly how much *tsampa* goes with how much tea; until you get these proportions right the end product is apt to turn into either a lump of desiccated dough or else a semi-liquid paste which sticks to your fingers . . . The whole process, in a country where nobody bothers much about washing, has the incidental advantage that, however dirty your hands may be when you embark on it, they are generally quite clean by the time you have done.'[8]

As a discovery, the grain-paste may fairly be described as epoch-making.* Everything suggests that it was invented long before the kind of flour-and-water flatbreads that, in various shapes and forms, have been the staples of much of humanity for the last 5,000 years. The Mexican *tortilla* and the Scots oatcake, the Indian *chapati*, the Chinese *po bin*, the Amerindian jonnycake, the Norwegian *flattbrød* and the Ethiopian *injera* are all direct descendants of later Neolithic bread; it is mainly the difference in the grain used – maize, oats, wheat, rye or millet, all of which have different cooking characteristics – that makes the end products seem so dissimilar.

Despite the options of earlier times, the cook's horizons expanded considerably when pottery at last came into use. A regular supply of fire- and waterproof containers, easily breakable but as easily replaceable, made it possible to boil food or stew it; to bake good flatbreads; to invent a number of entirely new dishes and improve on a number of old ones. And when pottery was succeeded by

---

* One of its subsidiary virtues was that it was useful for travellers, since it could easily be carried either ready-mixed or needing only the addition of a little water to make it edible – the first convenience food in history, antecedent of the Cornish pasty, the sandwich and the astronauts' rehydratable pumpkin pie.

unbreakable metal containers, the development of more ambitious cooking could begin.

THE DOMESTICATION OF ANIMALS

From the earliest days of the Neolithic period grain did more than feed humanity; it also attracted a number of the smaller herbivorous animals that had begun to multiply in the open margins of the forests as the climate mellowed.

The newly settled villagers, the raw materials of their diet under threat, had the choice of defending the fields, mounting a campaign against the raiders or bringing them to heel. The third option was undoubtedly the most appealing, guaranteeing as it did not only the grain supply but the meat supply as well.

Taming the wild sheep and goat may have been comparatively easy. Both were gregarious, comfort-loving and quick to breed, though which of them was domesticated first remains an open question. In the Near East the balance of probabilities favours the goat, maligned through the ages for its destructive browsing habits as much as for its pungent smell. When deliberate farming began and scrub had to be cleared to make way for cultivation, its talent for killing plants by defoliation must have made it a valuable helpmeet.

By just after 9000 BC the inhabitants of Zawi Chemi Shanidar in Iraq and Dobrudja in Romania[9] are known to have had sheep that were at least partially domesticated, but since the main progenitor of the domesticated sheep was the Asiatic moufflon, it seems likely that taming had begun earlier in cooler regions like the Karakum, east of the Caspian.* The first herdsmen would find themselves committed to a roving life – a single sheep can clear the land of a hundredweight of greenstuff in a week – and as they fanned out in search of fresh grazing, to the north and south of the Caspian and then westward, they took with them not only their huge, half-tamed flocks but knowledge of herding and, almost certainly, of milk and how to use it.

The pig, contrary by nature, arrived in the farmyard at least 2,000 years after its predecessors, perhaps because pigs, unlike the rumi-

---

* Where its wool would be almost as valuable as its meat. Primitive breeds of sheep needed no shearing; their two coats, hair on top and wool beneath, were both moulted in spring. One of the long-term results of domestication was to be the single coat of unmoultable fleece.

nants, cannot digest straw, grass, leaves or twigs, and were therefore no threat to the fields. They did have a taste for the same food as humans, however, so that pig farming was further delayed until the people of the Neolithic era were sure enough of a surplus to invest some of it in the enterprise.

The last major food animal to be domesticated was the cow, not in the heartland areas of the Neolithic but in Turkey or Macedonia at some time between 6100 BC and 5800 BC. The task may not have been easy. Though the ancestral type of the domesticated breed died out in the seventeenth century, attempts have since been made to re-create it,[10] and if the fiery and agile modern version is anything to go by, Neolithic man must have had his hands full with the original. Once brought under control, however, cattle were reduced to submission by poor feeding, close penning, hobbling and usually, in the case of bulls, castration.

Man had known since his hunting days that, as well as meat, the goat provided glossy, waterproof hair and a skin that made a first-class water container; that the sheep supplied wool and substantial quantities of fat, useful not only for cooking but also for medicinal salves and as tallow for rushlights; that the pig's bristles were as valuable as its lard and its skin; and that cow's hide was tough and strong, and its dung an excellent fuel for the fire. But only after the first of them had been domesticated did people learn that the goat, sheep and ox could also be pressed into service as agricultural labourers, made to tread seeds into the soil, pull the plough (when it was invented) and thresh the grain. The farmyard animal became, in effect, humanity's first power tool.

MILK ...

The second unlooked-for benefit of animal domestication (and one that was to be of supreme importance to later generations) was milk. The fact that animals suckled their young, just as humans did, must have been known from the earliest times, but the full value (and volume) of the milk that animals could be induced to supply to their new masters must have come as a revelation.

Milk being highly perishable, of course, a few hours would be enough to start it fermenting in the climate of the Near East. Depending on the temperature and the kind of bacteria in the air, the curds might develop into something pleasant and refreshing, or something quite uneatable even by the Neolithic peoples, whose tastes were necessarily less rigid than those of their modern counterparts. The curds might also be either fine or coarse. The finer type was to develop ultimately into the sharp, creamy substance represented today by the yoghurt of the Balkans, the *taetta* of Scandinavia, the *dahi* of India. The coarser kind, strained off, would make the first soft, fresh cheese.

A dairy five thousand years ago. It is just possible to see, here, that animals were milked from the back, not the side.

Cheese of a firmer kind probably also appeared early, even before the days of pottery. It, like other dairy products, seems to bear the hallmark of the pastoral nomads of Central Asia, who used animal stomach bags and untanned leather pouches as containers. Since the lining of a calf's stomach contains the enzyme (rennin) that produces the curdling agent, rennet, milk kept in a calf's stomach bag would turn into cheese more or less of its own accord.

Butter must have evolved in a cooler climate, and the traditional picture of some traveller taking a container of milk with him on a journey, only to find it turning into butter on the way, is as likely an explanation as any of how churning was discovered. In time it was found that the palatable life of butter (except in Tibet, where it was palatable only when rancid) could be extended by heating it, evaporating the water, and straining off impurities; this was the Indian method. In Europe salt was added during the making.

Throughout much of history, and especially in hot climates, milk has always been most used in one or other of its soured or fermented forms. The process of fermentation would not have been new to the early farmers. It must have been discovered very early in human history, since most substances, even if only slightly moist, will in time ferment if left to themselves. There would be a painful process of trial and error as *Homo sapiens* experimented to discover which fermented substances were palatable and which poisonous, and another long period while he tried to reproduce the palatable versions with reasonable consistency. Many of the fermented grain, vegetable, meat and fish dishes still known today probably had their origins in the Stone Age, even if written references to them are much later. (Sauerkraut rated a mention in Pliny.)

Whatever the background to the early discoveries, however, curds, cheese, yoghurt and butter all developed into useful ways of preserving milk that was surplus to people's immediate requirements,* cheese and butter having a special value in the days before farmers discovered how to manipulate their animals into giving milk most of the year round.

. . . AND HONEY

If, as seems probable, the nomadic peoples of Central Asia were responsible for disseminating knowledge of milk and milk products, it is even more probable that they introduced the world to honey. There is a universality about Eurasian words for it that suggests a single source of diffusion. The Sanskrit word *madhu* and the Chinese word *myit* are related to the *mit* of the Indo-Europeans, the *medhu* of the Slavs, and the mead of the English.[11]

Originally, honey was collected by smoking bees from their nests, a method illustrated in Egyptian tomb reliefs of the third millennium BC but dating back much earlier. Having discovered its pleasant flavour and energy-giving properties, people soon found that it had other virtues. Since it is almost pure sugar and ferments very readily, even the debris of a honeycomb left to soak in water is enough to produce a delicious and mildly intoxicating liquid. Honey ale, generally known as mead, was to be popular for thousands of years, especially in countries where the grape did not grow and ale-making grains were scarce.

Until the end of the Middle Ages honey was the sweetener *par excellence* in much of the world, although by no means the only one. Some countries used date syrup or fig syrup, others malted grains, still others grape juice, and a few had sugarcane. In England honey did not lose its hold until the monasteries – where bees were kept for their wax (used for votive candles), the honey being a commercially valuable by-product – were dissolved in the sixteenth century.

---

* There is nothing new about the EEC's surpluses except their scale.

The Birth of Civilization

Slowly – sometimes very slowly – knowledge of plant and animal domestication spread throughout the Old World. Sometimes it was carried by migrating clans, complete with a baggage train of livestock, seed grains and domestic impedimenta, sometimes by a few stray wayfarers who did no more than stimulate the minds of those they met by telling them what *could* be done.

But as the first migrants from the heartlands – children of the population explosion that inexorably resulted from the expansion in the food supply – moved, settled and then in turn sent out secondary waves of emigrants to even more distant lands, they had to adapt to new conditions. Sometimes their seed grains failed, not once but consistently; sometimes their livestock sickened and died.

About the livestock they could do little except wait and hope for the survivors to become acclimatized. In the case of crops, wheat proved strong enough in warm, lowland regions to defeat the particular kinds of weed that competed for its fields, but in cooler areas or at higher altitudes the weeds flourished. Ultimately, farmers found themselves harvesting the weeds rather than the wheat or, at best, a mixture of the two. One of the weeds was rye, later to become a staple grain in northern Europe; another was oats; in Central America, the tomato originated as a weed of maize and bean fields.

The early millennia of the Neolithic era were years of discovery, expansion and destruction. In the heartlands, wheat and barley were under cultivation by 7000 BC; peas, lentils and other pulses a thousand years later; olives and figs, dates, grapes and pomegranates by between 4000 and 3000 BC. But as the crops multiplied, so did the insect pests, while silos of dry grain stimulated a population explosion among the smaller rodents. Cultivation itself (though the experts are divided on this, as on so much else) may have devitalized the soil almost completely, giving nothing back except – without its value being recognized – manure from the animals who helped to work the fields and were allowed to graze on the stubble.

It takes only a few years to exhaust a patch of soil, as much as fifty for that soil to regenerate itself. In the Near East and elsewhere land that had first been stripped of trees and scrub, then overworked and overgrazed, began to turn to desert.

But then, at some time after 5000 BC in the region now known as Khuzistan, at the head of the Persian Gulf, farmers evolved a technique of breaching the banks of existing streams so that water flowed out and bedded itself into narrow canals – a primitive system of irrigation that could be used to water fields for three miles in either direction. The first result was richer and finer crops than had ever been seen before, and the second a concentration of population on the only lands, flat and near fresh water, that were suitable for it.

Gradually, irrigation techniques improved, with unforeseeable and far-reaching consequences. First, an administrative system came into being to handle the maintenance of ditches and canals and allocate fair shares in the waters, and then the administrative centre developed into a town, the town into a city. Civilization had been born.

An early development in irrigation. Instead of flowing freely from the source, water was raised by means of a counter-balanced baling bucket (or swape, or shaduf) and then tipped into the irrigation channels.

There are still many mysteries about the 7,000 years that pitchforked humanity from a Stone Age existence into a state of civilization. One is that, beforehand, women and men appear to have been more or less equal politically, whereas by the time society emerged from the Neo-lithic mists into the full light of recorded history, most institutions, most inventions and all power were the prerogative of the male.

Part of the explanation may be found in the division of labour during the agricultural revolution. The changing pattern of life increased woman's burdens while it lightened man's. Instead of living in a cave, bearing and burying children, and gathering such food and

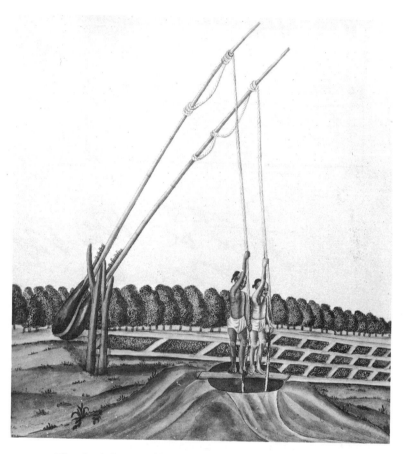

The shaduf was still in use in nineteenth-century India.

fuel as she could find, woman now had a primitive house to look after, essential crops to cultivate and care for, and most of the responsibility for husking and grinding the grain. Man, by contrast, was released from the physical and mental strains of the hunt to the peaceable tending of his flocks, which gave him both time and opportunity for constructive thinking, formulating plans, setting up and attending village councils, and criticizing woman's lack of inventiveness in the matter of crop-raising. In the end he took over.

In view of the snowball effect it is possible – even probable – that the superficially minor differences between cultivating crops and caring for livestock may have played a major role in bringing about the transformation from an egalitarian society into what was indisputably a man's world.

Even so, humanity had come a long way. It has been estimated that when the ice sheets first advanced a million years ago, there were about half a million ape-men on earth. By 10,000 BC, the eve of the Neolithic Revolution, *Homo sapiens* numbered around 3 million. By 3000 BC, after 7,000 years of farming, the world population had exploded to reach the 100 million mark.

Some things, however, had not changed. Average life expectancy in Sharh-i-Sokhta, one of the great new trading cities, was still no more than 18 years.[12]

BULLS OF HEAVEN AND GODS OF THE EARTH

Despite, or perhaps because of, their increasing technological expertise, people became ever more aware of how little they really knew about the forces of nature. Long before the Neolithic Revolution they had summoned up gods whose existence would explain the inexplicable – gods of air, fire, earth and water, friendly deities whose worship brought food in abundance, unfriendly ones who called down scarcity, drought, pestilence or plague. By the beginning of recorded history most of these gods had been slotted into place in one of humanity's two great religious legends, the legends that explained the functioning of the universe.

Which of them came first, if either did, is a matter for conjecture, but by late Neolithic times it was usually the creation myth (a magical explanation of the making of earth and heaven, people, beasts and birds) that preoccupied the hunting peoples and herdsmen, and the resurrection myth (explaining the annual death and rebirth of the soil) that obsessed agriculturalists as they waited for the barren winter ground to spring to life again. The fertility myth, subsidiary to both, could be accommodated in either.

The resurrection myth appeared in its basic form in the mythology of the predominantly agricultural Sumerians (*c.* 3500 BC). Inanna, goddess of love and war, set off to conquer the nether regions; while she was away the land remained infertile, but when, after many adventures, she returned to earth, everything came to life again.*

During the last 3,000 years BC, however, the whole area from Sumer (under its more familiar name of Babylon) to north-west India was subject to a series of invasions by the nomad pastoralists of Central Asia. The gods of the nomads were very different from those of the settled agricultural peoples – positive and dynamic, gods who did things, creator gods, not saviours. As the invaders settled down and achieved a *modus vivendi* with their new subjects, so too did their gods, making a place for themselves in the agriculturalists' pantheon and forcing a merger between the resurrection and creation myths.

At Thebes, bulls had to be officially inspected and registered.

Even so, the pastoralists' Bull of Heaven – worlds away from the patient castrated beast who drew the plough – was to sustain an independent role in many mythologies for thousands of years. Sometimes the role was half-playful, a cover for the amorous energies of Zeus. Sometimes it was symbolic, as in the Zoroastrian creed of Persia, where the original war between good and evil, light and

* With regional variations, the same tale of human dependence on a semi-mortal god appears throughout most of the early world. In Egypt the god Osiris died and was resurrected; in Canaan Baal was below ground for seven full years during which drought and pestilence reigned on earth; in Greece Persephone spent six months out of every twelve in the underworld. Even the Jesus of the New Testament, dead and then resurrected, echoed the early farmer's need to know that seeming death was not the end, either for nature or mankind.

darkness, was fought between cattle and wolves. Sometimes, as in Egypt, it was more direct, with a live domesticated animal representing Apis, bull incarnation of the god Ptah. And occasionally, the bull himself was immolated on the altar of a greater god, as in China, where the king sacrificed a red bull to the Sovereign on High in spring and, later in the year, one black bull to the Sun and another to the Ancestors. Only once did the farmyard animal triumph over his more dynamic brother, when St Luke was represented in the symbolism of the Christian Church as a winged ox, an image that survived until as late as the fifteenth century.

But domestication, in the end, conquered most of the animal gods – except in India, where religion, politics and economics helped to turn the cow, the great provider, into an object of love, gratitude and a peculiarly democratic kind of worship.

THE NEOLITHIC IN AFRICA

Although the people of the Upper Nile had been just as quick to learn how to grind wild grain as those of the Near Eastern heartland, the wider discoveries of the Neolithic world spread to Africa only in the fifth millennium BC. It was a propitious time. The encroaching desert sands had already begun to drive the primitive communities who lived on the fringes of the Nile Valley down towards the flood plains, and when cultivators armed with the new tools and knowledge began to clear the valley floor, the effect was dramatic. They found that the river itself did the farming for them.

Rising in mid-July, the Nile waters reached their fullest extent in September. When they retreated they left behind them a coating of rich black soil deposits (nowadays trapped behind the Aswan High Dam) from the Ethiopian plateau. As Pliny later reported, it became usual 'to begin sowing after the subsidence of the Nile and then to drive swine over the ground, pressing down the seed in the damp soil with their footprints . . .* This is done at the beginning of November,

---

* Thus creating natural containers that would hold water and attract dew, providing excellent conditions for germination. This idea, as a way of preventing dry areas from turning into a dust bowl, has just been re-discovered by the modern world. Students of jargon will be pleased to know that it is now called Holistic Resource Management, and extolled by the Food and Agriculture Organization (FAO) as 'a classic example of man's inadequate but developing comprehension of the co-evolution/cohabitation and mutually beneficial relationship between the forage resource and the foraging beast'.[13]

and afterwards a few men stub up the weeds – their name for this process is *botanismus* – but the rest of the labourers only visit the fields a little before the first of April, taking a sickle with them. The harvest is completed in May.'[14]

Domesticated animals helped to sow the grain, and later to thresh it by treading. The grain was thus fertilized at both stages. Fortunately, the Egyptians regarded dung as an antiseptic.

Wheat and barley flourished and the population multiplied more than a hundredfold in the course of a few centuries. By a thousand years after the first planting of crops in the Nile Valley a new civilization had appeared and Egypt had entered on its first dynastic period.

It has been estimated that in the third millennium BC the Egyptian peasant was capable of producing three times as much food as he and his family needed to sustain them,[15] which left a sizeable surplus for feeding the armies of workers engaged on flood control projects, public buildings and the tombs designed to ensure a deferential welcome in paradise for Egypt's greatest nobles and dignitaries.

From about 3000 BC Egyptian traders were in regular contact with Eritrea and Somalia, bartering knowledge, seeds, tools and domesticated animals for the frankincense and myrrh so much valued in the early world, and it was these traders who helped to stimulate cultivation and domestication over wide areas of Africa. Gradually, the knowledge filtered south and west over much of the continent. Animal domestication was adopted wherever the fauna were suitable, but in many places the wheat and barley of the Nile would not grow and cultivation techniques had to be adapted to other crops – millet in the light woodland belt south of the Sahara, 'red rice' in the great hook of the Niger, and 'finger millet' in the dry tropics. In the Congo basin there are hints of a primitive cultivating society that was not to burst into full, influential flower until new and suitable plants were introduced directly from south-east Asia around the beginning of the Christian era.

THE AMERICAS

Although the subject of the Neolithic Revolution is no less contentious in the Americas than in the Near East, it is clear that by some time between 7000 and 5000 BC the inhabitants of a group of caves in the Tamaulipas Mountains of Mexico, while still gathering wild plants in the shape of runner beans and the agave (or American aloe), had also begun to domesticate a number of others. Among these were the summer squash, which was both a flesh and a seed food; the chilli pepper, then as now a much-used seasoning in Central America; and the bottle gourd, whose young fruits could be used as a vegetable but which was probably more valued for the dry, hard shell of the mature plant, which made a useful water container. There are signs that maize (sweet corn), one of the most important plants of later times, had been brought under cultivation in the Tehuacan Valley between 6000 and 5000 BC, and beans were being grown around the same date in the Ancash department of Peru, where by 3000 BC the potato had also been domesticated.[16]

Plants were one thing, animals another. Climatic changes at the end of the eighth and last of the major ice ages, allied with the destructive nature of American hunting – partly attributable to the innocence of the indigenous fauna, which, unfamiliar with humans, learned too late to be afraid of them – had ensured that few of the larger species (and only the most recalcitrant of them) survived.

The early Americans were not, however, wholly deprived of animal protein. The evidence shows that the people of Catalina Island, California, consumed so many abalone in the fourth millennium BC that the colonies were almost wiped out and they had to make a start on mussels instead.[17] Elsewhere, insects were much eaten. An analysis of digestive remains from one prehistoric site shows that Mexicans were not averse to a meal of grasshoppers, ants or termites[18] – nor is there any good reason why they should have been. Several insects were considered delicacies in Classical times in Europe, and others, including silkworms, lake flies and witchetty grubs, are eaten with enjoyment in China, Africa and Australia today.*

---

* Insects can be a useful source of protein. Dried locusts provide 75 per cent protein and 20 per cent fat, as well as a number of vitamins; termites 36 per cent protein, 44 per cent fat and some valuable phosphates.[19]

ASIA

In Asia, as in America, archaeologists are hampered by problems of sheer scale; the number of potential excavation sites is formidable.

Even so, an increasing amount of information has been coming to light in recent years, some of it ignored by historians committed (as many still are) to a Western origin for all human progress. Pottery, for example, one of the key advances of the Neolithic, was being produced in Japan in 10,000 BC (3,000 years before it was known in the Near East), and stone tools with ground, as distinct from flaked, cutting edges were in use in northern Australia 20,000 years ago – something like 10,000 years before the technique appeared in the Near East.[20]

Until about 1970 so little was known about the Neolithic era in Asia that it seemed as if even the great civilizations of the Indus and the Yellow River had sprung like dragons' teeth straight from the ground, fully equipped, fully developed and apparently without antecedents. Excavations at scattered sites had produced evidence of 'probably cultivated' peas, beans, cucumbers and water chestnuts at Spirit Cave in Thailand (provisionally dated at *c.* 9750 BC), the bones of 'possibly domesticated' sheep (*c.* 5500 BC) in the Adamgarh hills of central India, and proof of 'semi-cultivated' rice at Non Nok Tha, also in Thailand, *c.* 3500 BC.[21]

But with the late 1970s discovery of two sites in Pakistan – a settlement of mud-brick huts at Mehrgarh (*c.* 5000 BC) and a fully evolved town, Rehman Dehri, flourishing on the Indus plains during the fourth millennium BC – a radical re-assessment became necessary. If Tepe Yahya and Sharh-i-Sokhta in Iran were at the western end of some major prehistoric trade route, then Mehrgarh, at the foot of the 6,000-feet-high Bolan Pass, could have been a staging post on it, and Rehman Dehri, the eastern terminus.

Unfortunately, food is less amenable to study than pottery or tools, and much work still remains to be done. But it appears likely that what is known about the great Indus cities of Harappa and Mohenjo-Daro – at their peak between 2300 BC and 1500 BC – may also have been true, on a less sophisticated scale, of the earlier Rehman Dehri.

If so, its people ate wheat and barley and the field pea, cooked their meat in sesame oil, and seasoned it with mustard and, possibly, turmeric or ginger. They would be familiar with sheep, goats, buffalo and pig, and may even have begun on the domestication of the Indian jungle fowl, later to become the world's 'chicken'. Since they had spice-grinding stones, it is possible that they also ground their grains into flour. In the matter of fruits the Indus Valley was more favoured than Mesopotamia; as well as dates there were melons, coconuts and bananas, pomegranates and, possibly, lemons and limes.

Chinese imperial edicts once began, 'The world is based on agriculture', which seemed to reinforce the belief that China, until a very late stage, was exclusively centred in the village, having nothing that could even begin to match the cities of the Euphrates, the Nile and the Indus. But in 1985 Chinese official sources triumphantly announced the discovery and preliminary excavation of Xibo, the formerly legendary capital of the Shang dynasty, with radiocarbon dates and stylistic evidence placing it somewhere in the seventeenth century BC.[22] Comparatively, this dating is still 'late', but a discovery of such magnitude encourages the hope that there may be other equally important, and earlier, finds that remain to be made.

Cities apart, the archaeological record shows that there were a number of settlements in the loess lands* of central China by as early as 6000 BC, all using pottery and experimenting with plant and animal domestication. As far as is known, however, it took another thousand years for cultivation to expand into the Yellow River valley. Although the river ('the Father of Floods') carried a rich sediment of loess down with it to the plain, serious farming there was not practicable without drainage, flood control and a sizeable and disciplined workforce. All this had come into being by 4500 BC, and there was a thriving village economy, the wooden houses crowded so close together that their roofs were almost touching.

The basic grain in north China at this time (when south China was still a foreign country) was millet, a dry-land crop, and there may have been experiments – though no more than that – with wheat and hemp. It is common today to think of rice as the main Chinese food almost to the exclusion of everything else, but this is partly the product – as are so many myths about food – of a Victorian misapprehension. China, an exclusive society, kept the West at arm's length until the middle of the nineteenth century, and one result was that foreign traders, confined to the southern port of Canton (now Guangzhou), assumed that the food of Canton – based on wet-farmed rice – was representative of China as a whole. It was an error later reinforced by the geographical accident that took emigrant Cantonese to Britain

* Loess is a fine dust of clay, sand and limestone that tends to erode into natural terraces. It is highly fertile and, by its very nature, self-regenerating.

and America, so that Chinese and Cantonese cooking were virtually synonymous during the early days of the fashion for Chinese food in the West.

The date of rice domestication remains doubtful. Wet-field cultivation is thought to have begun in the river valleys of the south by about 5000 BC,[23] but most dates in China, as in India and south-east Asia, are closer to 3000 BC. Nor is there any real certainty about origins. The wild plant is found across a wide swathe of land stretching from the Gangetic plain of India across Upper Burma, north Thailand and Laos, to North Vietnam and the monsoon area of southern China.*

Rice could, in fact, have been domesticated almost anywhere, especially as it lends itself to different methods of cultivation; early rice-users are known to have been ingenious at raising it in superficially unlikely conditions. The known dates, in relation to the domestication of other grains, suggest that rice was a late starter, which means that it could have been domesticated independently in several places.

The precise where and when are not, of course, of overriding importance to anyone save the expert, but they are still of interest. After all, rice today is the basic and sometimes the only food of more than half the world's population.

At the most famous of China's Neolithic sites, Banpo (formerly written as Pan-p'o-ts'un), freshwater fish, notably carp,† were a major item of diet, and there were semi-domesticated cattle, sheep and goats, and such game as wild dog, boar, horse, bear, bamboo rat and monkey. Remains of the small breed of pig peculiar to China – mostly slaughtered at less than a year old – were found in every hut.[25]

The prolific little pig was an ideal food animal in the context of China's developing social system. When large populations are involved in intensive crop cultivation, their animal husbandry usually extends only to keeping a few draught animals, certainly not to rearing grazing stock for food.‡ The Chinese pig, however, was small enough to be

---

* The swathe continues across northern Australia, Central America and tropical Africa, which conforms with the theory that the southern continents once formed a single landmass, Gondwanaland.[24]
† The first fish in the world ever to be 'farmed'.
‡ Cattle, for example, were always to be expensive in China, a capital investment to be worked for many years. Indeed, by the early Han period (the last two centuries BC) a contemporary history estimated that a man who could raise and sell 250 cattle a year would be as rich as the head of one of the great hereditary families.[26]

kept in the house, could be fed on scraps at no cost to the owner, matured at the age of a year, and produced two bountiful litters annually from then on, each consisting of up to a dozen piglets. It was hardly surprising that, for the Chinese, the words 'meat' and 'pork' became, and remain, synonymous.

PART TWO

THE NEAR EAST, EGYPT AND EUROPE
3000 BC–AD 1000

In the course of the Neolithic era much of humanity had been converted from a predominantly meat to a predominantly grain diet, a change significant in that it immobilized people, tying them to the land they farmed and increasing their awareness of boundaries and frontiers – an awareness that in turn stimulated a sense of social unity and a recognition of communal need. The nomadic herdsmen, whose concept of frontiers was linked to natural topographical features, to plains, watering-holes and mountain barriers, might respond to difficulties with their food supply by direct invasion of neighbouring territory, but the civilized peoples at first took a more civilized course. It was Sumer and Egypt that first systematized the long-distance trade that was to have such a profound influence on all subsequent development; Greece that, in need of grain, opened up much of the Mediterranean; Rome that, similarly inspired, expanded its imperial frontiers until they marched closely with the wheat-growing boundaries of the known world; and Rome, too, whose hunger for spices sent its mariners all the way to India and led to the discovery of the monsoon winds. At last, when Rome and world trade foundered, it transpired that Rome's successors, the barbarian nomads, had their own lesson to teach. It was they who sponsored the renewal of animal husbandry that was to influence Western food and farming for all the centuries to come.

— 4 —
The First Civilizations

Historically, cities are the index of civilization, admired for their palaces and temples, poetry and philosophy, art and aqueducts, but seldom for their granaries. Yet the whole magnificent structure of the world's first great civilizations rested on the granaries and the people who worked to fill them.

Seven thousand years of experiment had taught man which crops he was able to grow and how best to grow them. He – or more probably she, in the early days – had evolved not only the harrow, rake and mallet that were needed to break the light soil of the Near East, but the hoe, originally a hooked branch that did no more than scrape a shallow groove on the surface of the earth. This, in time, developed into a scratch-plough pulled by one man while another walked behind, forcing the tip into the soil, and when it was discovered in the third millennium BC how to harness oxen and put them to work, a heavier plough at last became practicable. Its deeper cut helped, if only temporarily, to slow down the rate at which the soil was being exhausted.

And the ingeniously irrigated soil of Mesopotamia *was* being exhausted. Unless there is perfect drainage, constant irrigation precipitates from the soil salts that destroy fertility. In the Near East the wheat began to fail, and then – although more resistant to salinity – the barley. The states that had been built on irrigation were soon to be forced to look beyond their frontiers towards new lands that could redress the deficiencies of the old. Irrigation, which had helped to found cities, was also to encourage the first tentative steps towards trade and exploration.

In the meantime, however, as well as the harrow and hoe, the armoury of the Sumerian agriculturalist also included a harvesting tool invented in the earliest days of grain usage, and so well designed that its fined-down successor still serves a purpose today. This was the sickle, a curved blade made from wood or horn, fitted with flint teeth and bearing a striking resemblance to that most functional of grass-cutting mechanisms, a sheep's jaw.[1] Only when tempered metal blades came into use was the flint-toothed sickle superseded.

Farming technology did not, of course, stop at tool design, and since the Sumerians were the first people in history to have a coherent system of writing – and thus the first people in history to speak in their own words to later generations – theory and deduction at last move into the realm of certainty, even if it is, at times, a limited certainty. Patiently incising their words on small, heavy, half-dry clay tablets, the scribes who were the secretaries of the ancient world understandably considered brevity one of the cardinal virtues.

It was the scribes' daily task to record everything that needed recording, including laws, legends, taxes and, perhaps surprisingly, the ancient equivalent of the export declaration. Clay tablets mentioning grain and cattle, timber and precious stones have been dug up from sites as far apart as south-east Iran and the eastern coast of the Mediterranean.

The scribes also recorded the medical practices of the day. One prescription (c. 2750 BC) included thyme, pears and figs. The physician was instructed to pulverize the dry ingredients into a thick paste, then 'pour ale over it, rub with oil, fasten as a poultice' – from which it may be seen that at least one of the products of fermentation was regarded as healthful, externally if not always internally. Drunkenness was a familiar phenomenon even 4,000 years ago.

There are interesting political sidelights, too. Sumerian temples had their tributary lands and draught cattle, as religious institutions have had throughout history, and one inscription from about 2400 BC makes it clear that civic dignitaries were sometimes guilty, then as now, of misappropriating temple funds. 'The oxen of the gods ploughed the *ensi*'s [city governor's] onion patches; the onion and cucumber patches of the *ensi* were located in the gods' best fields.'

In addition to all this, by 2500 BC the scribes had collated most of the accumulated expertise of the agricultural past into the *Farmer's Almanac*, one of the world's first reference books. 'When you are about to plough your field,' it says, 'keep your eye on the man who puts in the barley seed. Let him drop the grain uniformly two fingers deep . . . Use up one shekel of barley for each *garush* [strip of land about six and a half yards long]. If the barley seed does not sink in properly, change the coulter [blade] of your plough.'[2]

By modern standards the tools and technology of the Sumerians and their near-contemporaries, the Egyptians, may seem primitive, but they were the product of a long period of trial and error and well suited to local conditions. It is worth noting that in Egypt land put down to grain in 1000 BC is estimated to have yielded as rich a crop as it did in the 1950s.[3]

FOOD IN SUMER

Not surprisingly, Sumerian records are less than expansive on the matter of everyday eating; the scribes were not to know how eagerly their tablets would be studied by later generations.

The raw materials of the Sumerian diet, however, were barley, wheat and millet; chick-peas, lentils and beans; onions, garlic and leeks; cucumbers, cress, mustard and fresh green lettuce. By the time Sumer was succeeded by Babylon a special delicacy had been discovered that was dispatched to the royal palace by the basketful. Truffles.[4]

Everyday meals probably consisted of barley-paste or barleycake, accompanied by onions or a handful of beans and washed down with barley ale, but the fish that swarmed in the rivers of Mesopotamia were a not-too-rare luxury. Over fifty different types are mentioned in texts dating from before 2300 BC, and although the number of types had diminished by Babylonian times, the fried-fish vendors still did a thriving trade in the narrow, winding streets of Ur.

Onions, cucumbers, freshly grilled goat, mutton and pork (not yet taboo in the Near East) were to be had from other food stalls. Meat was commoner in the cities than in the more sparsely populated countryside, since it spoiled so quickly in the heat, but beef and veal were everywhere popular with people who could afford them – there were rich and poor even in Sumerian times – although most beef is likely to have been tough and stringy. Cattle were not usually slaughtered until the end of their working lives, and according to a palace inventory of about 2400 BC really 'old oxen' were fit only for feeding the dogs.[5]

Probably tenderer and certainly more common was mutton. The incomers who had first put the Sumerian state on its feet were originally sheep herders, and in the surviving vocabulary of Sumer there are 200 words describing sheep – fattened sheep, mountain sheep and fat-tailed sheep among them. The fat-tailed sheep, described centuries later by Herodotus, used to be regarded by scholars as no more than one of that enterprising geographer's flights of fancy, but it turned out to be perfectly genuine, the tail – a great delicacy, rich in high-quality fat – accounting for as much as a sixth of the total carcass weight of sixty pounds.[6] In a few parts of the Near East today 'tail fat' is still the preferred cooking medium.

THE ORIGINS OF BEER

Greek tradition has it that the god Dionysus fled from Mesopotamia in disgust because its people were so addicted to beer – or, more correctly, ale, since the preservative herbs used in true beer were not introduced until the end of the Middle Ages. Certainly, a staggering amount of the Sumerian grain yield went into ale; something like 40 per cent of the total. The ordinary temple workman received a ration of just under two pints a day, and senior dignitaries more than eight pints, some of which they may have used as currency.[7] There was, of course, no great range of alternatives at this time – no grape wine, no tea, no coffee, and water that, coming from irrigation canals rather than free-flowing streams, must have been badly contaminated.

Most of the brewers in the ancient world were women, who sold the ale from their homes and were under the nominal supervision of the goddess Ninkasi, 'the lady who fills the mouth'. It was she who baked 'with lofty shovel the sprouted barley'.[8] As well as barley ale, of which there were eight kinds, Sumer had another eight made from wheat and three from mixed grains. The quality of all of them seems to have been variable; indeed, the Code of Hammurabi (1750 BC) sounds very much like the Campaign for Real Ale (AD 1980) in its condemnation of understrength and over-pricing.[9]

It seems that the discovery of ale was stimulated by the process of bread-making. At some stage in the Neolithic era people had learned that if, instead of using ordinary grain, they used grain that had been sprouted and then dried, it made a bread that kept unusually well. Something very like this was used in brewing. The Egyptian process was to sprout the grain, dry it, crush it, mix it to a dough and partially bake it. The loaves were then broken up and put to soak in water, where they were allowed to ferment for about a day before the liquor was strained off and considered ready for drinking.[10]

Until about 1500 BC brewing remained a hit-or-miss affair, the presence of the micro-organisms responsible for fermentation being largely fortuitous. But brewers ultimately came to recognize that their old pottery ale jars (full of cracks and crevices that were an ideal home for natural yeasts) produced a much more consistent brew than new ones.*

---

* Today's brewers, following – in a scientifically controlled fashion – much the same process as their Egyptian predecessors, destroy any accidental spores by boiling, and then add specially cultivated yeasts.

In Egypt the commonest ale was *haq*, made from the red barley of the Nile. It seems to have been fairly weak, though other Egyptian ales were so sweet and aromatic that they were very little inferior to wine, and are thought to have achieved an alcohol content of about 12 per cent. Some of them, certainly, must have been potent or it would not have been necessary to warn drinkers, as an Egyptian papyrus of 1400 BC did: 'Do not get drunk in the taverns in which they drink ale, for fear that people repeat words that may have gone out of your mouth, without you being aware of having uttered them.'[11]

Ale continued to be the favoured drink on the Nile, but not in Mesopotamia, where, as irrigation soured the soil and even barley became difficult to grow, there was no grain to spare. It was then that the Sumerians' successors changed their drinking habits and took to date wine.

THE DATE PALM AND THE FIG

On favourable lands the date palm had flourished as far back as 50,000 BC, and developing man must always have found it valuable, although not, in the pre-technology era, quite the universal provider it is now, when it is said to have a different use for every day of the year – and five more besides. Two less obvious applications in early times were the reduction of date stones to charcoal for the fire, and the use of the fruit itself as a cure for asthma. 'Mix dates, sweet ale, and crocodile dung . . .'[12]

The network of irrigation canals in southern Mesopotamia provided ideal conditions for palm cultivation, the trees clinging to the banks, overhanging the water and leaving the rest of the land open for other crops. So productive were they that dates were the cheapest of staple foods.* They were also of superlative quality. Xenophon remarked on the size and succulence of the dates he ate during the Persian expedition in the fourth century BC. 'Their colour was just like amber, and the Babylonian villagers dried them and kept them as sweets.'[13]

Whether fresh, soft-dried or hard-dried, dates helped to give character to meat dishes and grain pastes, and were also a high-energy food for the traveller, with a sugar content of over 50 per cent. The juice was often pressed out and allowed to evaporate into a thick syrup,

---

* The average date palm produces 100 pounds of fruit a year for sixty years or more, and a good tree half as much again.

which was used in puddings and sweetmeats as a substitute for honey, or in the making of fermented or soft drinks.

The palm itself made other contributions to the diet, the crown being tapped for its sugary sap, which could be fermented to make palm toddy. During the useful life of the tree the tapping was done with moderation, but when it had passed its peak a good deal more was drawn off and, ultimately, the tree was drained completely. At the beginning of its last season those who cared to do so were able to feast on 'cabbage', the new foliage sprouting from the crown, which had a 'peculiarly pleasant' taste though it was apt to cause headaches.[14] It was taken only from palms already doomed, because the tree died when the 'cabbage' was cut.

Gathering figs. The apes may be artistic licence, although it is always possible that the fig-ape was a legitimate predecessor of the truffle-hound.

The fig, a native of western Asia and another fruit with a high sugar content, was also popular in the Near East and along much of the Mediterranean, although the tree did not have the 370 uses of the date.* Sometimes, however, it fruited well where the date did not, as in Greece, where it found a place in the diet of rich and poor alike, particularly in winter in its dried form.

* On the other hand, its leaves were a more convenient size and shape for the specialized requirements of the Garden of Eden.

'Nothing is sweeter than figs', Aristophanes declared,[15] and their reputation spread far beyond the lands in which they grew until, in the third century BC, Bindusara, king of the Maurya dominions in India, wrote to Greece asking for some grape syrup, some figs and a philosopher. Grape syrup and figs, he was told with cool courtesy, would be sent to him with pleasure, but it was 'against the law in Greece to trade in philosophers'.[16]

In Egypt basketsful of figs were numbered among the tomb furnishings of dynastic times. They were not always there for the gastronomic enjoyment of the *ka*, however. As a people, the Egyptians were much preoccupied by their digestions, believing that most illnesses had their source in the alimentary canal, and bombarding that organ with every remedy in their less than prepossessing pharmacopoeia. The fig, with its mild laxative properties, must have qualified as that rare substance – a food that not only tasted good, but also *did* you good. It was undoubtedly more palatable than the senna and castor oil that, then as now, were the main alternatives.

THE DISCOVERY OF RAISED BREAD

It was reputedly in Egypt that the art of making modern bread was discovered, although the evidence is elusive and the date even more so. Conditions, however, were favourable, because wheat was the important factor* and specifically wheat that did not have to be parched before threshing.

The starchy endosperm of wheat contains gluten-forming proteins. Yeast, the other essential ingredient of raised bread, in favourable conditions produces carbon dioxide gas. If the two ingredients are brought together in a bread mix, the result is a spongy mass consisting of tiny gas bubbles each enclosed in an elastic skin of gluten. When heat is subsequently applied, the gluten becomes firm instead of elastic, and this is what holds the bread in its raised form. If, however, the gluten-forming proteins have been subjected to heat before they come into contact with the yeast, their nature has already been changed; they have become inelastic and unable to 'rise'.

Since most of the early grains needed some degree of toasting before they could be threshed, raised bread was a chemical impossibility, but

---

* Other grains would not do. Barley and millet, because of their chemical composition, are unresponsive to leavening, and so are oats – which were, in any case, unknown in the Near East. Rye, the best alternative, was also unfamiliar in the civilized world before the first millennium BC.

by the beginning of the dynastic period in Egypt a wheat had been developed that could be threshed raw. It seems to have remained scarce for a considerable period; certainly, it did not become common in Greece until the fourth century BC,[17] although the Greeks had been trading with Egypt for 300 years and importing grain for most of that time.

Leavening, according to one theory, was discovered when some yeast spores – the air is full of them, especially in a bakehouse that is also a brewery – drifted onto a dough that had been set aside for a while before baking; the dough would rise, not very much, perhaps, but enough to make the bread lighter and more appetizing than usual, and afterwards, as so often in the ancient world, inquiring minds set about the task of reproducing deliberately a process that had been discovered by accident.

But there is an alternative and even more likely theory – that on some occasion ale instead of water was used to mix the dough. The rise would be more spectacular than from a few errant spores and the effect would be easy to explain and equally easy to reproduce.

As the idea of raised bread became familiar beyond Egypt's frontiers, other peoples evolved their own leavens. The Gauls and Iberians, according to Pliny the Elder, simply skimmed the foaming head off their ale, which was why they had 'a lighter kind of bread than other peoples'. The Greeks and Italians, who were not ale drinkers, used millet flour soaked in grape juice, kneaded and then set aside until it fermented; wheat bran steeped in white wine; or wheat flour made into a kind of porridge and then left to go sour. 'Manifestly,' said Pliny, 'it is natural for sourness to make the dough ferment.'[18]

The commonest method, however, was to keep a piece of dough from the previous day's baking and add it to the new mix, and this sourdough starter has continued popular ever since. Despite the fact that it has now been generally superseded by commercial block or dried yeast, it still makes a uniquely characterful bread.

Although leavened bread did not turn rubbery as quickly as the soft flatbreads, and though its texture was superior to the grain-paste's, this did not mean that the ancient world was instantly converted. Coarse flour, even when leavened, still makes a heavy, close-textured loaf, and the worn teeth of surviving skulls show that most Egyptians went on chewing their way through bread made from the old flours, rough with bran and spiky with splinters of chaff (sometimes with splinters of grinding stone as well).[19] The relatively demanding process of making high-raised bread, and the fact that it worked only with some kinds of grain, meant that it remained a restricted food for many centuries. In northern Europe it was still uncommon as late as the Middle Ages.

EGYPTIAN FOOD

It is clear that Egyptians enjoyed their food. Nobles and priests were particularly well served, with at least forty different kinds of bread and pastries, some raised, some flat, some round, some conical, some plaited. There were some varieties made with honey, others with milk, still others with eggs. And tomb excavations show what a wide range of other foodstuffs the great had set before them even as early as the beginning of the third millennium BC – barley porridge, quail, kidneys, pigeon stew, fish, ribs of beef, cakes, stewed figs, fresh berries, cheese . . .[20]

Much time was spent on organizing supplies. Until about 2200 BC the Egyptians persevered with attempts to domesticate a number of animals like the ibex, oryx, antelope and gazelle, and then, abandoning this fruitless occupation, turned to the more entertaining pursuits of hunting in the marshland preserves, collecting exotic vegetables like wild celery, papyrus stalks and lotus roots, trapping birds and going fishing.

The Nile marshes and canals contained eel, mullet, carp, perch and tigerfish, as well as many other aquatic species that have not been

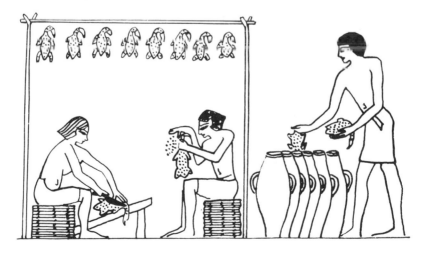

Birds were hung, cleaned, seasoned and then immersed in a brine tub.

identified. Fish were, in fact, so plentiful that the Egyptians dried and salted them for export to Syria and Palestine. Herodotus reported that another popular food was small birds, some of them pickled in brine for a few days and eaten without further preparation.[21]

The origins of salting as a preservation process remain obscure, although in Egypt there was a positive link between salt's use in preserving food for the living and embalming the bodies of the dead. Preservation by drying presents fewer questions, if only because figs, dates and grapes fallen from the tree or vine would dry themselves on the hot sandy soil, and no lengthy period of experiment would be needed to establish that fish, for example, responded well to the same treatment, even if it had to be buried a little deeper. The precise where and when of the discovery may be missing, but not the why or how.

The peasants' food, like their way of life, was more circumscribed than that of the great officials, but they seem to have been badly off only by comparison. Their standard fare may have been ale, onions and the common flatbread, *ta*, bought from a stall in the village street, but they could look forward to quite frequent days of plenty when they feasted on the surplus from temple sacrifices or one of the great high festivals.

They ate pork, too, regardless of government health warnings. It is often said that the common Near Eastern prohibition on pork – in the Jewish and Muslim religions, for example – had its origins in medical doctrine, and, certainly, pork can be a dangerous meat in a hot climate, which may well have been taken into account when dietary regulations were being formulated.

But although the peoples of the Near East (like their contemporaries in China) must have known this for something like 5,000 years, pork did not become taboo until after 1800 BC. The precise date is still debatable, but there is a clear correlation between the emergence of the taboo on pork and the arrival of the tribes of nomadic invaders who swept or drifted across great areas of eastern Europe and western Asia in the second millennium BC. These tribes, accustomed to sheep and cattle, seem to have had an almost pathological hatred for the pig – a wayward beast with little stamina, a constitutional objection to being herded and a tiresome inability to live on grass.

The Indo-European nomads disseminated much that was new throughout the lands they invaded and sometimes (if briefly) ruled, and one of their legacies was an institutionalized rejection of pork.

In 1985, therefore, it came as something of a surprise to archaeologists studying bones from a number of Egyptian sites when they discovered that a high proportion of the population were still, as late as 1350 BC, rearing pigs at home, in kennels.[22] It seems that neither the warnings of the physicians nor the exhortations of the priests had been enough to wean the peasant from his pork.

THE LAWS FROM SINAI

The Hebrews, formerly pastoral nomads themselves, had arrived in Egypt at the end of the seventeenth century BC, and departed from it without regrets in the thirteenth. The pastoralism, the Egyptian experience and the effects of the long exile were all integral to the dietary regulations that were subsequently imposed on them under Mosaic law, the law designed to reunite them by spelling out how they differed from the other peoples of their world and strengthening the single great bond that bound them – their worship of, and dependence on, Yahweh.

To unite a people, it is sometimes necessary to define them even to themselves, and this is successful only if the definitions make sense in terms of present or past experience, religious or social. This was certainly true of the Mosaic dietary regulations, even if among them was one that amounted to little more than an explicit rejection of a favourite dish of the land whose dust the Hebrews had just shaken from their feet. The prohibition on boiling a kid in its mother's milk* was to develop into a total ban on eating meat and dairy food at the same meal – presenting an enduring challenge to the kosher cook that has been eased only in recent years by the general availability of soy milk and similar products.

On a more fundamental level, many of the dietary laws (the *kashrut*) harked back to the origins of the Hebrew tribes and their concept of the world as it had been at the Creation (which they seem, not unreasonably, to have identified with the beginning of the Neolithic period).

Tradition had it that then they were vegetarians. 'And God said, "Behold, I have given you every plant yielding seed which is upon the

---

* One expert in semiotics suggests that this may have been partly linked to the laws against incest. 'You shall not put a mother and her son into the same pot, any more than into the same bed.'[23] Perhaps a more convincing back-up would be revulsion against cooking the slaughtered young in the very medium that had been designed by the Creator to sustain its life.

face of all the Earth, and every tree with seed in its fruit; you shall have them for food"' (Gen. 1:29).

But later, after the Flood – presumably when population pressures had begun to force some of the early agriculturalists (the sons of Noah among them) out of the good agricultural land to places where pastoralism flourished – Yahweh relented and granted permission to eat meat. 'Every moving thing that lives shall be food for you . . .' It was an acknowledgement of the realities of nomadism, as well as a concession to the many human imperfections that had shown up since Adam and Eve were created.

There was a proviso, however. 'You shall not eat flesh with its life, that is, its blood' (Gen. 9:33–4). The blood as the life was a constantly recurring theme in most early religions, and since, for the Hebrews, animals had souls and murder was forbidden, meat-eating could be rationalized only if the food animal's life-essence was returned directly to God in the form of a blood libation.

The ban on eating 'flesh with its life', strongly re-emphasized in the Mosaic laws, is still obeyed today through the ritual of kosher slaughter. Under rabbinical supervision, the animal's trachea, oeso-phagus, jugular vein and carotid artery are severed, reducing it to unconsciousness and resulting in the fullest possible outpouring of blood. Any that remains in the meat is later removed by the cook, who soaks it in cold water for a time and then salts it.

'CLEAN' AND 'UNCLEAN' FOOD

The second major provision of the Mosaic dietary regulations was something of an innovation. Where the unruly Hebrews were concerned, unity and social discipline could be imposed only through laws that were comprehensible, unequivocally stated and not open to argument. The legal systems of polytheistic lands had tended to evolve pragmatically, but the laws pronounced from Sinai were those of a single god, which made it possible to state them in terms of an absolute morality. There was right and there was wrong; and anything that was not wholly right was by definition wrong.*

Translated into dietary terms, right became pure or 'clean', and wrong, impure, 'blemished' or 'unclean'.

* Anything that was neither one thing nor another, but a mixture, was of course also wrong, hence prohibitions on sowing a field with two kinds of seed, yoking an ox with an ass, wearing linen and wool together . . .

'You shall therefore make distinction between the clean beast and the unclean, and between the unclean bird and the clean . . .' (Lev. 20:24–25). Which was which?

Often enough, in the course of history, religious reformers have tried to sweep away centuries of human error by going back to divine beginnings, and this was what the Mosaic laws did. Anything that Yahweh had brought directly into being must, in its original state, have been pure and 'clean', and since at the Creation He had given 'to every beast of the Earth . . . every green plant for food' (Gen. 1:30), it seemed that 'clean' must be the same as herbivorous.

Moses, wearing a lightly horned nimbus, expounds the law of the clean and unclean beasts.

The herbivorous animals most important to nomad pastoralists were, of course, sheep and cows, and Mosaic law took these for prototypes. All beasts that ate grass *and* chewed the cud *and* had cloven hooves were assumed to be clean. Not the horse, camel or ass, whose hooves were not cloven. Not the pig, which had cloven hooves but did not chew the cud. Not the hare, which (the Hebrews believed) chewed the cud but had no hooves at all. Since animals with claws were mainly carnivorous, they were obviously unclean, and even a theoretically 'clean' animal could be rendered unclean if it had a blemish.

Where birds and fish were concerned, the Creation references to 'the birds of the air' and 'the fish of the water' were taken as definitive. Birds and fish that remained in their prescribed environment and behaved as birds and fish were supposed to behave were in general regarded as clean,* but fish that did not swim (shellfish and molluscs) and birds that rarely flew (ostrich, swan and pelican) were unclean. The groundbound chicken seems to have escaped the net of uncleanliness either because it was more ready to fly then than now, or because it had not yet been introduced from India.

Perhaps because laws that can be disobeyed in private weaken the whole edifice, the concept of 'clean' and 'unclean' was not applied to the entire range of possible foodstuffs. Relatively public acts such as killing a food animal, catching a fish or trapping a bird fell within the scope of the laws, but what the priest could not see or reasonably be expected to supervise was left alone except on ritual occasions.

The relationship between 'cleanness' and the Neolithic beginnings shows very clearly in the food ordained by Mosaic law for Passover, the commemoration of the flight from Egypt (Exod. 12:8–9). It was roast meat that was specified, not boiled (there were no pottery containers in the early Neolithic period); the herbs were bitter or wild (green plants had not then been brought into cultivation); the bread was unleavened because leavened bread was a 'modern' invention.

In the Old Testament itself, of course, the unleavened bread requirement was explained by reference to the exodus, when 'the people took their dough before it was leavened' (Exod. 12:34). The reference is not entirely clear. If it means 'before the dough had risen', many bakers might question it, since the dough could have gone on rising quite happily in the kneading bowls 'bound up in their mantles on their shoulders' (Exod. 12:34). If, on the other hand, it means 'before the leaven had been mixed in', this would suggest that the Hebrews used a sourdough, added near the end. Liquids – and most early leavens were liquid – are not easy to blend into dough that has

* With the exception of birds like the eagle that had talons/claws and were therefore carnivorous.

already been mixed, whereas a piece of dough left over from the previous day's rising could be incorporated quite easily.

In the last analysis the laws handed down from Sinai reinforce one of history's lessons: dietary regimes established for doctrinal purposes have more to do with doctrine than with diet. From one point of view they are statements of exclusivity; from another, isolating factors – and sometimes for that very reason invitations to persecution.

— 5 —

CLASSICAL GREECE

Although by 3000 BC the peoples of the Tigris-Euphrates and Nile valleys had adapted their diet to fit their farming,* in Greece almost 2,000 years later memories of nomad pastoralism were still recent and romantic. Athenaeus might complain that the epic heroes knew nothing of even such commonplace delicacies as 'appetizers served in vine leaves',[1] but Homer drew on as sound a tradition for his characters' food as for their exploits.

When Achilles played host to Odysseus outside the walls of Ilium, he gave him a meal that might have been offered by any nomad chief for a thousand years before, or after, the Trojan Wars.

Patroclus 'put down a big bench in the firelight, and laid on it the backs of a sheep and a fat goat and the chine of a great hog rich in lard. Automedon held these for him, while Achilles jointed them, and then carved up the joints and spitted the slices. Meanwhile, Patroclus, the royal son of Menoetius, made the fire blaze up. When it had burned down again and the flames disappeared, he scattered the embers and laid the spits above them, resting them on logs, after he had sprinkled the meat with holy salt. When he had roasted it and heaped it up on platters, Patroclus fetched some bread and set it out on the table in handsome baskets; and Achilles divided the meat into portions.'[2]

This heroic predilection for roast meat was not to survive the problems posed by the landscape of Greece. In the early days wild boar was still there for the hunting, and settled communities were able to feed their pigs on acorns and beechmast from the trees that clothed the lower levels of the mountain ranges, but the long narrow valleys of the interior and the slender ribbons of fertile plain round the coasts set an irrevocable limit to stockrearing. Only in a few areas such as Boeotia (whose name means 'cow land') were there lands flat and wide enough to pasture cattle.

* And their style of government. The centralized organization of vast irrigation systems helped to make despotism (and the pharaohs) possible.

While the human population remained small, the farmer and his family lived off the land in modest comfort. They grew a little wheat or barley, tended their fig and olive trees and a few vines, reared pigs and kept a goat to provide milk and cheese. If they were rich, they might have some sheep and a pair of oxen or mules.

The farmer-poet Hesiod painted an idyllic picture of life in the eighth century BC.

> Then in a great rock's shadow, with milk-bread, let me lie,
> And Byblian wine, and milk from goats just going dry,
> And flesh of an uncalved heifer, fed in a forest glade,
> Or kids first-born of their mother. So let me sit in the shade,
> With a bellyful within me, sipping at my ease
> The fire-red wine, and turning to face the western breeze.[3]

As the population increased, however, everything changed until by about 650 BC the Attic peasant was leading a marginal existence on marginal land. The hillsides had been denuded of their trees to provide the timber needed for houses, for the ships on which the economy of the Greek states depended, and for the charcoal that was being swallowed up in ever-increasing quantities by the demands of metalworking.

Tree-felling may have seemed beneficial at first, providing valuable timber while at the same time clearing new land for cultivation. But the light soil of Greece, no longer fed by dead leaves or held together by living tree roots, soon began to be washed away by the torrential rains of winter. Formerly, the rains had been beneficial; filtering through the branches, they had soaked slowly and gently into the soil and then down to the limestone below, from which they drained gradually to the low ground. Now, instead, they poured onto the bare hillsides and thundered straight on downwards to flood the plains. Gradually, the hills lost their soil and the valleys their fertility.

Those who tried to carry on traditional, self-sufficient farming on the increasingly barren lower ground were plunged into debt. In the old days a family short of grain in the lean period before the harvest had been able to borrow a sack or two from a neighbour, but after money was introduced in 625 BC, things changed. Instead of borrowing grain, the peasant had to borrow money – a very different psychological proposition – and use it to buy what he needed at high, pre-harvest prices. When the time came to repay the loan, he either had to raise cash by selling his own produce at low post-harvest prices, or hold on until the market improved, paying punitive rates of interest in the meantime.

THE OLIVE

At the beginning of the sixth century BC Solon forbade the export of any agricultural produce other than olive oil. It was a wisely intended policy, but it struck the final and fatal blow at the Greek landscape.

The few remaining fibrous-rooted trees were felled for the sake of the olive, whose long tap root struck deep down into the limestone and did nothing to knit, conserve or feed the topsoil. By the fourth century BC Plato was gloomily contrasting the bare white rock of the Attic countryside he knew with the green meadows, woods and springs of the not-too-distant past.[4] In effect, the pure and brilliant light that is so startling a characteristic of Greece today had been bought at the expense of the trees that had once kept the land fertile. It had taken thousands of years for the Neolithic Revolution to desiccate the countryside of Mesopotamia; it took only a few hundred in the topographical context of Greece.

Cultivation of the olive is said to have begun 6,000 years ago at the eastern end of the Mediterranean. The straggly, spiny wild plant, poor in oil, had been widely distributed even before that time, but it needed the agricultural and mercantile genius of the Syrians and Palestinians to develop the thornless, compact, oil-rich cultivars that were to spread all along the shores of the Mediterranean.

Oils were everywhere in demand in the ancient world, for cooking, lighting and medicine, the lustrations of Egypt and the perfumed unguents with which the early Mediterranean peoples anointed their bodies. The olive was by no means the only provider, of course, even if it was the most productive known during the Bronze Age. In Greece oils were also extracted from the walnut and the opium poppy; in Mesopotamia and Africa, from sesame;* from almonds in Anatolia; flax and radish seeds in Egypt; flax and cameline (dwarf flax) in northern Europe. In South, Central and North America respectively, there were groundnut, maize and sunflower-seed oils, while in

---

* Sesame is thought to have been a native of Africa, though it found its way to India at, or soon after, the time of the Indus Valley civilizations. There are claims for it in China in the fourth millennium BC, but it appears more likely that it was introduced considerably later, during the early Han era.[5]

Asia the soy bean and the coconut palm were among the early sources.

But in a small country dependence on a single export crop brings, as a natural sequel, dependence on foreign trade for the necessities of life and a resultant defencelessness in wartime. Crete, which had grown rich during the third millennium BC on the produce of its olive groves, discovered this, and Athens in the end was to do so too.

During the century and a half after Solon, Athens appeared to flourish on the smooth green-gold oil of the olive and silver from the mines of Laurium. But as first the olive and then the vine, supplemented by fig and nut trees, took over the Attic landscape, livestock became few and wheat and barley virtually disappeared. The trade of Greece and the Greek empire itself expanded to meet the country's urgent need for the basics of life.

VINTAGES OF THE GREEK WORLD

The olive, the first great export crop of Greece, was followed a few centuries later by the product of the vine. From about the fifth until the latter part of the first century BC, Greece and the islands were the Burgundy of the Mediterranean world.

There are many picturesque tales about the origins of wine, but what probably happened was that at some time during the Neolithic era a container of *vinifera* grapes* was left neglected in a corner. The juice would run, and in the right conditions ferment and then settle; someone (tradition often makes it a woman) had the courage to taste the result and found it congenial. This suggests that the grapes in question may originally have been dried for keeping, but not quite enough. If they had been fresh, the accidental 'wine' would probably have been very rough, whereas fermentation of dried grapes would produce something sweeter, less alcoholic and more palatable.

The wild vine flourished in the Caucasus, and it may have been there that it was first brought under cultivation. It is unlikely that wine was made regularly until pottery was invented, since its making and storage would take up a disproportionate number of containers even if (as it probably was) it was of the ferment-for-a-day, mature-for-a-week variety.

* *Vitis vinifera*, the parent of more than 3,000 modern varieties of wine grape, is attested several thousand years before the Neolithic era.

By 3000 BC grape wine was known in Mesopotamia (whose rulers seem to have taken a personal interest in it) and Egypt, where it was at first used mainly in temple rituals. It did not find its place as a popular drink until the first millennium BC, when Greek influence began to be felt in Egypt. Egyptian temple vintners had been expert long before then, however, and it is perfectly possible that the Greeks simply exported to secular Egypt a fashion they had earlier imported from priestly Egypt.

In the Mediterranean during the Greek golden age most countries produced some kind of *ordinaire*, although rich men everywhere preferred the expensive vintages of Lesbos and Chios. The great wines are thought to have been sweet, and it has been suggested that the most famous wine of antiquity, the Pramnian so frequently mentioned by Homer, may have been as rich as Tokay.[6] They were. also thick and sticky, partly from evaporation through the walls of the earthenware amphorae in which the finer vintages were kept for as long as twenty-five years, and had to be heavily diluted with water.

There seems little doubt that the wine had a characteristic tang that might not find favour today. It was fermented in vats smeared inside and out with resin, and the goatskins or pigskins into which it was subsequently filtered no doubt made their own contribution to both flavour and aroma. Since fermentation was not a scientifically controlled process, the unadulterated wine did not keep well, and by early Classical times most regions had developed their own additives to rectify this. One formula involved a brew of herbs and spices that had been mixed with condensed sea water and matured for some years; another used liquid resin blended with vine ash and added to the grapes before fermentation. Wine was often matured in the loft where wood was seasoned and meat smoked, but although reasonable smoking was thought to improve a wine, the later Romans were united in disapproval of French vintners who over-smoked wines in order to make them seem older than they were.[7]

Greek wines began to go out of fashion after the first of the great Italian vintages, the Opimian, appeared in 121 BC, and in the centuries that followed many other Italian wines, including Falernian, became household names. The competition was too stiff for Greece. Italian vineyards were capable of producing over 1,600 gallons an acre[8] – far more than those of Greece, which were never very productive and always old-fashioned in their methods. Also, as the boundaries of the Roman Empire expanded, the taste for Italian wine, even the vines themselves, were carried to many new lands.

GREEK FOOD AND COOKING

The Greek peasant family never saw much profit from their vines and olives, but in time of peace they could rely on a solid, if monotonous, diet.

Even so, Sir Alfred Zimmern's oft-quoted definition of the Attic dinner as consisting of two courses, 'the first a kind of porridge, and the second a kind of porridge', was unduly severe.[9] Although the Greek word *maza*, like the Latin *puls*, is usually translated (according to the translator's fancy) as 'cakes' or 'porridge', the word *maza* carries the implication of 'kneaded things other than bread'[10] and both terms certainly included unbaked grain-pastes in the Neolithic tradition. *Puls* had a wider meaning than *maza*, since it covered pastes made from lentils and beans as well as grain.

From Pliny the Elder's Greek and Italian recipes for barley *puls*, it seems that in his day the term meant an oily, highly seasoned paste rather than a porridge.

The Greeks, he said, 'soak some barley in water* and then leave it for a night to dry. Next day they dry it by the fire and then grind it in a mill ... When it has been got ready, in the mill they mix three pounds of flax seeds [which produces linseed oil when warmed and pounded], half a pound of coriander seed, and an eighth of a pint of salt, previously roasting them all.' Everything was then mixed together. Italians, unlike the Greeks, did not steep their barley first; instead, they baked it and then ground it 'into fine meal, with the addition of the same ingredients, and millet as well.'[11]

It was still one of the virtues of the grain-pastes, especially in these sophisticated forms, that they stayed palatable for quite some time. Pliny recommended packing *puls* into a container for long-term storage and covering it with a layer of flour and bran.

Until the middle of the fifth century BC the diet of rich and poor was essentially the same. The peasant ate barley-paste, barley gruel or barley flatbread, with a handful of olives, a few figs, some goat's milk cheese or occasionally salt fish for added savour. Water and goat's milk were the usual drinks and meat a rarity except at times of

---

* Typically, he does not say how much barley, how much water or for how long the barley was to be soaked; these were things everyone was supposed to know without being told. But the next two steps would have been pointless unless the grain had been kept moist until it was at least on the verge of sprouting, and the recipe nowhere refers to cooking the grain.

religious sacrifice and feasting. Then, the officiating priest, after giving due heed to the omens indicated by the shape and condition of the sacrificial animal's liver, divided the carcass into three parts – one (not usually the best) for the god, one for the priest and one for the donor or donors.[12] While the god's portion was cooking, the priest, under the reverent but watchful eye of the paying customers, prepared and roasted their share. Similar ceremonies continued to be held in Rome, although the reverence was less in evidence. According to

Soothsayer, consulting the liver of a sacrificed animal. There were instructional models for him to refer to, rather like modern acupuncture maps.

Suetonius, the emperor Vitellius 'thought nothing of snatching lumps of meat or cake off the altar, almost out of the sacred fire, and bolting them down'.[13]

The rich drank less water and more wine; they could eat goat, mutton or pork without having to wait for a sacrificial occasion; and they might have deer, hare, partridge and songbirds to add variety. But in country and city alike, early Greece was an outdoor society and its cuisine correspondingly simple. Morning and midday snacks were taken outdoors, or at the corner of a table, and the more substantial evening meal was equally unceremonious. The symposium or banquet so dear to literary tradition was a kind of supper party at which the food was swiftly disposed of to make way for the real business of the evening – talking and drinking.

The Greek ideal of food can be seen in a passage from Telecleides' *The Amphictyons*, which reconstructed an imaginary golden age. 'Every torrent ran with wine, and barley-pastes fought with wheaten loaves to be first to men's lips . . . Fish would come to the house and bake themselves, then serve themselves up at table. A river of soup, swirling along hot pieces of meat, would flow by the couches; conduits full of piquant sauces for the meat were close at hand for the asking . . . On dishes there would be honey cakes all sprinkled with spices, and roast thrushes served up with milk cakes flew down a man's gullet.'[14] Shorn of the poetics, this was no more than good plain cooking. Fruit and vegetables, it may be noted, had no place in Telecleides' vision.

But although the evidence suggests that the average Greek was no great gourmet, even he shuddered at the diet of the Spartans, whose 'black broth'– reputedly made from pork stock, vinegar and salt – was infamous throughout the civilized world. Athenaeus reported the tale of the citizen of Sybaris invited to dine in the Spartans' public mess hall, who, as he lay on the wooden benches and ate with them, remarked that he had always before been astounded to hear of the Spartans' courage. But now he was forced to conclude that they were not, after all, superior to other peoples. 'For any man in his senses would rather die ten thousand times over than live as miserably as this.'[15]

After the fifth century BC and especially during the magnificent, self-assured days of Pericles and the Parthenon, Aeschylus, Sophocles and Euripides, Athens became a centre of art and culture, very conscious of its intellectual eminence. The contrast between rich and poor became apparent – which it had seldom been before – and so did the difference in their diet.

It would have been surprising if the new awareness of splendour had not struck an echo in the Greek kitchen. Although no recipe books remain, titles and extracts have been preserved in other works. There appear to have been at least a dozen books titled *The Art of Cooking*, and others on *Gastronomy*, *Pickles*, *Vegetables* and *Sicilian Cooking* by authors such as Glaucus of Locris, Mithaecus, Heraclidus, Hegesippus, Eristratus and Euthydemus. The father of Greek cookery writing, however, and self-styled inventor of 'made dishes' was Archestratus, who, in the fourth century BC 'diligently traversed all lands and seas in his desire . . . of testing carefully the delights of the belly' – the first in that long line of gastronomic pedants who have guided the world ever since. The style remains familiar today. While most Athenians who liked tuna fish had to make do with the dried or

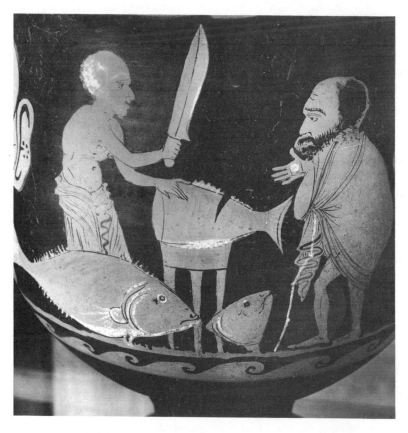

Greek fishmonger topping and tailing a fresh tuna fish.

salted variety from the Black Sea, Archestratus laid it down that none but the fresh kind from Byzantium would suffice, and that it should be eaten only in the autumn, 'what time the Pleiades are setting'.*[16]

As Athenian tastes became more exotic, they also became more cholesterol-full; fortunately, olive oil has the effect of lowering cholesterol in the blood. One much-prized delicacy in the later period was a pig that had died of over-eating; another, a goose that had been fed (probably force-fed) on moistened grain. The eggs of the peacock, a rare and much-admired bird, were claimed to be highly superior; 'fox-goose' eggs ranked second; and hen's eggs a distant third. The domestic hen was common in the Mediterranean by the fifth century BC and almost every Athenian had one, which may help to explain the poor gastronomic rating of its eggs.[17]

The Athenians were also responsible for inventing the original hors d'oeuvre trolley, which other Greeks adduced as proof of their miserly disposition. An Athenian dinner, claimed Lynceus, was an insult to a hungry man. 'For the cook sets before you a large tray on which are five small plates. One of these holds garlic, another a pair of sea urchins, another a sweet wine sop [probably some scraps of wine-soaked bread or marinated fish], another ten cockles, the last a small piece of sturgeon. While I am eating this, another is eating that; and while he is eating that, I have made away with this. What I want, good sir, is both the one and the other, but my wish is impossible . . . Such a layout as that', he concluded,† 'may seem to offer variety, but is nothing at all to satisfy the belly.'[18]

Satisfaction was a relative term. Within the walls of Athens in the latter part of the fifth century BC, Sophocles, Euripides and Aristophanes wrote comedies and tragedies that are still being performed today; outside, the Attic countryside was ravaged by the Peloponnesian Wars. The small peasant was ruined, reduced to a diet of pulses, greens and turnips, iris rhizomes, beechnut, lupin seeds (said to be sour but very nutritious), an occasional grasshopper, wild pears 'and that god-given inheritance of our mother country, darling of my heart, a dried fig'. If there was enough food for more than three of the family, said the poet Alexis of Thurii, it was unusual; as a rule, the others had to make do with a mouthful of barley-paste.[19]

---

* The setting of the Pleiades marked the end of the Greek sailing (and fishing) season, which put a very firm period to the availability of Archestratus-approved tuna.

† Sounding very much like John Bull in a *nouvelle cuisine* restaurant.

Recovery, as often as not, was impossible for such a family. It takes three or four years for a newly planted vine to produce a worthwhile crop, thirty years in the case of the olive. Ultimately, the small peasant sold out to the speculators and – like so many peasants in so many countries before and since – left the countryside for the doubtful haven of the city.

Officialdom made sporadic attempts to help the Athenian poor, but it was to be left to the Romans to embark on the first widespread – and, in the end, self-defeating – social welfare scheme.

6

IMPERIAL ROME

Juvenal was not the only one who complained that the Romans were interested in nothing but bread and circuses; it was just that he put it more succinctly than most. A little too succinctly, in fact, since it was not bread itself, but the *annona* – the distribution of *free* bread – that obsessed them.

The *annona* originated as an official attempt to relieve poverty, but soon grew into a huge public subsidy that distorted the whole economic and social structure of the state. From as early as the sixth century BC, Rome had suffered occasional shortages and famines, but it was only in 123 BC, when the cost of living rose to a dangerous level, that Gaius Gracchus set the precedent of allowing all citizens to buy their grain from public granaries at below the market price.[1]

By 71 BC not just cut-price but free grain was being dispensed to 40,000 adult males in the city of Rome, and in the decades that followed the number of people receiving it increased to such an extent that Julius Caesar thought it a matter for congratulation that he had succeeded in cutting the numbers back to a mere 150,000. Half a century later they had soared again – to 320,000, which meant that in Rome's imperial heyday one in three of the population was on the dole.[2]

Nor did it stop there, either in numbers or materials. Early in the third century AD Septimius Severus ingratiated himself not only with the Roman plebs but with his native city of Leptis Magna (suffering a trade recession) by buying up its oil and giving it away. Thirty years later Severus Alexander decreed that the people should have ready-made bread instead of grain.[3] Aurelian increased the daily ration to almost one and a half pounds, added pork fat to the list and, anxious to use up the wine paid as tax by the growers, threw that in too. When he proposed that this should form a regular feature of the *annona*, a scandalized official exclaimed, 'Before we know where we are, we will be giving them chickens and geese as well.'[4] In the latter days of the Empire, however, the state of the economy became so serious that free food distribution ceased, even though many basics continued to be made available at unrealistically low prices.

It took 14 million bushels* of wheat a year to feed the people of Rome in Augustus's time, representing the produce of hundreds of square miles of wheat fields.[5] One third of it came from Egypt, and

In second-century North Africa, horses (more vigorous than oxen) were employed to thresh the wheat.

most of the rest from Sicily and North Africa. Although when Rome defeated Carthage in the second century BC, it tore down the city and, with a fine sense of melodrama, ploughed its very foundations into the soil, there was no question of destroying the wheat fields. Indeed,

* There is no satisfactory urban yardstick for the rural bushel, a measure of volume. Perhaps it is easiest to think of 14 million bushels as equivalent to 112 million gallons – in other words, a lot.

to safeguard its hold over them, Rome embarked on a deliberate career of expansion, becoming suzerain of the Numidian kingdoms and going on to subdue the semi-nomadic tribes of the hinterland. In the first century BC Cyrenaica and Egypt also submitted, and Rome had all the cultivable land north of the Sahara in its grasp.

Wheat was a factor not only in territorial expansion but in the history of seafaring. Draught cattle might take a week to haul a ton or two of grain a hundred miles but, given a fair wind, ships carrying a thousand tons could make the 300-mile journey from North Africa to Ostia in four days or less, the 1000-mile one from Alexandria in thirteen. Special docks and lighthouses were built for the grain ships, and even Britain was not too far away to be an imperial granary.

Transporting the grain was a well-policed operation. The wheat was handed over in its country of origin to shippers whose contract stipulated that they carry it to Ostia by the shortest possible route – or, after Ostia silted up, to the adjacent artificial harbour of Portus; they were forbidden to put in to land at any intermediate point on pain of death or deportation. When the wheat reached port, it was

Frail though it looked, the Roman merchant vessel was capable of quite daring voyages.

unloaded and checked for quality and quantity; a sample of the shipment was usually sent separately in a sealed bag to insure against adulteration or fraud.[6] Finally, it was carried up river in hundreds of barges on the last three-day stage to Rome, where it was delivered to the millers.

This imported grain was specifically for the city of Rome, the rest of the country being left to manage as best it could (in which it succeeded very well), and the plebs knew as much as the authorities about the ships and when they were due in. On at least one occasion, when they were late, the whole city gave way to panic.

GRAIN INTO FLOUR

The Roman miller-baker was one of the first mass-producers in the history of the food industry,* and he owed it to the most important new application of rotary motion since the potter's wheel.

In the early days of the Neolithic period people had prepared their husked and winnowed grain by placing it on a large saucer-shaped stone and rubbing it with a smaller, bun-shaped one – a combination developed long before for pounding berries and dyes and, in principle, not unlike a very basic pestle and mortar. As grain usage increased, the saddle quern was evolved. Here, the protohistoric miller knelt at one end of a slanted, rectangular base stone and pushed his or her

The saddle quern, Egypt, c.2500 BC.

rubbing stone (now shaped like a rolling pin) backwards and forwards over the grain on the base stone. It was a task requiring much patience and stamina, but the next development showed that humanity was at last beginning to think technologically; the heavy rolling pin was changed for a small, thick, rectangular slab with a hole in the middle

* In the drink industry, of course, the vintners were well ahead of him.

through which grain could be fed onto the grinding surface. This hopper rubber meant that the operator no longer had to lift up the stone every time grain had to be added.

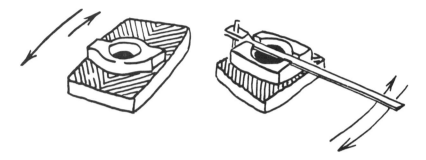

Hopper rubber and lever-operated hopper rubber.

Until the fifth century BC the grinding motion had been backwards and forwards, but then it was discovered that a side-to-side movement, with a lever attached to the rubbing stone, greatly improved the efficiency of the operation. It was at this stage that the professional miller entered on the scene, but he only came into his own when the swivel idea was carried to its logical conclusion in the rotary quern.

Rotary quern, still in use in nineteenth-century India. The central peg was a pivot, and the other a handle that forced the upper stone round.

The domestic model, which was also the military one – Roman legions on the march carried one quern for every ten men – consisted of a circular base stone with a spindle in the centre and an upper rubbing stone of roughly the same size, which had a handle and a feeding hole, and revolved round the spindle in the base.

The commercial donkey mill. The upper half was the hopper; the lower a revolving millstone that grated against an inner cone. The flour was channelled out through the grooves at the bottom.

Although the commercial queen looked very different, more like an hourglass, the principle was the same. For the first time large-scale, semi-mechanical grinding was practicable, powered by animal muscle. It had never been possible to drive draught animals backwards and forwards, or from side to side to match the action of the old millstones, but to keep them plodding round and round in a circle was an easy matter.

With the introduction of the donkey mill, the professional miller found himself profitably in business, and in the second century BC, by a kind of natural extension, he also became a baker.[7]

Even so, Romans were disinclined to place their full reliance on the millers. There were too many minor breakdowns, and an occasional major one as well. In the first century AD all the mills of Rome ground to a halt when Caligula commandeered the animals that turned them, and the same thing happened in the sixth century (by which time the mills were water-powered), when the invading Goths cut off the water supply. Most households therefore kept a saddle quern or a small rotary quern that could be used in emergencies.

By medieval times, some water-powered mills were no longer immobilized
when the level of the river fell; they were mounted on rafts or boats that rose
and fell with the tide.

ROMAN BREAD

The Classical world, taking its tone, perhaps, from Egypt – whose
views on diet were as obsessive as those of the West in the 1980s – had
strong opinions about the nutritional value of different flours and
breads. 'Bread made of wheat', declared Diphilus of Siphnos, 'as
compared with that made of barley is more nourishing, more digestible
and in every way superior. In order of merit, the bread made from
refined [thoroughly sieved] flour comes first, after that bread of ordinary wheat and then the unbolted, made of flour that has not been
sifted.'[8]

Cooking methods were also a matter for concern. Galen, the great
physician whose pronouncements were to remain basic to Western
medicine for another 1,500 years, said that 'bread baked in the ashes
is heavy and hard to digest because the baking is uneven. That which
comes from a small oven or stove causes dyspepsia and is hard to
digest. But bread made over a brazier or in a pan, owing to the
admixture of oil, is easier to excrete, though steam from the drying

makes it rather unwholesome. Bread baked in large ovens, however, excels in all good qualities, for it is well flavoured, good for the stomach, easily digested, and very readily assimilated.'[9]

Athenaeus, describing breads ancient and 'modern', native and foreign, threw out an endless list of what must have been the bloomers, baguettes, croissants and crumpets of his day. There were honey-and-oil bread, suet bread and cheese bread; large and gritty Cilician loaves, a soft, salty raised bread known as Cappadocian, and a mushroom-shaped kind covered with poppy seeds; pancakes; rolls baked on a spit (a military speciality); wafer bread, which was thin and crisp and had wine, pepper and milk among the ingredients; and *dice* – square loaves flavoured with aniseed, cheese and oil.[10]

In general, the flavoured breads were eaten on their own, with water, milk or wine, while the plain ones were dipped in wine or goat's milk for a *prandium* (midday snack) or eaten dry at the main meal (the *cena*), when they were used for mopping up rich sauces.

The concept of bread-and-butter, however, was still very far distant. Rome was as reliant on the olive as Greece, and butter was strictly a food of the barbarian pastoralists – 'your butter-eating gentry', as Anaxandrides called them.[11]

CLASS DISTINCTIONS

The Roman poor rarely, if ever, tasted Cappadocian bread or wine wafers. Grain-pastes were their staple, or sometimes a coarse home-made bread bristling with chaff, or a polenta-like porridge made from millet. Things may have improved slightly in the third century AD, when the *annona* began distributing loaves instead of grain; although the miller-baker was popularly thought to have a whole battery of fraudulent tricks at his command, the plebs knew their rights and it would have been a brave miller who tried to fob them off with bread no better than they could have made at home.

The plebs' usual drink was water, and their cooking was primitive because equipment was primitive, fuel a problem and fire a constant hazard in the tall, narrow *insulae* (tenements) in which most of them lived. Understandably, they avoided cooking whenever they could, buying their food instead from the 'grimy cookshops' that cluttered the streets – a slice of roast pork, some salt fish or goat's-milk cheese, or more often just a handful of olives, raw beans or figs.

Those who were a stage or two up from poor fared dispropor-tionately better. Juvenal, who claimed to be a modest man, contented himself with dining on 'a plump kid, tenderest of the flock, with more of milk in him than blood', some wild asparagus, 'lordly eggs warm in their wisps of hay together with the hens that laid them', and a dish of grapes, pears and apples to end with.[12]

The food of the rich, of course, was very different, and in the case of Rome – for perhaps the first time in history – radically different. Whereas in other societies differences had lain more in quantity and quality than in materials, the Roman rich had access to an astonishing variety of foodstuffs. Their passion for exotics is sometimes exaggerated by modern authors influenced by Classical gourmet texts (no more representative in the second century AD than in the twentieth), but it did exist and on a not inconsiderable scale. The only pike worth eating may have come, conveniently if unhygienically, from 'between the two bridges' at Rome[13] – the stretch separating the Tiber island from the *cloaca maxima* (the main sewer) – but pickles had to be imported from Spain, ham from Gaul, wine from the Jura, oysters from Britain and spices from Indonesia.

If Rome had known something of the Americas and more about Asia than the Asians themselves chose to tell it, the Roman gourmet – who had a distressingly vulgar streak – would have felt it necessary to send right round the world for the potatoes and 'French' beans of South America; the tomatoes, chocolate and maize of Central America; the limes and mangoes of India; the oranges – and the tea – of China. Fortunately for the economy, already under strain from the demand for spices, Rome knew nothing of these.

THE LANGUAGE OF FOOD

It is difficult not to be curious about the finished effect of a cuisine that remains persistently elusive, but before going into the matter of textures and flavours a caveat must be entered on the general subject of banquets and social eating.

Nowadays, when making a display of riches is often considered as anti-social as possessing them, it can be hard to conceive of a world in which extravagance was not only an adjunct of power but a necessary expression of it. Yet until less than two centuries ago the parade of wealth was, in itself, a declaration of the special qualities that set rulers and nobles above the common herd.* The royal banquet was as

---

* Even if the parade was frequently responsible for draining the treasury dry.

important an item in the public relations budget as the Field of
Cloth of Gold or, indeed, a presidential inauguration today – a
political and social statement that had only the most incidental
connection with gastronomy.

The banquet is just one example of the way in which food can be
used to make a general affirmation. Dietary exclusivity such as that of
the Hebrews and, to a lesser extent, the Muslims, is another. But it
can also be used in a much more precise context. Where a meal is
served to guests at home, the care taken in preparation can speak
volumes. As Alice B. Toklas neatly put it, 'If you wished to honour a
guest you offered him an omelette *soufflé* with an elaborate sauce, if
you were indifferent . . . an omelette with mushrooms or *fines herbes*,
but if you wished to be insulting you made fried eggs.'[14]

Nowadays, although an ordinary family supper may be shared with
very close friends, in most other cases potluck gives way to the silver
salver. Taking guests to eat out has at last become widely acceptable,
although until quite recently it was regarded as a reflection either on
the hostess's cooking or her willingness to exert herself. The choice of
restaurant also speaks volumes, wherever it may be. The ordinary
French bistro with its 75-franc, 100-franc and 150-franc menus has
up-market parallels; parallels, too, with the restaurants of China,
which in late imperial times offered 'first-class' meals of sixteen dishes,
'second-class' meals of ten dishes, and 'third-class' meals of eight
dishes. (Today, the distinctions are expressed, as in France, in
terms of price.) Systems of government may change, but the basic
language of food does not: to offer too cheap or commonplace a meal
is insulting; the opposite, ostentatious.

In the last analysis political eating has more to do with symbolism
than with the taste buds, and this has to be remembered when the
banquet is presented, as it too often is, as representative of food and
society at some particular period in history. Representative it is not,
nor ever was. All the banquet ever represented before the days of
royal democratization was the state of contemporary culinary expertise and the costliness (not the general availability) of its raw
materials.

One further proviso. In the matter of documentation it also has to
be remembered that professional gossip-columnists go back a very
long way – Athenaeus was one, Suetonius another – which means that
reports about the food served on great occasions have to be treated
with additional caution. Not until rulers began to make concessions
to the ruled were banquets reduced to something resembling the rich

man's dinner party; not until then were guests invited who had no particular axe to grind.

THE PROBLEM OF TEXTURE

All this having been said, let us return to the Roman banquet.

The standard text of Classical gastronomic literature is Trimalchio's feast from *The Satyricon* of Petronius, a fictional extravaganza built on an unmistakable and amusing basis of fact, during which guests were offered a hare tricked out with wings to look like a Pegasus, a wild sow with its belly full of live thrushes, quinces stuck with thorns to look like sea urchins, a hog stuffed with sausage links, roast pork carved into model fish, and several other frivolities of the kind.[15] It was satire, but only just, and its idiosyncratic grandeur proves on analysis to have been largely a matter of kitchen cosmetics, ruinously expensive only in the number of slaves employed to produce it.

The dish that the emperor Vitellius, a noted glutton, named after the goddess Minerva was, however, something entirely different. According to Suetonius, it required pike liver, pheasant brains, peacock brains, flamingo tongues and lamprey roe,[16] ingredients that had to be brought to Rome from every corner of the Empire. Cloying though the combination sounds at first, 'a dish of' could mean almost anything, and if it meant what would nowadays be called a terrine, it might have been excellent. 'If', however, is the operative word.

Guesstimating the finished effect of a dish from a bare list of ingredients is one of the major hazards in cooking history, and a bare list is usually all there is. Until the fifteenth century food writers (except in the Arab world) seldom mentioned quantities.

The nearest thing to a Roman cookery book that survives today is the work bearing the name of the first-century gourmet Apicius, who is reported to have poisoned himself when he realized that he had no more than 10 million sesterces left, on which it would be impossible to maintain his standard of living.*[17]

By no means all the recipes in the book, which was not compiled until at least three centuries after Apicius' time, can be attributed to the master himself. Some were certainly later, and a few of these were extracted from manuals of dietetics – fortunately for later generations, since medical writers sometimes did specify quantities. One such

---

* This would be equivalent to just under three-quarters of a ton of gold bullion.

recipe, for a sauce for roast meat, lists a quarter of an ounce each of pepper, lovage, parsley, celery seed, dill, asafoetida root, hazelwort (a bitter herb, emetic in large quantities), cyperus (turmeric), caraway, cumin and ginger, plus a little pyrethrum (a member of the chrysanthemum family, now used as an insecticide), a pint of liquamen (see below), and two and a half fluid ounces of oil.[18]

There is no indication of how much meat this lethal brew was intended to be sprinkled on, or to drown, but since the correct number for a full dinner party in Roman times was nine (the Greeks had a preferred maximum of five), it is possible that quantities were generally given for nine people. In that case there would be about a coffee-cupful of sauce for each diner, a reasonable amount if it were intended to be served separately as a kind of dip. Given the heavy spicing, it would also keep well, and might have been intended as the equivalent of one of today's bottled or 'store' sauces.

Although most recipes are inescapably cryptic about the texture of food, the Roman style of dining is suggestive. The nine guests, who were accommodated on three couches arranged in a U shape round the table, reclined at three-quarters length, propping themselves on their left forearms and stretching for food and drink with their right hands. Forks were unknown and knives and spoons rarely used, so most Romans ate with their fingers, a sticky proceeding if the meat were ready sauced. Although they did use fingerbowls, and sometimes napkins spread protectively over the edge of the couch, the most convenient food must have been something like roast meat with, on the side, a sauce with the sturdy independence of a good mayonnaise; many of the Apician sauces included wheat starch or crumbled pastry, which acted as thickeners.

Pastry had an additional usefulness in the days of finger-eating, since it served as both food and platter; even, when the need arose, as a scoop. One character in Petronius, describing a cold tart served with 'a mixture of some wonderful Spanish wine and honey', tells how he took 'a fat helping of the tart and scooped up the honey generously'.[19] Roman olive oil pastry presumably had a firmer texture than the modern version.

LIQUAMEN AND SILPHIUM

If Classical recipes are uninformative about texture, so they also are about taste, not only because of their reticence on quantities but also because they include ingredients that are either unfamiliar today or difficult to reproduce with any guarantee of exactitude. Even so, it is safe to say that in imperial times the Romans had very little enthusiasm for natural, unadulterated flavours.

One of the commonest and strongest seasonings was *liquamen* (or *garum*), a clear, golden, fermented fish sauce with a distinctively salty flavour. A keeping sauce, it was popular enough to be commercially produced; the best brews came from Pompeii, Leptis Magna and Antipolis (Antibes).

Of the several recipes for *liquamen*, the following seems to have been standard.

'It is best to take large or small sprats or, failing them, anchovies or horse-mackerel or mackerel, make a mixture of all and put into a baking trough. Take 2 pints of salt to the peck of fish and mix well to have the fish impregnated with salt. Leave it for one night, and then put it in an earthenware vessel which you place open in the sun for two or three months [eighteen months for large fish], stirring with a stick at intervals, then take it up, cover it with a lid and store away. Some people add old wine, 2 pints to 1 pint of fish.'[*20] If the sauce were made from especially fine fish, or from something like shrimps, the result was gastronomically superior (and correspondingly high in price).

There was a quick-brew version that could be made at home. 'Take brine and test its strength by throwing an egg into it to try if it floats; if it sinks the brine does not contain enough salt. Put the fish into the brine in a new earthenware pot, add oregano, put it on a good fire until it boils . . . Let it cool and strain it two or three times, until it is clear.'[21] This was no more than a salty fish stock, a poor substitute for the real thing.

The nearest modern equivalents to *liquamen* are probably the fermented fish sauces known in Thailand as *nam pla*, in Vietnam as *nuoc mam*, in the Philippines as *patis*, and in Cambodia as *tuk trey*. Ten million gallons a year are said to have been consumed in the 1950s – the last period for which statistics are available – in what was then French Indo-China.[22]

---

* As an example of the imponderables that make it difficult to assess and impossible to reproduce the dishes of the ancient world, *liquamen* is a good example. The final flavour would depend not only on the quality of the fish but, at least partly, on the quality of the salt – sprats, anchovies and mackerel being oily fish that go rancid very quickly. If, as seems likely, Roman salt had its ration of impurities, chemical decomposition may well have begun before the salt reached the centre of the fish – which would give the end product a character almost impossible to reconstruct with modern materials.

The scene at Eastern ports today may not differ greatly from that at the great *liquamen* factories of antiquity. A chain of labourers passes baskets of fish up from the boats to a foreman on shore, who levels the fish out in great wooden vats partially open to the air, alternating layers of fish with layers of salt until the vat is full. After a few days the liquid rendered from the fish is drained off from below and tipped back in on top of the heap, a process that has to be repeated several times over the course of the following days. Finally a wicker lid is placed on the vat and weighted down, and the brew is left to ferment and mature for several months, thickening slightly by a slow process of evaporation before the liquid is drained off and bottled.

Nutritionally, the resultant sauce is very valuable; as long as it is supplemented with vitamins, a few spoonfuls a day are said to provide almost a full quota of the nutrients required by the human body.

Nam pla tastes more of salt than fish, and a light soy sauce is usually recommended as the modern cook's alternative, but *liquamen* is generally believed to have been fishy as well as salty; the brine from salted anchovies, with a little anchovy creamed into it, might be the best option for anyone experimenting with Roman recipes. Other European fermented fish products – such as Norwegian *rakørret* (which tastes like strong cheese), Swedish *surströmming* and the *pissalat* of Provence – are no real substitute, since the Romans used the strained-off liquor rather than the fish (in which they are followed by the majority of south-east Asians), while Europeans prefer to eat the fish and ignore the liquor.

Liquamen may have been an acquired taste, but it was so commonly used that its absence from a dish must have been more noticeable than its presence.

Not quite as ubiquitous as *liquamen* but no less necessary to the Roman kitchen was the herb silphium, which came from the former Greek colony of Cyrene (Cyrenaica) in North Africa. Cyrene's economy was unhealthily dependent on two exports. 'I will *not* sail back to the place from which we were carried away', complained one character in an Antiphanes comedy, 'for I want to say goodbye to all – horses, silphium, chariots, silphium stalks, steeplechasers, silphium leaves, fevers and silphium juice!'[23]

Something happened to silphium, however – possibly there were crop failures as a result of overproduction – because it disappeared from the market in the middle of the first century AD, and no one today is entirely sure which plant it was. As a substitute, Rome began to import Persian asafoetida, the brown resinous juice of one of the giant fennels, a substance with the evil, penetrating smell of rotting garlic.

Silphium, a valuable product, was weighed and stored under the most careful supervision – although not, perhaps, that of the king, shown here.

Asafoetida was expensive, especially when a money-hungry government found it worth taxing, as happened in Alexandria in the second century AD. Apicius even gave a way of stretching it by keeping it in a jar of pine nuts to which it would communicate its savour (just as a vanilla pod flavours a jar of sugar). When a recipe needed silphium, a few of the pine nuts could be used instead.[24]

Despite the smell, a microscopic drop of asafoetida does give an indefinably pleasant taste to fish dishes, and it is much used (under the name of *hing*) in Indian vegetarian cookery. It is also worth noting that among the ingredients of that long-lived modern favourite, Worcestershire sauce, there are very small quantities of both asafoetida and anchovy essence.

THE SPICE TRADE

Although the spice trade was of respectable antiquity – imported cinnamon had been known in Egypt as early as 1450 BC – it reached a peak in the first century AD when the Roman demand for spices began to seem insatiable. At that time they accounted for forty-four of the eighty-six classifications of goods imported to the Mediterranean from Asia and the east coast of Africa. (The others included elephant trainers and eunuchs, parrots and palm oil, cottons and cooks.)[25] Egypt was also in the market for spices, if not always for culinary purposes; one formula for the incense known as *kuphi* – literally, 'holy smoke'– included twenty-six different spices in all.[26]

It was the Arabs, strategically situated, who monopolized most of the traffic with the East until the first century AD. Much of the cinnamon bark came by the long and hazardous route from Malaya and Indonesia to Madagascar (4,500 miles of open sea in double outrigger canoes), and then on up the coast of East Africa to the Red Sea. The Arabs knew very well where it came from, and how, but since there was nothing wrong with their commercial instincts, they took care to protect their middleman's profit by giving currency to a number of magical myths about its origins.

Herodotus, in credulous mood, reproduced their account of the cinnamon harvest. 'Where it comes from and what country produces it, they do not know. What they say is that the dry sticks, which we have learned from the Phoenicians to call cinnamon, are brought by large birds which carry them to their nests, made of mud, on mountain precipices which no man can climb, and that the method the Arabians have invented for getting hold of them is to cut up the bodies of dead oxen, or donkeys, or other animals, into very large joints which they carry to the spot in question and leave on the ground near the nests. They then retire to a safe distance and the birds fly down and carry off the joints of meat to their nests which, not being strong enough to bear the weight, break and fall to the ground. Then the men come along and pick up the cinnamon, which is subsequently exported to other countries.'[27]

There were equally disarming, action-packed tales about frankincense and cassia, this time featuring flying snakes and belligerent bats.[28]

Cassia leaf, known in Rome as *malabathrum*, was a more pungent version of cinnamon. It was carried in tightly balled bundles from China to the great market at the mouth of the Ganges, and shipped from there to other parts of India and to the West. Strangely, Apicius mentions *malabathrum* only three times, and cinnamon bark not at all, but there is scarcely a single recipe that does not make use of pepper.

Pepper was the spice *par excellence* of the Classical, as of the modern, world. It was already well known in Greece by the fifth century BC, although less for cooking than as an item in the pharmacopoeia. Hippocrates recommended it, blended with honey and vinegar, for the treatment of feminine disorders, and Theophrastus as an antidote to hemlock or, mixed with vinegar, for reviving a victim of suffocation.[29]

The level of market demand was to break the Arab monopoly in the end. Rome began building ships hardy enough to sail from the Red Sea coast of Egypt all the way to India, a long and dangerous journey. Spices at first remained scarce, pepper at one stage reaching a price that would be equivalent today to about £250 or more per Roman pound (twelve ounces),[30] but by the middle of the first century AD Roman mariners had discovered the monsoon winds, which carried them to south India and back in less than a year. 'The beautifully built ships of the Yavanas [foreigners]' soon became a familiar sight in the ports of Malabar. They 'came with gold and returned with pepper, and Muziris resounded with the noise.'[31] Roman demand was such that it soon began to drain Malabar of its spices, and Indian merchants had to make up the deficiency by buying in from places like Takkola ('Market of Cardamoms') and Karpuradvipa ('Camphor Isle') in south-east Asia.

A few decades after the discovery of the monsoon winds, the Han emperors of China imposed an arbitrary peace on the warring nomads who infested the wastes of Central Asia, and opened up the long and difficult land route known as the Silk Road. Rome's desire for the luxuries of China became insatiable. By the second century caravans regularly left the Chinese city of Luoyang (Lo-yang) with silk, ginger, cassia and cassia leaf, winding their way over the miles by Tunhuang, Lop Nor and Kashgar to the Stone Tower, a great meeting point somewhere north of the Pamirs. There, close to the roof of the world, exquisite Chinese silks and exotic spices were bartered for all that Rome was able to offer in exchange – glassware, pottery, asbestos cloth, coral beads, intaglio gems, grape wine for the emperor, and (the only things the Chinese really wanted) gold and silver.

Even before the monsoon winds had been discovered or the Silk Road opened, Pliny estimated that Rome was losing the equivalent of about £50 million of today's money to Asia every year. Later, the drain on gold increased dramatically and money became so seriously devalued that a measure of wheat that had cost six drachmae in first-century Egypt by the fourth century cost two million.[32] The subsequent retreat to a barter economy was to help ruin not only international trade but the Roman Empire itself.

THE FLAVOUR OF FOOD

The fact that no one even knows what Roman food was *intended* to taste like has never acted as a bar to speculation. There are two schools of thought. The first is revolted by an Apician recipe that recommends saucing cold chicken with dill, mint, dates, vinegar, *liquamen*, oil, mustard, asafoetida and boiled-down grape juice, forgetting that some of the ingredients of a modern *Salade à la Geisha*, if set down in the same random and unquantified fashion, would sound even less appetizing – crab, tomato ketchup, grapefruit, eggs, skimmed milk cheese, prawns, sunflower oil . . .*

The second, more sophisticated view is that the ingredients listed in Roman recipes, if judiciously balanced, could produce a very acceptable result. But from this perfectly tenable† position, apologists often go on to imply that the food actually served on Roman tables in Classical times would be acceptable today, which is not the same thing at all. 'Balance' and 'acceptability' are matters of taste and conditioning, and who is to say what a modern cook's taste has in common with that of a chef in a Roman villa?

Despite all this, it is possible to make at least a few deductions from the atmosphere of the recipes, and to integrate them with what is known about Roman life and attitudes of mind.

---

* With apologies to Michel Guérard's *Cuisine Minceur*, pp. 133 and 200.
† Within limits. There remain fundamental problems about the quality of Roman raw materials, not only in the case of salt and *liquamen*. How fatty was Roman pork compared with today's? How aromatic (or how musty) were the old, semi-wild spices, sun-dried and carried on camel-back and on months-long voyages in foul-smelling, leaky ships? And so on.

The very size of the city had an influence on the cuisine. In Sumer, Egypt and Greece even the greatest centres of population were relatively small, still intimately linked with the countryside that continued to provide most of their perishable foodstuffs. But imperial Rome expanded until it covered an area about quarter the size of modern Paris. The countryside receded. Transport was slow. 'Fresh' foods had to be stockpiled in warehouses. There was no refrigeration.

For the rich, these problems were not insurmountable. Indeed, there was no great emphasis in the cookery manuals on the dried and salted foods that might have been expected to figure largely on the winter menu, and although smoked meats were there it seems to have been less of necessity than because the Romans enjoyed their taste and texture. The rich had their own methods of dealing with seasonal food shortages. They had *piscinae*, or fishponds, in which fresh or salt water fish were kept alive until needed for the table, and aviaries in which thrushes were reared on millet, crushed figs and wheat flour. Fieldfares, counted as the finest of the thrush family, were even raised commercially. It was also possible, within limits, to control the timing of fresh supplies by setting slaves to tasks that could be slowed down or speeded up as the situation required – feeding snails on milk until they were too fat to slither back into their shells, stuffing dormice with nuts until they were plump enough to satisfy even the most demanding chef, clipping pigeons' wings or breaking their legs to immobilize them, and then fattening them for the table on chewed bread. (There is nothing new about the battery hen.) And the Roman fondness for fish was matched by the all-the-year-round availability of at least some of the multitude of kinds that swam in Mediterranean waters.

Even so, slow transport meant that the cook must often have been faced with the problem of having to disguise rancidity. The fishy/salty flavour of *liquamen* would certainly be useful in masking the milder fishiness of meat and poultry that had begun to go off. It would be valuable, too, for dressing up commonplace foods like eggs when, of necessity, they had to stand in for oysters or sea urchins, as well as for livening up wilted vegetables from the master's country estate. And the sometimes hard, dry flesh of exotics like the peacock undoubtedly needed improving; it was characteristic of the strongly competitive Romans, if by no means unique to them, that what was expensive or rare had to be good, by definition – even if the cook had a hard time making it so.

Spices fulfilled the same function as *liquamen*, especially in the rare (by Roman standards) cases where *liquamen* might have been too much of a good thing. Indian pepper was so important that it was numbered among the five 'essential luxuries' on which the whole foreign trade of the empire was said to be based. The others were Chinese silk, African ivory, German amber and Arabian incense.

Of the five, pepper came nearest to being a true essential, not because spices were vital to Roman *haute cuisine* but, on the contrary, because they transformed the food of everyday life. Lucullus, dining alone and presented by his cook with a plain supper, might reprimand the man with, 'What, did you not know, then, that today Lucullus dines with Lucullus?'[33] but in other households a line seems to have been drawn between family eating and social dining.

Whatever the impression conveyed by Roman recipe books (and Roman gossips), the simplicity of the Roman breakfast (*jentaculum*) and lunch (*prandium*) suggests that even the rich retained memories of their rustic origins. Breakfast was bread with a few olives or raisins, lunch something quick and easy – leftovers, perhaps some cold meat or eggs. The main meal (*cena*) may have been little more extravagant except in households where it was necessary to give a multitude of slaves something to do.

Far more than company food, plain food like grain-pastes, beans and bread *needed* spices. A strong sauce, even in small amounts, has the ability to transform disproportionate quantities of starchy food. The most intense of the world's repertoire of sauces – the soy mixtures of China, the curries of India, the chilli pastes of Mexico – developed basically as seasonings for bulky carbohydrates, which both absorb and dilute them. Only when the rich enter on the scene, the people who can afford to have meat or fish every day, are sauces like these eaten with flesh foods, which dilute them scarcely at all; so the whole essence of the cuisine is changed. This may have happened in the case of Rome, a plain, rural society transfigured by the vision of its legislators and the success of its legions.

The theory that most of the Roman aristocracy suffered from lead poisoning (which contributed to the decline of the Roman Empire)[34] emphasizes the impression of Roman food given by literary sources and suggests that city Romans, at least, may have had a need, as well as a desire, for strong flavours.

The people of Rome absorbed lead from the water that ran through their pipes, from cups and cooking pots, from cosmetics such as the white lead women used as face powder, and from their wine. To improve the rougher Roman wines, a sweet grape syrup was often added that had been boiled down in lead-lined pots; during the process, it became strongly contaminated. When the poet Martial drank five pints of wine at a sitting, therefore, he consumed, even allowing for the Romans' habit of watering their wine, not only the alcoholic equivalent of well over a bottle of whisky but something over fifty milligrams of lead.*

Among the symptoms of lead poisoning, many of which fit the Roman situation with impressive exactitude, are loss of appetite and a metallic taste in the mouth. It may be supposed that chronic sufferers would go to some lengths to find dishes that would stimulate their appetites and kill the taste of lead.

But whatever the truth about the flavour of Roman food, it was a fitting irony that the barbarians who materialized outside the gates of the city at the beginning of the fifth century AD should have demanded as tribute not only land, subsidies and military titles for their chiefs – but 3,000 pounds of pepper.

* The lead concentration of the syrup (before blending with wine) has been estimated at between 240 and 1000 milligrams per litre.[35]

7

The Silent Centuries

It was 'the funeral of the world' claimed Sidonius Apollinaris when the barbarians overran Europe in the fifth century AD, and for a while it seemed that he was right.

The tribes of Goths, Vandals, Gepids, Alemanni and Franks who brought a breath of fresh air into the stifling atmosphere of the Romanized world had been milling around the frontiers of the Roman Empire for centuries. Pushed at last into action by population pressures, the pursuit of year-round grazing for their herds and the shunting effect of nomad incursions from the east, they found themselves victorious not, in the main, because they were numerically superior – in Spain, there were only 200,000 Visigoths in relation to an estimated native population of 6 million[1] – but because they were more mobile and more dynamic, and their needs were imperative.

One of the immediate effects on the invaded territories was to accelerate a return to the land by townsmen who recognized that large centres of population acted as a natural magnet for the invader. Although in Classical Europe, as everywhere else until the full flood of the Industrial Revolution in the West, more than 90 per cent of the population was engaged in agriculture, this flight from the towns had a powerful influence on events, since every townsman made some contribution, however small, to the particular urban life-style that is the nucleus of civilization. As the towns emptied, civilization itself began to falter.

In the fifth century, however, life in the country was no more stable than in the towns. It was only partly the fault of the barbarians. The currency crises that had for so long bedevilled imperial Rome had brought about a widespread return to a barter economy, and the final disintegration of the Western half of the empire led to the dislocation of such organized trade as remained. Almost more than the invasions, economic factors had a repressive effect on rural life and the rural kitchen.

The day-to-day affairs of the silent majority are ill documented in comparison with those of the monarchs and merchants, abbots and aristocrats who have always formed the tip of the social iceberg, but conditions may not have been quite as bad as the 'Dark Ages' label makes them seem.

The diet of the rural poor in the less favoured northern regions of Europe was certainly less monotonous than the usual catalogue of 'bread, porridge, herbs and roots' suggests. Rivers and lakes gave up their fish, and coastal communities continued to gather shellfish as they had always done. Only the most incompetent countryman would fail to trap (legally or illegally) an occasional hare for the pot, while in many areas peasants were able to fatten their pigs on the acorns and beechmast in the local woods, and the domestic fowl pecked for provender in every hamlet. On the other hand, those same pigs, which were of the lanky, slow-to-fatten medieval breed, were by no means as prolific as their smaller Chinese counterparts, and neither was the hen the reliable egg factory she was to become in later centuries.

Among the root crops common during the first millennium AD were turnips, radishes, onions, leeks, carrots (of a sort) and an under-nourished form of parsnip, while 'herbs' included cabbage, spinach and cress, root tops, and the early sprouts of nettles, thistles and similar plants. Some of these were, of course, markedly seasonal and others none too plentiful; they also had to be cultivated or gathered.

In effect, there was always a possibility of variety during the fruitful seasons. But during the last months of winter the ground was barren and both humans and animals languished and sickened because their diet was lacking in essential nutrients. At such times the most common meal for the northern peasant added up to bread or grain porridge and ale, with perhaps some stewed winter cabbage, kale or onions, and occasionally a piece of salt pork.

EARLY MEDIEVAL COOKING

There is a popular belief – much favoured by gourmets of one country when they are being derogatory about the food of another – that most nations have the cuisine they deserve. It is, however, a matter of historical record that good plain cooking in any particular country, at any particular time, has always been logically and sensibly adapted to the materials, equipment and fuel available.

While the fluctuations of trade influenced some of the materials of both northern and southern cooking (the south suffering more than the north when *liquamen*, asafoetida and spices became unobtainable), it was fuel that dictated what were subsequently to become fundamental differences in cooking styles.

Around the Mediterranean a roaring fire was not only undesirable but progressively more difficult to maintain as the metalworkers' demands for charcoal swallowed up the forests of southern Europe at an ever-increasing rate. One result was the development of simple, enclosed charcoal stoves that gave southern cooks a unique expertise with quick-cooking stove-top dishes of all kinds. In the north, in contrast, there was as yet no shortage of timber.* In pre-Norman Britain cattle, sheep, horses and pigs grazed in the woods and even the peasants had access to whatever firewood they could gather 'by hook or by crook' (usually dead or fallen branches). The great halls of the nobility – built, until the eleventh century, more often of split logs than stone – were warmed by blazing central fires where cauldrons boiled, spits were turned and hotplates sizzled at the side. When there was no fire in the hall, cooking was done outdoors or in a separate kitchen shed.

What style of cooking was practised in the cauldrons that hung permanently in place in peasant huts as in lordly manors remains to some extent a matter for conjecture. There is a serious hiatus in food records between Roman times and the twelfth century and, for once, the food of the rich is almost as inadequately documented as that of the poor. The emperor Charlemagne 'almost hated' his doctors, it was said, 'because they advised him to give up the roast meat to which he was accustomed, and eat boiled instead'. His main meal of the day 'was served in four courses only, exclusive of the roast, which the hunters used to bring in on spits'.[3] And that was it; contemporary literature had little more to say about cooking styles in the Dark Ages.

From other sources, however – administrative archives, inventories and ecclesiastical records – there emerges a picture of a plain-living society scattered over much of Europe north of the Alps, dining most days on bread, water or ale, and a *companaticum* ('that which goes with the bread') from the cauldron, the original stockpot or *pot-au-feu* that provided an ever-changing broth enriched daily with whatever was available. The cauldron was rarely emptied out except in preparation for the meatless weeks of Lent, so that while a hare, hen or

---

* Even when the forests of north and west began to show signs of exhaustion at the end of the first millennium because of increased crop cultivation, the German successors of the Frankish Empire were able to push east across the Elbe and tap the seemingly limitless forests of the Slav hinterland.[2]

pigeon would give it a fine, meaty flavour, the taste of salted pork or cabbage would linger for days, even weeks. Except in really hard times, this system meant that there was generally something hot and filling to eat, even if it was no more than a soup thick with the shreds of past dinners.

Hares could be trapped in nets, caught by dogs, sometimes (if this picture is any guide) hunted by the more plebeian kinds of hawk.

Dumplings – including large ones tied in a flaxen cloth and suspended from a pot hook – could also be cooked in the cauldron. Most were made from rye flour, but from the eleventh century onwards the most common came to be the mess of dried legumes known as pease pudding that went so well with the commonest flesh food of the Middle Ages, boiled salt pork. Just as bread, rice or tortillas blunt the edge of a strong sauce, so legumes have the effect of neutralizing an excess of salt.

The old rhyme,

> Pease pudding hot, pease pudding cold,
> Pease pudding in the pot, nine days old,

suggests that pease pudding was not only a staple dish, but had keeping qualities that may well have recommended it more to the housewife than to her family.

As well as the cauldron, most households had some kind of shallow earthenware pan that could be set on the hot hearthstone at the side of the fire and used for special dishes. Though an egg might with a little ingenuity be boiled or even poached in the stockpot, it could scarcely be fried or scrambled there, and there must have been some way of utilizing broken eggs. It is possible that such a pan might also have been used for rissoles made from left-over scraps of meat hashed with vegetables from the cauldron, then bound with flour and fried; and fish or eels could be cooked separately 'in their own brew'.

A shallow pan or bowl was all that was needed for a very different kind of dish, one that in various guises crops up everywhere from India to Cuba, and China to England. Recipes for frumenty (or fermenty, fromity or furmity) are many and various, but basically it was made with new season's wheat, cleaned and lightly crushed, then soaked in hot water or milk at the side of the fire until the mixture swelled and gelatinized into a spangled white aspic. At its best, it seems always to have been something of a delicacy, but an adaptable one, since it could be eaten cold with fruit or a little fresh milk and honey – a nourishing combination – or heated up and mixed with something savoury from the stockpot for a main dish.

At least as much frumenty as bread seems to have been made from the wheat grown in northern Europe during the early Middle Ages. Even though rye, a weed of the wheatfields, had become the main crop over a wide belt of the continent, many cultivators went on hopefully planting wheat. Finding that what usually came up was a mixed crop, they discovered also that some of the wheat, separated out, could be used to make more frumenty than it would have made pure wheaten flatbread. (The raised-bread era had not yet arrived.)

Ordinarily, however, no one troubled to sort out the wheat from the rye. The everyday brown bread of northern Europe was made, sometimes with the addition of pea flour and a little barley, predominantly from rye. Where the crop showed a higher proportion of wheat, the bread was correspondingly finer. The wheat-and-rye mixture came to be known as maslin (in French, *miscelin*) and was used in sophisticated households for pastry as well as bread; pure rye flour made a pastry that was too soft to handle, and barley, the other alternative, one that was too brittle.[4]

Pastry, however, was a luxury product. It was bread that mattered, as it always had done and always would do. Instructively, the word 'lord' is derived from the Old English *hlaford*, meaning 'keeper of the bread' or loaf, i.e., master of the household. 'Lady' comes from *hlaefdigge*, meaning 'kneader of the dough'– equivalent to 'second-most-important person'.*

Good plain fare for the Normans; cauldron-cooked and spit-roasted food sauced with an episcopal blessing.

The *batterie de cuisine* in the average north European household added up to a sharp knife (of dagger form), a ladle, a cauldron, a pan, perhaps a trivet and sometimes a spit. In time the rachyncroke (racking crook) was to be developed, a double-ended pot hook with a ratchet device that enabled the cauldron to be raised or lowered over the fire. In time, too, the spit was improved with a jack that allowed semi-mechanical turning. But the cauldron remained the central and essential feature of the northern kitchen until the eighteenth century, and it was the cauldron that dictated how the majority of everyday foods should be cooked. In America the cauldron (known as the 'kettle') was still the single most important and expensive item in the settlers' baggage during the westward expansion of the nineteenth century.

Where materials were concerned, the breakdown of the imperial Roman trading structure forced the housewife to fall back on what was to be had close to home. She may or may not have had an extensive repertoire. She may or may not have inherited recipes from her grandmother. But, certainly, she had no cookery books, no

---

* Until the word became obsolete in the nineteenth century, the German for 'employer' was *Brotherr*, or 'bread-master'. In contrast, no doubt because the extreme north was livestock rather than crop country, Swedish women used to be addressed by their servants as *matmoder*, or 'meat-mother'; it was the same in Denmark and Iceland.

imported delicacies, no commercially preserved exotica, no idea of cooking styles other than her own and no knowledge of nutrition other than what she learned from old wives' tales or her own observation. Some tenth-century families may have been consistently well fed; but for others, salt pork and pease pudding were the ancestors of fish fingers and chips.

MONKS AND MONARCHS

In a period when most communities were necessarily self-supporting, monasteries and royal courts had their own ways of dealing with the problem, and bishops became as adept as kings at persuading the faithful to bequeath them desirable vineyards and productive olive groves that would remedy any deficiencies of the ecclesiastical estates.

Transporting wine and oil from distant sources back to the monastery or court was simple enough, a matter of organizing relays of tenants along the route, but it was different with perishable goods. Fortunately or unfortunately, medieval kings and bishops were constantly on the road, inspecting lands and benefices, and they were usually willing – indeed, anxious – to accept tribute or taxes-in-kind on the spot. Their huge retinues had to be fed and it was convenient to be able to rely on free supplies at every stage on the journey.

When, for example, the eighth-century King Ine of Wessex chose to break his journey in an English village, he could do so in the knowledge that it was legally bound to supply him with 300 round loaves, 10 sheep, 10 geese, 20 chickens, 10 cheeses, 10 measures of honey, 5 salmon, and 100 eels.[5] In his case, the village knew in advance what it was liable for, but this was not always so. In AD 844 Charles the Bald of France decreed that bishops were entitled to requisition, at any halt in their pastoral progress, 50 loaves, 10 chickens, 50 eggs, and 5 suckling pigs[6] – a heavy burden on a village if the visit were unheralded.

The monks and minor nobles who remained at home while their masters indulged in a gastronomic tour of the countryside had their own ways of varying the menu. The nobles went hunting, while the monks, sometimes just as strenuously, exacted what tribute they could from nearby hamlets. In the ninth century St Riquier in Picardy found itself committed to supplying the local monastery, every week, with 100 loaves, 30 gallons of fat or tallow, 32 gallons of wine and 1 gallon of oil, as well as 60 gallons of ale a day.[7]

Vegetables and herbs were grown within the walls of the monastery itself. According to a plan drawn up between AD 820 and 830 for St Gall in Switzerland (though never put into execution), the ideal was to have a physic garden close to the apothecary brother's house, planted with sixteen medicinal herbs; a kitchen garden with nine large beds each devoted to a different kind of food plant; and in the cemetery fifteen fruit trees planted between the graves. There were also pens for sheep and other livestock, although the sheep were possibly there only for the sake of their wool and the other livestock for their milk.[8]

Or possibly not. The monastic diet by the ninth century was more varied than it had been in the early days, when the Church Fathers had attempted to regulate their disciples' diet in such a way as to suppress hunger without acknowledging even a twinge of appetite; as they saw it, appetite for food led inexorably to appetite for sex.

As time passed, however, the number of monastic communities increased and became richer. Food, now, had to be taken more seriously. Monks who were wasting away on a 1000-calorie-a-day diet – consisting mainly of dried biscuit soaked in broth or thin porridge, with an occasional snack of bread and *liquamen* – made poor cultivators of fields and tenders of vineyards. After the introduction of the Benedictine rules in the sixth century, things improved and monks were allowed two meals a day, each consisting of two cooked dishes and one raw, supplemented with a Roman pound (12 ounces) of bread and a measure of wine. The dishes were mainly of vegetables and pulses but sometimes included meat. On Sundays and holy days, eggs, cheese and small fish were added, but on fast days – and by this time there were 200 of them a year – only one meal was allowed and that had to be vegetarian.

More time passed, and the quality of fast-day meals improved considerably as the monasteries began to acquire grants of land and fishing rights. Previously, fish had not been considered fast-day food, but by the tenth century many a monastery was able to boast a *vivarium* in which captured fish swam around peaceably until they were needed in the kitchen. The very existence of the *vivarium* – the monastic successor of the Roman *piscina* and predecessor of the modern fish farm – shows that fish had become of real and regular importance.

Although the first literary reference to a fast-day dish of fish dates from as late as the twelfth century, fish had become fast-day food long before then. It had even become one of the two rather flexible standards – the other was 'not meat'– against which other fast-day foods were measured. Frogs and beavers were counted unequivocally

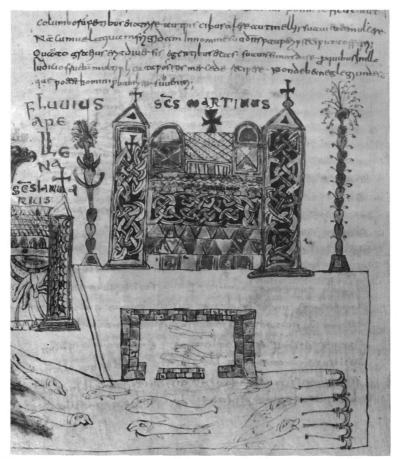

The strapwork decoration might be barbarian in influence, but the *vivarium* represented civilization, careful man with a store cupboard.

as fish; the fully developed foetus of the rabbit was classified, like eggs, as 'not meat'.*⁹

Only when the Church was afflicted by one of its periodic attacks of asceticism – brought on, as a rule, by the sight of too many over-weight abbots – were eggs, rabbit foetuses, milk and butter brought under the fast-day umbrella.

* The Romans had bred rabbits in *leporaria*, or special hare gardens, for their foetuses, and monasteries (especially in France) did so too.

THE YEARS OF FAMINE

There were many black years in northern Europe in the ninth and tenth centuries. Sometimes humans were at fault, as when the Scandinavians erupted suddenly and destructively into history, reducing churches and monasteries to smoking ruins, razing crops and carrying off cattle.

Sometimes the damage was done by nature. In the Rhine valley, in AD 857, came the first serious recorded outbreak of ergotism, in which thousands of people died, poisoned by their daily bread.[10] Rye is susceptible to a particularly virulent fungus known as ergot, which contains twenty poisons including lysergic acid diethylamide – the hallucinogen LSD. If the grain is badly contaminated, cooking is not enough to kill the fungus, and eating bread made from it can produce intense abdominal pain, delirium, gangrene and death, or else the acute inflammation of the skin that in the ninth century drove its victims to insanity and gave ergotism its common name of 'holy fire'.

In the century following the first outbreak of ergotism Europe endured twenty 'grievous famines', some of them lasting for three or four years in succession.

The south was no more fortunate than the north. It had suffered fifteen waves of plague between AD 541 and 750, some of them catastrophic, and simultaneously with the later waves had come the Arabs, bearing their new faith violently along the southern shores of the Mediterranean and up into Spain. In their triumphal progress they also carried with them a small bush that was to bring havoc to the agriculture of south-western Europe.

Until the early Middle Ages the deadly black stem rust that can lay waste to a whole harvest had been virtually unknown in Europe, but with the advent of the barberry bush – which plays host to the rust parasite at certain stages in its development – disease began to ravage the wheat fields.[11] As the barberry spread, valued for the curative potion that could be extracted from its stems and for the bright red berries that made a welcome foil to the ubiquitous mutton of the south, so did wheat rust, flourishing wherever there were warm rains, fogs or heavy dews. In the early part of the tenth century Spain had a series of disastrous wheat harvests, which brought the great famines of AD 915 and 929 in their wake.

Where there was famine, there was also cannibalism. What was said of India a few centuries later was scarcely less true in the darker parts of tenth-century Europe. 'Life was offered for a loaf, but none would buy; rank was to be sold for a cake but none cared for it . . . Destitution at last reached such a pitch that men began to devour each other, and the flesh of a son was preferred to his love.'[12]

Demand produced supply. In some of the more isolated regions killer bands roamed the countryside, waylaying travellers, cooking their flesh and selling it to the highest bidder. They may have claimed that it was pork (which cannibal communities of the modern world say it resembles), or mutton – even 'two-legged' mutton, which was what the twelfth-century Chinese called it when there was famine in the northern provinces.[13] Cannibalism born of hunger was to persist in Bohemia, Silesia and Poland until the end of the Middle Ages – an actuality that later helped to lend colour to the myths of werewolf and vampire.[14]

Nevertheless, during these dark and often despairing years new developments in agriculture were taking place that were soon to bring about a revolution in the diet of Western Europe, as well as in the whole fabric of society.

PART THREE

ASIA UNTIL THE MIDDLE AGES, AND THE ARAB WORLD

Rome's influence had stretched over a wide arc from England to the Near East, but there was another arc, its mid-point in Central Asia, which extended almost 4,000 miles from the west coast of the Black Sea to the borders of China. It was an empire of nomad pastoralists, highly complex and highly mobile, an economy of the steppes that depended first and foremost on grass, water holes and the weather. When these failed, the herds died and the nomads were faced with starvation. It was then that their need set up reverberations all the way across the Eurasian landmass. China, under strong dynasties, held them at bay, but the Song (formerly written as Sung) allowed one of the tribes – the Qitan (or Khitai), from whose name the word 'Cathay' is derived – to settle inside the Great Wall, a concession that was to alter the course of Chinese history. Long before that another horde of nomadic invaders had changed the course of India's history, too, and its diet. One product of the Indo-European incursions was the Indian caste system;
another, the sacred cow.

The nomads of the Eurasian steppes took what they wanted from the countries they overran, but the Arabs – when, in the seventh century AD, *they erupted out of their arid homeland onto a wider scene – took and also gave. Some things they destroyed, but they also returned to Europe much of the knowledge that had been lost in the collapse of the Classical world.*

— 8 —

INDIA

If any country in the world can be said to have come near to being vegetarian on principle, it is India, all of whose major religions reject at least one, sometimes all, of the meats that help to sustain the rest of humanity. Hindus eat neither beef nor pork; Muslims reject pork; orthodox Buddhists and Jains touch nothing that has had to be slaughtered. That, at least, is the theory, even if in practice there are, and always have been, a good many lapses.

As so often, beliefs like these developed against a background that was as much political and economic as it was religious. In the days of the Indus Valley civilization India's inhabitants seem to have been as ready as the next man to eat any meat that was available; there is archaeological evidence of mutton, pork, buffalo and goat. But although the mists that for so long enshrouded the origins and development of the Indus Valley civilization are at last beginning to disappear, the fact that its script has not yet been deciphered means that a whole dimension of history is still missing. Both of its great cities show signs of having been built to an elaborate, preconceived plan, with markets, granaries, dockyards, temples, public and private baths and an intricate system of drainage. Except that there were no major irrigation works, it would seem possible that Harappa and Mohenjo-Daro were little inferior to the great cities that flourished elsewhere in the centuries before and after 2000 BC. In the absence of words, however, the institutions, beliefs, philosophy, religion and even the everyday lives of the Indus peoples must remain a matter for speculation.

In the present context this might be of no more than abstract interest if it were not for the fact that the sacred cow cult, which has been a feature of Indian life through all the centuries of recorded history, may well have had its origins in the Indus Valley.

THE SACRED COW

Among the archaeological relics of the Indus Valley are almost 2,000 seals, miniature wads of clay impressed with a pictorial image and a short legend, which were used for trading or taxation purposes. Most of the images are of animals, probably symbolizing craft units or particular groups of citizens, and among the most common is a bull.

If the bull were always of the indigenous humped type (the zebu), there would be no great mystery, but in fact what appears with far more frequency is the flat-backed breed (*bos primigenius*) from which the domesticated cattle of the West are descended. On the seals, the primigenius bull is usually shown with a standard or incense-burner before it.

One theory is that the foreign bull was the symbol of a group of incomers who were in the process of being assimilated into the Indus Valley civilization – merchants, perhaps, or even an early wave of Indo-Europeans – while the incense-burner suggests that the living animal behind the symbol had a particular value. Assuming that the immigrants had fallen victim to the common early experience of driving their cattle into a climate in which they did not thrive,* it would have been natural enough to protect the survivors by stating their value in semi-religious terms that everyone would understand.

The humped and bearded zebu bull, and the flat-backed primigenius type, with a standard or incense-burner before it. Indus Valley seals.

Whether or not this was how it all came about, the primigenius bull was accepted as having some particular significance in the time of the Indus Valley civilization, and this left the way open for the next development, which occurred following the collapse of Harappa and

* In modern times when nomads in the Sahara and elsewhere have changed to a sedentary life, as much as 80 per cent mortality has been recorded among their livestock; animals can be less adaptable than humans.[1]

Mohenjo-Daro in about 1750 BC and the virtually simultaneous arrival of a great wave of Aryan invaders.*

The Aryans were pastoralists, their food mutton and beef, milk and curds, their cooking medium *ghi* – clarified butter that, unlike ordinary butter, can be kept for months even in a hot climate. What the Aryans introduced into India was not an increase in meat-eating but a heavy dependence on dairy products, and Indians took to them with such enthusiasm that there seems to have come a point when too many consumers were chasing too few supplies. Consequently, as the Aryans spread over the subcontinent they found it convenient to build on the Indus Valley precedent by giving all cattle the full protection of religious law. Even in the *Rig-veda*, the sacred text relating to the Aryans' early period in India, goat, horse, sheep and buffalo are all mentioned as food, but only *barren* cows.[2] A fertile cow's milk, like a fertile hen's eggs, could feed more people than its carcass.

By about 500 years later the eating of even barren cows was forbidden, the *Atharva-veda* declaring that to eat beef was to commit an offence against one's ancestors.[3]

From then on, the cow's sacredness moved in cycles, each restatement being followed by a period of rigidity, a period of relaxation and then a new restatement. There was a relaxed period around 700 BC, when it was generally accepted that cattle could be killed to meet the requirements of hospitality or for ritual sacrifice to the gods and spirits.[4] The priests, however, were soon demanding so many sacrificial beasts that the drain on the farmer's draught and milk cattle became intolerable. Indeed, the impositions of the Vedic system developed harshly enough to provoke a strong social reaction. Fundamental to the two new religious political systems that then emerged – Buddhism and Jainism – was a belief in the sanctity of all life, including that of the cow, and a resultant advocacy of vegetarianism (see below).

The emphasis against cow-killing was renewed, yet again, in the fifth century AD, this time on a secular level. It was a period of territorial expansion, when groups of pioneers were being sent out beyond the old frontiers, equipped with the necessities of life and accompanied by a few cattle and a brahmin adviser who knew all

* This is not the 'Aryan' of Nazi ideology, but the name for an offshoot of the Iranian branch of the Indo-European hordes who infested the area from the Caspian to Turkestan. The word Aryan comes, instructively in terms of the history of the caste system, from the Sanskrit *arya*, meaning 'of noble birth'.

about the calendar, the mysteries of planting, the techniques of sowing and the breeding of livestock. Cattle were so few in relation to the stretches of territory involved, and conditions so difficult, that it was necessary to place a total ban on cow slaughter. Wherever the brahmin went, the cow's sacredness was upheld.

And so it went on. The Muslim invasion of India in the Middle Ages (a conquest by foreigners who had no hesitation about eating beef) helped to place the final imprimatur on the Indians' own, and by now instinctive, reverence for the cow, and the Muslim conquest was followed by that of another people whose very image was inseparable from beef-eating, the British.

In 1857 the British even succeeded in precipitating the Great Mutiny by disregarding the strength of Hindu India's devotion to the cow and at the same time, with rare genius, ignoring the Muslims' hatred of the pig.* Though a deep social unease had made the Mutiny almost inevitable, it was the matter of the greased cartridges that set it in motion.

THE VEGETARIAN PRINCIPLE

Buddhism and Jainism, India's two great alternative religions, emerged in reaction to the class-conscious, colour-conscious,† violent society that had grown up under the influence of the *Vedas*, the Bible of the Aryans. The Vedic religion, Hinduism, divided society into four unequal classes. Brahmins (often priests) were superior to kshatriyas (warriors), who were superior to vaisyas (merchants), who were superior to sudras (everybody else); and all were superior to the dark-skinned, conquered peoples, who had no status at all.

This socio-religious class system was reinforced by the highly sophisticated doctrine of *karma*, a version of transmigration of souls that may have its roots in the early resurrection myths. It holds that if a living thing – man, beast, bird or insect – dies after having lived its life

---

* The cartridges for the Enfield rifle, a new weapon being issued to the East India Company's army, had to be bitten open before loading. They had a protective coating of grease on them which, according to rumour, consisted either of beef or pork fat. For a caste Hindu to bite on the fat of the sacred cow was an inconceivable sin, while the lard of the unclean pig meant insufferable pollution for a Muslim.
† The Aryans were light-skinned; their predecessors – those they had conquered and driven down to the south of the peninsula – dark-skinned.

'correctly', its soul is afterwards reincarnated at a higher level; if 'incorrectly', at a lower one. Even the least of men, therefore, may by virtuous living during a number of incarnations so improve his *karma* that he can rise to the highest level and achieve the paradise of release from the cycle of rebirth. Even an insect is inhabited by what may formerly have been, and may again become, a human soul.

Buddhism and Jainism both rejected caste, but not *karma*. It was belief in *karma* – not fastidiousness, nor any sentimental belief in kindness to animals – that led the Jina Mahavira to forbid his disciples, the Jains, to eat even fruit or vegetables without first making sure they contained no living thing. It was belief in *karma* that permitted the Buddha merely to recommend his followers not to allow animals to be specially killed for them; it could never be in a Buddhist's *karma* to be responsible for killing, but it might be in an animal's *karma* to be killed.

Jainism therefore insisted on, and Buddhism encouraged, a vegetarian diet, a diet not too far removed from the everyday realities of Indian life, where the only animal protein that occasionally interrupted the routine of the peasant table came from the goat, the hen or, on the coasts, fish and seafood. Sheep did not respond well to the climate, and the domestic pig seems, predictably, to have disappeared not long after the arrival of the Aryans.

So influential was the new religions' anti-slaughter campaign that by the first century BC even the brahmin priests had come round to it. And it was they, vegetarians themselves by the end of the first millennium AD, who took their food creed with them when, as missionaries, they penetrated beyond the Vindhya Mountains and laid the heavy hand of Hindu orthodoxy on the south. As a result, the south was introduced not only to a matured Hinduism, but to a Hinduism that equated vegetarianism with meritorious living. Perhaps because of this, south Indian vegetarian cooking remains today one of the world's most distinguished cuisines.

DAIRY PRODUCTS

An accurate picture of the important elements in the Indian diet is given in the *Puranas* ('ancient stories'), a curious compilation of legend, religious instruction and obscure geographical information dating from somewhere in the early centuries of the present era.

The human world, it was said, formed a series of concentric circles round Mount Meru, a succession of ring-like continents separated from each other by seven oceans. The ocean immediately surrounding the mystic mountain was composed of salt; the next of *jaggeri*, a very coarse, sticky, dark brown sugar (sugarcane had been introduced to India from New Guinea in Neolithic times); the third of wine; the fourth of *ghi*; the fifth of milk; the sixth of curds; and the seventh of fresh water.*

Of these seven magical oceans, representing the staple needs of humanity (apart from grain), no less than three were of dairy products. *Ghi* was the essential cooking medium, although the not-so-rich made do with sesame oil (one of the earliest seed oils) or mustard seed oil, and the very poor with safflower oil. Milk, though occasionally drunk fresh, was more often boiled down to thicken it and then used to make a porridge of whole grains or toasted barley meal. Curds, one of the most popular of all foods, had a tartness that was refreshing in a hot climate; Indians hastened the curdling process by adding pieces of a creeper called *putika* or the bark of the *palas* (gold mohur) tree.[6] In most other countries until late medieval times 'milk' might as easily mean sheep's or goat's as cow's. But where India was concerned, it always meant cow's. Tropical goats gave very little milk, sheep were scarce, and although the buffalo was productive, the higher castes in particular had an aversion to the rich, greenish milk with its highly distinctive flavour.

Once the sacredness of the cow had been unequivocally established, its products began to assume more than their face value. *Ghi*, in fact, was to be the religious salvation of the higher castes, who went in ever-present fear of ritual pollution (the brahmin had much further to fall than the sudra in the cycle of rebirth). Anything cooked in *ghi* was automatically purified.

'CLEAN' AND 'UNCLEAN' FOODS

The Hebrews were not alone among early peoples in embracing the concept of 'clean' and 'unclean' foods, but in India – characteristically – both the purpose and the logic were rather more intricate.

---

* This view of the world appeared highly comical to later Western minds. Nevertheless, when the nineteenth-century English explorer John Hanning Speke first tracked down the sources of the Nile, he had with him a map based on the geographical information in the *Puranas* and found that it gave local names in the African interior with an accuracy that astonished him.[5]

It was a common belief throughout much of the world until long after medieval times that food was more than mere nourishment; its own qualities were closely linked with the physical and moral qualities of those who prepared or ingested it. In India, because of the caste system and the doctrine of *karma*, this belief took an acute form. Indeed, by the middle of the first millennium BC, so many items were listed as unclean that rigid adherence would have been almost impossible for the poorer peasant. If he were of low caste, it did not perhaps matter very much, but the high-caste brahmin could be just as poor in financial terms as the most despised sudra.

To eat food prepared by a murderer was to become a murderer; to eat food prepared by someone of a lower caste was to be reduced to the same level. By the Gupta period (*c.* AD 300–750) the roster of those from whose hand no man should accept food included henpecked husbands, prostitutes, eunuchs and usurers.[7]

Food in its natural form was generally clean; it was preparation that was the problem. Peeling, slicing and cooking were believed to 'open' it to contamination from outside,* so that while a brahmin might safely buy his fish from an untouchable, there was no question of the untouchable cleaning and gutting it for him.[8]

Other foods were unclean by definition – rice that had turned sour through being left to stand overnight; ready-cooked dishes; food that had been sullied by mice or insects, or sniffed at by a dog, cat or humans; meat that had been cut with a sword, dog meat, human meat, the meat of carnivorous animals, of locusts, camels and hairless or excessively hairy animals.[9]

While a few of these beliefs now appear eccentric enough to lend an air of unreality to what would otherwise be fairly ordinary quality control laws, there were other market regulations that were unequivocally based on hygiene. It was, for example, forbidden to sell the meat of an animal that had died of natural causes (the Chinese and Hebrews took the same view), and the only meat permitted to be sold had to be specially and freshly slaughtered.[10]

In Hinduism, however, there were religious escape routes from secular hygiene, and official views on impurity were not absolute. If a dish had been defiled in some way, it was possible to 'purify' it by removing the defiled portion and sprinkling the remainder with water, curds or *ghi*. In terms of food poisoning these were noticeably less satisfactory correctives than the cooking, recooking or throwing away

---

* Which is perfectly true in its way.

Dining off interlaced leaf plates. The woman appears to be either raising a cooling breeze or waving away insects.

preferred by the Chinese. On the other hand, since the human system is capable of tolerating a surprising number of bacteria once it has become accustomed to them, faith has probably saved as many lives as hygiene over the centuries.

Preoccupation with the idea of purity in India extended to plates and dishes as well as the food itself. If someone ate from an earthenware dish, the laws stated that it had to be broken afterwards so that it could not be used again. Most Indians, even the richest, skirted the issue by using thick, unabsorbent leaves as plates. A tenth-century Arab merchant who visited the country said that princes and nobles sat down each day at 'tables made with the interlaced leaves of the coconut palm; with these same leaves they make kinds of plates and dishes. At mealtime the food is served on these interlaced leaves and, when the meal is finished, the tables and leaf plates are thrown into the water with whatever may remain of the food.'[11]

It was also customary to wash mouth, hands and feet before sitting down to eat; to make a small sacrifice to the gods (the equivalent of a prayer, or grace); to eat politely, facing east; and never on any account to complain about either the food or the cooking.

FOOD AND COOKING

In the early centuries AD Indians ate two meals a day and were advised that each meal should consist of thirty-two mouthfuls. They were to visualize their stomachs as being divided into four parts, two to be filled with food, one with liquid, and the fourth left empty to allow for the movement of wind.[12] It was a wife's duty to prepare her husband's food and serve it to him, she herself ate afterwards unless she were newly married or pregnant, in which cases she ate first.

What people ate depended not only on their means but where they lived. Wheat and barley could be grown in the south in winter, and at almost any time of year in the cooler parts of the north. Rice, first cultivated in about 2000 BC around the Ganges delta, was the staple on plains where there was natural or artificial irrigation; millet where there was none. Gourds, peas, beans and lentils were widely grown, as were sesame, sugarcane, mango, plantain and the pod-bearing tamarind, sharp-flavoured and refreshing. Essential spices such as pepper, cardamom and ginger were distributed throughout the country from the plantations and entrepots in the south.

Beyond such generalizations as these, the list of indigenous raw materials is endless and frequently meaningless, since India has as great a diversity of regional foods as the continent of Europe. To talk of 'Indian food' is as inappropriate as to talk of 'European food'; to link fine Punjabi cooking with that of the Naga hills as incongruous as to bracket *nouvelle cuisine* with the food of an Albanian village. The raw materials may have something in common, but not much more.

On the Malabar and Coromandel coasts during the first millennium AD, however, India's food was subjected to many outside influences. Malabar was the spice country, trading with the Arab world and the Mediterranean, while Coromandel faced east to the islands of Asia and, through them, to contacts with China. To widen the repertoire of spices already used in south Indian cooking, nutmeg, mace and cloves were imported from the Indonesian archipelago during the early part of the period, while coriander and cumin came from the west. Rice, spices, vegetables and fish formed the bases of south Indian cooking.

In the north-west of the country the effects of foreign contact were more profound. Through the passes of the Hindu Kush over a period of 2,000 years had come a succession of invasions and infiltrations – of ideas, attitudes and techniques; Aryan, Persian, Greek and Central Asian. These were absorbed into the area of the former Indus Valley civilization to produce a culture that was a strange but not in-harmonious mixture, and because the land was fertile and the foreign influences either nomadic or highly civilized, meat was more commonly eaten here than anywhere else in India.

In heartland India things were different. The very poor peasant probably ate nothing but stale boiled rice with half-cooked gourds or other vegetables, or perhaps a grain porridge mixed with mustard stalk, and washed down this unpalatable fare with an unidentified alkaline liquid that reputedly tasted like water from a salt mine.[13] It may have been rice-boiling water left to ferment.

The less poor would begin their meal with an appetizer of one or two pieces of ginger and some salt; then there would be boiled rice and bean soup, with a hot butter sauce; then small cakes with fruit and more butter; a piece of sugarcane to chew; and finally some spices wrapped in betel leaves to act as a digestive and sweeten the breath. Drinks were water, whey, buttermilk or gruel.

The rich man's meal followed the same basic pattern, with additions, but the quality was finer, the soup a rich golden broth and the rice shining white. In the south, curds and spicy meat sauces took the place of *ghi*, and drinking water was perfumed with camphor from Borneo. There were also mango syrup and lime juice, and a wide range of fermented liquors. Grape wine, imported first from Rome and later from Kapisi, north of Kabul, was a luxury only kings could afford, but lesser men made stimulating brews from 'sugarcane juice, *jaggeri*, honey, molasses and the juice of the rose-apple'. There was also an intricate brew made from 'the juice of the breadfruit infused with a decoction of *mesasringi* [the bark of a tree] and long pepper, kept for one month, six months or a year, [and then] mixed with two types of cucumber, sugarcane stalk, mango fruit and myrobalan [an astringent fruit]'.[14] Rice ale was more common, and a mild toddy and stronger arrack were fermented from the sap of the palmyra and talipot palms.

Another fermented drink called *madhuparka*, which had honey, sugar, *ghi*, curds and herbs among the ingredients, was strictly for special occasions, the correct thing to offer guests, especially suitors about to ask for a girl's hand in marriage; it was also given to women who were five months pregnant and used to moisten the lips of a newly-born first son.

A surviving menu for a royal banquet shows how varied the diet could be, since Indians made use not only of dairy products (which China generally ignored) but of fruit (of which Europe was intractably suspicious).

King Srenika's banquet began with pomegranates, grapes and dates, and continued with oranges – the sweet variety seems to have been introduced from China during the first centuries AD – mangoes, with their peach-coloured flesh and plentiful juice, and finger lengths of tender young sugarcane. Then came something cooked and creamy, then sweet cakes, then boiled and scented rice, then a selection of stew-like dishes, probably vegetarian. In the north there would instead have been *kosali*, delicate mouthfuls of spiced roast meat rolled in a purée of raw meat, re-rolled in rice, then cooked over the fire, or perhaps *mandaliya*, a sausage of bone marrow and spices roasted on charcoal.[15] After the main course the plates were removed and the royal hands washed. Dishes of flavoured curds followed, and the royal hands were washed again. The final course was a rich liquor made from milk boiled down until it thickened, then sweetened with sugar and honey, and tinted with saffron.[16]

THE BEGINNINGS OF CURRY

The true Indian curry bears very little resemblance to the parodies of it still served in the West (by Indians themselves, as well as by

Mixing, kneading, baking and toasting chapatis. The processes are illustrated from bottom to top, rather than (as in the West) from top to bottom.

Europeans) even in these reputedly enlightened times. Save for the Nepalese and a few other regional versions, it should not, by and large, be designed to paralyse the palate.

For Indians curry is a sauce intended to add relish – no more – to bland basic fare like rice or the wheaten pancakes known as *chapatis*. A little of it goes, and is meant to go, a long way.* A typical pre-medieval curry might have consisted of a *brinjal* (aubergine) and a couple of onions or a handful of *dal* (lentils) cooked in *ghi* or vegetable oil, flavoured with a mild blend of cardamom, cumin, coriander and turmeric, or a hot one of white pepper and mustard seed, and then diluted with coconut milk or *dahi* (yoghurt). Chillis, today's 'hot' element, were not introduced to India from tropical America until the sixteenth century.

The original south Indian *kari* (meaning 'sauce') from which the word 'curry' is derived, seems to have been of a fairly liquid consistency; when Europeans first encountered it they usually described it as a broth or soup that was poured over the rice. There were other kinds, however, with other names; some were more like a spicy stew of vegetables, fish or meat, some as dry as if they had been grilled.

It is as difficult to arrive at any true assessment of the flavour and texture of early Indian food as it is with Roman food. Working from the *Code of Manu*, a compilation of laws dating from about the first century AD and relating to a small district in modern Bihar, scholars have calculated equivalents for such measures as the *prastha* and the *pala*.[17] Unfortunately, when these are applied to (slightly earlier) recipes from the same area, the results are alarming. One recipe for a curry to accompany rice seems to require 27 ounces *each* of meat and spices, a little fat, salt and sugar, and a mere 10½ ounces of curds.[18] It looks as if the *dharana*, the specific measure used for spices, may (like many other historical weights and measures) have been regionally variable in practice.

Whatever the case, ordinary peasants would have one curry with their rice or chapatis, while the rich had several – liquid ones first, dry ones last. With spices freshly ground and individually blended, the flavours amalgamated and smoothed out with coconut milk or *dahi*, it was possible to produce an infinite range of sauces to ring the changes on the staples that have always formed the life-support system of the Indian peoples.

---

* Thinking (in non-gourmet terms) of curry on rice as one of the predecessors of tomato ketchup on chips helps to put it in perspective.

— 9 —

CENTRAL ASIA

Piecing together the hard facts about the nomads who changed the course not only of India's history but also that of all the countries surrounding their Central Asian heartland is a task that has so far defeated historians. These were peoples who left no writing to be deciphered and no great settlements to be excavated; even the earliest burial sites that have been discovered (some of them including superb examples of grave goods) cannot be dated much before 1000 BC[1] – long after the nomads had begun to make their mark in the world.

In general terms they seem to have been neither relics of a remote past nor rebels against an ordered present. Towards the western end of the steppes an earlier hunting way of life developed naturally into a pastoral economy; farther east some groups of nomads are believed to have gone through an intermediate stage as unsuccessful farmers. Later, as the wide, pale landscape that stretched from Hungary to Manchuria ceased to be an unpeopled void, it became clear that pasture land was too important for its boundaries to be settled according to the ancient law of survival of the fittest, and a complex organizational system grew up until, in the end, the steppe economy came to resemble a vast and intricate square dance, in which at a given moment all the tribes struck their black felt tents (plastered with tallow or sheeps' milk to keep out the rain) and moved on towards the new stretch of grazing that had been allocated to them.

By Classical times the steppes had become an empire (without an emperor) consisting of a number of different 'nations'. At the western end were the Scythians, who, said Herodotus, were 'a people without fortified towns, living . . . in wagons which they take with them wherever they go, accustomed one and all to fight on horseback with bows and arrows, and dependent for their food not upon agriculture but upon their cattle.'[2] More than most of their kind, the Scythians enjoyed a lively social life, trading for luxuries with the prosperous towns of the Classical world, ranging the fertile lands round the Caspian and the Black Sea, and supplementing the products of their herds with tuna and sturgeon, onions, garlic and beans. Hippocrates characterized them as 'a fat and humorous people'.[3]

The same could hardly have been said of their fellows at the Chinese end of the great ocean of grass: harsh, energetic men, bow-legged from constant riding, with large heads, blazing eyes and massive chests built to withstand the *buran* – the white wind of winter – and the freezing nights and parching days of the Gobi Desert, where, 'gazing on all sides as far as the eye can reach in order to mark the track, no guidance is to be obtained save from the rotting bones of dead men, which point the way.'[4]

But however different the temperament and living conditions of the various tribes, their grazing needs were much the same, and so too were their basic foods.

THE DIET OF THE NOMADS

Most of their needs were supplied by their flocks and herds – felt for their tents, hide for their armour, meat for their stewpots, milk for their drinks.

Mutton may have been the commonest meat, but there were enough animals in the steppe economy to allow for variety; veal from an orphaned calf, beef from an injured steer, roast hump of camel –

Sheep and goat, essential animals in the steppe economy, drawn by a Chinese scholar.

which was, and is, a great delicacy – and, of course, horseflesh, thought by the nomads (as by a number of open-minded gastronomes in later times) to be superior to beef. It was certainly a more common meat in Central Asia than beef, camel or yak, since cattle are not ideally adapted to nomadic life in its more rigorous form and it is uneconomic to kill slow-breeding camels for food. The yak, too, is more valuable alive than dead because of its rich and abundant milk.

Marco Polo's detailed description of how the thirteenth-century Mongol armies went on campaign would probably have been equally apt hundreds of years earlier. Every man had a string of eighteen remounts, he said, and they travelled 'without provisions and without making a fire, living only on the blood of their horses; for every rider pierces a vein of his horse and drinks the blood.'[5] An animal could afford to lose half a pint every tenth day – quite enough to sustain its owner – without its strength or stamina being impaired.

This system of provisioning, however repellent it may seem to the cosseted city-dweller, had a number of very practical advantages. No supply wagons, no preparation, no cooking were needed and, as Marco said, no fire had to be lit. Fire was often a problem for the men of the steppes, either because fuel was scarce or because the flames could be seen for miles. When William of Rubruck, emissary of Louis IX of France, passed through Central Asia forty years before Marco, he wrote, 'Of hunger and thirst, cold and weariness there was no end . . . Sometimes we were compelled to eat flesh half sodden [boiled] or almost raw, for want of fuel to boil it, especially when we lay in the plains or were benighted before we came to our journey's end, because we then could not conveniently gather together the dung of horses and oxen, for other fuel we found but seldom, except, perhaps, a few thorns in some places.'[6]

Blood drinking, or eating, has been common in pastoral communities throughout most of recorded history. Before Islam laid a taboo on it, the Arabs were fond of a composite dish of camel hair and blood mixed together and then cooked on the fire;[7] the hair presumably acted as a temporary binder, frizzling away to nothing as the blood coagulated in the heat. A few hundred years later, according to a ninth-century Chinese traveller, the peoples of the Berber country, south of the Gulf of Aden, were accustomed to 'stick a needle into the veins of cattle and draw blood, which they drink raw, mixed with milk'.[8] In the eleventh century the Byzantine scholar Michael Psellus reported of the Patzinak tribes that if they were thirsty and there was no water available, 'each man dismounts from his horse, opens its veins with a knife and drinks the blood . . . After that they cut up the fattest of the horses, set fire to whatever wood they find nearby, and, having slightly warmed the chopped limbs there on the spot, they gorge themselves on the meat, blood and all.'[9]

Time passed and civilized Byzantium vanished, but there were other critics waiting in the wings, equally anxious to observe the habits of primitive peoples. In seventeenth-century Ireland, said a French traveller, the peasants 'bleed their cows and boil the blood with some of the milk and butter that came from the same beast; and this with a mixture of savoury herbs is one of their most delicious dishes'.*[10]

In Tyrone and Derry the blood was preserved for the lean months by being allowed to thicken in layers 'strewn with salt until a little mound was formed, which was cut up in squares and laid by for use as food in the scarce time of the year'.[11]

Until a dozen years ago (and probably still today) the Masai of Tanzania tapped the blood of cattle or sheep by shooting a special arrow – with a stop below the point to prevent it from penetrating too far – into the jugular vein, draining off as much as they needed, and then closing the wound with a plug. The Masai drank the blood fresh, but the Nuer tribe of the Upper Nile either boiled it to thicken it, or allowed it to coagulate into lumps, which could then be roasted in the embers of the fire.

MILK PRODUCTS

More conventional 'dairy' products were also, of course, familiar in Central Asia in the first millennium AD, the most important among them being mare's milk – not only because milk, as such, was the basis of many other foods but because mare's milk, in particular, seems to have been an unrecognized factor in the nomads' exuberant good health.

Except in Scythian territory and the small, favoured kingdom of the Ferghana (north of Afghanistan), where the most luscious fruits in the world were said to grow, the nomads' access to fresh fruit and vegetables was limited. Although the meat in their diet supplied them with plenty of protein, fat and vitamins A and B, they ought to have died

* It is also a version of 'drisheen', a kind of black pudding still known in County Cork and elsewhere today. Black pudding is also (or was, when the real thing was to be had) a blood sausage.

like flies from the vitamin-C deficiency disease of scurvy – or, at the very least, have displayed signs of the lethargy characteristic of it. Not even their worst enemies, however, could have accused the nomads of lethargy, and part of the reason must have been their high consumption of mare's milk, which has twice as much vitamin C as human milk and four times as much as cow's. A pint a day would have been enough to take the nomads over the 30 milligrams that the World Health Organization estimates to be sufficient for the average adult today, and in the absence of other drinks (with one notable exception, see below) it seems likely that the nomads drank a good deal more than a pint. Days spent on horseback in an arid landscape make for a powerful thirst.

The nomads' baleful energy may have stemmed, in part, from another factor in their diet. The amino acid tryptophan (contained in meat) is necessary to the biochemical manufacture of serotonin, a neurotransmitter that operates in the parts of the human brain that control aggression, sleeplessness and response to pain. Recent research suggests that reducing the tryptophan in the diet helps to reduce aggression.[12] If the reverse is also true, it would contribute a further biological reason for the dynamism most nomadic peoples have shown throughout history.

The nomads took milk from all their animals and made a number of foods of the curd or yoghurt type. Dried milk, however, had a special value for them. Marco Polo described the Mongol version. 'First they bring the milk [almost] to the boil', he said. 'At the appropriate moment they skim off the cream that floats on the surface and put it in another vessel to be made into butter, because so long as it remains the milk can not be dried.* Then they stand the milk in the sun and leave it to dry. When they are going on an expedition, they take about ten pounds of this milk; and every morning they take out about half a pound of it and put it in a small leather flask, shaped like a gourd, with as much water as they please. Then, while they ride, the milk in the flask dissolves into a fluid, which they drink. And this is their breakfast.'[13]

---

* When creamy milk is heated in shallow containers to a few degrees below boiling, the cream becomes thick and crumpled, easy to skim off. This is today's 'clotted cream' or 'Devonshire cream', and not unlike butter even without churning. If the Mongols had not taken the trouble to skim off the cream, their dried milk would have turned rancid very quickly.

KUMISS

The nomads also converted their mare's milk into the fermented liquor most commonly known by its Mongol name of *kumiss*.

The milk, on the edge of fermenting, was poured into a great bag and beaten, according to William of Rubruck, with 'a piece of wood made for that purpose, having a knot at the lower end like a man's head, which is hollow within; and so soon as they beat it, it begins to boil [froth] like new wine, and to be sour, and of a sharp taste; and they beat it in that manner till butter comes'.* Faintly surprised, William went on, 'After a man hath taken a draught, it leaves a taste behind it like that of almond milk, going down very pleasantly, and intoxicating weak brains, for it is very heady and powerful.'[15]

It seems that medieval *kumiss* must have been stronger than the modern variety, which has an alcohol content of only about 2 per cent – scarcely enough to intoxicate even the weakest brain and certainly not enough to account for its popularity in China (even in the imperial palace) when it was introduced during the Song (Sung) period (960–1279).

---

* The Kazak peoples of Russian Turkestan, who still make *kumiss*, churn it sporadically over three or four days.[14]

— 10 —

CHINA

Every now and then scientists engaged on research into contemporary nutritional problems come up with results that have interesting historical implications. The indigestibility of milk is a case in point.

What research has shown is that all new-born babies, regardless of ethnic origin, produce an enzyme (lact*ase*) that enables them to digest the lact*ose* (milk sugar) in milk. Ninety-six per cent of people who come from West European stock continue to produce the enzyme throughout life and are therefore able to drink fresh milk without discomfort. But 75 per cent of Africans, Indians, Persians, Arabs and East Europeans* stop producing lactase in early maturity and thereafter suffer nausea, flatulence, abdominal pain or diarrhoea when they drink more than the smallest quantity.[1]

The question is why, and the obvious (though simplistic) answer is that in temperate climates, and with a mixed agriculture, it has been usual over many generations for infants to go straight on from mother's milk to cow's (or sheep's, or goat's). Continued production of lactase therefore has a purpose. But where children usually stop drinking fresh milk after they are weaned – perhaps because milk-giving animals are few, or because heat and humidity quickly turn it sour – they also stop producing lactase.

Some biologists reject this idea. Their alternative theory is that West Europeans, strangers to the sun, are prone to a deficiency of vitamin D, which, in turn, inhibits the body's utilization of calcium and often leads to bone malformation. Lactose, however, during the course of its breakdown in the intestine, has the effect of improving utilization. The argument is that there would therefore be genetic pressure on West Europeans to continue to produce the lactase that encourages the useful breakdown of the lactose.[2] This explanation appears to overlook the fact that lactose still has to be introduced into the intestine in the first place, which means – unless the lactase con-

* Unfortunately, no figures are available for the Republic of China, but it would be surprising if they departed radically from this pattern.

tinues to be produced for generation after generation in the Micaw-berish hope that, some day, some lactose will turn up – a milk-drinking population.

Undoubtedly, the reasons for lactose intolerance are complex and unlikely to be fully identified for some time yet, but the acknowledged fact of its existence, and the scale of it, are illuminating in the Chinese context.

The general absence of dairy products from the diet of China's people used to be attributed, *faute de mieux*, to their hatred for the nomad pastoralists who for so long harassed their frontiers; it was China, more than any other nation, that took the continuing brunt of the Central Asian nomads' restlessness when their activity in the west was curbed by the growth of strong civilizations there. But it is also the case that, for nearly one-third of the two-thousand-plus years since the nomads first began to trouble China, nomad-originated dynasties have ruled the northern half of the country. It seems unlikely that the conquerors, even when they settled, would have stopped using milk merely because the conquered peoples disliked it; nor is it probable that the Chinese – a rational race – should have sustained a purposeless hatred over such a long period for something as important as a plentiful new foodstuff. In effect, if milk had been readily available and dietetically acceptable, it must, however slowly, have been adopted by the Chinese in the end.

But it was neither. Because of the intensive crop farming of the Yellow River heartlands, grazing livestock were scarce and so was milk. As a result, the Chinese were not in the habit of drinking milk (or, indeed, of making any other use of it); therefore they must have found it indigestible when they did; therefore they had no dietary incentive to expand the livestock farming that would, in the end, have overcome the intolerance.*

None of this means, however, that milk was totally unavailable or totally rejected. In small, digestible quantities, and usually heated or cooked, it was thought to be quite nutritious. It even became fashionable (among the rich) in Tang (T'ang) times. One Tang emperor was prescribed a decoction of 'long' pepper (a particularly potent variety) simmered in milk to cure an intestinal disorder, and a later one cooled off in hot weather with a frosty dish of rice cooked with cow's milk and two preparations of camphor known as 'dragon's eyeball powder' and

* It was a pity that the entire output of Chinese sows was needed to feed their litters. Of all animal milks, pig's is nutritionally closest to human.

'dragon's brain fragments'.[3] In the mid-thirteenth century, too, a Chinese traveller described coconut flesh as being of 'a jade-like white,* and of an agreeable taste, resembling that of cow's milk'.[4]

Most of the limited quantity of milk, however, went, as in other warm countries, into soured products. In terms of hygiene this was sensible, and in terms of intestinal comfort even more so, because the organisms responsible for fermentation have a lactose-digesting enzyme of their own that relieves the consumer of the need for it. Even lactose-intolerant people can therefore face yoghurt, curds or cheese without a qualm.

In Tang times (AD 618–907) China had dairy products roughly equivalent to curd cheese, lightly fermented skimmed milk, clotted cream and butter-oil. The latter two were the most coveted items. Thick, rich *su* (clotted cream) made a dish on its own when mixed with honey, or was used as the shortening in luxurious pastries, while *tihu* – the fine oil sweated out of *su* when it was heated gently over the fire – added the ultimate touch of perfection to a really grand dish. Such, indeed, were its virtues that it came to be used as a literary metaphor for finesse.

But although dairy products were to be introduced and re-introduced to the Chinese cuisine more than once during the course of history, they were never really to catch on except in the days of the Tang as a passing fashion.

The people of China, like other non-pastoral societies, had their own perfectly satisfactory alternatives to milk products (even if the milk products themselves may sometimes have suggested the alternative versions). Basic milks were made the world over – even in societies ignorant of dairy products – from nuts and pulses. In India and south-east Asia the grated flesh of the coconut was soaked in hot water for a while, and the creamy juice pressed out. North American Indians extracted a milky liquid from hickory nuts and pecans. In Europe walnuts and almonds, blanched, pulverized and soaked in water, provided a much-used milk in many households until the end of the eighteenth century.†

---

* The Chinese put a higher value on creamy-coloured 'white jade' than on the common green variety.

† Most almonds came from Italy and Provence, to which the trees had been introduced during the Arab conquests, and were correspondingly expensive elsewhere. As a result, almond milk had a high nutritional reputation and was poured down the throats of privileged infants in astonishing quantities.

But although China may, on a local basis, have made milks from hazelnuts, pine nuts and one or two others, bean milk was much more common. The fluid from several different kinds of bean (cooked, puréed and strained) can be used as milk, but in Chinese terms bean milk meant milk extracted from the soy bean, the great provider (see below).

TEA

Curiously enough, although the Chinese never put milk of any kind into tea, the drink that swept the country in the second half of the eighth century, they did sometimes use *su* (clotted cream) and also *fagara*, the mild Chinese pepper. It was left to the nomads, temporarily on good terms with their neighbours, to develop a passion for tea made by boiling up the leaves with milk and butter, and it seems to have been in this form that the Russians – the world's most dedicated tea drinkers after the Chinese themselves and possibly the English – first encountered it almost 900 years later.[5]

Tea, a native of south-west China, had been drunk in the north as early as the Han period, though not with any great enthusiasm; millet wine was far more popular. But by the later days of the Tang, it was a commodity important enough to be taxed. There were a good many varieties by then, some flavoured with ginger or tangerine peel, some esteemed for their leaf shape, some sold in cake form and some powdered.

Already, too, there were tea rituals and tea snobs, worthy predecessors of the modern wine snob. For a fine tea, only cups made from porcelain (the new, luxury kind of pottery) were admissible; the ideal water for tea-making came from a spot near the mouth of the Yangtze, though second-bests might be sought out in certain areas of Zhejiang (Chekiang) and Anhui; and the water from springs near some of the great Buddhist monasteries had particular virtue.[6]

EARLY CHINESE FOOD

If spiritual purity was a transferable asset where tea water was concerned, so it also was with food. In common with the people of India, the Chinese had come to believe that food and drink were intimately bound up not only with the health of the body, but also with that of the mind and soul. To eat and drink correctly was as much an instrument of virtue as an expression of it.

The origins of the Chinese cuisine are obscure, but society was already uniquely food-oriented when it emerged into the light of recorded history in the first millennium BC.[7] Just as an ancient Athenian was expected to be politically aware, and a medieval German knight to have acquaintance with all the rules of chivalry, so a sensitive knowledge of food and drink was, from the very earliest times, one of the essential qualifications of a Chinese gentleman.

Shooting game birds and cultivating grain in the highlands of Sichuan.

Among the oldest surviving Chinese texts is the *Shih ching* (Book of Songs), a collection of traditional ballads and fragments gathered together some time after 600 BC and describing the life of the warrior-farmers of the north-western highlands of Shanxi (Shensi). In winter the men hunted animals for their furs, and cut and stored ice for use in the summer months.* In early spring, after ploughing, there came the rite of expiation when a lamb was cooked on a bed of southernwood as a sacrifice to the gods.

* The Chinese were well ahead of the rest of the world where refrigeration was concerned.

High we load the stands,
The stands of wood and earthenware.
As soon as the smell rises
God on high is very pleased:
'What smell is this, so strong and good?'[8]

In summer boiled beans and mallows formed part of the evening meal, and there were plums and cherries for sweetness. When winter approached, the rice wine was set to ferment, rats were smoked out of the houses, the millet, bean and wheat crops were brought inside, windows and doors were blocked up against the weather to come and roofs rethatched with freshly gathered reeds. Finally,

With twin pitchers they hold the village feast,
Killing for it a young lamb.
Up they go into their lord's hall,
Raise the drinking cup of buffalo horn:
'Hurrah for our lord; may he live for ever and ever!'[9]

Tradition has it that the *Shih ching* was compiled by Confucius himself, and there is further information on early Chinese food and customs in his *Lun yü* (Analects), one of which described how a man ought to prepare himself before making a sacrifice to the spirits. His behaviour, his clothing and his interior economy were all required to be ritually correct – which was the same as saying socially correct.

'There is no objection to his rice being of the finest quality, nor to his meat being finely minced. Rice affected by the weather or turned he must not eat, nor fish that is not sound, nor meat that is high. He must not eat anything discoloured or that smells bad. He must not eat what is overcooked nor what is undercooked, nor anything that is out of season. He must not eat what has been crookedly cut nor any dish that lacks its proper seasoning.'

A summary of general hygiene and health regulations, in effect. Then the ordinary laws of polite behaviour:

'The meat that he eats must at the very most not be enough to make his breath smell of meat rather than of rice. As regards wine, no limit is laid down, but he must not be disorderly. He may not drink wine bought at a shop or eat dried meat from the market. He need not refrain from such articles of food as have ginger sprinkled over them; but he must not eat much of such dishes.'[10]

Among the spirits to whom a Chinese gentleman might find himself making sacrifice were 'the ancestors'– and when a man reached the age at which his conversion into an ancestor was becoming imminent, he was treated with the greatest consideration by both his family and the state.

In the *Li chi*, a handbook of traditional ritual, recipes (more or less the only recipes that have survived from this period) were given for the Eight Delicacies considered appropriate for the aged on ceremonial occasions. There was nothing here to compare with the milk-and-slops to which the toothless ancients of the West were doomed. Luxuries like fillet of beef, mutton, elk and venison were all on the menu, tenderized by marinating, pounding or mincing; there was a savoury fry-up of soaked rice and crisp morsels of fat from a wolf's breast; and dog's liver barded with its own fat, roasted and given a final searing on the charcoal.

The *pièce de résistance* was the suckling pig stuffed with jujube 'dates' (*Zizyphus jujuba*). The stuffed piglet was wrapped in a jacket of straw and reeds coated with wet clay, then roasted until the clay dried, by which time the juices had been sealed in and the skin had softened. The clay was discarded, and the skin stripped off and pounded to a paste with rice flour and a little liquid. Re-coated with this paste, the piglet was deep-fried until it was cooked to an appetizing golden brown. Then came the final stage, when the meat was sliced, placed on a bed of herbs and steamed gently for three days and three nights. When it emerged, exquisitely tender and aromatic, it was served with (something of a jarring note, this) pickled meats and vinegar.[11]

With so much culinary activity involved on important occasions, it comes as little surprise to discover that the royal kitchens in the second century BC employed 2,271 persons, including 128 everyday chefs and another 128 for entertaining; 335 grain, vegetable and fruit chefs; 162 master dieticians; 94 ice men; 62 pickle and sauce chefs; and 62 'salt men', who were presumably responsible for cleaning and pounding.[12]

The rich, as always, had access to a great variety of foods, especially in regions further south, and a number of them were enumerated in the third century BC poem 'The Summons of the Soul' – an invocation to the soul urging it to return home to the pleasures of the good life.

> . . . all kinds of good food are ready:
> Rice, broom-corn, early wheat, mixed all with yellow
> millet;

Bitter, salt, sour, hot and sweet: there are dishes of all
flavours.
Ribs of the fatted ox cooked tender and succulent;
Sour and bitter blended in the soup of Wu;
Stewed turtle and roast kid, served up with yam sauce,*
Geese cooked in sour sauce, casseroled duck, fried
flesh of the great crane;
Braised chicken, seethed [boiled] tortoise highly seasoned,
but not to spoil the taste;
Fried honey cakes of rice flour and sugar-malt sweet-
meats;
Jade-like wine, honey flavoured, fills the winged cups;
Ice-cooled liquor, strained of impurities, clear wine, cool
and refreshing . . .[13]

The concept of balancing bitter, salt, sour, hot and sweet (the Five
Flavours) – and, indeed, of producing dishes in which balance and
combination were more important than the individual elements –
seems to have become established early, and so well established that it
turned into a philosopher's cliché. It has remained characteristic of
the Chinese cuisine ever since, as has the care taken in cutting and
preparing food before it is put to cook; the numerous Chou words
meaning 'to cut' or 'mince' show this very clearly. And long before the
third century BC (possibly as far back as 1750 BC) Chinese food and
Chinese chopsticks went together,[14] though which came first – if either
did – remains one of the great unanswered, and probably un-
answerable, questions in gastronomic history.

There was as yet no record of the stir-fry cooking that for so many
people epitomizes Chinese food today. The essential pot in both Chou
and Han kitchens consisted of a cauldron – in which *keng*, the
everyday soup/stew, was set to simmer – with a clay steamer resting
on top, in which the grain was cooked. Neither vessel was adapted to
stir-frying. But social conditions in the later Han period produced a
situation that was ripe for the development of some quick and easy –
though, in Chinese terms, not very refined – style of cooking. If stir-
frying first evolved as a kind of impromptu field cookery, this
would explain why it did not find its way into the literary record until
long after its beginnings.

* The true yam (probably *Dioscorea opposita* or *esculenta*), not the sweet
potato, which reached China only in the sixteenth century AD.

Social conditions for the great mass of the population during the first two centuries AD were geared to farming, and a kind of farming that was technically and scientifically more than a thousand years ahead of that practised in Europe. The land was turned by heavy mouldboard ploughs and there were mechanical seed distributors to help with the planting; fertilizers and insecticides were in use.[15] It was a system of intensive cultivation that required all the peasants who worked the land to move out of their villages in early spring and live in temporary huts in the fields until the harvest was gathered in September or October.

There must certainly have been some central organization of supplies, perhaps even a kind of field canteen, but fuel was a problem and cooking time limited. However, if the starchy element was communally supplied – possibly in the form of the old travellers' standby of cooked and dried grain that could be eaten as it was or easily rehydrated – all that was needed was a savoury sauce that took little time and less fuel to cook. Stir-frying (*chao*) could have been the answer. Something very near it had certainly been developed by the Tang era.

If *chao* originated with the peasants, so also did noodles. Wheat, for most of the early period, had been a food of the common people, used mainly in its whole-grain form and coming a very poor third to rice and millet in popular favour. But when grain mills were introduced in the first century BC (probably from the West), a whole new vista opened up. Within a few decades boiled noodles, swung noodles, steamed buns and baked cakes had been invented, and the street noodle-seller was well and truly in business. According to the Chinese historian Shu Hsi, writing 300 years later, 'noodles and cakes were mainly an invention of the common people', but by the end of the Han period, even the emperor was eating them.[16]

THE SOY BEAN

Just as wheat became respectable under the Han, so did the soy bean, formerly regarded as a coarse, rustic food; nothing but soy beans to chew and water to drink was the index of extreme poverty.

The primary recommendation of the bean correctly known as *Glycine max* was that it produced a good crop even in bad years, but a few of its many other virtues seem to have been made manifest in the early days of the Han. One of the bamboo slips found in Han Tomb No. 1 at Mawangdui (Ma-wang-tui), dated at about 160 BC, makes reference to soy sauce and fermented black bean sauce,[17] and since the occupant of the tomb was a wife of the first Marquis of Tai, it would appear that the soy bean was already becoming upwardly mobile.

Whether the Lady of Tai's soy sauce bore any resemblance to today's is debatable. The modern version is made by puréeing cooked beans with a modicum of wheat flour and straining off the liquid.* The drained purée is shaped into loaves and put away for the winter months to ferment in a cool dark place. Afterwards, the fungus is scraped off and the loaves are soaked in brine for a few weeks. The briny liquid, carefully strained, is soy sauce. The debris of the loaves is made into a thick 'cheese' that is partially blamed for the high incidence of stomach cancer in Asia.[18]

Another product as familiar as soy sauce in the Han period, and probably first made about 200 BC, was *shi*,† salted and fermented black bean sauce. It was said to be the only relish that the rural population could afford, but the fact that it was widely available in the towns testifies to its general popularity.

Over the centuries the soy bean has become a complete food industry in itself, providing milk, curd, sauce, cheese, cooking oil, flour with an unusually high protein and low carbohydrate content and, of course, bean sprouts. In January 1987 plans were announced for a Chinese economy car – to run on soy bean oil.[20]

IMPORTED DELICACIES

During the Han period China imported more than just flour mills from beyond its western frontiers. The grape vine was introduced, as were the pomegranate, walnut and lychee; so were sesame and caraway, and coriander from Bactria; peas, cucumber and a new kind of onion; and alfalfa from the Ferghana – though that was intended to feed not humans but the Heavenly Horses the emperor Han Wudi (Han Wu-ti) was so anxious to acquire; it was said to be the only thing they would eat.

Despite the centuries of disruption that succeeded the fall of the

---

* This, when boiled, throws a sediment that forms the basis for bean curd, which, with cabbage, remains as fundamental to Chinese home-cooking as bangers-and-mash used to be to English. Whether it was known in Han times is still an open question.

† The word 'soy' seems to have been a Japanese corruption of *shi*.[19]

Han, China's trade with Persia and the outward-looking attitude of India during the golden age of the Guptas combined to sustain the Celestial Empire's awareness of the world beyond its frontiers, and when the Tang dynasty emerged in the early seventh century AD, China again began to play an active role.

There were some moderately improbable results. When, for a brief space, China found itself allied with the Turkish nomads of the steppes, the people of Xian (Ch'ang-an) and Luoyang (Lo-yang) the two imperial capitals, became obsessed by Turkish fashions. They studied Turkish-Chinese dictionaries, wore Turkish clothes, set up elegant sky-blue tents in the city centres. The emperor's son even camped out in the grounds of the imperial palace and with his own sword hacked off slices of boiled mutton for his dinner.[21] It was not at all what a Chinese gentleman was accustomed to.

Cooking over a charcoal brazier in Tang times; note the handy little frying pans and the use of chopsticks for stirring.

More refined foods were also adopted from foreign parts, little cakes fried in oil becoming especially popular. The recipes for these – even the cooks themselves – may have come from India, as did 'light and high' steamed wheat buns.[22] Wine was imported from the Tarim basin, the fertile oasis towards the western end of the Silk Road, while the king of Nepal sent gifts of some spinach plants and a 'vinegar leaf vegetable'. Kohlrabi came from Europe by way of the Silk Road, and pistachio nuts from Persia. Indian pepper was not as essential in Tang China as it had been in imperial Rome – the Chinese had their own *fagara* – but seems to have been almost as expensive. 'Stone honey' was another luxury import, the juice of sugarcane boiled down and then dried in the sun; the whitest sugar cakes came from Bokhara, where a judicious dash of milk and careful skimming contributed to the beauty of the end product.

EVERYDAY FOOD

As in most societies, there was a world of difference between the food of the rich and that of the poor. Most of China's population ate what was immediately available, and would never hear of, far less see or taste, the capital's 'Brahmin bread' or the 'Western plate' meat dishes, for which Indian black pepper was the requisite seasoning. They would not have *su* in their tea – if they had tea. Nor would they kneel at leisure round the mat, supping off a morsel of this and a fragment of that. They ate, more probably, in the manner of the Japanese carpenters who appeared so extraordinary to Sei Shonagon, the great court lady of eleventh-century Kyoto.

'The moment the food was brought, they fell on the soup bowls and gulped down the contents. Then they pushed the bowls aside and polished off all the vegetables. I was wondering whether they were going to leave their rice; a second later there wasn't a grain left in their bowls. They all behaved in exactly the same way and I suppose this must be the nature of carpenters.'[23]

By Song times reliance on rice had become so general that bean curd soup and bowls of rice had replaced soy beans and water as literary shorthand for poverty or the virtuous simple life. In practice, they were foundations to be built on as availability decreed. Throughout China the most common extras were spring onions, bamboo shoots and beans, with soy sauce, sweet-sour plums or fermented black beans to add savour. Pork and chicken were occasional luxuries and fish another – sturgeon, bream or tench, and the large, fat carp, semi-domesticated and as ready as the pig to gorge itself on kitchen scraps.

Vegetables and fish were either lightly cooked or eaten raw. The eighth-century Chinese traveller I-ching commented favourably on the food in India compared with that at home, where 'people of the present time eat fish and vegetables mostly uncooked; no Indians do this.'[24]

At a later stage in history, however, the Chinese came to categorize all non-Chinese peoples as 'cooked' or 'uncooked', depending on their sensitivity to Chinese civilization. It took a long time for the Mongols to earn the word 'cooked', and the Europeans never did.[25]

REGIONAL SPECIALITIES

Local specialities – though perhaps not the coolie's 'brushwood eels' (snakes), 'brushwood shrimps' (grasshoppers) or 'household deer' (rats) – found their way to the imperial kitchens in the form of tribute, and since specialities often grow out of superfluity it is likely that what was considered a rare delicacy in Xian may have been so commonplace in its native village that even the poor could eat it almost every day.

Because of China's great diversity of climate and vegetation there was a wide range of such specialities. Indeed, the history of Chinese food is much complicated by the fact that what is now called China originally had – and to some extent still has – three or more separate cultures. The first of these was in the crowded north and centre. According to the Tang census of AD 754, roughly 75 per cent of the total population of the country lived north of the Yangtze. Xian had 2 million inhabitants, and more than twenty-five other cities well over half a million.[26] The country peasants of the north may have had readier access than the rich to venus clams; the 'sugar crabs' of the Yangtze; the dried flesh of the 'white flower snake', a kind of viper found in Hubei (Hupei); and the cherries and pickled melons of Shaanxi (Shensi).

To the south the people (and their diet) were closer to south-east Asia than to heartland China. Only in the last two centuries BC did the Han begin to colonize the south, and for a long time the colonists remained strangers in a strange land. Rice, however, was always plentiful, and dried oysters made a sauce for it, while among the most admired regional dishes in the Tang period were barbecued elephant's trunk (said to taste like pork, but to be more digestible) and sliced python in vinegar. There seems to have been just one southern favourite that northerners were unable to stomach – the frog.

Westward, in the enclosed valleys of Sichuan (Szechuan) and the mountains of Yunnan, the people were different again, independent, self-sufficient, scarcely even in contact with the rest of the country. When Marco Polo passed through Yunnan in the thirteenth century, he found that meat – mutton, beef, buffalo – was the mainstay of the diet. 'The poorer sort go to the shambles and take the raw liver as soon as it is drawn from the beasts; then they chop it up small, put it in garlic sauce, and eat it there and then. And they do likewise with every other kind of flesh. The gentry also eat their meat raw.'[27]

Since Marco was prone to refer to all Chinese as 'Tartars', here perhaps, in the secret valleys of Chinese Yunnan, was eaten the original *steak tartare*.

MARCO POLO'S CHINA

In 1176 Genghis Khan had been born, son of a minor leader of the wild but not wholly uncivilized Mongols. When he died sixty years later, much of north China was in his hands, and in 1276 Hangzhou (Hangchow) itself, the beautiful southern capital of the Song, finally submitted to Genghis' grandson, Kublai – Marco Polo's 'Great Khan'. The campaigns of the preceding 150 years had reduced China's population from 100 million to less than 59 million.[28]

Marco saw China before the glory of the Song had time to fade, and Hangzhou, its capital, appeared to him very much like a Chinese Venice. It was a teeming, cosmopolitan city, a jewel set among rivers and lakes, outlined against a background of tortuously shaped mountains and deeply cleft valleys – the landscapes of the great Song painters who set the standard against which all later artists were to be judged.

To the harbours of Hangzhou came ships bearing spice from the Indies or carrying away silks for the Levant. Arabs and Persians and Christians haggled over prices, the shops overflowed with precious goods and transactions were carried out with paper money – unheard of in Marco's native Italy. The rich even had their own specially selected varieties of rice imported daily into the city.

Hangzhou's residents were gourmets where rice was concerned, and they could afford to be, since the eleventh-century introduction of hardy, early-ripening Champa rice strains from Annam had given a significant boost to rice production. It is difficult for Westerners to appreciate all the subtleties of rice in Asia, where it plays a central rather than a supporting role, but among other varieties Song China had pink rice, white rice, yellow rice, mature rice and winter rice, each with its own characteristics and some with an almost flower-like fragrance. The custom of serving rice and other foods in separate bowls made it possible for the finer rices to be appreciated as they deserved to be.

The rice intake of the people of Hangzhou is said to have averaged out at a gargantuan 2 pounds 5 ounces per head per day.[29] Not all of it, of course, was consumed in the form of grain. Some was made into rice flour and some into rice wine (of which fifty-four varieties were recorded at the end of the Song period) while a good deal went in one shape or other into the snacks that, eaten out, were an important social feature of the Chinese day, especially for the great army of Song bureaucrats and scholars.

Most countries had their cookshops, but none at this period were as advanced and varied as China's. As well as ordinary eating houses, there were fast-food restaurants, hotels, taverns, tea houses, noodle shops and wine shops, all with their own chef's specials – chilled fruits or honey fritters, steamed pork buns, *won ton*, barbecued meats, fish soups and so on. Every morning between 1 a.m. and dawn the proprietors hurried off to one of the ten great specialist food markets of Hangzhou for the pork or silkworms or shrimps from which they made pies to serve with their drinks, or the oysters, mussels, or bean curd that nourished the poorer classes.

The fish market, according to Marco, was an extraordinary sight. Every day 'a vast quantity of fish is brought upstream from the ocean, a distance of twenty-five miles. There is also abundance of lake fish, varying in kind according to the season, which affords constant occupation for fishermen.' So many fish were on sale at the market that 'you would imagine they could never be disposed of. But in a few hours the whole lot has been cleared away.'[30]

A century later Friar Odoric de Pordenone was also dazzled, this time by the cheap ginger and plump geese. 'Here you can buy 300 pounds of fresh ginger for less than a groat! The geese too are bigger and finer and cheaper than anywhere in the world. For one of them is as big as two of ours, and 'tis all white as milk . . . And these geese are as fat as fat can be, yet one of them well dressed and seasoned you shall have there for less than a groat.'[31]

One reason why Hangzhou's eating houses flourished was that only the wealthiest homes were equipped to produce the variety of dishes requisite to even a modest feast. China's cuisine was by now almost fully evolved, and although in Europe it was also customary to set several dishes on the table at the same time, only at royal banquets did the number of them approach what the Chinese would have regarded as acceptable for a simple family celebration.

So, as Friar Odoric reported, when a man wished to give a dinner to his friends, he went to 'one of the hostels which are established for

The sweetmeat vendor in Song times. His bamboo table carries covered jars and open dishes of candied fruits and tiny cakes; it is protected by a canopy and decorated with peony blossoms in a red lacquer vase.

this very purpose, and saith to the host thereof: "Make me a dinner for such a number of my friends, and I propose to expend such and such a sum upon it." Then the host does exactly as ordered, and the guests are better served than they would have been in the entertainer's own house.'[32]

At a respectably lavish supper in thirteenth-century China there would have been a dozen soups, about forty dishes of boiled, stewed, stir-fried, steamed, roasted or barbecued meat, poultry and seafood;

the same again of fruits and sweetmeats; twenty vegetables and a dozen differently prepared and flavoured rice dishes; up to thirty variations on dried and pickled fish; and a wide choice of drinks that performed the same function as the sorbets of later French dinners – cooling the palate and reviving the appetite between courses. Since pre-Han times ice had been used as a refrigerant in China; by the days of the Tang chilled foods and drinks were an almost commonplace luxury.

Imperial banquets offered hundreds of dishes rather than scores, but in recent years the National Palace Museum of Taiwan has tarnished the image by claiming that much of the food served on such occasions not only remained uneaten at the end, but was unfit to eat in the first place. Many dishes, it seems, were stale leftovers, set before the guests (well out of reach) in order to keep up appearances.[33]

This was possible because diners were never expected to sample more than a selection of the offerings. In Song times, as now, the Chinese meal consisted of a number of different dishes designed to ensure that each guest would find a few to his or her taste. Until the nineteenth century the same civilized custom ruled at European tables.

THE ARAB WORLD

While the Tang ruled in China and the Rashtrakutas in India, the Arabs sallied forth from the desert and, under the banner of Islam, swept away the Persian Empire, conquered the whole northern coast of Africa and crossed the straits of Gibraltar to take possession of the Visigothic kingdom of Spain.

Even during the austere centuries of desert living their commercial instincts (especially in the matter of spices) had been noticeably well developed. Now, their ambitions expanding with their horizons, they found themselves engaged in a continuing war with the Byzantines for economic control of the Mediterranean. When they succeeded in diverting Egyptian wheat from Byzantium to the holy cities of Islam, the administrators of Byzantium were forced to take their custom elsewhere, to the Balkans and southern Russia. And when, in turn, a Byzantine blockade passed sentence of death on the old Syrian/Egyptian trade route to Asia, the Arabs were compelled to move their capital from Damascus to Baghdad.

There, in AD 763, they built their Round City in the valley of the Tigris where Kish and Babylon, Seleucia and Ctesiphon had once flourished. Outside the walls of the city gathered an extraordinary medley of peoples, Arabs and Syrians, Persians and Turks, a population in whose veins ran the blood of Greeks, Parthians, Sassanids, even of Romans.

Soon Baghdad became the great warehouse of its time, filled with the products of the East. From it Arabs and Rhadanite Jews journeyed to China for cinnamon and rhubarb (important in medicine) and to India for coconuts; others went to Bactria for grapes; to Isfahan for honey, quinces, apples, saffron and salt; to Mosul for quails; and to Hulwan for pomegranates, figs and vinegar sauces.[1]

Some of these goods were destined for onward transmission to paying customers in Europe. Others went with Arab officials to the colonies they administered, notably Spain, where with the aid of a new system of canals they began to re-create the tinkling fountains and green gardens of the Tigris Valley. Those same administrators, missing the fresh tang of the citrus fruits they had become familiar with in Persia and the sweet crispness of almonds, planted them wherever they would grow in the new lands. They took rice seed with them, too, and cuttings of the sugarcane the Persians had introduced from India, and saffron, whose golden glow was soon to suffuse the cooking of the western, as it did of the eastern, end of the Mediterranean. And as the years passed, many of the foods carried to new lands by the men of Islam for their own enjoyment became commercial crops, the financial support of later generations.

BYZANTIUM

The emperors of Byzantium and the caliphs of Baghdad, despite their continuing animosity, had at least one problem in common – the heterogeneous nature of the peoples they ruled. When the Roman Empire had been divided into western and eastern halves in AD 395, the western half had inherited the hungry and demanding plebs of Rome, an even greater drain on the economy than the epicurean rich, while the eastern half – centred on Constantinople (later Byzantium) – had a populace more than capable of fending for itself, both socially and gastronomically.

Greeks and Jews, Armenians, Syrians, Macedonians and Italians jealously guarded their own ways of life and, in face of the Roman cuisine imported by the court, their traditional cooking styles, so that as the centuries passed even some of the complex Roman dishes favoured by the upper ranks of Byzantine society took on (as did society itself) an increasingly eastern tinge. The fermented fish sauces of Classical times remained popular, as did hams, game birds and 'variety meats', but the Near Eastern and Greek cooks' lavish hand with the heavier olive oils ultimately brought about a transformation in the cuisine.

That the cooking of Byzantium had become entirely 'foreign' by the tenth century is clear from the brief but venomous description left by Liutprand, Bishop of Cremona, when at the table of the emperor Nicephorus Phocas he was served with food he described as 'foul and stinking . . . soused in oil like a drunkard's mess and sprinkled with some horrible fishy liquid'.[2] *Liquamen* might have vanished from the Roman scene but not, it seems, from the Christian world.

THE COURT OF THE CALIPHS

Liutprand was by no means an unprejudiced observer, having a violent dislike of all things Byzantine, but it may be doubted whether he would have been any more charitable about the food of the caliphs, perfumed with mutton fat and rosewater, and combining with a fine free hand meat and fruit, nuts, vegetables and poached eggs all in a single dish.

Surrounded by the luxurious debris of the Persian Empire, the Arabs had unhesitatingly abandoned their tents and camels, barley and dates in favour of instant civilization. Most of Europe might still be sunk in a barely literate daze, but the banquets given at the court of caliphs were renowned for the extravagance of the food, the poetry and the gastronomic erudition of the conversation.

Fairly typical, perhaps, was a banquet given by the tenth-century caliph Mustakfi, at which all the guests were put through a stiff *viva voce* on different kinds of food and the poetry that had been composed about them. One guest was able to recall a set of verses written by Ibn al-Mu'tazz about a tray of hors-d'oeuvre:

> Here capers grace a sauce vermilion
> Whose fragrant odours to the soul are blown . . .
> Here pungent garlic meets the eager sight
> And whets with savour sharp the appetite,
> While olives turn to shadowed night the day,
> And salted fish in slices rims the tray . . .*

The caliph promptly instructed his cooks to prepare the dishes described, while another guest launched into some lines by Mahmud ibn al-Husain al-Kushajim:

> First a roasted kid, a yearling,
> With its innards firmly strung,
> And upon it, well to season,
> Tarragon and mint are hung . . .
>
> Lemons, too, with *nadd* [perfumes] besprinkled,
> Scented well with ambergris,
> And, for garnishing the slices,
> Shreds of appetizing cheese . . .[3]

---

* All this sounds remarkably like something out of Athenaeus, but that may be due to some quirk of translation.

In the golden age of the caliphate, cookery books were written by princes of the blood as well as by distinguished philosophers – although the earliest known works to have survived cannot be dated before the thirteenth century – and even the most exalted courtiers were expected to have not only a literary but a practical acquaintance with cookery. On one occasion the caliph al-Mu'tasim set his boon companions to the task of cooking a variety of dishes on which an unwelcome guest was then required to pass judgement,[4] a challenge that, in the climate of a city where life was held cheap, must have played as much havoc with the guest's nerves as his digestion.

FOOD, THE RAW MATERIALS

In the religion of Islam were blended elements of Judaism, Christianity and the traditional beliefs of the tribes, and the Arabs were equally eclectic about their food. Although according to the Koran, the collected wisdom of Muhammad, pork was impure, animal blood a pollution and wine an abomination,* these were minor prohibitions in the rich context of all the other foods available.

Egypt was the place for vegetables and citrus fruits, while in Iraq and Syria there were orchards filled with apples, pomegranates, plums, figs, pears, cherries and twenty-one varieties of apricot. Syria and Palestine produced olive oil in abundance. Raisins came from Jerusalem, olives from Palmyra; wheat from Egypt, millet from southern Arabia; sheep and goats from Palestine, fish from Shihr (near Aden) and pigeons from special fattening towers everywhere. During the early Islamic period sugarcane, spinach, mangoes and bananas were among the new crops introduced from Asia,[6] and, since the Arabs still controlled the spice trade, there were also spices in plenty.

A substantial increase in rice production took place during the early days of the caliphate, notably in the valley of the Jordan, but rice remained expensive. 'White rice with melted [ewe-milk] butter and white sugar is a dish not of this world', said al-Asma'i in the ninth century.[7] Wheat, millet and barley were still the commonest grains, though their flours were as variable in quality as they had been in

* The first two embargoes were derived from the Old Testament, while the third was traceable to an historic occasion on which some of the Prophet's levies had been found drunk and incapable on the eve of battle.[5] The last was also the most frequently ignored of the dietary regulations, by both rich and poor. Muslims, however, seldom went so far as to become tavern-keepers; that was left to Jews and Christians.

Despite the Koran, the Arab world had its taverns. The vintage is illustrated at bottom right; final consumption in the gallery above.

Classical Rome and were soon to be in an expanding Europe.

Great rose gardens supplied the rose water used in all kinds of cooking, not only in sweets and drinks. Where it was added to meat dishes it seems to have been used with reasonable discretion, when a dry ingredient needed to be lightly moistened or a touch of freshness added to something rich – as in the following *makhfiya*, a 'simple dish' from the thirteenth-century collection of recipes by a gentleman-gourmet known as al-Baghdadi.

'Cut red meat into thin strips about four fingers long . . . Put the meat into the oil, with a *dirham* [roughly $\frac{1}{8}$ oz] of salt and finely milled dry coriander, and fry lightly until browned. Then cover with water, adding green coriander leaves, cinnamon bark, a handful of peeled chick-peas and a handful of onion chopped fine. [Bring to] boil, and remove the scum. Now mince red meat fine and make into meatballs with seasonings. Take hard-boiled eggs, remove the whites, and place the yolks in the middle of the meatballs; place in the pot [with the meat strips]. When almost cooked throw in fine-ground cumin, pepper, mastic [an aromatic plant resin] and ginger. Take more eggs and beat well: remove the strips of meat, dip them while hot in the egg, and return them to the pot. Do this two or three times until the slices are well coated with egg . . . When the liquor [in the pot] has all evaporated, sprinkle with a *dirham* of fine-pounded cinnamon, spray with a little rose water, and leave to settle over the fire for an hour.'[8]

PERSIAN AND OTHER INFLUENCES

Many recipes, well-spiced, highly complex and time-consuming to prepare, seem (like their ingredients) to have been derived from the court cooking of the caliphs' Persian predecessors.

The Sassanid Persians had been particularly fond of *ahbisa*, which meant any kind of jelly, and from which the modern Turkish Delight (*rahat lokum*, 'giving rest to the throat') is descended. They also enjoyed sweet-sour combinations; the strong, fatty mutton of the Near East benefited greatly from being sharpened with fruits like the pomegranate, apricot and lemon.* This idea was gratefully adopted by the Arabs, the new fruits adding a new dimension to the old, familiar combination of meat and dates. Indeed, the Arabs seem to have had a penchant for decisive flavours, sweet, spicy or salty; the physicians were constantly warning them against using too much salt, which was almost an addiction with them.

From the Persians, too, Arabs learned the trick – as the Romans had before them – of using ground almonds, walnuts and pistachios to thicken dishes both sweet and savoury. This became a characteristic of the caliphate's *haute cuisine* that was carried to Western Europe by the Arabs themselves as well as by Italian merchants and homebound Crusaders, there to develop into an exotic and then a commonplace feature of the bourgeois table. Tenth-century Baghdad dishes like *harisa*, a mixture of meat and vegetables simmered in a creamy, almond-thickened sauce, had by the fourteenth century become equally familiar in Europe.

As well as princely and Persian dishes, the Arabs adopted meat

---

* Here Persia seems to have been closer to China and India than Classical Rome, since the Romans used not fruit but honey and vinegar to achieve the sharpening effect.

recipes from the Caucasus, cakes from Egypt, *couscous* from the Maghrib, and 'Frankish-style' roast lamb from Western Europe. *Maghmuma*, the ancestor of the layered dish of mutton, onions and aubergines now known as moussaka, came from Central Asia.[9] There were also recipes for rice cooked in milk that suggest Indian origins.

The pastoral peasant tradition of the Near East contributed the oil in which almost every Baghdad dish was put to cook – *alya*, the fat rendered from sheep's tails. Time after time al-Baghdadi began his instructions with the words, 'Cut meat into middling pieces; dissolve tail and throw away the sediment. Put the meat into this oil and let it fry lightly . . .' The popularity of tail fat may have had something to do with the existence of the local fat-tailed sheep, though whether as cause or effect remains a matter for debate.

From the same tradition came reliance on *laban*, a preparation not unlike yoghurt,[10] and 'Persian milk', which seems to have been yoghurt in actuality; the constant use of fresh and dried dates; and the habit of cooking even the most complex dishes in a single pot.

Some dishes, too, survived in a refined form from the desert past, occasionally described, like *hais*, as excellent fare not for nomads but for their less dashing successors, 'travellers'. To make it – and it was certainly both convenient and sustaining – 1 pound of dried bread-crumbs was kneaded with ¾ pound of stoned dates, the same quantity each of almonds and pistachios, and a few spoonfuls of sesame oil. The mixture was finished by being shaped into balls and dusted with powdered sugar.[11]

The fat-tailed sheep's main asset had to be protected from wear and tear.

DIETETIC MEDICINE

Receptive to all that the older, more settled civilizations had to offer, the Arabs also developed an interest in dietetic medicine, which they studied largely from Greek sources and later helped to transmit back – in slightly amended form – to a Western world that had forgotten it.

The Greek language had lost its cultural currency in the West after the fall of Rome, though not in Byzantium, heir to the Greek tradition. Byzantium, however, had been rent by controversies over Christian dogma, and during the subsequent persecutions a number of heretics fled to Jundishapur in Persia, then an international centre of learning patronized by scholars from India as well as Syria and Persia. There they began to translate important Greek works on science and medicine into Syriac, the new language of knowledge in the Near East. When Persia fell to the Arabs and the caliphs of Baghdad gave their imprimatur to all things cultural, a number of these works, including the vast corpus attributed to the second-century Greek physician Galen, were again translated, this time from Syriac into Arabic.

The third and final stage in the transmission took place at Salerno, near Naples, where – in a pocket of land surrounded by Byzantine, Italian and Islamic possessions, and open to all the intellectual winds that blew along the Mediterranean – a medical school had grown up during the centuries after the fall of Rome. Although under the aegis of the Benedictine monks of Monte Cassino, the school was remarkably free from Christian dogmatism and was noted at an early stage for the wide range of its teachings.

To Salerno late in the eleventh century came a man who, born in North Africa, had travelled extensively in the Near East and India. Known as Constantine the African, he settled at Salerno and began translating and editing great works of medical learning from Arabic into the tongue of Western Christianity, Latin. Among these works were the treatises and commentaries of Galen.

The Greek medicine that was now restored to Western Europe had acquired on its travels a number of Persian, Arabic, Hindu and even Chinese glosses, some of them relating to new diseases and drugs that had come to light as the known world expanded, some reflecting the religious and social attitudes of the Koran and some – no doubt as a result of Constantine's own experience of Asia – placing a more profound emphasis on diet than had been present in Galen's original.

THE SALERNO REGIMEN

Salerno might well have taken as its motto the statement by a Chinese physician that 'experts at curing diseases are inferior to specialists who warn against diseases. Experts in the use of medicine are inferior to those who recommend proper diet.'[12]

The predominantly Graeco-Arabic-Italian 'regimen of health' that was to be disseminated through Europe by Crusaders cured at Salerno of their ills or wounds was to form the basis of most of Western medicine until well into the eighteenth century.

This regimen was founded on the simple proposition, no less appealing then than now, that it was possible to look younger and live longer on the right diet. Why, its theorists asked, were people dying younger these days when Adam had lived to be 930? They concluded that it was because modern man was indulging in 'mis-diet' and 'much surfeiting'.[13]

Salerno's 'mis-diet' had nothing to do with saturated fats, excess salt or insufficient fibre. Instead, it was based on the theory that human beings and their food contained within themselves the same four elements as made up the cosmos. These (air, fire, water and earth) manifested themselves in the human body in the form of four 'humours' (blood, bile, phlegm and black bile) and some people and some foods suffered from an excess of one or other of them. It therefore counted as 'mis-diet' when a man of choleric (fire/bile) temperament gorged on 'hot' foods, or when the elderly (who were assumed to suffer from a surplus of water/phlegm) ate cold or moist foods. The choleric man was told to balance things out by restricting himself to cool foods, and the elderly – meaning anyone over 40 – to hot.

The 'four humours' theory had been evolving for 2,000 years. Although first propounded in the Salerno form by Empedocles in Greece in the fifth century BC, and later amplified by Galen, the thinking behind it was common to much of the ancient world. In China a hundred years before Empedocles, Ho the Physician had divided diseases into six groups, each of them derived from an excess of one of the six aspects of *ch'i* – the 'breath of life' or 'subtle wind', which was a concept similar to the Greek *pneuma* and from the layman's point of view even more abstruse.* Later, Ho's six were reduced to

---

* The confusion it still aroused even in Victorian times, and especially among Europeans in Asia, was eloquently demonstrated when a certain Mr Gilmour's Chinese teacher mentioned to him that a particular drug was good for 'inside and outside HEE [*ch'i*]'. What, demanded Mr Gilmour, was HEE? 'Inside HEE', he later noted, 'is wind ascending and descending, evidently colic; what outside HEE is I can't discover. After pursuing my teacher over the verge of his knowledge, the old man admitted that he had never seen outside HEE, though he had often suffered from inside HEE.'[14]

five – fire, water, earth, wood and metal – which were subclassified as *yin* (cool, moist, contracted, female) or *yang* (hot, expanded, male), the two most important facets of diet as of life. In India medical writers such as Caraka also settled on five as the magic number.[15]

Even in the early days the idea of four (or five, or six) humours had raised problems. There was no difficulty in classifying a fire/bile or choleric man. He was hot-tempered, bold and always hungry. The phlegmatic type was also recognizable at a glance, stolidly built and slothful. Nor was there any uncertainty about children, who were classified not (as they might be in the self-expressive context of the late twentieth century) as fire/bile personalities but, like the elderly, as subject to an excess of water/phlegm.

But classifying foods was by no means as easy as classifying people, and the physicians had no Larousse to guide them. As a result, lacking a full list of foods – lacking, too, any straightforward dividing line of the kind that would suggest itself to the modern mind, with fatty and starchy foods on the hot side and astringent ones on the cold – they laid down lists of 'hot' and 'cold' foods that now appear more arbitrary than perhaps they originally were. In India even today, for example, though meat and strong spices are predictably considered hot, butter and honey, wheat flour, rice and sugar are all classified as cold. In China, pepper, fried foods and oily legumes like peanuts are hot, but beans are cold.[16]

It is not difficult to understand why Salerno should have accounted fruits as cold food, even if in nutritional terms it was regrettable, especially where children were concerned. Since they were thought of as 'phlegmatic', fruit was banned not only for them but even for their wet nurses.

The problem of wet nursing was a very old one in the curious composite of myth and medicine that, until as late as the nineteenth century, decreed what was to be fed to a baby. From as far back as the first millennium BC, when the Indian *Upanishads* put into words ideas of even greater antiquity, no one ever questioned that children imbibed temperament and morals as well as physical nourishment from their mother's milk.[17] In medieval times careful mothers would not have dreamed of employing a gipsy or a Saracen to suckle their infants,* and even at the beginning of the twentieth century the authors of a housekeeping manual dedicated to 'the English girls to whom fate

---

* 'Suitable' and 'unsuitable' wet nurses varied according to the political climate of the times.

may assign the task of being house-mothers in our Eastern Empire' felt it necessary to air the matter. What other than racial prejudice, they asked with acid logic, could account for fears that 'the milk of a native woman should contaminate an English child's character, when that of the beasts . . . is held to have no such power'?[18]

If children and wet nurses (who, of course, included mothers) had been encouraged to eat fruit instead of abstaining from it, history's long and tragic tally of infant and female mortality might have been much reduced. Unfortunately, although dietary dogma was less widely disseminated than it is today, fashions in it did not change annually, with the result that such prejudices, once established, were difficult to eradicate.

The scholars of Salerno seem to have inherited their suspicion of fruit directly from Galen, who claimed that his father had lived to be 100 because he never ate it. Galen's prejudice (and theirs) may have arisen from the fact that, consumed in quantity, fruit has a laxative effect, which must have appeared to link up with the dysentery common in hot climates during summer and autumn, the time when most fruits are available.

Even so, and perhaps because of the Arab glosses, the Salerno regimen did pay a rather backhanded compliment to some of the fruits native to the Near East and Asia.

> Cool damsons are, and good for health, by reason
> They make your entrails soluble and slack,
> Let peaches steep in wine of newest season,
> Nuts hurt the teeth, that with their teeth they crack,
> With every nut 'tis good to eat a raisin,
> For though they hurt the spleen, they help the back.*[19]

It should, however, be added that, if physicians had been successful in imposing the Salerno regimen on the population at large, the mortality rate would have soared.

> All pears and apples, peaches, milk and cheese,
> Salt meat, red deer, hare, beef and goat, all these
> Are meats that breed ill blood, and melancholy . . .[20]

In Western Europe at least, anyone who rigidly abstained from all of them would have been high on the list for death by starvation.

* It was, and is, usual in non-literate societies to couch useful information in the form of verse, which is easier to memorize than prose.

— Part Four —

Europe AD 1000–1492

Even in the year 1000 it would have been difficult to conceive of such an enterprise as the Crusades, but the agricultural revolution that had already begun north of the Alps was to bring, before the turn of the next century, not only a substantial increase in the food supply but an unprecedented improvement in its nutritional value. The result was a growing population that was better fed and more energetic than ever before – dynamic, ripe for action, ideal tools for the aggressive imperialism of the Crusades. On a more mundane level, the new system of agriculture also contributed to a revival in village and urban life and a consequent revival of local markets, while the desire of returning Crusaders for the luxuries they had discovered on their Mediterranean travels fuelled the rebirth of international trade. The spices of the East began once more to flood into a Europe that was now in the process of profound cultural transformation. In little more than 400 years Western society moved from its age of darkness into one of the most brilliant periods in history, the Renaissance. And soon after, driven by its continuing hunger for spices, the Old World ventured abroad – and discovered the New.

12

SUPPLYING THE TOWNS

The tool that shaped the agricultural revolution of the Middle Ages was, prosaically enough, a new kind of plough. The 'scratch' plough that had turned the earth since Sumerian times had been improved over the centuries, most effectively by tipping the point with metal, but it was still a clumsy implement, no more than a heavy stick that, dragged along the ground, scraped a shallow V-shaped furrow out of the soil. Where the soil was light and dry, the scratch plough worked reasonably well, but on the damp, heavy clay of the north it gave poor results in return for back-breaking labour.

In the sixth century, however, the Slavs of the north-east introduced to mainland Europe a new plough that cut deeply into even heavy soil;[1] in its fully developed form it became known as the mouldboard plough. It had three working parts – a knife blade (the coulter) that slashed vertically into the ground; another (the ploughshare) that cut horizontally through it at grassroots level; and behind the two blades a shaped board (the mouldboard) that turned the cut slices of turf neatly over to the side. The technologically advanced Chinese had had an even better plough of the same general type (with a 'board' made of metal) since Han times,[2] but Europe's wood-boarded plough was still a powerful implement compared with what had gone before. With the new plough and a strong team of oxen it was now possible to farm formerly virgin land, to clear forests and cultivate waste ground.

The scratch plough.

Food production increased and so did population. In one part of Germany it is estimated that by the end of the seventh century the population had expanded to four times what it had been in the Roman period.

The mouldboard plough.

But the new plough imposed new disciplines. It was expensive to make and maintain, needed six to eight oxen to pull it, and was unhandy in restricted spaces. As a result, cooperatives had to be formed, with the joint owners of the plough and its team merging their own patches of land into larger, workable fields. This led to radical social adjustments. What a man now and henceforward took from the land was related not, as it had been in the past, to his needs, but to the relative value of what he was able to subscribe towards the corporate enterprise.

CROP ROTATION

Although rotation of crops is a subject that has killed many a school-child's interest in history, the unexciting fact that people began growing wheat or rye in one field, legumes in another and leaving the third to lie fallow had a far from unexciting result. The people of the early Middle Ages became, in every sense, full of beans.

Much of the soil that was now tilled for the first time was put to far better use than ever before. The Greeks and Romans had known that land soon became impoverished if the same crop was grown on it year after year, but though they also observed that legumes – plants of the pea and bean family – seemed to invigorate rather than exhaust the soil, they made no real use of the discovery. This may have been partly because upper-class Greeks and Romans had an ambivalent attitude to beans, which some believed to contain the souls of the dead and others blamed for causing defective vision,* but whatever the reason, and despite the recommendations of such enlightened agronomists as Cato the Elder, the Classical world seems generally to have settled for planting half the land with grain in the autumn and leaving the other half fallow; in the following year the roles were reversed.

Soon after the mouldboard plough appeared in the north, however, and almost by accident, it became clear that the two-field system of rotation could be improved on. Using a three-field system – one field planted at the end of the year with wheat or rye, the second put down in spring to peas, chick-peas, lentils, broad beans, oats or barley, and the third left fallow – it was possible to make a given acreage of land productive for two years out of three, instead of just one out of two.

Without recognizing it, farmers who adopted this system produced not only more food but also better food. Peas and beans contain amino acids that dovetail neatly with the elements in grain to produce the kind of protein that grain alone cannot supply. More protein meant better health, increased energy, greater stamina. In the empire of Charlemagne, where the system was first applied, society itself became more forceful, and when the system became widespread the results were even more dramatic.

Historians now recognize that the Crusades were stimulated as much by population pressure as by Christian zeal or the prospect of loot. When Anna Comnena, daughter of the Byzantine emperor, described the multitudes who arrived in the Near East on the first Crusade, she was guilty of no more than pardonable exaggeration. 'The whole of the west', she wrote, 'and all the barbarians who lived between the Adriatic and the Straits of Gibraltar migrated in a body . . . marching across Europe country by country with all their households . . . Full of enthusiasm and ardour they thronged every highway, and with these warriors came a host of civilians, outnumbering the sands of the seashore or the stars of heaven, carrying palms and bearing crosses on their shoulders.' A touch sourly, she concluded, 'The arrival of this mighty host was preceded by locusts, which abstained from the wheat but made frightful inroads on the vines.'[3]

This was only the beginning. According to modern estimates, fully half the knights of France set off either for the Levant or the Islamic

* Broad beans, the type common in early Europe, are now thought to be responsible for a disorder of the red blood corpuscles known as favism – rare in most of the world but common in the Mediterranean – which is signalled by headaches, weariness and sometimes blurred vision.

territories of northern Spain during the thirty years covering the end of the eleventh and the beginning of the twelfth centuries.[4]

THE HORSE

Northern Europe's new crop system also gave new vigour to the horse. First domesticated somewhere in the steppe lands of Eurasia in about 2000 BC, it had become by early medieval times a mount for the knight rather than a traction animal for the farmer. Its hooves were not adapted to moist soils, its strength was inferior to that of the ox and it did not thrive on a restricted diet of hay and grass.

The first problem was solved with the introduction of heavy nailed horseshoes, and the second when farmers discovered that a new style of collar harness (originating in China) almost quadrupled the horse's draught efficiency.[5] The answer to the feed problem lay with the three-field rotation system, which could be adjusted to produce a regular crop of oats.

Its strength and endurance much improved, the horse began to take over some of the field labours of the ox. It also justified its reputation as a riding animal and gave a small measure of freedom to the peasant who had formerly had no transport other than his own feet. Although the location of towns and their outlying villages continued to conform to the old pattern of a day's walk to market and back, it was now possible to make the journey more quickly, and therefore more often, whenever the horse could be spared from the land. People became more mobile, and therefore more gregarious, than ever before, which helped to lead to an expansion not only of the markets but of the towns themselves.

TOWNS OF THE MIDDLE AGES

Because most dwellers in the new towns were peasants used to working the land these towns at first remained deeply embedded in the countryside. Pigs rooted in the refuse littering the 'streets' (the passages between the houses) while sheep grazed on patches of muddy pasture. There were areas of garden where the conscientious housewife grew a few vegetables and the strong-smelling, pesticidal herbs she strewed on the floors of her home, while the land immediately outside the town perimeter was put down to grain and beans; in wine country there were individual vineyard plots. As time passed, however, overcrowding set in and newcomers began building outside the walls until their dwellings spread over much of the area that had formerly produced the inhabitants' basic foodstuffs.

Even so, until the sixteenth century town dwellers continued to keep cows, pigs and hens. Cows were often shackled and hens did not wander far, but the scavenging pigs who roamed the streets were prone to trip up pedestrians and tangle up traffic. In twelfth-century Paris one of them dived between the legs of a horse ridden by the heir to the throne; royalty sustained a fractured skull and an edict was passed forbidding pig-rearing in towns. No one paid much attention; four centuries later the inhabitants of Paris were still keeping their bacon pigs. One of the public executioner's subsidiary duties was to capture as many unattached pigs as possible and take them to the *Hôtel-Dieu* for slaughter.

Elsewhere, it seems to have been the pigsties rather than the pigs that were unpopular. In Frankfurt in 1481 an edict was passed against the pigsties cluttering the streets in front of the houses but, again, little attention seems to have been paid. Even in nineteenth-century New York the wandering hog was still a familiar sight. The urban pig in fact performed a useful function in the days before city cleansing departments, clearing the highways of a good deal of refuse that would otherwise have lain there and rotted.

THE MARKETS

As the towns grew, small markets that had evolved for the neighbourly bartering of produce developed into major trading events where coinage, spices, wine and silks replaced baskets of apples and day-old chicks as currency. Frequently, so much of a town's prosperity depended on the market that stringent precautions had to be taken to guard the stall-holders against robbery, violence and the medieval equivalent of the protection racket. The Greeks had enforced a 'market peace' in Classical times; in this new Christian world the same ideal was symbolized by the setting up of a cross in the market place.

The great cities of France, Germany and England grew at speed as kings and princes tightened their disciplinary hold over the once independent barons. Formerly, rulers had been constantly on the move, supervising their estates and their subjects, but as the paraphernalia of administration increased this became impracticable. Armies of clerks and libraries of documents had to be housed somewhere, and where the records were, there the rulers of mid-medieval times set up their courts.

Where the courts were, there too were the merchants and tradesmen. Control over the great city markets soon became, in every sense, a right royal headache. Imposing some kind of order and guaranteeing the market peace were feasible only if the place of sale was subject to regulation, and the usual practice was to establish different areas for different kinds of merchandise.*

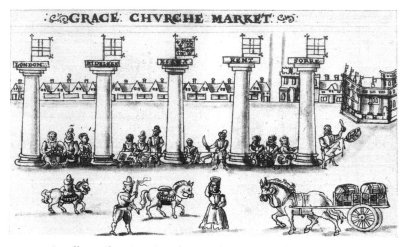

GRACE CHVRCHE MARKET

Small retailers in a London market, grouped by county.

Although many of the early regulations were designed for administrative convenience, others grew out of the pressures brought to bear on the authorities by the increasingly powerful merchant associations and guilds. In London in 1345, for example, the poulterers, incensed by competition from out-of-town henwives who wandered the streets selling to people who had neither the time nor the inclination to go to market, insisted on the passage of an edict prohibiting 'folks [from] bringing poultry to the City' and selling it in 'lanes, in the hostels of their hosts, and elsewhere in secret'. Anyone with poultry to dispose of was obliged to take it 'to the Leaden Hall and there sell it, and nowhere else'.[6]

Just as the merchants knew how to force through edicts that suited them, so they knew how to disregard, with impunity, those that did not. It was to take more than two centuries before butchers finally surrendered to the demands of the law and began selling meat by

---

* This, the traditional system in the markets of Asia, had also been adopted in Byzantium.

weight rather than by 'the piece'; in the meantime they played every trick imaginable on their customers, and got away with most of them – for a while. They padded out their veal in a quite literal sense, inflated stringy mutton by blowing air between the membranes and plumped out kidneys by stuffing the internal tubes 'with rags and other foul things'. Since no one wanted lean meat, with its inferior taste and texture,* they removed a layer of fat from good stout oxen and sewed it on to lean ones.[8]

Sharp practices like these affected only a minority of customers – not all butchers, it seems, were double-dyed villains – but there was a continuing outcry against the general messiness of the trade. In 1369 'Edward by the Grace of God' put it to the dignitaries of the City of London that he had received 'grievous complaint' from those of his subjects who had the misfortune to live near the slaughterhouse (shambles) of St Nicholas, whose butchers thought nothing of killing their beasts in the public streets. The nuisance did not stop there, since the complainants spoke of 'the carrying of the entrails and offal of the said beasts through the streets, lanes and places aforesaid to the said banks of the river . . . where the same entrails and offal are thrown into the water aforesaid'. By the 'dropping of the blood of such beasts between the said shambles and the waterside aforesaid – the same running along the midst of the said streets and lanes – grievous corruption and filth have been generated . . . so that no one, by reason of such corruption and filth, could hardly venture to abide in his house there.'

Despite an earlier warning from the throne, the mayor, recorder, aldermen and sheriffs had failed to take action by the specified date of the Feast of St Peter's Chains (1 August), and the king now suggested that they would be well advised to get something done by the Feast of the Assumption of the Blessed Virgin Mary (15 August). But the city dignitaries ignored the whole thing. Two years later the shambles of

---

* People knew what they were about in medieval times. Scientists have recently proved what discerning customers have known for years, that the modern demand for lean meat has had an adverse effect on tenderness and taste. The explanation is that in pigs, for example, selection for leanness has produced animals with greater thyroid activity, a characteristic that results in an increase in the number of beta receptors in the skeletal muscles and an accelerated breakdown of glycogen.[7] Briefly, lean pigs are tense pigs; the effect is the same as if the animal had been exhausted or terrified at the time of slaughter (see note p. 8).

St Nicholas were still causing 'corruption and grievous stenches and abominable sights', and 'Edward by the Grace of God' was still fruitlessly threatening retribution.[9]

In Paris fifty years later 'Charles by the Grace of God' was having much the same kind of trouble. 'We have commanded, and we command, so that the air of our said city be not infected or corrupted by these slaughterhouses and knackers' yards, and also that the water of the River Seine be not corrupted nor infected by the blood and other filth of the said beasts falling or being thrown into the said River Seine, that all slaughterhouses and knackers' yards establish themselves outside our said city of Paris . . .'[10] The language was marginally less abundant, but the message was the same.

QUALITY CONTROL

Although it was generally impossible, in view of the commercial politics involved, to put an end to offences against health and hygiene, officialdom everywhere worked hard at imposing quality control and a number of guilds were far-sighted enough to try to regulate their members' trade practices.

In France the authorities took a close interest in the condition of all pork offered for sale; there were even *langueyeurs* (tongue inspectors), whose responsibility it was to examine the pigs' tongues for ulcers, which were thought to cause leprosy in consumers. In Venice all fish had to be taken to 'the tall pole' in the markets at San Marco and Rialto to be valued and pay duty before they were put on sale, and the fishmongers' stalls were inspected daily for stale fish, which the law required to be taken away and destroyed. Nevertheless, it seems that Italian 'fishfags', banned from freshening up the look of their fish by sprinkling water over them, still resorted to the old dodge described by Athenaeus. Two of them would quarrel, the quarrel would develop into a fight, one would knock the other out and then some helpful bystander would toss a bucket or two of water over the dazed victim – and, coincidentally, his fish.[11]

The majority of merchants were probably honest and God-fearing citizens, but a minority were either inept or corrupt. Some kinds of offence were spotted and reported very quickly. The medieval nose being peculiarly sensitive to the smell of decay (it was generally thought that bad odours were responsible for transmitting disease), amateur malefactors like John Gylessone, who tried to sell the 'putrid and stinking' flesh of a sow he had found dead in a London gutter, found themselves in instant trouble.[12] Less easy to detect, though still a product of ignorance rather than knavery, was the kind of violation that cropped up in a particularly lurid form in Venice in 1498, when a number of small traders were charged with selling 'cooking oil' that had been used for bathing sufferers from venereal disease.[13]

As long as towns remained small the deliberately crooked trader had to be either transient or highly ingenious. The itinerant pedlar might still be able to pass off his wooden nutmegs and juniper-berry peppercorns on unsuspecting housewives in the countryside, but in the towns once a particular swindle had been discovered it ceased to work. As the cities grew, however, calculated fraud became more common.

There were many ways by which a determined miscreant could evade detection, and the food inspectors spent a good deal of time assessing the quality of wine, ale, flour and oil – which were particularly liable to adulteration – and investigating what went into sausages and blood puddings. Catching a wily London baker like John Brid, however, was a matter of almost pure luck.

In the medieval period (even today in some places) it was usual for the oven-less housewife to make her own bread dough and take it to a baker to be cooked. Mr Brid's bakehouse appeared to be no different from any other. The customer tipped the ball of risen dough out of her apron on to the counter, had a brief chat with the baker and then watched him slide her dough onto his shovel and from there into the oven. There seemed to be no opportunity for trickery. But the counter had an almost invisible trapdoor cut out of it, and while customer and baker exchanged gossip, the baker's assistant was crouched underneath withdrawing dough from the underside of the loaf, 'piecemeal and bit by bit', so that the loaf that went into the oven was appreciably, if not visibly, lighter than it had been when it arrived in the shop. By this means, said the indictment sternly, John Brid collected great quantities of dough, 'falsely, wickedly and maliciously, to the great loss of all his neighbours and persons living near'.[14] With an ounce of dough here and an ounce there, the loaves of his own that Mr Brid offered on general sale were pure profit.

As it happened, one of the commonest food crimes in the later Middle Ages was selling underweight bread, the price of a loaf being fixed in relation to its weight. In early fourteenth-century London a halfpenny maslin loaf (a mixture of wheat and rye) was supposed to weigh twenty-eight shillings; the shilling had a standard weight of three-fifths of an ounce. If it weighed less, the guilty baker – with the offending loaf slung round his neck – was condemned to be drawn through the dirtiest streets in town on a hurdle (a kind of mobile pillory), a target for anything the populace cared to throw at him.

PUBLIC COOKSHOPS

Just as lack of domestic cooking facilities sent most housewives to the baker, so it encouraged the proliferation of cooked-meat vendors.

There was nothing new about the cookshop. It had been known in Mesopotamia in the days of Nebuchadnezzar, and the people of the Near East continued to buy their forcemeat balls, roast mutton, fish, fritters, pancakes and almond-paste sweetmeats from the market. It may have been from the Arab world, by way of Spain or as a result of the Crusades, that the custom of buying ready-cooked food was reintroduced to a Europe that had forgotten it since Roman times, although it would have made little headway if the revival of a monetary economy had not already begun.

A dishonest baker dragged round the streets with an underweight loaf tied round his neck.

In London by 1183 there was already one famous cookshop, where 'according to the season you may find viands, dishes roast, fried and boiled, fish great and small, the coarser flesh for the poor, the more delicate for the rich, such as venison, and birds both big and little. If friends, weary with travel, should of a sudden come to any of the citizens, and it is not their pleasure to wait fasting till fresh food is bought and cooked . . . they hasten to the river bank, and there all things desirable are ready to their hand.'[15]

There is no record of twelfth-century prices, but in 1363 a leg of roast mutton was to be had for $2\frac{1}{2}d$ (a day's wage for an agricultural labourer), as were three whole pigeons. A whole roast pig cost $8d$, ten roast finches less than $\frac{1}{2}d$, and a customer could have her own capon baked in a pasty at a charge of $1\frac{1}{2}d$ for 'the paste, fire and trouble'.[16]

Preparing tripe in a tavern or cookshop.

HYGIENE

Though the people of the Middle Ages knew that disease could be spread by either contagion or airborne infection (which they equated with bad smells), the standard of hygiene in cookshops, markets and private homes was anything but stringent.

Except during epidemics, even the most fastidious housewife – accustomed to hens in the house and sewage in the streets – seems to have given no thought to the perils of the market place, which were not, in essence, very different from those enumerated centuries later by an Englishman in India. 'Jones of the club, as he takes the cover off one of M-'s best entrées, may for once think of the leprous hand that has handled it; Brown may fancy for once he will catch smallpox from his beefsteak; Robinson may think of the dog licking the leg of mutton from which his whack is taken.'[17] Such were the hazards of all markets when medical knowledge was a luxury for the few and regulations about hygiene an irritating, additional burden for the many.

The very existence of the market could endanger a whole city. The merchants' food stores, the waste from the slaughterhouses, the refuse from the stalls – all these were breeding grounds for pestilence, havens for the omnivorous black rat, which by the thirteenth century infested most of the new towns of Europe. All that was needed was for a diseased rat to pause in the gutter and scratch itself, displacing a flea on to some passing human, and the result – if the human, like most people in medieval times, already had lice (which are transmitters of the typhus virus) – could be an epidemic. When something of this sort occurred, people died by scores, often by hundreds, occasionally by thousands.

The people who lived on the river banks also risked contracting dysentery or paratyphoid from the water. Although some towns, such as Göttingen in central Germany, enforced street-cleaning regulations from as early as 1330,[18] in most places the rubbish simply lay in the streets until it was washed away by a good downpour – usually into the wells from which drinking water was drawn or into the river. Historians used to think that sunlight and the small organisms that feed on bacteria must have purified the sewage in the rivers, but this has now been disproved. On the evidence of antibodies found in fish, it seems that not only the water but also the fish that swam in it (carefully protected by the authorities) were potent carriers of disease.[19]

Plague and typhus spread by rats in the market place, dysentery and paratyphoid from the fish in the river, food poisoning from the take-away stalls – it was hardly surprising that the Dance of Death should have taken such a hold on the medieval imagination. That nightmare pestilence, the Black Death, had a scarcely more traumatic effect on the survivors than the steady erosion of family and friends by the dangers of everyday life.

SPICES, THE MAGIC INGREDIENT

The rich and the new middle classes, having more living space than the poor, escaped some of the more intimate hazards of city life, even if they occasionally seem to have gone out of their way to court disaster. Parisians, for example, thought that sour wine could be improved by filtering it through sand that had first been thoroughly washed in the waters of the Seine.[20] Fortunately, they also spiced their wines – which may have helped to compensate for the sewage factor; their most popular spices, cinnamon and cloves, have an antiseptic influence in the intestine.

Although it is customary to account for the huge medieval consumption of spices in terms of their culinary usefulness, there are two other, minor factors that ought also to be taken into account. Firstly, the people of the Middle Ages – who knew a great deal about the medicinal properties of herbs – recognized that spices, too, could have a generally beneficial effect on health.* And secondly, until about 1490 and the advent of the Little Ice Age, the temperature in Europe may have been high enough to make spicy food biochemically desirable, even if not as essential as it can be in hot countries today.†

The fashion for spicy food – which had died with the death of international trade – seems to have been reintroduced to northern and western Europe by returning Crusaders, who, dazzled by the warmth and brilliance of the lands they had visited, carried a taste for new foods, as well as for many other luxuries, back to their native fastnesses. At the beginning they may have displayed their taste for foreign dishes very much as the modern tourist exhibits his souvenirs from abroad, but in the growing towns and cities of the West, where more and more people were condemned to a winter diet of unrelieved salted and dried foods, and a summer one of variable freshness, spices filled a real and obvious need. Soon Europe was depending on them so heavily that they became a common currency, as negotiable as silver. Today the phrase 'peppercorn rent' is sometimes used to denote a nominal sum, but in late medieval times there was nothing nominal about it. A pound of pepper was the barter equivalent of two or three weeks' labour on the land.

---

* Doctors, of course, used spices in many of their prescriptions, but usually as adjuncts to more potent ingredients like eye of newt and horn of toad.
† Spices encourage perspiration, which, evaporating, has a cooling effect on the body.

In political as well as monetary terms, the cost of spices was high. As the taste for them returned, they became a key factor in the development of international trade.

The trade routes of the Western world had been radically altered by the continuing hostility between Arabs and Byzantines. Spain and Egypt had suffered badly in the process, while the cities of southern France, north-western Italy, Cyprus and North Africa had been virtually abandoned for a while, and the old Rhône Valley trade route had faded into insignificance.

By the end of the so-called Dark Ages it was Venice that had become the waist in the hourglass of east-west commerce. Although its original prosperity had rested on the salt from its lagoons, Venice had followed Genoa and Pisa in supplying the Crusades with transports and warships, arms and siege engines, even the money to subsidize the troops, and it had turned out to be a profitable investment. Repayment came in the form of valuable concessions in the Near East that enabled Venice to build up a uniquely advantageous trading position.

The pepper and cinnamon, saffron and cloves, ginger, sugar, cardamom, costly medicines and exquisite silks that reached Venice from Constantinople travelled on from there to Pavia, the crossroads at which the busy highway of the River Po connected with the long-distance land routes to Germany and northern France by way of the Alpine passes of the Septimer, Mont Cenis and Great St Bernard.

In Pavia, a thriving city until Milan began to displace it in the eleventh century, the abbot of St Gall was among those who found it worth while to set up his own market to serve the transit trade – the Anglo-Saxon merchants ceaselessly complaining about the routine at border customs houses, the ingratiating representatives of distant courts intent on their middleman's rake-off and the great Venetian merchants themselves, every one of them obliged to buy off the master of the treasury with an annual one pound each of pepper, cinnamon and ginger.[21]

Across the Alps and beyond Switzerland cargoes were transferred to the Rhine, a route opened up first by the Frisians and later taken over by the Vikings, whose long commercial tentacles stretched east along the Baltic and west along the North Sea coasts of Europe towards England. Amber, furs, fish, tallow, honey, wool and wine were among the commodities with which they paid for the exotica of the East. As time passed, however, Scandinavian supremacy gave way to that of the enterprising townships that were later to form themselves into the Hanseatic League.

GRAIN SUPPLIES

Just as the Venetians came to monopolize the spice trade, the Hanseatic League succeeded in taking a grip on Europe's supplies of an even more important commodity – grain.

The early growth of towns had been matched by grain production on land increasingly distant from the centres of consumption. But when there was a bad harvest, the lords on their great estates and the peasants on their smallholdings kept what there was for themselves, and the townspeople – the new class who owned no land, worked no land and had no access to land – suffered shortages and inflated prices.

When real famine threatened, however, those who ruled in Europe did as the Romans had done so many centuries earlier and tried to silence the townspeople clamouring on their doorstep by sending out to appropriate as much grain as they could find, even if it meant stripping the reluctant countryside.

It had long been clear to the world's rulers that they could not afford to let their subjects die of hunger (provided the cost of keeping them alive was not too exorbitant). The earliest recorded food handouts had been designed to help the portionless widow; both the Old Testament and the *Shih ching* mention the custom of leaving a little grain in the fields for her to glean. After that came the Roman *annona*, foreshadowing not famine relief but unemployment benefit. Then, at the end of the eighth century, Charlemagne approached the problem of shortages from a different direction by banning the export of grain.

But one of the first rulers to make a systematic attempt to deal with recurring food shortages was the eleventh-century Chinese emperor Ying Zong (Ying-tsung), who resurrected an idea originally advanced by the Han usurper Wang Mang in AD 10 and established 'regulative granaries'.*

The state bought up surplus grain in good years, releasing stocks when times were bad and the market price would normally have risen too high for the average citizen to afford. This method had the twin virtues of building up food reserves and frustrating speculation, but it did demand a sizeable investment by the state. In other countries

* A more intelligent version of the EEC's grain mountain.

various civic bodies also made the attempt to guarantee grain supplies for their cities and to ensure that prices were kept down to an acceptable level.

The quantities of grain involved were considerable at a time when bread was a major item of diet for even the richest families. In England in the thirteenth century the Earl of Leicester's household used up 300 pounds of grain a day, even when the master was not at home,[22] and the lesser gentry consumed proportionately almost as much. One citizen of Genoa, whose family and servants numbered no more than ten, still had to buy in roughly five and a half tons of grain every year.[23] With consumption running at this level, a town with 3,000 citizens had to be able to call on something like 1,500 tons of grain annually – the produce of 10,000 acres of cultivated land.

It was fortunate that a huge new granary had been opened up in the twelfth century when the Germans expanded onto the plains of Eastern Europe. So plentiful and cheap were supplies from the Baltic that, courtesy of the Hanseatic League, there was now grain enough and to spare – even for brewing. In fact, by the end of the thirteenth century so much grain was coming through the Baltic that the farmers of Western Europe found it hardly worthwhile to go on growing their own. In Gascony and Poitou the vine took over; elsewhere there was a huge increase in stock breeding.

SHEEP FARMING

To the late medieval European the sheep was the most attractive commercial proposition. It supplied milk and meat, fat for cooking and tallow for lighting, wool to clothe the people of the north, and skins that were much in demand by the parchment makers, whose business had begun to boom as literacy spread outside the walls of the monasteries and into the realms of business and everyday life. Less temperamental than the cow and nimbler on rough pastures, the sheep also cropped the grass more closely and was marginally more fecund.

Abbeys and monasteries owned huge flocks – Fountains Abbey seems to have had something like 19,000 head, and Rievaulx 14,000 – while the wool merchants were the wealthiest traders in England (and the most heavily taxed). But the small investor also looked into the possibilities of sheep farming and found them good. Butchers and burgesses advanced capital to enterprising peasants, sometimes on a profit-sharing basis, sometimes on a head-count system under which the peasant was supplied with a flock, free of charge, which he

returned to his backer in two or three years, keeping for himself half
the lambs born in the interim.

Long before, the nomads of Central Asia and the barbarian hordes
of Europe had been equally enthusiastic about the sheep, and their
herding techniques had not been forgotten. Harking back to the
summer–winter migrations of the animals in the wild (which had kept
Palaeolithic man on the move), the nomads had always shifted their
flocks seasonally. The Visigoths took the system to Spain, where it
was well established by the seventh century and a key element in the
economy by the tenth. Historians today believe that the northern
Spaniards fought to free the rest of the country from the Arabs less for
doctrinaire reasons than because they wanted to be able to take their
flocks south to winter pasture again. In Castile alone there were an
estimated 1.5 million sheep at the beginning of the fourteenth century;
2.7 million by 1467.[24]

Moving millions of sheep over hundreds of miles during two brief
periods every year was an exercise requiring the most sophisticated
organization, and it is hardly surprising that the *Mesta*, Spain's
supervisory association, should have developed into a major power in
the land, with interests not only in national but international politics.

In France, as in Spain, tens of thousands of sheep were moved
annually from the mountains of Provence to winter pasture at Arles;*
in Italy from the Abruzzi to the Apulian plains. Everywhere there
were acrimonious exchanges between the herdsmen with their flocks
and the wayside farmers whose fields they ravaged.

Wool was the sheep's most important item of trade, but sheep
farming on the medieval scale did much to improve general standards
of nutrition, since meat, milk and cheese were now readily available.
The meat may have been less than tender, especially in the transhu-
mance (seasonal-migration) countries, where their twice-yearly mara-
thon ensured that the sheep remained lean and muscular, but there
was still protein in the stringy flesh and, since medieval cooking was
largely synonymous with long, slow simmering in the cauldron, tenderness was not too much of a problem except for the rich, who
preferred their meat roasted.

Some idea of levels of consumption is given by fourteenth-century
statistics, although statistics at this period are so rare that they cannot
be taken as generally representative. However, the 90,000 inhabitants

---

* The people of Provence, stout-hearted souls, also drove their pigs across
country every October to fatten on the acorns of Vaucluse.

of Florence consumed annually '4,000 oxen and calves, 60,000 mutton and sheep, 20,000 she-goats and he-goats, 30,000 pigs',[25] which was equivalent to one-and-a-third food animals per head of population – a very adequate intake. In France the royal household of Charles VI accounted for 200 sheep every week;[26] in addition to these, there would be other farmyard animals and, as in all noble households, a strong emphasis on the product of the hunt.

With so many fast-days in the year (for laity as well as monks and priests), cheese was as important as meat. In the fourteenth century it was estimated that twenty ewes could produce enough milk each week to make half a gallon of butter and fourteen pounds of cheese.[27] Since there were roughly 8 million sheep in England at that period[28] – nearly three times as many sheep as people – the existence of a cheese mountain cannot be ruled out.*

Milking sheep (centre left) in fourteenth-century England.

Simple excess may have been one reason why over the next 300 years the English peasant took an ineradicable dislike to ewe-milk products. When Tudor landlords began to appropriate the peasants' common grazing lands, the peasants complained that they would starve if they had nowhere to keep their cows, for *only* the cow could provide the 'butter, cheese, whey, curds, cream, sod [boiled] milk,

---

* There must certainly have been a lake of whey, the by-product of cheese-making. It is as well, perhaps, that the people of the medieval world did not know that whey could be used to make short-term building materials such as chipboard,[29] otherwise Westminster Abbey and Salisbury Cathedral might no longer be with us.

raw milk, sour milk, sweet milk and buttermilk' that were essential to their diet.[30]

It was an index of the changes taking place in society that even the least of its members could insist that they had a right not only to enough food, but also to enough food of the kind they liked.

13

THE LATE MEDIEVAL TABLE

Literacy and learning had been two of the most critical victims in the centuries following the collapse of the Classical world, centuries during which reading and writing became the preserve of the monasteries, and what was read and what was written were at the sole discretion of churchmen and kings.

One result was that relatively little of the Roman culinary tradition survived into late medieval times, and then mainly in the form of everyday techniques eroded by the passage of a thousand years and forty generations of cooks. Despite superficial resemblances, food in Europe in the Middle Ages – like food everywhere at every period up to the present – was an adaptation to current circumstances rather than a remembrance of things past.

Current circumstances for most people, especially in the north and west as towns grew and society changed, meant dependence on salted and dried foods for six months out of the twelve. This was because, with beans, dried stems, chaff and straw as the only feedstuffs, it was difficult to keep food animals alive throughout the winter. Where draught animals were concerned, it was usual to buy them, in part-nership, in the spring and sell them in late autumn to speculators who could afford to feed them during the bad months and resell (at a healthy profit) when the new farming season began.

The peasant's stock of fodder was estimated on the basis of keeping the household cow alive, while the pigs were expected to survive on kitchen scraps and whatever they could find by foraging. If their stamina was in doubt, they were slaughtered in November, before they began to lose weight. Some of the meat was eaten fresh, but most was salted down for the months to come.

PRESERVATION BY SALTING

There were two time-honoured methods of salting – dry-curing, in which the meat was bedded down in granulated salt, lightly spiced or herbed; and brining, where the preserving medium was a strong

Autumn slaughter and subsequent feasting.

solution of salt and water. The dry method gave good results, but the labour of pounding the lumpy medieval salt into crystals fine enough to pack closely round the meat may have ruled it out for the ordinary family. Noble households, on the other hand, had a servant known as the 'powderer', whose primary task that was.

Soaking and rinsing the gut destined to be used for sausage skins.

Meat was scarcely worth preserving unless it was in prime condition, which helps to explain why less mutton was salted than might have been expected. The elderly wool sheep was, quite literally, not worth her salt when, even without such desirable additions as peppercorns and cloves, salting added 40 per cent to the cost of the meat. At late thirteenth-century prices it took 2d-worth of salt (2 pounds) to cure 5d-worth of meat (20 pounds).[1] In the country there were no direct costs for the meat, but the expense of rearing and fattening the animal still had to be accounted in the reckoning.

Salting had had a long and somewhat chequered history. Although its origins remain obscure, in pre-Classical times both Egypt and Spain ran a thriving export trade in salted fish, and Roman Gaul was renowned for its salted and smoked hams. Christianity, however, with its meatless fasts, eventually did more for the fish-salting business than even the Church Fathers could have foreseen. Lent (the forty-day fast that precedes Easter) was the most profitable time for the merchants, but Fridays throughout the year were almost as good. Until as late as the mid-sixteenth century it remained legally possible for an Englishman to be hanged for eating meat on a Friday.[2]

The most important item in the salt-fish trade was the herring. In the fourteenth and fifteenth centuries the Baltic and the North Sea swarmed with it, a fatty fish whose oils turned rancid so quickly that salting had to be begun within twenty-four hours of the catch. This required a high degree of organization in the days of sail and oar, even in the Baltic, where most of the fisheries were close enough to land for the catch to be brought in daily. The Baltic commerce was dominated by the Hanseatic League.

In the scarcely less lucrative North Sea, Brielle in Holland vied for leadership with Yarmouth and Scarborough on the east coast of England. The problem with the North Sea catch was that it had to be salted on board, so the Norfolk doggers that set sail for Icelandic waters in early summer carried enough grain and ale, bacon, salt fish, beef and butter to feed their five- to ten-man crews for several months, as well as over a ton of salt and as many barrels (or materials for making them) as the ship would hold.[3]

Salt herring from the North Sea was notorious for having the best fish at the top of the barrel and the little tiddlers stuffed down towards the bottom, but the Hanse merchants made very sure that their customers – even if they had to pay extra for the privilege – could buy safe in the knowledge that the grading and packing of every barrel had been carefully supervised.

VARIETIES OF SALT

The three main sources of salt in medieval times, as today, were ordinary sea water, the rock residues of prehistoric seas, and natural salt springs.

The commonest was plain sea salt, which had been made for centuries all over Europe (and, indeed, the world) either by natural evaporation or by boiling sea water down in artificial pools or 'pans'.* But a vast increase in demand in the middle of the fourteenth century – partly attributable to economic conditions and partly to the trading damage caused by the Hundred Years War – brought about a crisis in north European salt production from which the merchants of Bourgneuf Bay, at the mouth of the Loire, emerged victorious.

Their victory had nothing to do with the quality of their product, which, made from sea water containing a good deal of debris, seaweed and probably sewage, was coarse and gritty, sometimes black in colour, sometimes grey, sometimes even green. But it was cheap, and for well over a century great convoys of ships travelled back and forth to the bay in the last months of winter to collect what was needed for the summer herring season in the north.

In time 'bay salt' ceased to mean salt from Bourgneuf Bay itself and became a generalized term for coarse salt made by natural evaporation on any sea coast. It seems never to have been anything but lumpy and impure, but it sold for half the price of good white salt. When its use became common, replacing the purer products of Luneberg and Lincolnshire, the quality of salted meat and fish deteriorated abruptly. Polluted sea salt did not penetrate the flesh as quickly, so that there was time for the inner parts of a fish or a piece of meat to turn rancid before the salt reached them.†[4]

Rock salt, which first had to be mined and then, usually, reboiled with sea water to increase its saltiness, was much less common than

---

* Town names are often informative, even if it may need a map to tell which town was likely to have produced which kind of salt. Saltcoats, Salzburg, Salt Lake City and the innumerable towns and villages called Salinas all carry their history in their names. Others such as Prestonpans – which means 'the salt-boiling pans at the priest's town' – are less easy to recognize.

† A consideration that troubled the king's justices in seventeenth-century England less than it troubled the housewife. Before being put on public display *pour encourager les autres*, the heads of villains who had been hanged, drawn and quartered were parboiled 'with Bay salt and cumin seed – that to keep them from putrefaction, and this to keep off the fowls from seizing on them'.[5]

either sea salt or the superior salt from the springs, which was known as brine salt. The saline content of brine salt was higher than that of sea salt and the end result was free from the calcium, magnesium salts and other less salubrious ingredients that marred the common sea-water kind, but it was expensive and supplies were by no means inexhaustible.

Almost as expensive was a complicated variation on sea salt known as 'peat salt', which was made mainly in the Low Countries from peat impregnated with sea water, dried and then burned to ashes. The ashes, in which most of the salt was precipitated, were subsequently mixed with more sea water and then boiled down over a turf fire. The result of this intricate production process was a fine white powder over which the Middle Ages rhapsodized, but peat was unfortunately in limited supply, could be dug only at certain times of the year and had to have sunshine to dry it out before it could be burned.

Extracting brine from salt springs in China, and sending it through a conduit to the evaporation pans.

SALT IN HISTORY

Salt-winning – the deliberate production of salt – is known to have been practised in the Neolithic era, but the naturally occurring variety had probably been gathered tens of thousands of years before that, even if only by coastal communities that, subsisting largely on shell-fish, found other foods insipid without it.

However the taste originated, salt was to become a more powerful factor in the world economy than any other food material apart from basic grains. As Cassiodorus, the fifth-century Goth administrator, put it: 'It may be that some seek not gold, but there lives not a man that does not need salt.'[6]

The contexts in which the word itself crops up are an index of salt's fundamental importance. The word 'salary', for example, is derived from the Roman for 'salt rations'. In Russia the term for hospitality (*khleb-sol'*) literally means 'bread-salt'. To the Arabs, eating a man's salt creates a sacred bond. The salt of the earth, being true to one's salt, if the salt have lost its savour ... Phrases of this kind can be counted almost *ad infinitum* in every one of the world's languages. Modern health advisers who would ban all salt from the diet are, in effect, recommending rejection of a substance that humanity has been genetically and socially programmed, over a period of tens of thousands of years, to desire and need.

Salts, in a generalized sense, have always been not only stimulating to the taste buds but also biological necessities. When a human being perspires, he loses some of his natural body salts and these have to be replaced from the food he eats. Raw meat is the best provider; cooked meat less so, because salt is usually lost in the cooking process. A diet based on cooked grain and vegetables contains few natural salts, even less if the vegetables are cooked in unsalted water, since some of their own salts are then leached out; contradictory though it may appear, salt in the cooking water actually helps to reduce this loss.

In parts of the world where food is mainly vegetarian, mineral salt is essential to remedy the deficiency. In 1936 the Chinese Communists had to evacuate some of the territories south of the Yangtze, which they had held for eight years, because the Nanking government blockade had cut off salt supplies;[7] salt hunger succeeded where military strength had failed. In Uganda during the reign of Idi Amin in the 1970s the appearance of salt in the markets of Kampala was enough to trigger off riots.[8] Examples of this kind could be multiplied indefinitely.

Although the need for salt is not always demonstrated quite as sharply as this, control of the salt pans and mines has always been a powerful political weapon. By the first millennium BC it was an essential feature of the administration in China, as it was for the Ptolemies in Egypt and the Seleucids in Persia. Venetian trade supremacy was built on salt, and in the eleventh century the Berbers joined in a great campaign against the Ghanaian Empire because they had long had their eye on the salt mines of Ankar. In the fifteenth century a whole African nation, the Vakaranga, trekked hundreds of miles north from Great Zimbabwe because the salt supplies there had been exhausted. Salt taxes, such as the hated French *gabelle*, were as profitable to many governments as tobacco taxes today.

Even in the twentieth century salt was still a government monopoly in British India. Indeed, it stimulated one of the great political demonstrations of modern times when, in 1930, Mahatma Gandhi marched with his followers on a pilgrimage to the seaside at Dandi, there – illegally – to make salt. His example fired the public imagination so effectively that other Congress leaders were caught on the hop. 'We knew precious little about it,' Jawaharlal Nehru confessed a few years later, 'and so we read it up where we could, and issued leaflets giving directions, and collected pots and pans and ultimately succeeded in producing some unwholesome stuff, which we waved about in triumph, and often auctioned at fancy prices.'[9]

PRESERVATION BY DRYING

The second major preservation process of the Middle Ages was drying, which may also – assuming that freezing was discovered during the ice ages – have been the second food preservation process known to history. In the Near East from very early times fruits such as dates, figs and grapes had been dried by the simple expedient of burying them in the desert sand, while meat was beaten with stones to extract the juices and then exposed to the sun.

Drying was not an easy proposition in mild, damp countries, where protection from the weather and plenty of fuel were needed, but the Scandinavians discovered that cool, crisp air and a stiff breeze were almost as good drying agents as the desert sun. Oily fish like herring and mackerel did not dry well, but cod, haddock, pollack and ling could be processed satisfactorily, cheaply and on a highly commercial scale. Norwegian *stokkfisk* – cod that had been gutted and hung to dry on wooden racks – ultimately provided the people of the Middle Ages with a cheap and almost indestructible food reserve.

It seems to have needed an equally indestructible cook to deal with it. One fourteenth-century author said of ten- to twelve-year-old stockfish, 'it behoves to beat it with a wooden hammer for a full hour and then set it to soak in warm water for a full two hours or more, then cook it and scour it very well . . .' The end product was best eaten with mustard or soaked in butter.[10]

Deep-sea fish were neither salted nor dried at home, except perhaps by fishermen's wives, but smoking was another matter. If it had not been documented from Roman times, it would be tempting to argue that the early medieval peasant discovered it independently. In the chimneyless, eye-stinging, often windowless peasant dwelling meat and fish (like people) may well have been smoked willy-nilly. The usual method with the two great protein staples of the medieval diet, bacon and red herring – the predecessor of the kipper – was to put them in the brine pot for a while, and then hang them over or near the fire to dry and smoke, after which they would keep for some months.

COOKING TECHNIQUES

Salt and smoke were the predominant flavours in the European kitchen for the whole of the winter and spring seasons; it must have been like living today on nothing but cheap factory bacon for half the year. The poor had little choice but to put up with it. The rich, on the other hand, became highly ingenious in the matter of taste improvers.

Most of what is known about medieval food comes from court catering records or the kitchen account books of monasteries and noble households, which are informative about raw materials, prices and quantities. For recipes and general culinary lore there is a handful of works on cookery and etiquette. All of them, with the notable exception of the domestic manual compiled by a fourteenth-century Parisian merchant known as the *Ménagier*, have one serious historical failing – they relate to the kitchens and dining halls of the great nobles and landowners.

From the historical point of view these manuscripts also have other failings. Still, as of old, the recipes are carefree about quantities, seldom specify whether salted or fresh meat should be used and never trouble to spell out heat intensities or cooking times. Not that the authors can be criticized for this. Such manuscripts were originally intended as *aides-mémoire* for the cooks (usually royal) who wrote them, or for assistants or successors who would know without having to be told not only how to deal with the preliminaries when salted or dried foods were being used, but also most of the other essentials necessary to the production of dishes with which they were already, in general terms, familiar. What the cooks' manuals do, in effect, is supply the details of medieval food preparation without the guiding principles.

The first principle, of course, was to ensure – in days when an instruction to 'soak in several changes of water' involved some scullion in numerous trips to the well – that salt meat and fish were as thoroughly desalted as soaking could make them. That this first principle was often flouted is shown by the number of remedies in the medieval cook's armoury.

The basic expedient was to hang a linen bag of oatmeal in the cauldron to absorb some of the excess, but the cook commonly ensured that the menu as a whole had a salt-neutralizing bias. Some dishes were routinely offered as accompaniments to others for that very reason.

Where potatoes or rice might be used today as side dishes that help to soak up the salt without themselves becoming salty, the Middle Ages relied on dried peas, dried beans, breadcrumbs or whole grain. Pureed beans with bacon was the standard combination in poorer households, but the rich preferred frumenty, mortrews or blamanger – the forerunners of today's bread sauce.

By medieval times frumenty had become a thick pudding of whole wheat and almond milk sometimes enriched with egg yolks and coloured with saffron. It was the standard accompaniment for venison. Mortrews, which took its name from the mortar in which the ingredients were pounded, was made by mixing boiled and puréed white meat or fish with breadcrumbs, stock and eggs, and then reducing it over the fire; a sprinkling of pepper and ginger added the finishing touch. For blank mang or blamanger (the scarcely recognizable ancestor of the modern blancmange) shredded chicken was mixed with boiled rice and almond milk, then seasoned with sugar and salt; aniseed and fried almonds were the correct garnish.

The cook's other recourses were to employ spices or fruit to offset saltiness, and/or creamy sauces to smooth it out. Some medieval recipes look almost as fearsome as Roman ones, with unspecified quantities of ginger, pepper, saffron, cinnamon, cloves and mace, but although these may, in truth, have been no more than the equivalent of 'a pinch of mixed spice', it seems as if medieval cooks may have used rather more than a pinch. The starches and creams that reduce saltiness also reduce the intensity of the spices themselves, and in some types of dish the spices would scarcely have been discernible unless they were used generously. Nor had the medieval host any more desire to hide his expensive spices under a bushel than his Roman predecessors had done.

'Pumpes', for example (which, except for the choice of meat, sound very much as if they might have come from a kitchen in Baghdad) were a fairly typical dish, and made as follows:

'Take and boil a good piece of pork, and not too lean, as tender as you may; then take it up and chop it as small as you may; then take cloves and mace, and chop forth withall, and also chop forth with raisins of Corinth; then take it and roll it as round as you may, like to small pellets, at two inches about, then lay them on a dish by themselves; then make a good almond milk, and blend it with flour of rice, and let it boil well, but look that it be quite runny; and at the dresser, lay five pumpes in a dish, and pour the pottage thereon. And if you will, set on every pumpe a flower, and over them strew on sugar enough and mace: and serve them forth. And some men make the pellets of veal or beef, but pork is best and fairest.'[11]

Much of the rich man's time was taken up with hunting. He enjoyed the exercise as much as the game he came home with, and for the cook game was certainly less trouble all round, although even the finest roast had to be accompanied by one or more spicy dipping sauces. The dipping sauce was so generally useful that in Paris the professional saucemaker had become a familiar figure by the fourteenth century.[12] Included in his repertoire were 'yellow sauce', in which ginger and saffron predominated; 'green sauce', with ginger, cloves, cardamom and green herbs; and 'cameline sauce' – the great fourteenth-century favourite – in which cinnamon was the essential ingredient.

According to Guillaume Tirel, cook to Charles V of France and compiler of the 1375 cookery book *Le Viandier de Taillevent*, cameline was made as follows. 'Pound ginger, plenty of cinnamon, cloves, cardamom, mace, long pepper if you wish, then squeeze out bread soaked in vinegar and strain all together and salt it just right.'[13] The English version had one or two additional refinements. 'Take raisins of Corinth, and kernels of nuts, and crust of bread and powder of ginger, cloves, flour of cinnamon, pound it well together and add it thereto. Salt it, temper it up with vinegar, and serve it forth.'[14]

Dried fish, the other mainstay of the menu, was a pallid food that needed to be livened up with mustard or vinegar or disguised with spices or fruit. It was one of the greatest challenges to the cook's ingenuity during periods when the Church took a firm stand on fasting. Then, meat, eggs and dairy products were forbidden on

Wednesdays, Fridays, Saturdays and the whole of Lent – half the days of the year.

One masterly way of dealing with stockfish was 'Lenten ryschewys', a kind of fruity rissole encased in batter. 'Take figs and boil them up in ale; then take when they be tender and pound them small in a mortar; then take almonds, and shred them thereto small; take pears and shred them thereto; take dates and shred them thereto; and take [dried haddock or ling] that is well soaked and shred thereto.'[15] The resulting paste was shaped, floured, dipped in batter and fried in oil.

Medieval Europe faced much the same culinary problems as Rome and used many of the same meats, spices, fruits and grains, but although memories of Roman cooking may have survived the lapse of centuries, the reality of it had vanished in the long scarcity of spices, the disappearance of *liquamen* and silphium – and the continuing absence of flamingoes' tongues. If the late medieval cuisine of the West was directly indebted to any one source, it was to the Arabs, the cultural middlemen of the post-Classical world. From their synthesis of Roman, Persian and desert-nomad foods, Europe's cooks borrowed many, perhaps most, of the techniques and materials they needed to solve their own pressing problems.

THE MENU

There is a dismal monotony about the peasant menu across the continents and across the centuries that is probably more apparent than real: in China rice, vegetables and perhaps a mouthful of pork; in India rice, vegetables and a spicy sauce; in Mexico maize pancakes or beans, with tomatoes and peppers; in northern Europe dark bread, cabbage, beans or salt pork from the stockpot, with curds to round off the meal.

These, however, were only the basics, and because they sound dull it is too easy to assume that they *were* dull. Yet there must have been good cooks in the fourteenth century, as in the twentieth, cooks who knew how to make use of the seasonal bounty of the countryside. Some peasants in some places may have eaten consistently well.

Even so, the servants in the castles and fortified houses of the countryside were more reliably catered for. Most of their meals might consist of pease pudding, salt herring or dried cod, followed by cheese and washed down with ale brewed on the estate, but their bread was a decent maslin and occasionally they had beef or goose to eat with it, or even a few leftover delicacies from the lord's table (though the beggar at the gate had first call on these).

By the fourteenth century, however, there was a new class in the population, still closer to the peasantry than to the nobility, but with a positive identity of its own. In the dinners given by its members, especially the prosperous town merchants, the particular character of the medieval cuisine is displayed more clearly than in the banquets of the great.

The menu at this time bore very little resemblance to today's. It was as if *table d'hôte* and *à la carte* were one and the same thing, with the alternative dishes in each course all being placed on the table at the same time. A 'course' was a more or less haphazard assortment, its only real consistency that it offered a wide choice within itself; not until the sixteenth century did there emerge some degree of unity (see menu, pp. 231–3). The diner surveyed what was on offer, and made his own choice – some of this, some of that – with no compulsion to take a platterful of everything, even if the option existed.

In Paris in 1393 a merchant's guests might have been offered the following.[16]

FIRST COURSE

Miniature pastries filled
with cod liver or
beef marrow

A cameline 'brewet'
– pieces of meat in a
thin cinnamon sauce

Beef marrow fritters

Eels in a thick, spicy purée

Loach in a cold green
sauce flavoured with
spices and sage

Large joints of meat,
roasted or boiled

Saltwater fish
Fritters
Roast bream and darioles
Sturgeon
Jellies

SECOND COURSE

'The best roast that may
be had'

Freshwater fish

Broth with bacon

A meat tile
(see below)

Capon pasties and crisps

Bream and eel pasties

Blank mang (blamanger)

THIRD COURSE

Frumenty

Venison

Lampreys with hot sauce

After the meal the board was cleared to make way for dessert, which encompassed a variety of sweet and spicy confections. Either then or later, spiced wines and wafers were served, as well as dry whole spices 'to help the digestion'.*

Ready and waiting in a corner of the kitchen, a crowned and garlanded swan, perched on a pie.

It is the menu rather than the individual dish that divides the fourteenth century so irrevocably from the twentieth. A 'meat tile', for example – pieces of sautéd chicken or veal, with a spiced sauce of pounded crayfish tails, almonds and toasted bread, and a garnish of whole crayfish tails[17] – might be quite acceptable at a modern table if the rest of the meal were light and fresh-flavoured. But balance was lacking from the medieval menu.

On the tables of the rich there would be fewer fish dishes (except on fast days) and more game birds and beasts. The overall number of dishes would also be much greater than those offered on the middle levels of society. But where the aristocratic table differed most strikingly was in presentation. The medieval world, still only marginally

---

* The same custom had existed in India for a thousand years (and still does), the spices being wrapped in betel leaves for convenience.

literate, compensated by being intensely visual, and its delight in architecture, painting, silverware and costume overflowed onto the rich man's table in the form of gilded swans, peacocks in all their plumage and extravagant 'soteltes' (subtleties) – sweets, jellies or pastries moulded into splendid and fanciful representations of lions, eagles, crowns or coats of arms. When sugar became readily available in the sixteenth century, Italian confectioners won a high reputation for the intricacy of their spun-sugar sculptures.

As the Middle Ages merged into the Renaissance and became fascinated by Classical antiquity, even more exotic conversation pieces were invented, including one that harked back (in an improved form) to Trimalchio's feast.

To make pies that the birds may be alive in them
and fly out when it is cut up

Make the coffin [piecrust] of a great pie or pasty. In the bottom thereof make a hole as big as your fist, or bigger if you will. Let the sides of the coffin be somewhat higher than ordinary pies. Which done, put it full of flour and bake it, and being baked, open the hole in the bottom and take out the flour. Then, having a pie of the bigness of the hole in the bottom of the coffin aforesaid, you shall put it into the coffin, withal put into the said coffin round about the aforesaid pie as many small live birds as the empty coffin will hold, besides the [small] pie aforesaid. And this is to be done at such time as you send the pie to the table, and set before the guests: where, uncovering or cutting up the great lid of the pie, all the birds will fly out, which is to delight and pleasure show to the company. And that they be not altogether mocked, you shall cut open the small pie.[18]

KNIVES AND FORKS

Most medieval food fell into one of five textural categories. There was the plain, dry roast. There were small pies, pasties and fritters consisting of meat, sauce and plate, all in one self-contained package. There was the thickly sauced mixture, sometimes custardy like mortrews, sometimes a whole-grain pudding like frumenty. There was the 'brewet' of meat, poultry or fish in a spicy, creamy sauce. And there was the simple soup, a flavoured liquid with a few 'sops' of bread or meat swimming around in it.*

Texture was as important in medieval times as it had been in Roman because there were only two pieces of cutlery. Most people carried a knife of the traditional, general-purpose dagger shape, and spoons were not uncommon, but the dinner fork was an oddity in most of Europe until the eighteenth century.

Kitchen forks had been familiar for hundreds of years, even if most of them were only marginally smaller than a farmer's pitchfork. By the tenth century, however, small gilt ones were being used at select Byzantine tables, mainly for sweetmeats,[20] and they were known in Greece 300 or 400 years later.[21] From Greece they travelled to Italy, a country whose refined manners had again become the envy of Europe, but in Italy, for a while, they stuck. A French silk merchant, Jaques le Saige, noted them favourably at a ducal banquet in Venice in 1518. 'These seigneurs, when they want to eat, take the meat up with a silver fork.'[22] Yet although Catherine de Medici appears to have taken not only her cooks but also her entire kitchen with her when she went to France in 1533 to marry the dauphin, the fork did not catch on. Nor did it in England seventy years later, when the traveller Tom Coryat flattered himself that he had introduced a new fashion.[23]

Until after 1700, although a few eccentrics used a fork for dining, most north Europeans continued to eat with fingers and knives, or spoon and bread, using them as a child does a spoon and pusher. Even as late as 1897 the British Navy was forbidden the use of knives and forks, which were considered prejudicial to discipline and manliness.[24] In America, however, nineteenth-century etiquette manuals were so severe about people who ate peas off their knives that those with better manners went to the other extreme – with the result that America became a nation of dedicated fork-eaters.[25]

---

* The number of sops per serving was an index of the host's meanness or generosity. On one occasion, when a certain Sieur de Vandy dined at a friend's, 'they placed before him a soup in which there were only two poor sops chasing each other around. Vandy tried to take one up but, as the plate was enormous, he missed his aim; he tried again, and could not catch it. He rose from the table and called his valet.

"You there! Pull off my boots!"

"What are you going to do?" his neighbour asked him.

"Allow me to have my boots removed," said Vandy coldly, "and I propose diving into that plate in order to seize that sop!" '[19]

The bread trencher, clearly illustrated; there was a pile of spares to replace any that became sodden during the course of the meal.

Table Manners

The absence of the table fork would have been of minor interest if it had not been for the way in which the service of food was organized.

Only the great man was served individually. Others ate in pairs if only one side of the long table was occupied, or in fours if there were people on both sides of it. Each two or four was known as a 'cover'. Every guest had his own trencher (from the Old French *tranchier*, to cut), which was originally a thick slice of stale bread measuring about six inches by four that served as an absorbent plate. The greedy diner would eat his trencher himself at the end of the meal, but it was more often given to the poor or to the dogs. By the fifteenth century the bread trencher was being superseded by a square of wood with a circular depression in the middle.

When there was roast meat or game, the carver placed the best pieces on the important guests' trenchers, and the rest on platters on the table, but other kinds of food came straight from the kitchen or dresser in dishes containing portions for two or four. From these, diners helped themselves with the aid of knife, spoon or (most often) fingers, transferring each morsel separately from serving dish to trencher to mouth.

The cleanliness of one's neighbour's fingers was therefore a matter of personal interest. Indeed, as Giovanni della Casa said, 'Before meals it is right to wash your hands openly, even though you have no need to do so, in order that those who dip their fingers in the same dish as yourself may know for certain that you have cleaned them.'[26]

But it was one thing for a man to wash his hands before a meal, and quite another to keep them clean during the course of it. In late medieval and Renaissance times a number of 'courtesy [etiquette] books' were produced for the children of the nobility, which give a hair-raising picture of the table manners of the time. Although much of the material in them was probably exaggerated, the fact that authors found it necessary to condemn certain habits as undesirable suggests that those habits, though not necessarily common, were not entirely unknown.

'Let thy hands be clean', said Fra Bonvicino da Riva in 1290. 'Thou must not put either thy fingers into thine ears, or thy hands to thy head. The man who is eating must not be cleaning by scraping with his fingers at any foul part.'[27] Although Brother Bonvicino chose not to define 'foul parts', later writers were less inhibited, instructing their readers not to blow their noses with their fingers and not to go scratching at that segment of the male anatomy generally known as the 'codware'.

Scratching, when fleas and lice were omnipresent, was one of the habits most thundered against in the courtesy books. If it could be done surreptitiously, well and good. But to remove one's fingers from a shared bowl of food and promptly start scratching was not at all the thing. 'If it happen that you cannot help scratching,' recommended a fourteenth-century German writer, 'then courteously take a portion of your dress, and scratch with that. That is more befitting than that your skin should become soiled.'[28] The scratcher's dinner partner, it

Despite the formal elegance of most representations of banquets, this was much more like the reality.

may be supposed, was probably less concerned with smudges on his neighbour's chin than with having a scratched-at louse transferred back to the brewet-bowl on the tip of a soupy finger.

Napkins, like forks, were not used at this time, but if Della Casa is any guide they had not done a great deal for cleanliness even 200 years later. After discussing gluttons who dipped their hands into a dish almost to the elbow, Della Casa remarked that they made a fearful mess of their napkins. 'And these same napkins,' he added, 'they will use to wipe off perspiration, and even to blow their noses. You must not so soil your fingers as to make the napkin nasty in wiping them; neither clean them upon the bread which you are to eat.'*[29]

There were other undesirable habits, too. It was offensive 'to poke about everywhere when thou hast meat or eggs or some such dish. He who turns or pokes about on the platter, searching, is unpleasant, and annoys his neighbour at dinner.' Some people were also inclined 'when they have gnawed a bone, to put it back in the dish',[30] whereas the proper place for such debris, even in the most august households, was the floor, thoughtfully carpeted with rushes to smother the rubbish and strewn with sweet-smelling basil or southernwood. When Cellini was a young man, his employer made 'a very large vase designed for the table of Pope Clement, into which at dinnertime were to be thrown bones and rinds of fruit'. But it transpired that even the Pope had no particular aversion to a floorful of bones. The vase, Benvenuto went on, was only for display.[31]

DIGESTIVE WIND

A medieval banquet can have been restful to none of the senses. Servants scuttled back and forth bringing wine, carved meats, sauces, fresh trenchers and sweetmeats from the boards set up round the walls, frequently colliding with the guests' own retainers, brought along to fetch and carry for their masters. Great men's 'tasters' hovered close to their lords, assaying every dish for poison. Dogs scavenged among the rushes on the floor. And senior household dignitaries anxiously supervised everything that went on, from the clearing of one course and setting of the next to the decent conduct of the troubadours and acrobats who entertained the company in the intervals.

But despite the noise, the bustle, the spicy aromas of the food and

* Della Casa's Victorian translator could not here restrain himself from interpolating, 'We should hope not!'

the no less spicy aroma of unwashed humanity, the courtesy books still found it necessary to make mention of digestive wind.

Of all the rules of etiquette through the ages that against breaking wind has had the longest life. Surviving texts are not always specific about which aspect of the subject they are discussing (or perhaps it is just that translators are too genteel), but it is clear that while a delicate burp has been acceptable, sometimes even commendable, in most societies,* the audible release of what Dr Johnson disarmingly referred to as 'an ill wind behind' most certainly has not.[33]

'Scientific researches! . . . or – an Experimental Lecture on the Powers of Air'. Vintage 1802.

Farting in public was forbidden to the Chinese as early as the sixth century BC, while in India, 400 years later, Kautilya laid down that anyone appointed to the king's service should take care not to 'indulge in bellicose talk, nor make statements that are uncultured . . . nor indulge in loud laughter when there is no joke, nor break wind'.[34] The emperor Claudius, it was said, 'planned an edict to legitimize the breaking of wind at table, either silently or noisily – after hearing about a man who was so modest that he endangered his health by an

* Save when being breathalyzed in the twentieth century. A burp at the wrong moment has been known to take the burper over the limit.[32]

attempt to restrain himself'.[35] (Sadly, there is no record of who had made it illegal in the first place.)

There were always, of course, men of independence who would have no truck with such rules and regulations. When one of the caliphs of Baghdad paid Ibn al-Junayd the signal honour of inviting him to become an official boon companion, he declined. He felt happier, he said, in the company of ordinary men, 'where one can pass gas in this or that direction without much fuss being made about it.'[36]

In this he would have had the support of Salerno:

> Great harms have grown, and maladies exceeding,
> By keeping in a little blast of wind:
> So cramps and dropsies, colics have their breeding,
> And mazed brains, for want of vent behind.

It was perhaps unfortunate that beans, cabbage, onions and garlic should have been the commonest vegetables of the Middle Ages, even if they were not all potent in precisely the same way. References to garlic go even further back in history than references to farting. In India the priestly brahmins were forbidden to eat it, while in the first days of Islam the Prophet Muhammad – fearful of offending his hosts by rejecting a dish with garlic in it – explained disarmingly, 'I am a man who has close contact with others.' Salerno, however, believed (rightly) that it was efficacious against many 'poisons' and infections.

> . . . For they that it devour
> May drink, and care not who their drink do brew;
> May walk in airs infected every hour.
> Since garlic then hath powers to save from death,
> Bear with it though it make unsavoury breath,
> And scorn not garlic, like to some that think
> It only makes men wink, and drink, and stink![37]

The truth was that, however often medieval man was told to 'beware of [his] hinder part from guns blasting',[38] there was very little he could do to prevent it.

He might have been helped (though not very much) by modern research on the internal environment of spacecraft. The US Department of Agriculture has developed a system for measuring the 'flatus-producing effect' of individual foods,[39] while another researcher, Dr Michael Levitt, has gone into the subject of food intake as a whole. It seems that the answer to excessive gas output is a two-day diet of water. If that does not appeal, a high-fibre diet makes it odourless.[40]

A few years ago one French astronaut – apparently unaware of these findings – took some garlic-laden delicacies along with him on a Soviet space flight. The air conditioning, it was subsequently reported, proved unable to cope.[41]

— PART FIVE —

THE EXPANDING WORLD 1492–1789

By the fifteenth century spices had become so important to the West that half the nations of Europe were determined to do what Rome had done so long before, break the middlemen's monopoly. They were more successful than they could have dreamed of, because, in the process, Columbus discovered America and Vasco da Gama opened up the sea route to India. Although the New World was found to have none of the spices that had helped to stimulate the voyages of discovery, it provided a number of new foodstuffs that were to be of the greatest importance to the Old in the centuries to come. India, however, did have spices, and one result of the trade wars that ensued was the founding of the British Empire. The West's great era of imperial enterprise had begun and no part of the world was to remain untouched by it. Even the countries that escaped physical occupation became the victims of competition and sometimes war; victims, too, of the new awareness of national identity. 'The world is a bridge', said the Mughal emperor Akbar in 1602. 'Pass over it but build no house upon it.' Formerly, the peoples of the West had built no theories of racial superiority on the bridge of other people's worlds. Now they did.

14

NEW WORLDS

During the fifteenth century chaos descended on the spice trade. The Mongols, who had succeeded the Arabs as overlords of the land routes to the East, were replaced at key points by the inflexible Ottoman Turks. Although Venice and Florence continued to trade profitably at Alexandria and Damascus – Venice alone bringing back to Europe an estimated 2,500 tons of pepper and ginger annually and almost as much again of other spices – the future was beginning to look less than rosy.

The merchants of the Italian cities were, of course, only the last link in a long chain of middlemen who all exacted profit from the trade. What this profit amounted to in the fifteenth century remains uncertain, but in 1621 a knowledgeable Englishman reckoned that 3,000 tons of spices could be bought in the Indies for £91,041, whereas by the time they reached Aleppo the price had soared to £789,168[1] – which was a substantial mark-up by anyone's standards. The Venetian profit had to be added on top of that.

It seemed to the other nations of Europe that if they could bypass the established trade routes by sailing direct to the Spice Islands and buying at source, nothing but benefit would accrue. Always before there had been too many difficulties, not least those of ship design, but now there were sturdy merchantmen that could withstand the buffeting of the open sea and had three masts instead of one – an innovation that made oars unnecessary – which overcame the most serious of the problems.

The psychological turning point came when the last remnant of the once great Byzantine Empire, Constantinople itself, was captured by the Ottoman Turks in 1453. Three years later Athens too, the *sanctum sanctorum* of the Classical world, fell to the infidel. Men who lived on the Atlantic coasts of Europe, visualizing complete closure of the Mediterranean, looked again at what had been said in the past about the physical shape of the world and some became convinced that, as the ancient philosophers had claimed, the western coast of Africa could not be far removed from the eastern coast of India.

Personal fame, the glory of God and a share in the spice trade – an unbeatable combination in fifteenth-century terms – all played a part in sending Columbus off on the voyage that was to end in the New World. For the admiral himself, the first prospect was perhaps the most enticing. Luis de Santangel, who lent Queen Isabella of Castile the money to subsidize the voyage, seems to have been more interested in the second. But it was the possibility of breaking into the highly lucrative spice trade that almost certainly swung the balance for Isabella, her treasury dangerously depleted by the campaign against the last Muslim garrisons in Spain.

When Columbus reached what he thought were the Indies in 1492, he found no spices that he recognized, nor any of the 'powerful kingdoms and noble cities and rich provinces' that one of his advisers had told him to expect. On the second voyage, however, he persuaded himself that, in Haiti, he had discovered 'different kinds of wild spices that could be brought to perfection by cultivation, such as fine-coloured cinnamon (though bitter to the taste), ginger, pepper and different kinds of mulberry trees for producing silk'.[2] Whatever the 'cinnamon' and 'ginger' may have been, only the pepper – which was entirely different from the East Indian species – was to make any useful contribution to the spice chests of the Old World.

Vasco da Gama was more successful. When, in 1498, he reached the true Indies, he sent a man ashore to prospect. Greeted by the local population with an improbable 'May the Devil take thee! What brought thee hither?' the man replied, equally improbably, 'We came in search of Christians and spices.'[3] The farce was compounded by a misunderstanding that led da Gama to think he had found both, but although the 'Christians' of Calicut turned out, in the end, to be a myth, the spices were perfectly real.

Within twenty-five years, however, the nations of Europe were complaining just as loudly about the Portuguese stranglehold on the spice trade as they had earlier done about the Venetian. In 1523 a Nuremberg decree commented sourly on the fact that over 100 tons of ginger and almost 2,000 tons of pepper had come into Germany from Lisbon alone, and 'the king of Portugal, with spices under his control, has set ... prices as he will, because at no manner of dearness will they rest unsold among Germans.'[4]

Later in the century the Dutch began to whittle away the Portuguese monopoly, and by 1599 the English were so disgusted at the price of pepper having gone up from three shillings to eight shillings a pound that eighty London merchants met to establish the East India Company

– and, however unwittingly, the British Indian Empire. Soon, France, Denmark and Austria also found footholds in Asia, and Spain reached the Indies by the Pacific route.

Europe's discovery of America and conquest of southern Asia were only two of the surprising results of its hunger for spices. There was another, less direct but no less far-reaching. In the urgently entrepreneurial climate of the Old World just after Columbus's first voyage, Pope Alexander VI chose to settle the question of imperial rights in formerly unknown and unmapped territories by drawing a line on the existing map from north to south through the Atlantic, allocating to Spain all new lands west of the line, and to Portugal all those to the east.

This, by chance, gave Brazil to Portugal, and it was Portugal's possession of Africa on one side of the Atlantic and Brazil on the other that made the joint expansion of the sugar and slave trades inevitable.

— 15 —

THE AMERICAS

The 'Indies' where Columbus made his landfall were in fact the Bahamas,* islands 'full of green trees and abounding in springs' with 'gardens that were as beautiful as Castille in May'. Although relieved to find the inhabitants a 'gentle, peaceful and very simple people' who gratefully accepted the 'little red caps and glass beads' he bestowed on them, he soon realized 'that this was not the land he sought; nor did it offer such promise of riches as to hold him there'.[2]

In search of better things the Spanish ships cruised south during the months that followed, touching at many of the Caribbean islands, looking for spices and gold, surveying the territory, learning a little about the people and – of necessity – more about their food.

Some of the things they ate appeared revolting to the Europeans, unaccustomed to 'large fat spiders, white worms that breed in rotten wood, and other decayed objects'.[3] Tropical America, of course, had always been short of food animals, so there was a long tradition of eating, instead, the insects that abounded. The agave worm (*meocuilin*), considered a great delicacy at the court of the Aztecs, remains one in Mexico today.†

Among the groups of tribes the Spaniards encountered was the Taino, which suggests that the 'other decayed objects' may have included a speciality of theirs, zamia bread, whose preparation was by no means unsophisticated. It was made by grating the stems of the zamia plant, then shaping the pulp into balls and leaving them in the sun for two or three days until they began to rot and turn black and wormy. When sufficiently ripe, the balls were flattened into cakes and baked over the fire on a griddle. If the bread was eaten before it became black and wormy, said the Tainos, 'the eaters will die'. In this

---

* At a spot recently identified by the National Geographic Society's computer (with 98 per cent certainty) as sixty-five miles south-east of San Salvador on Samana Cay.[1]

† Mexican gourmets have their worms. In France the great new delicacy of 1986 was snails' eggs (selling at roughly £35 per 1 ¾-ounce jar).[4]

they were right; unless zamia pulp is either intensively washed or else fermented, it can be toxic.

In Cuba the Spaniards found a more acceptable bread, cassava, although it, too, was made from a plant that was poisonous when raw, the bitter variety of manioc, which contains cyanide. The technique here was either to boil the roots very thoroughly and then mash them, or to peel and grate the roots, and then squeeze out the juices under heavy pressure.* The pulp was sieved, shaped into flat cakes, and cooked slowly on a griddle.

Soft and flexible when fresh, cassava bread could be dried and kept for two or three years. The Spanish, and later the French, adopted it with enthusiasm; there were even some who claimed it to be superior to wheaten bread. Manioc was to be introduced into Africa by the Portuguese during the sixteenth century, where its lack of protein was more than compensated for by a virtual immunity to locusts and an ability to remain in the ground for as much as two years after maturity without deteriorating, making it a valuable insurance against scarcity.†

As well as objectionable insects and breads of dubious provenance, the people of the Caribbean ate 'cooked roots that had the flavour of chestnuts'[6] – probably sweet potatoes – beans in variety, wild birds, fish, and crabs in abundance. In Panama they wrapped a particular kind of small fish in leaves 'as apothecaries roll electuaries [medicinal powders] in paper, and after being dried in the oven the fish keep for a long time'.[7] There were also a great number of fruits, from which fermented drinks were made.

Maize

Of all the new foodstuffs Columbus found in the Caribbean, maize was to be the most important in later history. Europe now knows it by a version of its Taino name (*mahiz*), but the Pilgrim Fathers in seventeenth-century North America first learned of it from local Indians; then, as now, 'corn' was a catch-all English word for any kind of grain, so they called it 'Indian corn'.

* The juices, boiled hard, were used to make cassareep sauce and also threw a starchy sediment that, dried, was to become the bane of generations of European children, tapioca.

† Though not infallibly. In northern Mozambique as recently as 1981 an acute water shortage resulted in some manioc not being prepared as thoroughly as it should be; more than a thousand people suffered partial paralysis as a result.[5]

When Columbus first sighted America, its inhabitants had already developed more than 200 types of maize – one of the most remarkable plant breeding achievements in history. On his early visits to Cuba Columbus noted that it was 'most tasty boiled, roasted or ground into flour'.[8] When he arrived back in Spain, his most popular exhibits from the New World were a few specimen 'Indians' and some handfuls

By 1563, maize was familiar enough round the coasts of the Mediterranean for Arcimboldo to include it in his painting of 'Summer'.

of gold dust, but he seems also to have carried maize seeds in his baggage. Soon afterwards the Spaniards began distributing maize around the Mediterranean, although it was the Venetians who took it to the Near East, from which it travelled up to the Balkans and also back to France, Britain and Holland. For a time Britain, Germany, Holland and Russia called it 'Turkish wheat'. In parts of France it was Rhodes, Spanish or Barbary corn; in Italy, Sicilian or Turkish corn. And in Turkey? '*Rooms* corn' – foreign corn.

When, in 1519, Magellan set out on a new Spanish attempt to reach the Spice Islands by a westward route, he took maize with him. It was known in the Philippines soon after, and by 1555 was sufficiently important in some parts of China to rate a mention in a regional history of the province of Henan (Honan).⁹ In the seventeenth century it was to transform agricultural life in Yunnan and Sichuan (Szechuan) and become a life-saving crop for migrants forced out into the hills from the overpopulated Yangtze delta.

To Portugal, however, belongs the dubious credit for having introduced maize farming to Africa to provide ships' stores for the slave trade. Among history's many ironies is the fact that a cheap food designed to feed African slaves on their way to America should have resulted, in Africa itself, in a population increase substantial enough to ensure that the slavers would never sail empty of human cargo.

Maize was accepted quickly in Africa because, in comparison with other grains, it grew rapidly and its cultivation was undemanding (which is not, however, true of the modern, heavy-cropping varieties). A woman working alone could plant her seeds, leave them to grow and harvest the crop as and when she needed it; when one patch of soil became exhausted, she moved on to another. It was poor agriculture, but it sustained life and made few demands.

In time the health of the Old World peoples who adopted maize as their staple began to deteriorate. Africa today is still only too familiar with the 'disease of the mealies', otherwise known as pellagra, which results from eating too much maize and not enough foods containing the vitamin C and nicotinic acid that maize lacks. In much of the African interior, except in banana-growing regions, useful fruits and vegetables were in short supply until the American introductions (including manioc, the sweet potato, groundnuts and French beans) became widely established, while in Europe foods with a high nicotinic acid content were not, with the exception of cheese, easy for the poor to come by, especially when they were unaware of the need for them. As a result, maize soon lost much of its initial popularity in Europe (if not in Africa, where the options were fewer) and did not regain it until a wider-ranging diet became common.

BEANS, TOMATOES AND PEPPERS

In Central and South America pellagra was rare because the deficiencies in maize were amply remedied by other items in the diet – tomatoes, avocados, beans, capsicums and fish.

Beans, which provided useful protein when eaten in conjunction with maize, were usually boiled, though if they were young and small they may have been eaten raw. The *refrito* beans that are a speciality of Mexico today – boiled, mashed, fried and served with a topping of grated cheese – evolved only after the Spaniards introduced the cow and other domesticated animals to Central America. Before that, there seems to have been no reliable supply of fat or oil; what little fat there was came from dry-fleshed game animals or birds, and although oil was sometimes extracted from groundnuts, maize or sunflower seeds, there is some academic doubt as to whether technology was far enough advanced for this kind of extraction to be practised on any scale.

Tomatoes had made their first appearance as weeds in prehistoric times, but careful cultivation had enormously increased both yield and varieties by the time Cortés and his 400 Spaniards reached Mexico in 1519. Like maize, tomatoes were utilized at every stage of growth; thin shavings of the green and unripe fruit were incorporated in many dishes, while the ripe fruits were mixed with chillis to make a strong-tasting sauce to go with cooked beans.*

The tomato introduced into Europe in the sixteenth century may have been an orange-yellow variety, which would account for one of the early names, 'golden apple', although apples can seldom have been as heavily ribbed and misshapen as tomatoes were until the beginning of the twentieth century. Another name was 'love apple', which derived either from the fruit's reputation as an aphrodisiac or from the French *pomme d'amour*, itself a corruption either of *pomi di Mori* ('apple of the Moors'),† or of *pomodoro* ('golden apple'). The

---

* Mexico's 'sauce to go with the beans' was an exact reflection of the European's *companaticum* and the Indian's *kari*.

† In the sixteenth century northern Europe was very hazy about where all the new foods were actually coming from and, from long centuries of habit, tended to attribute them to the eastern end of the Mediterranean, and call them Turkish (see p. 210); occasionally, if a Spanish connection was suspected, they compromised on Moorish.

Spaniards, better informed, called it *tomate* (from the Aztec *tomatl*) and adopted it as readily into their diet as they did all other introductions from their American empire.

Italy also acquired a taste for it some time later, when two Jesuit priests brought a red variety back from America. 'Apples of Love', reported the Quaker merchant Peter Collinson in 1742, 'are very much used in Italy to putt when ripe into their Brooths & Soops giving it a pretty Tart Tast. A Lady Just come from Leghorn says she thinks it gives an Agreeable tartness & Relish to them & she likes it Much.'[10] Tomato sauce as an accompaniment to pasta put in an appearance a few decades later.

Not until the twentieth century did Britain acquire a taste for tomatoes – and, with it, a passion for tinned tomato soup – and America was almost equally slow, possibly influenced by the same arguments that discouraged the peoples of northern and western Europe.* Tomatoes were described as being an extremely 'cold' food (in terms of the four humours), a cause of gout and lacking in both nourishment and substance.

The Central American capsicum 'pepper', which like the tomato has a high vitamin C content, bore no family relationship to the *piper nigrum* of India, but the Spaniards were swift to apply the old name *pimienta* to the hot-tasting capsicums they found in Mexico – an excusable piece of wishful thinking, on the whole, since it was the search for pepper that had taken them to the New World in the first place.

The inevitable confusion over names and classifications of peppers has not diminished with the centuries but, loosely, chilli peppers – which come in various sizes and shapes, the small ones being most familiar – are used for seasoning; the gamut of flavour runs from inflammatory to blistering (and the seeds can in fact, burn). Some are dried to make chilli powder or the more refined cayenne paper, some pickled in vinegar for Tabasco sauce, and others can be used in sauces and chutneys, or as direct flavourings in meat dishes. The large, sweet, fleshy bell pepper is the one that is used, green, yellow or red according to ripeness, as a vegetable or in salads. Special varieties of it are dried to make the mild spice known as paprika, which has none of the searing pungency of the chilli.

---

* The United States (as distinct from the native Americas) were at first predominantly WASP, or white Anglo-Saxon Protestant, and took much of their culture and many of their attitudes from the Old World of their ancestors.

The people of tropical America used, and still use, capsicums with everything. In early post-Columbian times capsicums went into soups, stews, sauces and vegetable preparations, sometimes four or five different kinds in the same dish; they were dried and pickled, too, as a portable relish for travellers. In the early seventeenth century it was estimated that there were at least forty varieties of capsicum;[11] in Mexico today there are said to be ninety-two.

FOOD IN MEXICO

In Aztec times most Mexicans breakfasted long after they had begun the day, stopping only at about 10 a.m. for a bowl of maize porridge flavoured with honey or capsicums, which sustained them until the main meal taken in the early afternoon, when it was too hot to do anything else. This commonly consisted of tortillas, a dish of beans and a sauce made from tomatoes or peppers.

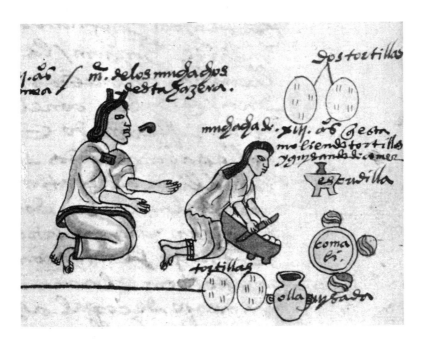

A Mexican girl learning to make tortillas. She grinds the boiled kernels on a saddle quern (*metate*), moistening the paste with water as she works. Then she will knead it and pat it into flat cakes to be cooked on the *comalli*, an earthenware platter resting on three hearth-stones.

When the conquistadors reached the Aztec capital, Tenochtitlan, and saw the market there, one of them, Bernal Diaz del Castillo, reported how astonished they were 'at the number of people and the quantity of merchandise that it contained, and at the good order and control that was maintained . . . Each kind of merchandise was kept by itself and had its fixed place marked out.' Some stallholders sold 'beans and sage and other vegetables and herbs', some 'rabbits, hare, deer, young ducks, little dogs [bred for the table] and other such creatures', some fruit, some salt, some honey and some 'cooked food, dough and tripe'.[12]

The 'cooked food' would consist of stews, spiced maize porridge and stuffed tortillas; the 'dough' would be tortilla paste. Tortillas were Mexico's daily bread. Kernels of dried maize, boiled in water with a little charcoal or lime to loosen the skins, were crushed to a paste with a stone roller. The paste was then kneaded and slapped into thin round cakes, and cooked on a special hotplate, the *comalli*, that rested over a small fire.

Tortillas could be rolled and stuffed, when they were known as tacos (or enchiladas), or the mixture could be made into tamales, in which the uncooked dough was plastered onto corn husks, spread with a mixture of beans, capsicums, green tomato shavings and shreds of meat or fish, folded like an envelope and then steamed. The result, after the husk was stripped off, was a portable individual pie, Mexico's answer to Scotland's Forfar bridie and China's spring roll.

When Bernal spoke of 'tripe' he probably meant 'tripes', or offal, since tripe (in the gastronomic as distinct from the political sense) refers to the stomach lining of ruminant animals, and the only Mexican ruminant in the early sixteenth century was the wild deer, which was probably not slaughtered in sufficient numbers to keep a tripe seller in business. There would, however, have been business enough and to spare for a vendor of giblets, because although game animals were scarce, there were great seasonal migrations of ducks, geese and other wildfowl, and birds were trapped in considerable numbers.

There were some foods that gave the conquistadors pause, especially those drawn from the lakes on which the capital was built. As well as conventional pond life such as frogs and freshwater shrimps, there were tadpoles, water flies, larvae, white worms and a curious froth from the surface of the water that could be compressed into a substance not unlike cheese. At the court of Montezuma, a variety of newt peculiar to Mexico (the *axolotl*) was something of a delicacy and so, too, were winged ants and the large tree lizard, the iguana, which even Columbus's sailors had thought 'white, soft and tasty'.[13] That other luxury, the agave worm or maguey slug, was often served with guacamole, the sauce that even in Aztec times was made with tomatoes, capsicums and avocados – rich in protein, fat and A, B, C and E vitamins.

Mexico's only domesticated livestock were the turkey and the dog, which was regarded as a useful but inferior meat. 'The turkey meat was put on top and the dog underneath, to make it seem more.'[14] After the Spanish conquest and the introduction of European cattle, the dog began to lose its usefulness as a food animal, but the turkey entered on a wider stage.

THE TURKEY

It is possible – just – to make sense of how the turkey got its name. The bird itself seems to have reached England soon after its first arrival in Europe (in about 1523–4) through the agency of the Levant or Turkey merchants, who usually touched in at Seville on their way to and from the eastern Mediterranean. Not familiar with its Mexican name, *uexolotl*, or understandably reluctant to pronounce it, the English solved the problem in the usual way and called it the 'turkie cock'.

Unfortunately, in about 1530 the Portuguese brought the guinea-fowl back to Europe from one of its homelands in West Africa, and the Levant merchants seem to have picked it up, too, and transported it onward to an England that had forgotten it since Roman times.

Confusion ensued. The guinea-fowl was not unlike a miniaturized version of the turkey in looks and in its reluctance to fly, and it seems to have been assumed that they belonged to the same family. But although some sources claim that in sixteenth-century England any reference to 'turkey' really meant guinea-fowl, this is not the case. When Archbishop Cranmer framed his sumptuary laws of 1541 he classed turkey-cocks with birds of the size of crane and swan, not – as he would have done with guinea-fowl – with capons and pheasants. At much the same time a certain Sir William Petre was keeping his table birds alive until wanted in a large cage in his Essex orchard, 'partridges, pheasants, guinea-hens, turkey hens and such like'.[15] And the heraldic arms granted in 1550 to William Strickland of Boynton-on-the-Wold – the crest 'a turkey-cock in his pride proper' – show a bird that is, without doubt, a turkey proper.[16]

None of the other nations of the Old World called the turkey a turkey except the Egyptians, who ought to have known better (*dik-rumi*, the 'fowl of Turkey'). No one else called it a guinea-fowl, either, except – regrettably – Linnaeus, the eighteenth-century Swedish botanist who undertook the superhuman task of giving a Latin title and classification to everything in nature. On the turkey he bestowed the generic name of *meleagris*, which had been Classical Rome's name for the guinea-fowl.

Elsewhere in Europe there was confusion of a different kind. In France the name most generally favoured was *coq d'Inde* ('cock of India'; not, it should be noted, 'of the Indies'), which was later corrupted to *dinde* or *dindon*. In Italy it was *galle d'India*; in Germany, *indianische Henn*. The sex of the names might vary, but the principle was the same, and it was, on the whole, reasonable enough that the bird should have been attributed to India – even (or perhaps especially) by the Turks, who called it *hindi*. The New World stubbornly remained 'the new Indies' long after the error had been discovered.

But it was a pity that the Germans, Dutch and Scandinavians should have chosen to embroider further on the Indian theme, producing the *calecutische Hahn*, the *Kalkoen* and the *Kalkon* that suggest an origin in Calicut, the place where da Gama first landed on the south-west coast of India. The Persians also had a contribution to make, calling the turkey the *filmurgh* or 'elephant bird' – without specifying whether it was an Indian or an African elephant they had in mind. No doubt they simply meant 'large'.

As if all this were not enough, in India itself the bird became known as *peru*, which was geographically a good deal closer to the mark than most, even if still a few hundred miles out. The bird, as it happened, was no more Peruvian than it was Turkish (or Indian). It seems to have reached India, as something new and exotic, in the second decade of the seventeenth century, probably by way of the Philippines, a Spanish possession ruled direct from Mexico.

At least one thing all these names do make clear: the turkey established itself quickly and firmly on most of the tables of the Old World.

CANNIBALISM

There was one among the wealth of new American foodstuffs that failed to recommend itself to the Spaniards, and indeed gave them an ineradicable dislike for the whole of Aztec civilization. Ceremonial cannibalism came to them as a profound culture shock.

Rumours of it had started with Columbus, who, misled by the 'gentle, peaceful and very simple' Tainos of his first encounter, had been totally unprepared for the Caribs, the red-painted, cannibal Vikings of those sunny waters. It did not take long for the legend of the Caribs to grow and be improved on, so that when the Spaniards

A barbecue in sixteenth-century Brazil.

captured four anonymous islanders and discovered that they 'had had their virile members cut off', they deduced that the Caribs castrated their captives 'as we do to fatten capons, to improve their taste'. The Caribs were believed to deal with the carcasses as coolly as any European butcher, 'guts and limbs eaten, and the rest salted and dried like our hams'.*17 A further gloss was that the Caribs were not only cannibals but connoisseurs, though their preferences depended largely on the fancy of the chronicler. According to one (a Frenchman), the Caribs thought the French were delicious, the English so-so, the Dutch tasteless and the Spaniards so tough as to be virtually inedible.

No more, in truth, than a primitive tribe with an age-old belief in

---

* In fact, the peoples of the Caribbean knew nothing about salting until they learned the technique from the Europeans.

the symbolic power of anthropophagy, the Caribs were unfortunate enough to have their name and reputation immortalized in several European languages by the Spanish transliteration of Carib into *Calib* into *Canib*, whence the word 'cannibal'.

When the conquest of Mexico began just over twenty years later, the Spaniards discovered a whole nation where 'the sacrilegious desecration of the human body' was an instrument of government. The human body was desecrated in Spain, too, of course, but although the Spaniards executed their own prisoners and criminals in the most barbarous fashion, they killed them in the name of Christianity and did not eat them afterwards.

It is difficult today, more than 2,000 years after Judaism's final commutation of human into animal, and then into spiritual, sacrifice, to understand a belief in the *literal* offering of the human heart to the gods, and it was no easier for the sixteenth-century Spaniard, especially when faced with extensive evidence of the ancillary belief that man could increase his own strength by consuming, equally literally, the strength of someone who had been a worthy adversary in battle.

All along the way to Tenochtitlan Cortés and his men counted the neat piles of skulls in every temple forecourt, until they became convinced that they themselves were also destined for the pot. 'How anxious these traitors are', said Cortés, who, interloper though he was, took an engagingly one-sided view of the enterprise in which he was involved, 'to see us among the ravines so that they can gorge themselves on our flesh . . . In return for our coming to treat them like brothers, and tell them the commands of our lord God and the king, they were planning to kill us and eat our flesh, and had already prepared the pots with salt and peppers and tomatoes.'[18]

The Aztec blood-sacrifice rationale was highly sophisticated and in its own way perfectly logical,[19] but the Spaniards, their eyes on the skull racks of Tenochtitlan, would have been incapable of understanding it even if it had been explained to them. All they knew was that the Aztec gods demanded the living heart of their sacrifices; local wars were fought for the sole purpose of taking prisoners, who were ripped open alive by the priests so that their hearts could be taken out still beating. Afterwards, the head was hung on a skull rack, one thigh was presented to the supreme council and other choice cuts to various nobles. The remainder of the body was returned to the victim's captor, who took it home and had it cooked into *tlacatlaolli* (maize-and-man stew), which was reverently consumed by all the family.

The true extent of cannibalism in the Aztec world is a subject on which anthropologists cannot agree. Some, interested mainly in religion, ignore the lethal consequences. Others, obsessed by (largely unreliable) figures, are convinced that famine and meat-hunger were of predominant importance. But even if the true figures run into thousands rather than the hundreds of thousands sometimes quoted, they were far from negligible either in their immediate or, since most of the sacrifices were of young, fertile males, their long-term effect.

It was the ritual acceptance as much as the blood that appalled the conquistadors, because Europe had nothing to learn from the Aztecs as far as death was concerned. When Cortés landed, it is estimated that Central Mexico had a population of 25 million. Thirty years later it had been reduced to a little over 6 million. By 1605, less than ninety years after the conquest, just over 1 million remained.[20] War, economic upheaval, forced religious conversion, exploitation, new diseases to which the peoples of Central America had no resistance – all these had combined to produce one of the most comprehensive human catastrophes in the history of the world. But there were many at the time who saw it, coldly, as God's justice.

THE INCA OF PERU

Cortés had gone north from the Caribbean to Mexico. Francisco Pizarro went south on an even more extraordinary voyage of discovery. In Peru he found the dream of all adventurers – a land where emeralds were to be had for the asking and temples were panelled in gold.

There was a richness of food, too, with an abundance of fish along the coastal strip and in the mountain waters of Lake Titicaca, while communal game hunts tracked deer, wild llama and guanaco, bear, puma, fox and the large rodent called *vizcacha*. Guinea pigs were raised in almost every household, and ducks seem also to have been domesticated. The royal Inca disapproved of eating dogs, but their subjects had no particular aversion to them.

Even so, most Peruvian food was vegetarian, with fish and meat an occasional luxury. Maize and potatoes, squash and beans, manioc and sweet potatoes, peanuts, tomatoes, avocados and chillis were the foundations of the diet. The beans, peanuts and avocados supplied protein. Vitamin A came from winter squashes, tomatoes and avocados; B from peanuts and avocados; and C from tomatoes, peppers and, in smaller quantity, from potatoes.

Peanuts were already familiar to the Spaniards, who had encountered them in Haiti and were soon to be instrumental in introducing them to the Malay archipelago. (From there, before 1600, they travelled on to China to become second only in importance to the soy bean.) But the potato was something entirely new – 'a dainty dish even for Spaniards', admitted one of the conquistadors.[21]

Digging and bagging potatoes in Peru.

Climatically, Peru and its neighbouring Andean regions were very different from Mexico and the islands. In lowland regions maize was the staple food, cooked without much refinement; Peruvians did not trouble with the boil-and-bake process needed for tortillas, but simply ground the dried kernels into flour and boiled it in water to make a porridge not unlike *polenta*.

Above 11,000 feet, where maize would not grow, the main crops were potatoes or one of the other tubers such as oca and quinoa, which were never to travel beyond their Andean homeland. With several thousand years' experience behind them, Peruvians knew how to make the most of the potato and had even discovered how to preserve it by a process of freezing and drying. The harvested crop was spread out on the ground and left overnight in the biting air; next day, as if at some chilly vintaging, everyone gathered to tread out the moisture. This process was repeated every day for four or five days, by which time the potatoes had given up most of their water content and were in a state to be dried and stored. Known as *chuñu*, preserved potatoes were of the greatest importance to the highland peoples.

The usefulness of the potato as a food for the masses did not escape the conquistadors. In the silver mines at Potosi the workers subsisted almost entirely on *chuñu*, and before long speculators were streaming over from Spain to buy up supplies from the producers in the mountains and resell them at an inflated price to the mineworkers.

EUROPE AND THE POTATO

Once the wealth of the Peruvian mines began to be shipped to Europe, Spain adopted potatoes as basic ships' stores; as a result they were being cultivated in Europe soon after the conquest. By 1573 they were common enough for the Hospital de la Sangre at Seville to order them in at the same time as other stocks,[22] and from Spain they took passage to Italy where, by 1601, people no longer even treated them as a delicacy, but cooked them 'with mutton in the same manner as they do turnips and the roots of carrots'.[23]

Fortunately (in the matter of name), the Turkey merchants failed to pick up the new vegetable at Seville. Instead, it reached England direct from the Americas when Sir Francis Drake, on the way to Virginia in 1586, put in at Cartagena in the Caribbean to revictual and brought some home with him. Even so, there was confusion. Because of the description in Gerard's *Herbal* it was thought for centuries that the potato had originated in Virginia, and it was not until the 1930s that the geneticist N. I. Vavilov showed this to have been impossible.[24] It seems, in fact, not to have been known in Virginia until English settlers took it there.

In the early days opinion in Europe was divided. Dr Tobias Venner claimed that the nourishment yielded by potatoes, 'though somewhat windy', was 'very substantial, good and restorative',[25] and William Salmon thought they stopped 'fluxes of the bowels', were full of nutrients and cured consumption. 'Being boiled, baked or roasted,' he went on, they 'are eaten with good butter, salt, juice of oranges or lemons and double refined sugar . . . They increase seed and provoke lust, causing fruitfulness in both sexes.'[26]

In Burgundy, on the other hand, potatoes were banned in 1619 because of a belief that 'too frequent use of them caused the leprosy', and this was an idea that persisted in France until well into the eighteenth century. In the mid-1700s they were still thought of as fodder for animals, not for men – except for peasants. As Diderot's *Encyclopédie* put it, 'However it is prepared, this root is tasteless and starchy. One would not include it among the agreeable foods, but it does provide plentiful and sufficiently healthful nourishment for men who do not require more than sustenance. The potato is correctly held responsible for flatulence; but what is flatulence to the vigorous digestions of peasants and workers?' Even Switzerland, an early convert, still blamed the potato for scrofula.

Except in the countries where it became popular soon after its introduction, and a few other places like Ireland where its cultivation precisely met contemporary needs, it took well over 200 years for the potato to become widely distributed, and even then people could sometimes be remarkably obdurate. In 1774 the hungry citizens of Kolberg refused to touch it when Frederick the Great of Prussia sent them a wagonload to relieve famine, and had to have their minds changed by the militia. In 1795 when Count Rumford was making a scientific experiment into feeding the poor as well as possible for as little as possible, he concluded that barley soup was the answer, thickened with potatoes and peas, seasoned with vinegar and served with pieces of stale bread to encourage the steady chewing that, he believed, seemed 'very powerfully to assist in promoting digestion'.[27] But the poor of Munich were strongly resistant to the potatoes in Count Rumford's soup and it was some time before they could even be persuaded to taste it. In Russia in 1840 the government ordered the peasantry to plant potatoes on common lands and found itself with a number of pitched battles on its hands and major riots in ten provinces.[28]

Although that energetic advocate Antoine-Auguste Parmentier – 'the Homer, Virgil and Cicero of the potato'[29] – is usually credited with bringing it into fashion in France, his real efforts were directed towards persuading bakers to substitute potato flour for wheat flour in bread. In truth, increased usage of the potato was attributable not to one man, but to several decades of experimenting by gentlemen agriculturalists, followed by a levelling up in post-Revolutionary society that caused the food of the poor to take on a democratic glamour.[30]

In 1806 Antoine Viard included several potato recipes in *Le Cuisinier*

Impérial, and in 1814, with Antoine Beauvilliers' *L'Art du cuisinier*, the potato achieved full acceptance. In hurried deference, perhaps, to the nation that had just defeated Napoleon, Beauvilliers included such traditional British delights as *Woiches rabettes*, *plomb-poutingue* and *machepotetesse*.[31]

SUGAR AND THE SLAVE TRADE

Sugar and the slave trade became interdependent very soon after the discovery of the New World, first in the Caribbean and then in Brazil.

By as early as 1506 Spain had begun cultivating sugar in the Greater Antilles, the string of islands dominated by Cuba and Hispaniola, but the decline in the native population after the conquest soon led to a labour shortage. Spain solved the problem in the usual way. In Europe slaves were common enough; rich Spanish families owned as many as fifty, some of them Greeks, Russians, Albanians or Turks bought at the famous slave market of Caffa on the Black Sea, but most of them blacks from Africa.[32] So it was Africa the New World pioneers went to when they needed more workers in Cuba.

It was not long, however, before Spain began to be more interested in gold and silver than sugar, and it fell to the Portuguese to discover what profit could be made from combining slaving in Africa with sugar production in Brazil. They had papal authority for it. Nicholas V had not only given them leave, but actually ordered them to 'attack, subject and reduce to perpetual slavery the Saracens, pagans and other enemies of Christ southward from Capes Badajor and Non, including all the coast of Guinea.'[33] Better still, the monarchs and merchants of the Gold Coast were only too anxious to exchange people they didn't want for the cloth, firearms, hardware and spirits that they did.

Occasionally, there was a murmur of protest. In 1526 Mbemba Nzinga of Congo, an ardent Christian convert, complained to his brother monarch in Portugal that merchants were 'taking every day our natives, sons of the land and sons of our noblemen and vassals and our relatives' – kidnapping them, in effect – so as to exchange them for European goods. So busy were they that 'our country is being completely depopulated, and Your Highness should not agree with this nor accept it as in your service.'[34] But the voice of the Congolese ruler was too faint to compete with the demands of the Brazilian sugar producers. More and more slaves were required, to work for 'half a year together night and day like horses'.[35] In 1550 there were five sugar plantations in Brazil. By 1623 there were 350.[36]

It was at this stage that the Dutch began to take a hand in the game, invading and occupying the whole northern part of Brazil and then wresting the Gold Coast from Portugal's grasp. Although they held Brazil for only nineteen years, they learned a good deal about sugar production and their knowledge soon filtered through to the English, French and Danes, who had independently acquired several of the Caribbean islands.

The demand for slaves rocketed. It is estimated that during the course of the sixteenth century fewer than a million blacks were landed in the Americas; in the eighteenth century it was seven times that figure.[37] By then, of course, labour-intensive cultivation had proved its worth and spread to the North American mainland, where tobacco and cotton raising followed roughly the same pattern as sugar.

Countries and colonies dependent on the cultivation of a single crop could not feed themselves. Brazil and the West Indies were perhaps the first societies in world history to be dependent on imports for *all* food beyond the barest necessities. In 1783 Britain sent 16,576 tons of salt pork and beef, 5,188 flitches of bacon, and 2,559 tons of tripe to the West Indies, notably Jamaica. In Brazil the slaves lived on tons of cod from Newfoundland and tons of dried meat brought in from the south.[38]

Competition over sugar brought an end to the first phase of imperialism, which had begun with competition over spices. At the beginning sugar had been of little importance, a minor luxury, but there came a radical change when supplies of Europe's traditional sweetener, honey, began to fall off – partly as a result of the Reformation and the campaign against the monasteries, whose need for beeswax candles had placed them among the foremost honey producers. When sugar became readily available, it also became popular – and even more popular when it was discovered (about 1600) that fruit could be preserved in it and (some time before 1730) jam made with it.

By the 1670s sugar was a trading commodity of such importance that the Dutch yielded New York to England in exchange for the sugar lands of Surinam, while in 1763 France abandoned the whole of Canada to the British for the sake of Guadeloupe. But not even the most optimistic eighteenth-century sugar merchant could ever have foreseen that by the 1980s the British would be consuming 80 pounds of it per head per year, or the North Americans 126 pounds.[39]

THE SETTLING OF NORTH AMERICA

The potato, the tomato, maize, avocados, pineapples, haricot, kidney and butter beans, lima beans, scarlet runners, 'French' beans, chocolate, peanuts, vanilla, red peppers and green peppers, tapioca and the turkey, not to mention gold and silver, tobacco, rubber, chewing gum and quinine – what the Americas contributed to Europe added up to a formidable list.* Most of it came from the south, however; from the north, there was nothing new, only fish, furs and timber. All were valuable.

The early explorers of North America were still hoping to find some great waterway cutting right across the continent to the Pacific and thence to the Spice Islands. The Spaniards ventured, with disastrous results, into Florida. The French sent Jacques Cartier to take a look at Canada. But it was the English who made the most immediate profit from their forays after they dispatched the Cabots (in 1496) to 'seek out, discover and find whatsoever isles, countries, regions or provinces of the heathen and infidels wheresoever they be, which before this time have been unknown to all Christians'.[40] The Cabots discovered no heathen provinces within the meaning of the Act, but reported the existence of great cod-fishing banks off the coast of Newfoundland. From then on, fishing fleets from England, France, Portugal and Holland haunted the shores of Newfoundland, using the island as a base where they could dry their catch for transport back to Europe. The abundance of cod within easy range of what was to become New England later gave the infant colony a useful start in life.

In 1607, after two catastrophic earlier attempts, England managed to land some colonists in Virginia who proved capable of surviving – though only just. 'They chased out a few Indians', gossiped the Antwerp agent in London, 'and put up a three-sided fort, and planted . . . adjoining land with [grain], on which they could live a long time.'[41] It was a picture that did not stand up to closer inspection. Two years later an arriving settler found many of his predecessors 'dispersed in the savages' towns, living upon their alms for an ounce

* The Americas also benefited. Columbus took vegetable seeds, wheat, chick-peas and sugarcane to the Caribbean on his later voyages; Colombia's second governor introduced the first cows that had ever been seen there; settlers took bananas, rice and citrus fruits; yams and cowpeas crossed the Atlantic with the slaves. Coconuts were introduced to the Bahamas, breadfruit to the Caribbean, and coffee to Brazil.

An Amerindian town in what was later to be known as Virginia. At the top, a tobacco field; on the right, fields of maize sown serially, so as to supply a choice of green, semi-mature and mature ears.

of copper a day, and fourscore lived twenty miles from the fort, and fed upon nothing but oysters eight weeks space, having no other allowance at all, neither were the people of the country able to relieve them if they would.'[42]

The Jamestown settlers, according to all accounts, were argumentative, incompetent and ignorant, workshy, ill-equipped with tools and materials and over-conscious of their dignity. The land was rich in game, the waters alive with fish, the woods full of edible berries, but if it had not been for the generosity of the Indians they would have starved.

Fortunately, the Pilgrim Fathers who landed on Plymouth Rock in 1620 were made of sterner (if no less argumentative) stuff. They had brought wheat and rye seeds with them, but these proved difficult to grow on rough land, whereas maize was easy. From the Indians they learned not only how to cultivate it – being from northern Europe, none of them had seen it before – but also how to cook it in a variety of ways, as porridge, flatbread and a kind of frumenty. They were pleased, too, to recognize the turkey. True to tradition, there was some confusion over the bird's name, but this time it was unaccountably slight; the settlers' 'turkey' was the Indians' *furkee*.

Also from the Indians they discovered how to have a seacoast clambake by digging a pit, lining it with flat stones and lighting a fire on them. When the stones were white-hot, the embers were brushed away and replaced with a layer of seaweed, on which went alternate layers of clams and ears of maize, interleaved with more seaweed. When the pit was full, it was covered with a blanket of wet cloth or hide, which was kept moist throughout the hour or so of cooking time. This characteristically Polynesian technique may have reached America from the Pacific. The Maoris call it *umu* (earth oven) or *hangi*; in Honolulu it is *luau*.

From Caribbean sources, directly or indirectly, the colonists also discovered how to barbecue. The northern part of Hispaniola, one of the Spanish islands, had never been properly settled, the early pioneers having done little more than ship in some cattle and pigs. These, left to their own devices, had flourished, so that when ship-wrecked sailors, runaway servants and other kinds of vagabond began to take refuge on the island, the food supply presented no problems. From surviving Caribs they learned the old island trick of smoke-drying meat on greenwood lattices erected over a fire of animal bones and hides. The Caribs called the technique *boucan*, which passed into French as *boucanier* and gave the outcasts their name of buccaneers.

In Spanish the greenwood lattice was called *barbacoa*, which ultimately became 'barbecue'.

The once-familiar pattern of east-coast American eating – the food whose mention still brings a sentimental tear to the all-American eye – was laid down in the early days. Hominy (ripe maize, whole or reduced to grits), succotash (fresh or dried kernels cooked with beans), and cornpone (a thick, unleavened maize pancake) were the colonists' basic grain dishes. Shad, terrapin and oysters were not too hard to find, and there were canvasback duck and wild geese when they could catch them. Deer were so plentiful that they yearned for a plain joint of mutton, although it was the pig rather than the sheep that settled down most happily when domesticated livestock were imported from Europe, irrepressibly surviving the attentions of wolves, bears and the American Indians, who discovered an unhallowed passion for pork.

In Virginia especially, pigs found both climate and food so congenial that larders began to burst at the seams with pork and hams. Indeed, said William Byrd II in the 1720s, the people themselves became 'extremely hoggish in their temper . . . and prone to grunt rather than speak'.[43]

16

FOOD FOR THE TRAVELLER

From the early sixteenth century onwards shoals of tiny ships began to infest the oceans of the world. The mariners of Western Europe, who had formerly hugged familiar coastlines and put ashore for supplies almost anywhere they chose, now pointed their bows out to sea and hoped for the best.

When they sighted land, often after many weeks afloat, they were more immediately concerned with food and water than gold or spices. The ships' logs that survive from the era of maritime exploration often carry a running catalogue of what was to be found in various places. At the Cape Verde Islands there were 'no fruits nor good fresh water', although 'very small' goats were to be had. Off the Pacific coast of South America things were better; 'plenty of excellent fat goats, good fish'. And among the thousand islands off Java there was reputedly one with 'abundance of beeves [beef cattle]'.[1]

The preoccupation with food was not surprising. It took the new navigators a long time to discover the patterns of the oceans on which they now embarked, the tangled cross currents, errant gales, unexplained calms. Even the passage from Europe to America – which settled down to a maximum of about ten weeks once the action of wind and waves was fully charted – could last as long as eight months in the early days. When that happened, as on Columbus's fourth voyage, a ship's supplies could run dangerously low. 'And what with the heat and the dampness,' wrote Columbus's son Ferdinand, 'even the biscuit [dried bread] was so full of worms that, God help me, I saw many wait until nightfall to eat the porridge made of it so as not to see the worms.'[2] The fat black heads of the biscuit weevils, the need to eat shark or rats bought at an exorbitant price from the ship's ratcatcher – these were new hazards discovered at the same time as new lands.

CONVENIENCE FOODS

Travellers had known since prehistoric times how to provision themselves when they were away from home.* Some of the dried foods that helped to sustain settled communities in winter could be equally useful on long journeys, since they were light in weight and needed no special care in handling. The Chinese, more than 2,000 years ago, counted dried snake among the best convenience foods, while Indians took with them on their travels dried rice and the delicacy now known as 'Bombay duck' (dried bummelo fish). In countries where bread was the staple, methods were developed for preserving that too. It even seems that the unique Tibetan concoction of tea leaves and yak butter may have originated as a convenience food for mountain journeys. The mixing is still done in a section of bamboo, which is then stoppered and slung over the traveller's shoulder to be dipped into as necessary.

Special difficulties confronted the long-distance sea voyager, not least that of storage. With a capacity of only about 600 tons, the full-rigged ship of the sixteenth century could easily find itself over-burdened by cargo, guns, enough men to handle the increasingly complex system of sails and enough food and water to sustain them for an unspecified period. It was the food and water that were often cut back by owners in expectation of an easy landfall. But sailors, unlike land travellers, could not scatter and fend for themselves when supplies ran short. They might feed, in extremity, on the fish and seabirds they hated, but drinking sea water was the way to madness and death.

What the sailor ate was dictated by two considerations imposed by the construction of the ships themselves. Wooden ships floated because they were built from a substance that absorbed water, and this made it virtually impossible to keep food dry. Salt, or 'barrel' beef and pork came to no harm, but the dried peas and ship's biscuit that went with them were soon alive with weevils. The second consideration was the danger of fire, especially in latitudes where the sun dried out the fabric above the waterline. The only fire permitted on board was in the galley (and even that had to be put out every time the ship was hit by a storm or squall), so the sailor was almost entirely dependent for his food on the ship's cook.

Ship's biscuit (or hardtack, or pilot bread) was made from a flour-and-water dough baked and dried to a state of such immortal hardness that it was reckoned to remain edible, if not palatable, for as long as

* A fact often forgotten by those today who deplore potato crisps and pork pies not for their quality (which would be understandable) but for their contribution to 'the breakdown of family life'.

fifty years. It was also so hard that it would have been impossible to break had it not been for the weevils, which created a pattern of inner perforations.

Sailors did what they could with their 'bread', soaking it with a little of the water ration into a porridge-like mess, which they improved with pieces of salt pork or a dash of vinegar and dignified with names like skillygolee, lobscouse and Scotch coffee.[3] With the meat they could do little. It seems always to have been unpleasantly salty because there was little fresh water to spare for soaking, and sometimes so gristly that the sailors carved snuffboxes and trinkets out of it in preference to eating it. The beer soon soured; the butter was usually rancid before the ship even put to sea; and the cheese was said to be tough as old leather.

The shipowners and, later, naval officials responsible for provisioning were as unimaginative as they were parsimonious, their guiding principle to ensure a supply of solid, cheap, bulky food that would remain consumable even under adverse conditions. Not for the common sailor were the spices and seasonings that gave variety to the food of his betters, although a few relishes sometimes found their way on board in the guise of 'surgeon's necessaries' for the sick bay. Nor was there any attempt to cater for the sugar hunger that resulted from a diet dominated by salt and starch. Dried fruits would have helped, but the victuallers considered them luxuries. They were at one, perhaps, with that dogmatic wanderer William Lithgow, who felt nothing but contempt for men who could 'hardly digest bread, pastries, broth and (*verbi gratia*) bag-puddings' unless they had currants or raisins in them.[4]

THE SEAMAN'S DISEASE

The deficiencies in the sailor's diet were not only gastronomic. Indeed, most ships setting out from Western Europe on a voyage of any length soon counted a number of sick and dying among their crews.

Voyages often began in early spring, when most people were in a rundown state of health after months without fresh vegetables or fruit. Going to sea at such a time effectively extended the winter diet of preserved foods, and the result was scurvy, the vitamin C deficiency disease. On da Gama's first voyage to India more than half his crew died of it.

Even in its early stages scurvy was both debilitating and demoralizing. It was recognizable, wrote the sixteenth-century English sailor Sir Richard Hawkins, 'by the swelling of the gums, by denting of the flesh of the legs with a man's fingers, the pit remaining without filling up in a good space; others show it by their laziness'.[5] Wounds refused to heal. Swollen gums made a prolonged agony of chewing tough meat and biscuit, so that sufferers ate less and less and were soon weak from starvation.

The Chinese, as far back as the fifth century, had been accustomed to carry pots of growing ginger on board their vessels, and by the fourteenth century, by purely empirical means, had arrived at a general understanding of the role some kinds of food could play in preventing or curing diseases like beri-beri. The Dutch, in contact with Chinese-influenced south-east Asia, probably learned there that greenstuffs and citrus fruits could be important in a sea diet and passed the message on to Europe. Certainly, when the English East India Company dispatched its first ships to the Indies in 1601, the little fleet hove to off the southern tip of Madagascar and gathered 'oranges and lemons of which we made good store of water [juice], which is the best remedy against scurvy'.[6]

But the official mind could see no way of growing a sufficiency of green herbs on board heavily manned ships, and citrus fruits were much too expensive for economy-conscious owners. Many of them argued that scurvy was caused not by too little fresh food, but too much salt food – and that was something about which nothing could be done. For almost 200 years the only known remedies for scurvy were neglected while a search went on for others that would be cheaper and more convenient. Malt, cider, pickles and sauerkraut all had their advocates but since the physicians knew what worked without knowing why it worked, they came up with no satisfactory answer.

Finally, at the end of the eighteenth century it was accepted, by the British Navy at least, that the juice of citrus fruits was the only medicine that could conquer a disease that was killing more seamen than enemy action. The Admiralty decreed that a fixed amount of lemon juice should be issued daily to all sailors after their fifth or sixth week afloat, and stood by this decision to the tune of 1.6 million gallons of it in the period between 1795 and 1815. The mortality rate showed a gratifyingly steep decline.

The lemon juice was usually mixed with the rum ration, whose issue was the highlight of the sailor's day. After the capture of Jamaica in 1655, rum, which remained sweet longer, had begun to replace the Navy's beer in West Indian waters, but a neat half-pint a day proved too much for many of the men, especially when they were aloft in the rigging. In 1740, therefore, a certain Admiral Vernon – nicknamed 'old

Grog', from the old cloak of grogram cloth he wore in rough weather – formally introduced a diluted version. Subsequently, the grog issue became general in the Navy, and the lemon juice was added to it in 1795.*

In the mid-nineteenth century lime juice from the West Indies was substituted for lemon from the Mediterranean, an innovation viewed by many sailors with a jaundiced eye, especially when American seamen began to call them 'limeys'. And in fact lime juice – which has considerably less vitamin C than lemon or orange – proved to be less effective against scurvy.

THE LAND TRAVELLER

Most land travellers, except in the great deserts or the frozen north, expected to live off the terrain, but took a store of provisions with them by way of insurance.

Such provisions had to be light and compact when the traveller moved on his own feet and was his own beast of burden, and from native Americans, north and south, the European explorer learned the virtues of two sustaining and lightweight meat products, pemmican and *charqui*.

Pemmican was ideally suited to the chilly north. It was made by drying thinly sliced lean meat, usually from one of the larger game animals, over a fire or in the sun and wind. The dried meat was pounded to shreds and mixed thoroughly with an almost equal quantity of melted fat, some marrow from the bones and a few handfuls of wild cherries, and then packed in rawhide sacks that were tightly sewn up and sealed with tallow. Pemmican's name came from the Cree Indian word for fat, and its high fat content made it a valuable source of warmth and energy.

It was pemmican that sustained the fur trader Alexander Mackenzie during his pioneering journey of 1793, when he became the first European to cross North America from coast to coast. Half a century later Arctic explorers were to be furnished with a refined version in cans, scientifically prepared by Mackenzie's fellow Scot and successor in

---

* The British Navy's last rum ration was piped on 31 July 1970, the Sea Lords having come to the conclusion that for men entrusted with the sophisticated and extremely expensive equipment of modern times, the equivalent of four free double gins a day (Admiralty, or 'Pusser's', rum was 95.5 proof) was altogether too much.[7]

Canadian exploration, Sir John Richardson. Richardson found that if the meat were slowly dried over an oak fire it improved pemmican's keeping qualities, and that first-grade currants or sugar made an acceptable substitute for wild cherries.[8]

Charqui was the South American alternative and may have originated in Peru as a way of preserving some of the game slaughtered at communal hunts, although when cattle became established beef was more generally used. The method was to cut boned and defatted meat into quarter-inch slices, which were dipped in a strong brine or rubbed with salt. The meat was next rolled up in the animal's hide for ten or twelve hours for it to absorb the salt and release some of its juices, then hung in the sun to dry, and finally tied up into convenient bundles. It looked, said one German traveller, like strips of thick cardboard and was 'just as easy to masticate'.[9] When opportunity offered, most travellers preferred to pound the *charqui* vigorously between two stones and then boil it before eating. The 'jerked' in 'jerked beef' is derived from the word *charqui*.

As well as mass-production items like pemmican, *charqui*, salt beef, and pork, many travellers by land (and some by sea) also took with them a few luxuries prepared in their own kitchen. A container or two of potted meat, heavily sealed with fat, helped to postpone the moment of complete reliance on salted and dried foods. 'Pocket soup' was valuable, too, the ancestor of the modern bouillon cube – a highly concentrated stock made from meat trimmings and pigs' trotters, which set to the consistency of solid glue and kept for years. For a bowl of soup, all that was needed was to break a piece off and dissolve it in hot water. And many Americans travelled with supplies of the dried cornmeal pancake known as jonnycake, whose name came either from 'journey cake' or the Amerindian *shawnee-cake*.

Until the early nineteenth century all the known preservation techniques had been in use for at least 2,000 years. The way in which different peoples in different parts of the world – peoples often isolated from contact with others – varied the basic techniques to suit their own needs and materials makes a fascinating study.

Originally, most of the early convenience foods were designed for the specific purpose of storing present surplus against future need. What was convenient about them was that they were there at all. When canning was introduced in the nineteenth century, however, the idea of convenience foods began to take on an entirely new meaning and importance.

17

A GASTRONOMIC GRAND TOUR : 1

In the eighteenth century, even while explorers were still opening up new lands, gentlemanly travellers in Europe began to venture in increasing numbers on the Grand Tour, a pilgrimage to the shrines of established culture. By whichever route they went, they almost invariably ended up in Rome, where they admired the architecture and antiquities of the Classical world and complained about the food. 'Raw ham, Bologna sausages, figs and melons' were not enough. 'No boiled leg of pork and pease pudding', lamented one traveller. 'No bubble-and-squeak.'[1]

Despite all the exchanges of peoples and foods over the preceding 300 years, nothing even remotely resembling an international cuisine had emerged; rather the opposite, because the pursuit of empire had nourished a growing awareness of national identities within Europe as much as abroad. Formerly, the pattern of eating had been divided horizontally, with the food of the rich, like the food of the poor, having much in common all the way across the continent. But a vertical division had now also emerged, with the cuisines of different countries taking on their own individuality, so that it was possible, as it had rarely been before, to identify characteristic national styles.

The feeling of separateness was intensified by the reports of the occasional travellers-for-pleasure who had begun to haunt the highways of the world in the seventeenth century. Even a hundred years before, sailors, merchants and explorers had viewed foreign food with the eye of the hungry realist, but when the new breed of travellers appeared – book-writers all, and wise in the ways of their world – they consistently made the point that no country but their own had such superb raw materials, such delicacy in handling them or such refinement in consuming them. Their descriptions of foreign food were often very funny, almost invariably defamatory, and widely influential.

It would, however, have been not only possible but practicable in the late eighteenth century for an open-minded traveller, his pockets stocked with money and his mind with questions, to go on a far more stimulating Grand Tour than the orthodox one, a tour in which Italy would have come not as an end, but a beginning.

THE FOOD OF ITALY

It was the Italians who had emerged first from the medieval morass of sauces and spices. The riches of the spice trade and the Renaissance rediscovery of the Classical world had given back to them much of the power and influence of Roman times; the loss of the spice trade was to transform their cooking and, subsequently, that of the rest of Europe.

When spices for the first time in a thousand years became as expensive in Italy as they had always been elsewhere, its cooks adapted to the new situation with admirable promptitude. By 1570, less than three-quarters of a century after Portugal had captured the spice trade and a quarter of a century before the English and Dutch entered the fray, Italy had evolved a *nuova cucina* remarkable for its lightly-spiced simplicity. It could still be extravagant, as in the following banquet given by Pope Pius V, but the extravagance took a very different form from that of medieval times.[2]

FIRST COURSE
Cold delicacies from the sideboard

Pieces of marzipan and marzipan balls
Neapolitan spice cakes
Malaga wine and Pisan biscuits
Plain pastries made with milk and eggs
Fresh grapes
Spanish olives
Prosciutto cooked in wine, sliced, and served with capers, grape pulp and sugar
Salted pork tongues cooked in wine, sliced
Spit-roasted songbirds, cold, with their tongues sliced over them
Sweet mustard

SECOND COURSE

Hot foods from the kitchen: roasts

Fried veal sweetbreads and liver, with a sauce of
aubergines, salt, sugar and pepper
Spit-roasted skylarks with lemon sauce
Spit-roasted quails with sliced aubergines
Stuffed spit-roasted pigeons with sugar and capers sprinkled
over them
Spit-roasted rabbits with sauce and crushed pine nuts
Partridges, larded and spit-roasted, served with lemon slices
Pastries filled with minced veal sweetbreads and served with
slices of prosciutto
Strongly-seasoned poultry with lemon slices and sugar
Slices of veal, spit-roasted, with a sauce made from the juices
Leg of goat, spit-roasted, with a sauce made from the juices
Soup of almond cream, with the flesh of three pigeons for
every two guests
Squares of meat aspic

THIRD COURSE

Hot food from the kitchen: boiled meats and stews

Stuffed fat geese, boiled Lombard style and covered with
sliced almonds, served with cheese, sugar and cinnamon
Stuffed breast of veal, boiled, garnished with flowers
Milk calf, boiled, garnished with parsley
Almonds in garlic sauce
Turkish-style rice with milk, sprinkled with sugar and cinnamon
Stewed pigeons with mortadella sausage and whole onions
Cabbage soup with sausages
Poultry pie, two chickens to each pie
Fricasséed breast of goat dressed with fried onions
Pies filled with custard cream
Boiled calves' feet with cheese and egg

FOURTH COURSE

Delicacies from the sideboard

Bean tarts

Quince pastries, one quince per pastry

Pear tarts, the pears wrapped in marzipan

Parmesan cheese and Riviera cheese

Fresh almonds on vine leaves

Chestnuts roasted over the coals and served with salt, sugar and
pepper

Milk curds with sugar sprinkled over

Ring-shaped cakes

Wafers

This was a menu of some finesse, the Near Eastern influences still recognizable but subsidiary, and most materials – the sausages and songbirds of traditional cooking, fruits and a variety of cheeses – appearing in their natural guise. The whole atmosphere of the menu was very much simpler than it would once have been, with the diversity necessary on great occasions being supplied by basic ingredients rather than spices.

Ex-Queen Christina of Sweden dining with the Pope, half-hidden behind serried ranks of sculptures made of spun sugar, an Italian speciality.

PASTA

Revolutionary though the new Italian manner of cooking might be, what most travellers took note of was the macaroni.

Discussions about the history and origins of pasta are sometimes acrimonious. Who thought of it first? The Italians – or the Chinese?* The popular story that Marco Polo found it in China and brought the idea home with him stems from a simple (possibly even wilful) mis-reading of his text some hundreds of years later. When Marco said he had 'discovered' pasta in China, it was taken to imply that he had discovered something new; in fact, he had discovered that the Chinese had pasta 'which are like ours'.

It is claimed that macaroni in Italy goes back to Etruscan times, which would pre-date the Chinese noodle by about 500 years. But the evidence is not entirely convincing. Perhaps the knitting-needle-shaped objects found in Etruscan tombs were indeed meant to have dough rolled round them to make macaroni; or perhaps not. But the Apician cookery book certainly included recipes using lasagne, and by the twelfth century pasta was important enough to have attracted the attention of the quality-control legislators.

There is nothing surprising in the fact that Italy and China should both have been familiar with pasta. What is surprising is that there should not have been something of the sort in almost every country in the world, especially those where flatbread was common. Lasagne, the parent of most pasta shapes, is after all not much more than flatbread that has been boiled rather than baked, and flat tagliatelle and noodles would be an obvious enough progression from it.

There may, however, have been some exchange of ideas in the matter of variations on the basic model, especially the rounded kinds. Indians and Arabs had been eating thin pasta from AD 1200 at least, and probably earlier. The Indians called theirs *sevika*, meaning 'thread', and the Arabs *rishta*, which also meant 'thread' (in Persian).†³ The

---

* In 1972 the Italians very nearly won on points by exhibiting a spaghetti-making machine at a trade fair in Beijing (Peking); flour, water and tomato sauce were fed in at one end, and hot spaghetti, nicely cooked and with cheese and sauce on top, came out at the other. The *New York Times*, which recorded this provocative gesture, failed to record the Chinese reaction.

† The Arabs' method of cooking *rishta* would probably not have suited the Italians, since they simmered it in relatively little water and left it to settle for an hour before serving.

Italians, taking the larger view, opted for *spaghetti*, derived from *spago*, or 'string'.

The small, stuffed Italian shapes such as ravioli and tortellini (both attested from the middle of the thirteenth century) also had parallels elsewhere, including China (*won ton*), Russia (*pel'meni*), Tibet (*momo*), and in the Jewish kitchen, *kreplachs*. It has been suggested that

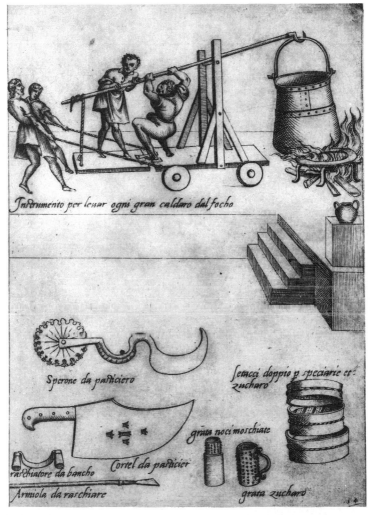

The Renaissance cauldron was no lightweight. Below, a variety of kitchen tools, including cheese and sugar graters, and a ravioli cutter.

some of the forms may have originated in the Near East and been
transmitted in an arc from there, which would certainly be consistent
with the general historical pattern.[4]

Despite the many varieties, the most common name for pasta in
later medieval Italy seems to have been 'macaroni', although this now
means the round as contrasted with the flat kind. The fourteenth-
century English *Forme of Cury* gives a recipe for 'macrows' (an anglicized plural) that unquestionably produces a flat result; the recipe
even recommends serving it strewn with morsels of butter, and with
grated cheese on the side.[5] In its native land it does not seem to have
been regarded as a very high-class food; in the sixteenth century
Teofilo Folengo said that the artificial language known as Macaronic
Latin – a mixture of Latin and Italian – was so called because it

A seventeenth-century spaghetti merchant.

reminded students of Venetian macaroni, 'a kind of coarse, rough, rustic pudding made of flour, cheese and butter'.[6]

By the eighteenth century and the days of the Grand Tour macaroni was firmly established in European mythology. Middle-class tourists of mature years might scorn it as they scorned most other foreign food, but the adolescent aristocrats who were dispatched, complete with tutor and chaplain, to complete their education in the heartland of Classical civilization, were not so insular. So weary did their less-travelled contemporaries become of the young men's sketches of ruins, antique busts, 'Italian' manners and poems in praise of pasta that they nicknamed the whole breed 'Macaronis'.

FRENCH COOKING COMES OF AGE

When Catherine de Medici arrived from Florence in 1533 to marry the heir to the French throne, she had with her – as was the aristocratic custom of the time – a number of her own chefs and pastrycooks. At the end of the century Marie de Medici imported more Italian cooks when she became bride to Henri IV. It was formerly thought that, between them, the two queens had been responsible for introducing the new Italian style of cooking to France, and that from then on the French had never looked back. But, as so often with the kind of history that is built on anecdote, this was an optimistic version of reality.

Certainly, in 1577 the Venetian ambassador found no Italian refinement in Paris. The people were quite immoderate, he reported, eating four or five times a day, as and when they felt inclined, and consuming very little bread or fruit but a great deal of meat. 'They load the table with it at their banquets . . . [they] ruin their stomachs and bowels by eating too much, as the Germans and Poles do by drinking too much.'[7]

The decisive change in French cooking did not become apparent until the middle of the seventeenth century, although the new cuisine codified by Pierre François de la Varenne in *Le cuisinier françois* (1651) had been evolving for some time before that. Even so, it had not entirely captured the courtly kitchen, which maintained the medieval tradition of lavish display, even if in a more refined form, for another eighty years. There were, however, two cooking developments of particular note at this time. One was the introduction of soup in the modern sense, with the soup itself becoming more important than the 'sops' it contained, and the other the appearance of the flour-and-butter *roux* as a thickening agent in place of the creamed almonds, breadcrumbs and crushed pastry of the past. The *roux* was such a convenient, all-purpose solution to so many culinary problems that it gained general popularity very quickly at all levels of society.

La Varenne, squire of the kitchen to the Marquis d'Uxelles, seems to have been unable to abandon the court tradition completely, but the atmosphere of *Le cuisinier françois* suggests that his heart was not in it. The old recipes were there, but the new ones, harbingers of what is now thought of as the classic French cuisine, were sharply contrasted. La Varenne began his book with a recipe for stock – in which most cookery writers have followed him ever since – gave sixty recipes for the formerly humble egg (some of them still used today), treated vegetables as food in their own right, made much use of the globe artichoke and very little of spices, and recommended simple sauces based on meat juices and sharpened with vinegar, lemon juice or verjuice (the juice of sour grapes, or sometimes of sorrel, green wheat or crab apples). He gave recipes for stuffed mushrooms – his employer's name is immortalized in mushroom *duxelles* – and even had a kind word to say for the truffle.

THE TRUFFLE

Truffles had been known in Babylon as well as in Rome, although the Romans were none too sure what they really were. Pliny the Elder had his own view. 'We know for a fact that when Lartius Licinius, an official of praetorian rank, was serving as minister of justice at Cartagena in Spain a few years ago, he happened when biting a truffle to come on a denarius contained inside it which bent his front teeth. This will clearly show that truffles are lumps of earthy substance balled together.'[8]

Although the people of medieval Baghdad feasted on truffles from the Arabian desert,* in France truffles remained sunk in obscurity until the fourteenth century, when they were pickled in vinegar, soaked in hot water and served with butter. That they were eaten at all was probably due to their reputation as an aphrodisiac (a label that was attached to most new or rare foods until the early modern period). There is a sad little legend that when, in 1368, the Duke of

---

* Desert truffles are not a fiction. The Kalahari, in Botswana, contains some of the richest truffle mines known today.

Clarence married an Italian wife whose dowry included the truffle hills of Alba, he so gorged himself on 'white diamonds' at the wedding banquet that he did not live to put their powers to the test.

La Varenne suggested cooking truffles like mushrooms, but although Louis XIV was one famous enthusiast and Napoleon another, it was not until well into the nineteenth century that the French really became converts. Then truffles became so fashionable that the demand trebled, and so did the price.

LA CUISINE BOURGEOISE

There were many changes in French food in the hundred-plus years between the time of La Varenne and the outbreak of the French Revolution. With the changes in society ushered in by the death of Louis XIV and the birth of the Age of Reason, everything suddenly became flexible. Even mealtimes changed; where formerly there had been two meals a day, now there was a third, breakfast, with a character of its own. The banquet as a form of entertaining gave way to the intimate supper of the *salons*. The Church contributed by abandoning most of its fasts. And the existence of the bourgeoisie was acknowledged at last.

Although the French had been slow to produce cookery books for ordinary households, a new note was heard in 1739 when François Marin, in *Les dons de Comus*, announced that the bourgeoisie could eat like princes if they had proper pots and pans, went to market every day and knew how to make a good bouillon. But the real breakthrough came in 1746 with the appearance of Menon's extraordinarily popular, 400-page *La cuisinière bourgeoise*. In an earlier book Menon had scorned 'third-class persons' but by 1746 had mellowed sufficiently to admit not only third-class persons to his confidence but third-class cuts of meat to his books.

In the second half of the eighteenth century cooking literature came into its own, with the most popular works even being distributed in the *Bibliothèque bleue* – the library of cheap reading matter, bound in blue paper covers, that found its way all over France, often in the satchels of travelling pedlars. New vistas opened up for housewives whose only previous teacher had been local tradition. By the end of the period, cooking in France had been elevated into food for philosophy as well as for the stomach. There might be occasional aberrations, such as the adoption of meat cooked *a l'anglaise* – *rostbif*, for example, and even that interesting variation, *rostbif d'agneau* – but, overall, no Frenchman had the slightest doubt that in matters of taste France was superior to all other nations.

THE IBERIAN PENINSULA

A visitor to Spain in the seventeenth or eighteenth century would have found himself oddly adrift in a society that ought to have belonged in the familiar European tradition, and yet did not. There was no real princely cooking of the kind to be found further north; instead of the rich man's foods filtering downward to the lower levels of society, the reverse was the case. The food of Spain was the food of the people – *del pueblo* – and common to all.

Peasant, poor knight and rich knight were all likely to eat a version of what had sustained the fictional Don Quixote in the sixteenth century – an *olla podrida*, or meat stew from the cauldron, with salad; lentils on Friday; boiled bones on Saturday; and pigeon on Sunday.

An excellent representation (by Velasquez) of the charcoal stove of the Mediterranean, made from pottery that looks as if it might have come from Vallauris. The woman is cooking her eggs in oil, and there is a shallot for flavour. The boy is about to cut into a melon.

The *olla podrida* is said to have had its origins in the Jewish *adafina*, where the protein element was supplied by chicken or hard-boiled eggs, but in the days of the Inquisition, when every man's Christianity had to be restated daily if he were to survive, it became customary in Spain to ensure that there was always either pork in the cauldron or the dried pork sausage called *chorizo* hanging from the rafters as a sure proof that no Jew or Muslim lived or ate in the house.

Spain and Portugal were also the fishiest societies the traveller in Europe was likely to encounter, except in Scandinavia. As with all coastal peoples in impoverished lands, they made extensive use of fish and seafood. The Portuguese even sailed (and still do) as far as Newfoundland for cod, which was salted on board and then taken back to Portugal to be sun-dried and used in some of the country's most popular dishes.

The foods of both Spain and Portugal were mirrors of trade and conquest. The cooking medium, olive oil, had been introduced from the eastern Mediterranean during the first millennium B C. Production of salt and dried fish had been greatly expanded to meet the demands of Rome. The barbarian invasions had led to a substantial increase in sheep farming and mutton eating. The Arabs had introduced rice, at once a staple foodstuff and an export crop, as well as citrus fruits, almonds and sugar, and a taste for such sweetmeats as marzipan and nougat.* Portugal's imperial adventures had brought it a richness of sugar and spices, while Spain's victories in the New World had introduced into the cuisine two new foods that quickly became naturalized – the tomato and the capsicum pepper.

But although many of the new foods from Latin America could be grown in Europe, the tropical cacao tree could not. Spain held most of the lands where the cacao already grew, Portugal the rest, and for well over a hundred years after the conquistadors first discovered the drinking chocolate of the West Indies both production and consumption remained a jealously guarded monopoly.†

Drinking chocolate was made by drying cocoa (or cacao) beans and roasting them over a fire. They were then pounded to a paste

---

* It is one of the minor and more enjoyable ironies of history that the secret recipe for the very special Moorish-Muslim confection known as *yemas de San Leandro* is now in the safe keeping of the nuns in a Catholic convent.
† In the Latin American economy cacao was one of the most important cash crops, in more senses than one. In the 1540s the charge made for their services by Nicaragua's ladies of pleasure was ten cacao beans.

with water and, sometimes, powdered flowers; by the end of the sixteenth century sugar seems to have been added. In Mexico little cakes of this paste, with spices incorporated, were shaken up with water in a gourd until they frothed. The drink was then gulped down 'in one swallow with admirable pleasure and satisfaction of the bodily nature, to which it gives strength, nourishment and vigour in such a way that those who are accustomed to drinking it cannot remain robust without it even if they eat other substantial things. And they appear to diminish when they do not have that drink.'⁹

In Spain by 1631 the preparation of a pot of chocolate had become a complex operation. 'For every hundred cocoa beans, mix two pods of chilli or Mexican pepper ... or, failing those, two Indian peppercorns, a handful of aniseed, two of those flowers known as 'little ears' or *vinacaxtlides* and two of those known as *mesasuchil* ... Instead of the latter one could include the powder of the six roses of Alexandria [an apothecaries' formula] ... a little pod of logwood [dye], two drachmas of cinnamon, a dozen almonds and as many hazelnuts, half a pound of sugar and enough annatto [a yellow-orange dye] to give colour to the whole.'¹⁰

By the early 1600s a considerable amount of chocolate paste was being exported to Italy and Flanders, but it was not until 1650 that chocolate drinking became the vogue in Oxford; a chocolate house opened in London in 1657, and Pepys (inevitably) tasted and approved soon after. In France the new drink became widely known two years later, though its popularity was at first erratic. French court circles, willing converts after the Paris faculty of medicine reported favourably on it, temporarily lost interest when strange tales began to circulate, culminating in one of the Marquise de Sévigné's most engaging pieces of gossip. 'The Marquise de Coëtlogon', she reported, 'took so much chocolate, being pregnant last year, that she was brought to bed of a little boy who was as black as the devil!'¹¹

For almost 300 years after its introduction into Europe, chocolate was thought of as a drink. Only in the nineteenth century was it to be mass-produced in block form for eating. West Africa is now the main producer, and Britain among the most avid consumers.

DRINKS

Chocolate, and the other two drinks that were introduced into Europe at much the same time – tea and coffee (see pp. 267, 274) – ushered in an entirely new era, one of relative sobriety. Before they became popular for everyday drinking, most Europeans had to choose between water, which was often unsafe; milk, which was no great thirst-quencher; and wine, ale, beer or cider.

Foods that were heavy in carbohydrates and fats, as most north European foods were, had to be washed down with plenty of liquids, and this was one of the reasons why Poles, Germans, Dutch and English all acquired a reputation for heavy drinking. Even small ale, with its low alcohol content, had a cumulative effect when drunk by the gallon.

For centuries most countries had had their own grain-based beers and ales, and where there was honey there was also mead. Such drinks were brewed on the manor during the Middle Ages and in most country households after the manorial system collapsed. Except in wine-producing areas, ale (or its hopped successor, beer) was the common drink whenever a drink was needed, even at breakfast.

France was the wine-producing country *par excellence*, and the names of Beaune, St Emilion, Chablis and Epernay can be found in manuscripts dating from as early as the thirteenth century. The Hansa towns, Flanders and England were among the steadiest markets for the wines of Gascony (Bordeaux), whose pale *rosés*, known as clairet,[12] were drunk only a few weeks old. By the end of the Middle Ages, however, Spanish and Portuguese wines had come into fashion; so had the red *vernaccia* (or 'vernage') of northern Italy; Malmsey from Crete, Malaga and, later, Madeira; and Rhenish from Germany.

In the sixteenth and seventeenth centuries immoderate drinking became a fashion in the north. Della Casa thanked God that in Italy, 'among the many pests which have come to us from beyond the mountains, this vilest one has not yet reached us, of regarding drunkenness as not merely a laughing matter, but even a merit.'[13]

Although fermented drinks had been known for thousands of years, the process of distilling was only discovered in the first century A D. Fundamentally, the process consists of converting a liquid into vapour through the application of heat, and then of condensing the vapour again. It can be used either to drive liquid off from a moist substance, leaving the substance dehydrated, or to extract a pure liquid essence (the condensed vapour) from some kinds of solid. The Arabs, for example, made kohl, the cosmetic eye-liner, by the first means, and rose water by the second. The word 'alcohol' itself is derived from Arabic *al-kohl* or *al-kuhl*.

Although there are literary references hinting that China may have been several hundred years ahead of Europe (as usual),[14] it is generally accepted that the distillation of spirits was discovered in the twelfth century by the alchemists – chemists rather than wizards – who were experimenting with the separation of liquids from solids. With careful temperature control and rapid cooling of the vapour, they found that it was possible not only to separate liquids from solids, but one liquid from another liquid. When they tried distilling wine in this way, they found they had pure water plus almost pure alcohol (which vaporizes at a lower temperature than water). Wine contains about one part alcohol to nine parts water and what distilling did, in effect, was isolate the active ingredient.

The alcohol produced from distilled wine and, subsequently, distilled ales, was at first regarded as a medicine and known as *aqua vitae* ('water of life'), a name immortalized in *eau de vie, akvavit, vodka,* and the Gaelic *uisge beatha* (abbreviated to *uisge,* which was then corrupted into 'whisky'). The Germans, less poetically, called it *gebrannte Wein* or *Brandewine* ('burnt' or distilled wine), which was anglicized as 'brandy'.

By the sixteenth century spirits in the north were being distilled mainly from fermented grains, and local variants were appearing. There were akvavit, schnapps and gin in continental Europe ('gin' was from *genever,* or juniper, the flavouring element) and whisky in Scotland and Ireland. Single malt whisky, drawing its flavour from pale golden grains of malted barley, aromatic peat smoke and rich brown water from hill burns, comes closest nowadays to competing with Cognac (made from the wines of the Charente) for the favour of connoisseurs.

EUROPE, THE CENTRE AND WEST

A sturdy solidity was the overwhelming impression conveyed by most of the northern cuisines or, as an English chef more flatteringly put it in 1710, a 'substantial and wholesome plenty'.[15]

In what was later to become Germany, pork and sausage, cabbage, lentils, rye bread and beer were the mainstays of the diet. A thick, hearty broth appeared on the table at almost every meal, and a fruit-stuffed goose on high days and holidays. Poland and Hungary, which had borne the brunt of most of the nomad incursions into European history, reflected it in their cuisines. Veal, fermented milks and pickled cabbage were old standbys, and the once-nomadic Turks who occupied Hungary for much of the sixteenth and seventeenth centuries had introduced maize and capsicums brought from the eastern end of the

Mediterranean. Austria, too, was a clearing house of foreign influences, and nowhere more so than in Vienna, whose food included dishes and cooking methods from all over the Hapsburg Empire. In Bulgaria rice, potatoes, capsicums, tomatoes and maize had all, by the end of the seventeenth century and much more swiftly than elsewhere, begun to revolutionize the old diet of flatbread, cheese, mutton, goat, beans, lentils and cabbage.

In the Low Countries much of the food was heavy and fatty but, inspired by the imports of their East India Company, the Dutch had begun to cultivate as many exotic fruits as could be induced to grow. They were notable horticulturalists in this part of the world; even before the era of colonial enterprise, the Flemish had been famous vegetable growers, supplying much of Europe with onions and salad materials. By 1636 the markets at Antwerp were so luscious that the great still-life artist Jan Davidsz de Heem felt compelled to go and live there, where there were 'rare fruits of all kinds, large plums, peaches, cherries, oranges, lemons, grapes and others, in finer condition and state of ripeness to draw from life'.[16]

The fine foods of Antwerp.

Across the North Sea, in England, fruit was a feature only of 'the tables of the great, and of a small number even among them'. At the end of the seventeenth century, beef, mutton, fowls, pigs, rabbits and pigeons 'infallibly' turned up at mealtimes, the mutton underdone and the beef salted for some days before being boiled and served up inside a rampart of 'five or six heaps of cabbage, carrots, turnips or some other herbs or roots, well peppered and salted, and swimming in butter'.[17]

Fifty years later the situation had improved a very little. In 1748 a Swedish visitor remarked that 'Englishmen understand almost better than any other people the art of properly roasting a large cut of meat', which was not to be wondered at, 'because the art of cooking as practised by most Englishmen does not extend much beyond roast beef and plum pudding.'[18]

At their best, many of the standard dishes of northern and western Europe may have been excellent, good filling food for a cold climate – this was still the Little Ice Age – but the evidence suggests that more often they were dull, heavy and as lacking in food value as in savour.

COOKERY BOOKS

If English cooking was as bad as everyone except the English said it was, it was not for lack of cookery books, which had been doing very nicely since the genre had first proved itself profitable. Gervase Markham's *The English House-wife*, published in 1615, was in its eighth edition by 1668, and *The Good Huswife* was also able to buy her *Jewell*, her *Treasurie*, her *Closet*, or her *Handmaid*. These little books were bursting with activity. As well as supervising the arrangement of a whole boar on a bed of parsley, the housewife had to instruct the servants, oversee the preserve-making, deal with the estate accounts, mix plague cures, weave and dye and brew and bake . . .

Although in the late 1600s many northern aristocrats dispatched their cooks to France to learn about refined cooking, the experiment was not a success. French *quelque chose* (anglicized as 'kickshaws') turned out to be a paltry substitute for real food, and the battle between French and English cooking was soon joined, in cookery books as in kitchens. By 1710 the veteran royal cook Patrick Lamb was firing the first salvoes in the war that was to rage for the next two centuries and more. Britain's raw materials, Lamb claimed, were unequalled anywhere, and 'the *quelque chose* of France, and the vines of Italy' were no recompense for 'the surfeits and fevers they usually bring on such as deal in them'.

Eliza Smith, one of the early women cookbook writers, was equally scathing about French kickshaws, besides having a word or two to say on the subject of French 'messes' and upstart French chefs, while Hannah Glasse, whose *The Art of Cooking Made Plain and Easy* was arguably the most successful cookery book of the eighteenth century, tactfully agreed with both of them without allowing it to stop her from borrowing French recipes and using fractured-French titles.

With the advent of Sarah Phillips in 1758, a glimmer of modern cooking techniques began to appear, especially in the treatment of vegetables, where Mrs Phillips' injunctions to use minimum liquid and minimum cooking times shone like a good deed in a naughty world. But in some ways she remained very old-fashioned; phrases like 'hack it with a knife' and 'rip open the belly' were very much in the tradition of the medieval cook's 'smite them in pieces' and 'hew them in gobbets'.

THE NORTHERN FRINGES

The contrast between the comfortably settled lands of temperate Europe and the sea-nibbled mountains of Scandinavia – still in the eighteenth century firmly locked into the early Middle Ages – could hardly have been more extreme. Famine in the extreme north was sometimes so near when spring came that the cattle, skeletal from their winter diet of straw and shredded bark, had to be carried out to the pastures. But within days of the new growth beginning, the land-scape had sprung into the lush life characteristic of places where summer is short, and the people had already begun working towards the next winter, which was not very far away.

The whole atmosphere of Scandinavian food reflected the reality of the latitudes, as dictatorial in the eighteenth century as in the time of the Vikings more than a thousand years before. Some Viking dishes were still common. The cured salmon known as *gravlax* may have been one of them. The velvety blood soup, *svartsoppa*, was certainly another, though it is unlikely that the Vikings ever troubled to cook it. In the later period it was made from the pig's blood that was available in quantity at the time of the autumn slaughter.

It was winter necessity that dictated what should be grown or caught or collected in the summer, when the only sauce fresh food needed was its freshness. Anything that could be satisfactorily dried, smoked or salted took top priority – fish in quantity, whale, pork, beets, cabbage, onions, apples, cheese, berries and nuts. Variety was more important than in most countries because winter trading was out of the question; the great range of Danish *smørrebrød* (the 'bread and butter table', with its open sandwiches) hints at a time when a varied display of foods was taken as evidence of good house-wifeliness. Sweden's *smörgåsbord*, which has the same meaning, was originally a pre-prandial snack of herring, cheese, bread and aquavit, laid out on a separate 'aquavit table'. Only in the late nineteenth century did it develop into the grand, multi-course buffet it is today.

There is a libellous comparison still current in Scandinavia that claims that the Danes live to eat, the Norwegians eat to live, and the Swedes eat to drink. Whether or not this is true of the Swedes, there was a period of history when it was unquestionably true further east.

DRINKING IN RUSSIA

'Drinke is their whole desire, the pot is all their pride,
The sobrest head doth once a day stand needfull of a guide.'[19]

When George Turberville, poet and minor diplomat, visited Russia in the late 1560s no one offered him vodka, which seems to have been not only new at that time,* but also very vulgar. Moving in elevated circles, as he did, he was treated instead to the noblest meads and finest beers.

Mead and *kvas* (a very small beer) had been the most important drinks from as far back as the sixth century AD, when the Slavs settled the Russian plain. Mead, of course, was brewed from honey, which was not always available, but *kvas* – 'a quenchy draught', according to one traveller[21] – could be made by anyone from the commonest ingredients. One basic recipe required two pounds of barley or rye meal to be stirred into a bucketful of water with half a pound of salt, and honey as available. Kept warm overnight, the mixture was stirred and left to settle. The liquid was then poured off, and after being kept for a few days was considered ready to drink – a lightly fermented thirst-quencher, almost non-alcoholic unless the honey content was high. Some people included fruit in the mixture, others varied the proportions, so that there were probably as many versions of *kvas* as there were people who made it.

With the introduction and rapid spread of spirits – brandy first

---

* Some authorities claim that spirits were introduced into Russia in the late fourteenth century, but the balance of probabilities seems to favour the early sixteenth.[20]

(apparently brought in by foreigners) and then vodka* — the idea of drink as a source of income for the royal treasury became of interest. Whereas even a lowly peasant could make *kvas* at home, distilling was an operation that required capital and organization.

As a result, the old inns and taverns soon gave way to the state drink shop, which sold no food but only state-produced or state-licensed drinks, particularly spirits; the whole atmosphere of drinking became more purposeful, less social. By 1626 there were twenty-five drink shops in Moscow alone,[22] and drink-shop officials everywhere had acquired police functions and acted as agents of the treasury.

In 1652, however, three years after the peasants of Russia had been legally declared serfs, the drink shop was abolished in favour of the 'pot house' (a kind of off-licence). There was to be only one in each town, and they were forbidden 'to sell more than the one cup decreed to [any] one man; and drinkers are forbidden to sit or to be allowed to drink at or near the pot house; and no drunkards and boozers and dicers are allowed at the pot house . . . Clerics and monks are not allowed into pot houses nor are they to be sold drink; no spirits are to be sold from the pot houses to any person on credit or against a deposit.'[23]

Although it has been argued that these new regulations were designed to increase the quantity of grain available for export by reducing home consumption, the details of the legislation make it just as likely that the intention was to abolish the kind of social centre that readily became a hotbed of discontent.

Fortunately or unfortunately, the effect was to reduce the state's profit so drastically that drink shops were restored just over ten years later. Immoderate drinking was even encouraged. 'On holidays they are allowed, even given the pre-eminent right, to make themselves drunk without punishment; one may then see them lying on the streets, frozen by the cold, or carried to their homes, piled one on top of another on carts and sledges.'[24] Paralytic drunkenness was not a danger to the state.

State control of the drink trade became increasingly profitable. Between them, salt and spirits brought in almost 20 per cent of Russia's total tax revenue in 1724, over 30 per cent in 1769.[25] It is estimated that towards the end of the eighteenth century the men of St Petersburg were swallowing something like ninety pints of spirits per head per

---

* Which was distilled originally from wine, later from rye, and only much later from potatoes.

annum, and those of Moscow thirty pints. Elsewhere, most seem to have contented themselves with an abstemious ten.[26]

FOOD IN RUSSIA

With a resignation almost too saintly to be credible, the Russian peasant of early modern times is reported to have felt that, 'If there's bread and *kvas*, then we have all we need.'

The bread, at least, could sometimes be excellent. Even prejudiced Western travellers noticed it when they overcame their astonishment at banquets that opened with bread and vodka. 'There were neither spoons nor plates on the table', reported a Bavarian guest at a formal occasion in 1606. 'They first served vodka and exceedingly tasty white bread, then they served various dishes of food, mostly hashes, but badly cooked; among them was a huge pie filled with small fish; the dishes were not served all at once, but one at a time: there were very many of them, but all tasteless, partly from an excessive amount of oil, partly from the honey which the Muscovites use instead of sugar.'[27]

Until the eighteenth century the diet of the upper classes (as in Spain) differed from that of the lower in quantity and quality rather than style. Where the peasant rarely ate fish, for example, the tsar was supplied from his own fishing grounds. From the Volga alone he had huge quantities of beluga and sturgeon, some delivered whole, some in the form of steaks brined in barrels and some carved into back and belly cuts, dried and cured. There were also barrels of brined sterlet (a small sturgeon); ling roes; beluga and sturgeon caviare, either granular or pressed in cheeses; and sturgeon gristle (probably the spine, used in the fish pie known as *coulibiac*).[28] Another 400 barrels a year of whitefish came from Greater Novgorod, and there were sea trout and salmon from Archangel and elsewhere. Anything surplus to imperial requirements was sold in the market.

At the end of the 1600s, during the reign of Peter the Great, the Russian court began importing not only luxury foods, but also cooks. 'Rich grandees visiting Western Europe brought back foreign cooks. At first, these were mainly Dutch and German, in particular Saxon and Austrian, later they were Swedish and predominantly French.'[29]

One sequel was a change in the first course at formal meals. Bread and vodka gave way (presumably when Swedish cooks were in fashion) to something with a marked family resemblance to the 'aquavit table'; the Russian version became known as *zakuski*. There were open sandwiches of herring, pickles in brine, caviare, cured salmon, cheese, cold ham, smoked tongue, salt beef and sausage. 'All this', remarked the Danish envoy in 1709, 'was very salt, with a lot of pepper and garlic'[30] – which suggests that it was indeed very salt, since Scandinavians had (and have) a high salt tolerance.

Such changes as these, of course, had no effect on the diet of the mass of the people, who went on eating what they had eaten in the sixteenth, and the fifteenth, and the fourteenth centuries, and were to go on eating until well into the nineteenth.

All over Russia, no matter what the local options, the peasants seem to have subsisted on the same rye bread, the same *kvas* and the same main course of soup made from pickled cabbage, with milk or fat in it on meat days, and groats or nothing on fast days. Sometimes there would be buckwheat *kasha*, sometimes milk (though that was mainly a food for children and invalids, a special seasoning for everyone else), soured cream, cottage cheese or eggs, usually onions or garlic and, as often as possible, fried or pickled mushrooms – flavour that could be had free for the gathering. Meat and fish were for festivals.

As an eighteenth-century English governess remarked of the Russian serfs, 'they need not lay by much to provide for Food; for they can make an hearty Meal on a Piece of black sour Bread, some Salt, an Onion, or Garlick.'[31]

18

A Gastronomic Grand Tour : 2

European gentlemen who crossed the Atlantic during the seventeenth and eighteenth centuries were overwhelmed not only by the vastness and emptiness of North America, but by its variety.

In the north, what is now Canada was an empire of fish and furs, inhabited by a handful of Europeans – most actively French until the eighteenth century – a few thousand Eskimos, and an estimated 200,000 Amerindians who still occupied most of the country, hunting, fishing and sometimes practising a primitive agriculture.

The south of the continent grew tobacco, sugar, cotton and slaves, 'Indians and Negroes being rated [as taxable assets] with Horses and Hogs'.[1] In the centre, rippling slowly and erratically outward from Jamestown and Cape Cod, lay the diverse and commercially astute heartland of what were to become the United States.

The first truly American dish – and, according to one historian, the first truly American word – may have emerged long before the Pilgrim Fathers sighted Cape Cod. Fishermen from many of the countries of Europe had been haunting the waters south of Newfoundland ever since the time of the Cabots. 'It must have been in their polyglot get-togethers ashore that, between fights, the proto-Yankee fisherman learned *chowder* . . . for the fish or clam stew that his French rivals made in large pots called *chaudières*. Those chowders lacked milk, for there were no cows within 2,000 miles, and potatoes, for that tuber had not yet triangled to North America . . . But ship's biscuit, salt pork and onions doubtless were available.'[2]

As new settlers arrived in America, they introduced their own traditional dishes, adapting them to suit the materials available. The English took apple pie; the Dutch, cookies (*koekjes*), coleslaw (*kool*: cabbage, and *sla*: salad) and waffles; and the Germans, sauerkraut. Inevitably, the American cuisine became in time a mirror of history, the names of its dishes reflecting the medley of its peoples, religions, wars, places and even occupations. There were ambushed asparagus, Shaker loaf, burgoo, Maryland chicken, snickerdoodles, spoon bread, cowpoke beans, hush puppies, jambalaya, pandowdy, Boston baked beans, Philadelphia pepper pot, Moravian sugar cake, Swedish meatballs, haymaker's switchel, whaler's toddy . . .

In the backwoods, until well into the nineteenth century, the visitor still found himself eating plain-cooked possums, racoons and other un-expected beasts, although on nothing like the scale of Canada, where he might have been offered stuffed moose heart, lynx stew, paupiettes of buffalo, woodchuck casserole (with biscuits) or roast polar bear.* Recipes for all these still appear in cookery books designed for the northern territories today.

For historical reasons French influence was to remain widespread in Canada, but in the United States it was mainly confined to the south. In New Orleans after the War of Independence a complete range of French specialities was soon to be had, traditional dishes enlivened by black and Spanish influences. Plantation slaves might have to make do with 'soul food' – black-eyed peas and leftovers from the big house, including turnip tops, ham hocks and chitterlings made from unwanted scraps of pig – but when their city brethren were able to exercise their talents on more rewarding materials they injected an entirely new gusto into the self-conscious world of classical French cooking.

Despite the War of Independence, domestic life in the thirteen colonies remained recognizably European. The city lady on the east-ern seaboard had her servants, her table silver, her coffee, white bread, imported cheeses and white loaf sugar. Even her cookery books were European, since all those published under an American imprint before 1796 were European ones in superficial disguise. Only when Amelia Simmons, 'An American Orphan', wrote *American Cookery* did such already established national dishes as Indian pudding, slapjack and jonnycake make their first appearance in print.

On a prosperous eastern farm the housewife lived almost as com fortably as her sister in the city, though her daily tasks were more demanding. The main household had to be supervised, as well as food and accommodation for the farmhands. There were dairying, pickl-ing and preserving to be seen to. The smokehouse had to be hung with meat and game for the winter; the root cellar to be filled with bins or barrels of potatoes, dried corn, beans, squash and apples.

The poorer farm wife and (later) the west-bound settler lived closer to American beginnings. They seasoned their stews more often with maple syrup than with salt, sweetened their pies with molasses, cooked

* Never eat the liver of a polar bear. It contains so much vitamin A that it is toxic to humans.[3]

cornmeal mush more often than bread, broiled fresh meat or fish only when there had been time to hunt or catch it. If staked-out land proved inhospitable, they upped stakes and moved on in search of better. Many women even learned how to make butter on the trail, 'by the dashing of the wagon, and so nicely to calculate the working of barm [leaven] in the jolting heats that, as soon after the halt as an oven could be dug in the hillside and heated, their well-kneaded loaf was ready for baking'.*⁴ But most people stocked up on dried corn, jonnycakes, pocket soup and preserved meats like jerky (*charqui*) for their journeys into the unknown.

RUM . . .

By the eighteenth century Scots and Irish settlers had introduced whisky distilling into North America. Lacking peat, the product was a poor substitute for the real thing, but still very different from the early rye whiskey or the maize spirit produced at the end of the century by the folk of Bourbon County, Kentucky.

Like their contemporaries in Europe, early Americans had a built-in resistance to water. This was not altogether surprising. Much 'fresh' water within range of human habitation was, if not actually poisonous, not far from it. One of the seventeenth-century colonists' first priorities had been to organize a supply of fermented drinks, but their initial experiments in growing barley and hops in New England proved disappointing; there was to be no beer until Pennsylvania was settled. In the meantime, however, thirst being the mother of invention, they very soon discovered that potable brews could be made from pumpkins, maple sugar and persimmons.

They found a good use for apples, too, when their first orchards came into full bearing. Cider intake soon reached gargantuan proportions, and so did the consumption of apple brandy and that rough and highly potent liquor correctly known as applejack though sometimes referred to as 'essence of lockjaw'.⁵

But of all the drinks that warmed the eighteenth-century American interior, rum was the most important. It is estimated that just before the War of Independence the colonists were downing twenty-four pints of it per head per year, women and children included.⁶

Some historians argue that it was not the 1773 tax on tea that was

---

* If the ancient Hebrews had been as housewifely on the flight from Egypt, there might have been no matzos today.

responsible for the final schism between Britain and its American colonies (even if that was the catalyst), but the Molasses Act of forty years earlier, which imposed a heavy tax on sugar and molasses coming from anywhere other than the British sugar islands of the Caribbean.

An eighteenth-century Massachusetts merchant with pipe, account book, and bowl of rum punch.

It is a persuasive argument, since rum (unlike tea at that period) was very much more than a drink. A substantial part of the colonies' trade was based on the molasses from which rum was made, the syrupy liquid left after the juice of the sugar cane was boiled once, twice or three times to produce sugar crystals. For several decades the shipowners of New England had found it profitable to sail with a cargo of rum to the slave coast of Africa and there exchange it for slaves, whom they took back to the West Indies for sale to plantation owners. In the West Indies, loading up their now empty vessels with molasses, they took the new cargo home to New England, where it was distilled into the rum that would supply the capital for the next round trip. Restrictions on the purchase of molasses therefore threatened not only the colonists' own favourite drink but a whole related trading cycle.

Alcohol in its various forms – the stronger the better – was the great lubricant of eighteenth-century America. It quenched the majestic thirst that resulted from too much preserved food; it was a social ice-breaker in new communities; it was, for many centuries, a surgeon's easiest and sometimes only recourse when an anaesthetic was needed;* and it even became a political tradition. When George Washington ran for the legislature in 1758 he expressed some concern that his agent might have been too niggardly in doling out only three gallons of beer, wine, cider or rum to each voter.[8]

. . . AND COCA

If rum was North America's stimulant, coca was the South's.

Coca was (and is) a leaf that South American Indians 'keep constantly in their mouths, chewing it together with a small amount of ground lime [as a digestive] . . . They say that chewing this leaf gives them strength and vigour, and such is the superstition and faith that they have in it that they cannot work or go on trips without having it in their mouths. And, on the contrary, having it, they work happily and walk a day or two without refreshing themselves otherwise or eating anything.'[9]

---

* During the Civil War a colonel of the 1st New York Infantry, who had an educated palate for anaesthetics, was to be cashiered for authorizing the purchase of a month's medical supplies of 96 gallons of bourbon, 33.6 gallons pale sherry, 17.2 gallons pale Otard brandy, 32 gallons Cabinet gin and 24 dozen Allsop East India ale.[7]

The fresh coca leaf contains cocaine, but research shows that although it can be fatally addictive it does not produce a simple 'high'; rather it deadens fatigue, pain and hunger, makes it easier to breathe at high altitudes (very important in the Andean regions), appears to sharpen the mind and enables people who chew it to endure much that would otherwise be beyond human tolerance. Its properties, half stimulant, half narcotic, are something of a mystery, but it is believed to be a valuable aid in a low-protein, high-carbohydrate diet, keeping up blood glucose levels and retarding the breakdown of blood sugar.[10] Even so, the coca leaf's hunger-suppressing properties in a land where food has often been scarce have been known to lead to involuntary self-starvation.

Historians have yet to agree on the relationship between coca-chewing in the Andes, *pan*-chewing in India and cola-chewing in West Africa. The custom may have developed independently in all three

Prepared betel quids being offered to the god Krishna.

places, but it seems more likely that it originated in Asia – possibly Malaysia, where the Chinese encountered it in 140 BC – was then transmitted to South America during the pre-Columbian period, and spread from there to Africa in the wake of the slave trade. An appetite suppressant would have ready appeal for slave-traders, who could squeeze in two or three extra slaves for every barrel of red herrings left behind.

In Africa there was no coca, but there was the cola nut, from a tree also to be found in tropical America. The nut kernels were wrapped 'in a thick green capsule' to make a quid that was 'very pleasant, bitter and astringent' and 'much esteemed for its stomachic powers'. Since the nut contained not only caffeine but the heart stimulant kolanin, it had an invigorating effect. As an appetite-suppressant it proved a poor substitute for coca, but was sufficiently pleasant for cola-chewing to have become habitual in West Africa by the eighteenth century – an 'innocent luxury', as one contemporary traveller mistakenly remarked.[11]

Pan-chewing in India is said to go back to the centuries before 200 BC. Like coca, its effect is partly narcotic and partly stimulating, but it is much less dangerous except in large quantities, when it is toxic. *Pan* is a small leaf package containing a mixture of shredded betel nut (the fruit of the areca palm), powdered lime and *catechu* (a highly astringent, tannin-rich, red-brown substance made from an infusion of chips of acacia wood). The effect of chewing *pan* is to reduce hunger, slightly anaesthetize the mouth, and create a mild sensation of exhilaration. Indians believe that it sweetens the breath, and women also claim that it has contraceptive qualities.*

For Indians *pan*-chewing was a pleasant, gently addictive luxury; cola for West Africans not much more. But in the Latin America of post-conquest times, the coca that had once been the prerogative of the Inca became a necessity for the rapidly dwindling native peoples.

Even so, the changes wrought by the Spanish conquest were not

---

* They could be right. A number of 'old wives' tales' of this kind have turned out to be well founded when tested in the laboratory. This seems the place to add that women in some developing countries use Coca-Cola (whose recipe, although a closely guarded secret, does not include coca) as a spermicidal douche. When the Harvard Medical School investigated this, they discovered to their surprise that classic-formula Coca-Cola did, in fact, stop 91 per cent of sperm in their tracks. The new formula made a poor showing by comparison – only 42 per cent.[12]

always to the peasant's disadvantage. There was a swift spread of Spanish livestock, which soon ensured that some, at least, of the surviving peoples had meat to eat, a horse to ride and a draught animal to work for them. Even the very poorest benefited, because the goat adapted itself well to Mexico and the slopes of the Andes.

Much of the continent east of the Andes was good land for livestock. Sheep and cattle breeders seem to have had no particular desire to own land – all they wanted was wide open pastures and permanent quarters for themselves and the hands – but inevitably they came into conflict with the new agriculturalists on their settled farms and, in the end, it became necessary to define the ranchers' grazing lands by fencing them in.[13] In the meantime, however, there had grown up a new breed of mounted vagrants who preyed on the free-ranging cattle. These, the gauchos, were part Spanish, part Amerindian in blood, and almost wholly lawless. Their life and diet had much in common with that of their nomadic predecessors in the Central Asia of a thousand years before.

To the European traveller the gaucho was more alien than any poor peasant, even after serious attempts had been made to civilize him. He fuelled his fire with cow dung held down with bones that singed but did not burn and smelled abominable, and 'on this material, with its loathsome effluvia, another bone, with some flesh on it, is laid and broiled; and if the gaucho is particularly kindly disposed towards you, he takes the bone for you from the fire, knocks the cinders off on his leg, tears off a morsel with his own teeth to see whether it is well done; and you, as a polite gentleman, say with a sickly smile: "*Muchac gracias, Señor*".'[14]

NEW ZEALAND

Temperamentally, the Maoris of New Zealand struck the innocent visitor very much as the gauchos did – brimming with personality, friendly within limits, homicidal when provoked.

By the end of the eighteenth century the Europeans – flushed with imperial success – no longer expected primitive tribals to answer them back, and were dumbfounded when they did. For the first few years everything went smoothly enough with the Maoris of the North Island coasts, who were natural traders and very ready to buy, sell and bargain. But then the Maoris discovered the quality of the people they were dealing with. Neither deserters nor escaped convicts seem to have offended them particularly, but many of the sailors they encountered represented the dregs of Western civilization, people to whom thieving and brutality were a way of life.

Since the Maoris took a passionate delight in war, and had developed it into something of a fine art, they responded in kind. A few gangs of seal hunters were massacred, two ships' crews were not only massacred but eaten, and for almost a decade after 1810 Europeans regarded New Zealand as one of the most dangerous places in the Pacific.

The earlier history of the Maoris remains unclear. They had no written language, and oral history – although it can be much more informative than is generally thought – often muffles reality in the multiple wrappings of mythology. It seems, however, that the Maoris arrived in New Zealand from Polynesia possibly in the fourteenth century or (equally possibly) much earlier.

Whatever the date, they successfully transported across 2,000 miles, and then persuaded to grow, a number of plants that were quite unsuited to the New Zealand climate. The most important of these were the sweet potato and the yam, all-the-year round crops where conditions were right. In New Zealand the Maoris had to learn how to grow them on a seasonal basis. They became skilful farmers, learning to save seed tubers of the sweet potato for planting at the right season instead of immediately replanting what remained of the harvested roots. They recognized the existence of micro-climates and discovered how to protect what they were trying to grow by surrounding the plants with warmth-retaining, moisture-draining ramparts of sand and shingle. They used burnt scrub as a fertilizer.[15]

But however effective they turned out to be as hunter-farmers, the harsh experiences of their early days in New Zealand – and the later days, too, when famines were frequent – had helped to shape both their society and their attitudes. By the time they swam into the orbit of the West, they had an obsessive interest in food preservation, storage and trade, and an admirable selection of materials to work on.

The Europeans who came to know the shores of New Zealand at the end of the eighteenth century were not convinced of this. They were not enthusiastic vegetable-eaters. Cabbage, carrots and turnips were what they were used to at home and what they hoped to find abroad. Although the botanist Joseph Banks, who sailed with Cook, was typically fascinated by such Maori vegetables as sow thistle, 'wild celery', a kind of 'sea cress', a herb not unlike Lamb's lettuce, and hearts of the cabbage tree palm,* his successors were well able to contain their excitement.

They were, however, impressed by the seafood, including lobsters and even *kina*, sea urchins, which they ate raw, like oysters. Unable to find out from the Maoris what the names of all the magnificent fish were, they gave them European names wherever they bore a rough resemblance to European fish, which has led to endless confusion ever since.

Maori bread, which was not unlike a sourdough, and *raupo*, steamed cakes made from the blossoms of the bulrush, were two local specialities that the newcomers found themselves perfectly able to stomach. They were interested, too, in the Maoris' cooking methods; there was roasting, of course, and pit-boiling of a kind, using a wooden vessel (the Maoris had no clay pots and no iron). Where there were thermal springs, the food was usually placed in baskets and lowered into the hot pools until it was done. But the cooking method that most appealed to the newcomers was the *hangi*, a version of the clambake that was to be adopted wholeheartedly by the new society that formed in New Zealand in the nineteenth century and still survives today as a tourist attraction. Everyone agreed that food cooked by this means in the *umu* (earth oven) was delicious.

There were some things, however, that were altogether too much for the Europeans. Possibly because the Maoris had found it necessary to experiment with every conceivable and inconceivable method of food preservation, sometimes less than successfully, they had become accustomed to strong flavours. The higher the food, the better they seem to have liked it. One traditional favourite was *paua*, a kind of tough abalone, which they buried in the ground for some weeks until it was soft enough to slice like cheese.

Quick to adopt new European foods, including the pig – a welcome addition to the local four-legged fauna, which consisted only of dogs and rats – they were equally quick to discover how to make them palatable in Maori terms. Maize and potatoes were given the full treatment. Maize was prepared by three-quarters husking it, and putting it in a bag in a running stream for up to six months.† The

---

* Not the same as the American palmetto, which provides most 'hearts of palm' today.

† Not, perhaps, as mad as it sounds. Fern roots had long been a useful food in New Zealand, and it is possible that some of the moisture-loving kinds may have been kept fairly successfully by this means.

evil-smelling mushy grains were then scraped off, cooked with salt in clean water, and eaten with more salt. This dish was known as *kaanga-pirau*. Potatoes were similarly immersed, then skinned, mashed, formed into cakes and baked in the ashes. This was *kotero*.[16]

It was not *kaanga-pirau* or *kotero* that killed off Maoris by the thousand, although by the end of the 1830s their numbers had been reduced by 40 per cent. Just like the Amerindians, many of them had fallen prey to European diseases against which they had no natural immunity – whooping cough, influenza, measles, typhoid and the venereal diseases imported in the baggage of the prostitutes.

AUSTRALIA

The European's early experience of the Australian aboriginal was very different. Instead of answering back, the aboriginal simply ignored him. A way of life hallowed by thousands of years of tradition was not to be disrupted by intruders in strange clothes and stranger hats.

There has been a radical rethinking of history over the last few years that suggests that the modern aboriginal may well be descended in direct line from the *homo sapiens* whose Australian remains have been dated at 30,000 BC, and everything about his way of life confirms it. When the Europeans arrived they discovered a people with no houses, no weapons, no kings, no concept of money; a race of hunter-gatherers who travelled light and had nothing much in the way of cooking equipment; who ate roots, seeds, bulbs and grubs; and who coated small animals and birds with clay before roasting them.

If the scene had been America and the time 200 years earlier, the newcomers would have been forced to learn from, and about, the aboriginals. But these were no Pilgrim Fathers. Indeed, when the First Fleet arrived in 1788 it resembled nothing so much as a Noah's Ark loaded with horses, cattle, sheep, goats, pigs and a whole army of squawking hens.[17] There were plants, too – figs, sugarcane, vines, apple and pear trees – seeds of maize, wheat, rice and barley, and back-up supplies (soon needed) of salt pork and dried beans.

Thus provisioned, the British looked briefly at the aboriginals and then dismissed them, convinced that such a primitive people could have no useful knowledge to impart. Yet, in truth, they had a vast fund of information about plants and wildlife, and at least some of the technology to match it. They knew, for example, which fungi were poisonous and that cycas seeds were toxic unless very thoroughly washed and then roasted. Some of their knowledge could have been useful to the British, if the British had wanted to know. But they did not.

Australian aboriginal women taking little part in the preparation of this meal.

They found out for themselves how good the turtles were, how tasty the reef clams and mud oysters. They shot, or caught, kangaroos, Solan geese, mullet, bream and snapper, and found them palatable. They made serious inroads on the cabbage palm, but since, like their contemporaries in the islands to the south-east, they were no great lovers of vegetables, they carried their researches little further. They had, after all, brought seeds from which they could grow the everyday foods they were familiar with.

It did not work out quite like that. Most of the plantings went wrong, and it was back to salt pork and beans again. Only the bread that went with the pork and beans was different, a new kind, adapted to the circumstances of life, that became infamous as the 'damper'.

Flour was mixed with water and kneaded for a minute or two. 'The dough is then flattened out into a cake, which should never be more than an inch and a half or two inches thick, and may be of any diameter required; the ashes . . . are then drawn off the hearth (for the fire is on the ground not in a grate) by a shovel; and on the glowing smooth surface thus exposed the cake is lightly deposited, by being held over it on the open hands and the hands suddenly drawn from under it. The red ashes are then lightly turned back over the cake with the shovel. In the course of twenty minutes or half an hour, on removing the ashes, the cake is found excellently baked; and with a light duster or the tuft of the bullock's tail, every vestige of the ashes is switched off and the cake, if the operations have been well-conducted, comes to the table as clean as a captain's biscuit from the pastry cook's shop.'[18]

CHINA

From the land of damper bread to the place where the people were said to eat anything with four legs except a table, and anything that flew except a kite – in other words, from Australia to China – was a journey to be measured in more than miles.

Although many new foods had been introduced to China in the thousand years between AD 700 and AD 1700, none had been revolutionary enough to change the essential pattern of the diet – grain foods in quantity; very little meat; protein-rich, calcium-rich soy beans; and, in winter as in summer, a wide range of vegetables. The north Chinese winter was only marginally more favourable than that of northern Europe, but the Chinese were not of a mind to settle down to a six-months' penance of salt pork and pease pudding. Instead, they found or developed varieties of vegetable that were resistant to cold. They protected the more delicate ones with straw mats that could be turned back when the sun shone. They had manure-based hot-beds to warm the soil. And as a result the poor as well as the rich had fresh vegetables all the year round.

Between the early eighteenth and the middle of the nineteenth century, however, the population of China increased from about 150 million to 450 million.[19] No one is quite sure why. But although the newly introduced American crops – maize, potatoes, sweet potatoes and peanuts – may not have been the cause, such a population explosion could not have taken place without them since the production of traditional foods had by then reached its limit. The new crops were suitable for land that had never before been farmed, and China embarked on a period of internal expansion roughly comparable with that of America in the years when the West was won.

Although there were still rural misery and hunger (and rebellions), philosophers of the culinary art continued to find a place in the pantheon of Chinese culture. And at least they were the practical kind of philosopher who warned the cook to be sure that no feathers were left in the bird's nest soup, and no mud in the sea slugs.

It was things like sea slugs that bothered the European traveller. Despite the eulogistic terms in which the Jesuits had described China, the traveller firmly expected to be confronted with weird and wonderful food. And indeed, economical even when rich, the Chinese made use of storks and cranes, magpies, ravens, cormorants, owls, dogs, horses, donkeys, mules, camels, bears, wolves, foxes and a variety of rodents. Bird's nest soup was prized for the delicate flavour of the gelatinous substance (extracted from a kind of seaweed) used by certain south-east Asian swallows to bind their nests; the best quality nests came from Java. Indonesia supplied the reputedly aphrodisiac sea cucumber (trepang, or *bêche-de-mer*), which, dried and smoked, was immensely popular.* And there were more conventional delicacies like plovers' eggs, sharks' fins and roasted snails.

The Chinese being a courteous people, it is unlikely that any guest at a Chinese merchant's table would have been offered red-cooked dog or stir-fried cat, though every European visitor until the end of the nineteenth century went in dread of it. It was a dread gleefully fostered by generations of humorists. One anonymous versifier, unable to communicate with his hosts, claimed that he was equally unable to identify what he was eating until the covers were changed and:

> . . . he brightened up
> And thought himself in luck
> When close before him what he saw
> Looked something like a duck!
>
> Still cautious grown, but, to be sure,
> His brain he set to rack;
> At length he turned to one behind,
> And pointing, cried 'Quack, quack?'
>
> The Chinese gravely shook his head,
> Next made a reverend bow;
> And then expressed what dish it was,
> By uttering 'Bow-wow-wow!'[21]

---

* *Bêche-de-mer* was also fished off the north coast of Australia. A twentieth-century Melbourne writer claimed that the soup made from it was like liquid golden velvet and quite delicious.[20]

Just occasionally, the humorist paused to imagine himself as a Chinese reacting to a European menu of soup, fish, meat, cheese and beer.

'Judge now what tastes people possess who sit at table and swallow bowls of a fluid, in their outlandish tongue called *Soo-pe*, and next devour the flesh of fish, served in a manner as near as may be to resemble the living fish itself. Dishes of half-raw meat are then placed at various angles of the table; these float in gravy, while from them pieces are cut with swordlike instruments and placed before the guests . . . Thick pieces of meat being devoured . . . the scraps [are] thrown to a multitude of snappish dogs that are allowed to twist about among one's legs or lie under the table, while keeping up an incessant growling and fighting . . . Then a green and white substance, the smell of which was overpowering. This I was informed was a compound of sour buffalo milk, baked in the sun, under whose influence it is allowed to remain until it becomes filled with insects, yet, the greener and more lively it is, with the more relish is it eaten. This is called *Che-Sze*, and is accompanied by the drinking of a muddy red fluid which foams up over the tops of the drinking cups, soils one's clothes, and is named *Pe-Urh* – think of that!'[22]

In the Europeans' opinion, most Chinese drinks were a good deal more regrettable than *pe-urh*. They were especially suspicious of the Chinese pharmacopoeia,* and the wines listed therein. Tortoise wine was said to be good for bronchitis, snake wine for palsy, dog wine for lassitude, and mutton wine for strengthening the stomach, kidneys and testicles.[24] In a spirit of purely scientific inquiry the Reverend J. Gilmour asked his Chinese lama how mutton wine was made.

One of the ingredients, it transpired, was what the Europeans chose to call 'cow's milk whisky' but the Mongols would have known as *kumiss*. The recipe ran as follows. 'One sheep, 40 catties [the catty was nominally equivalent to 1⅓ lb] of cow's milk whisky, 1 pint of skimmed milk, soured and curdled, 8 ounces brown sugar, 4 ounces honey, 4 ounces fruit of dimocarpus, 1 catty of raisins, and half a dozen drugs weighing in all about 1 catty. The sheep must be 2 years old, neither more nor less, a male, castrated.'[25]

---

* Which did, indeed, contain a number of interesting remedies, some of them not unlike the one being used in a London hospital in 1974 as an allergy vaccine, which contained extracts of ram's testicle, shark cartilage and the liver of South African limpets. 'It sounds like a witch's brew, but it works', said the specialist.[23]

The brewing process was complex and the end product, which smelled strongly of mutton, had an alcohol content of 9.14 per cent.*

Although they had serious doubts about Johnny Chinaman's food, many travellers in Asia found themselves reluctantly impressed by the way he handled it. Chopsticks had been in use since about the eighteenth century BC[27] and had spread to some of the Chinese-influenced countries of south-east Asia. Japan, too, had adopted them, as it had so many other aspects of Chinese food and culture. One early merchant visitor, Francesco Carletti, seeing them for the first time, described how ingeniously food was conveyed to the mouth with the aid of two slim sticks, 'made in a round shape and blunted, the length of a man's hand and as thick as a quill for writing . . . They can pick up anything, no matter how tiny it is, very cleanly and without soiling their hands. For that reason they do not use tablecloths or napkins or even knives, as everything comes to the table minutely cut up . . . When they want to eat it, they bring the bowl it is in close to their mouth and then, with those two sticks, are able to fill their mouth with marvellous agility and swiftness.'[28]

TEA

Tea had been a popular drink in China since the Tang period and was generally believed to have medicinal value and to contribute to longevity. When Haji Muhammad reported on it to the Venetian geographer Ramusio in 1550, he said that the Chinese believed 'one or two cups of this decoction taken on an empty stomach remove fever, headache, stomach pain, pain in the side or in the joints, and it should be taken as hot as you can bear it . . . And those people would gladly give a sack of rhubarb [greatly prized by European apothecaries] for an ounce of *Chiai Catai*'.†[29]

Tea seems to have been introduced to Europe from Japan rather than China, the first few pounds of it being imported to Holland in 1610 by the Dutch East India Company. At first only the medical profession was interested. Almost half a century later (in 1656) the

---

* Europe was not entitled to feel superior about wines featuring livestock. Eliza Smith, in *The Compleat Housewife* (1727), gave a recipe for Cock Ale – ten gallons ale, one large and elderly cock, raisins, mace and cloves – and there are modern works on home wine- and beer-making that strongly recommend adding a cockerel to the ferment.[26]

† From *chiai*, the British army derived 'char', the slang word for tea.

whole year's order from Japan still amounted to less than 200 pounds
– and that was a record. After an energetic publicity campaign, however, sales of 'hay-water' took a turn for the better and by 1685 usage
in Holland had surged to 20,000 pounds a year.[30]

In Britain it caught on more quickly. The first public tea sale was
held in 1657 and three years later Samuel Pepys tried his first 'cup of
tee (a China drink) of which I never had drank before'.[31] The merchants claimed, as they always did when offering something new, that

Dutch merchants sampling tea in a Chinese warehouse.

here was the ultimate panacea – an infallible cure for migraine,
drowsiness, apoplexy, lethargy, paralysis, vertigo, epilepsy, catarrh,
colic, gallstones and consumption. Whether or not the public found
such claims convincing, by the decade 1770 to 1779 18 million pounds
of tea a year (three-quarters of it said to be smuggled) were being
consumed by the English, which was the equivalent of about two
pounds per head.* It was still relatively expensive, but good value
since a pound of tea can make almost 300 cups – a fact that recommended it as much to the housewife as to the merchant who paid the
shipping costs.

* Today the figure has trebled.

An innocent drink, a necessary luxury, tea and the British demand for it were to be of immense imperial importance in the nineteenth century. It became India's major plantation industry; it was directly responsible for the Opium War with China, one of the great turning points in relations between Asia and the West; and it saved Sri Lanka's (Ceylon's) economy at the end of the nineteenth century, when rust put an end to the cultivation of coffee.

The other European nation that took to tea drinking on a large scale was Russia, although the ignorant young boyar who arrived in Peking in 1656 with instructions to establish diplomatic relations with China very nearly scuppered the whole future of Sino-Russian trade. First of all, he refused to kow-tow. 'They then presented me with some *Thee* made with Cow's milk and butter,* in the King's name, it being *Lent* I refused to drink it; they told me that I being sent from one great *Tsar* to another mighty Prince, I ought at least to accept it, which I did . . .'[32] By the 1730s, however, several different grades of tea were being imported into Russia, although it was not to become widely popular until the time of Catherine the Great.

For the Siberian nomads and others who infested the wastes of Central Asia, tea was a food rather than a drink. One eighteenth-century traveller described how it was made, and the complexity of the process is interesting in the context of nomadic tent living. 'The hospitable landlady immediately set her kettle [cauldron] on the fire . . . She took care to wipe it very clean with a horse's tail that hung in a corner of the tent for that purpose; then the water was put into it, and soon after, some coarse bohea tea, which is got from China, and a little salt. When near boiling, she took a large brass ladle and tossed the tea, till the liquor turned very brown. It was now taken off the fire and, after subsiding a little, was poured clear into another vessel. The kettle being wiped clean with the horse's tail, as before, was again set upon the fire. The mistress now prepared a paste, of meal and fresh butter, that hung in a skin near the horse's tail, which was put into the tea-kettle and fried. Upon this paste the tea was again poured; to which was added some good thick cream, taken out of a clean sheep's skin . . . The ladle was again employed, for the space of six minutes, when the tea, being removed from the fire, was allowed to stand a while in order to cool . . . The principal advantage of this tea is, that it both satisfies hunger and quenches thirst. I thought it not disagreeable . . .'[33]

* Mongol rule had left its mark on court taste.

For the Westernized gentry of Catherine's Russia, however, tea was much more delicate and something of a status symbol; it is estimated that the rich were drinking a little over a pound each a year in the early 1790s, and using with it about a quarter of a pound of sugar (which suggests that many people took no sugar at all).[34] But soon afterwards there was a sharp rise in consumption as the tea-drinking habit spread. From just over one and a half ounces per head of population per annum at the beginning of the nineteenth century – much of it the coarse leaf, steamed and pressed, known as brick tea – consumption increased to more than fourteen ounces in 1880. This was a result not only of changing taste but of cost. The opening of five Chinese ports to direct trade with Russia, the cutting of the Suez Canal, the development of Russia's merchant marine, and the opening of the Trans-Siberian Railway all combined to ease the trade situation and make tea so cheap that almost everyone could drink it.

None of the new tea-drinking nations, however, quite appreciated how much difference the quality of the water made to the final infusion. China, which had always known it, seems to have passed on the knowledge only to Japan. There is even a permanent reminder of the fact in Tokyo, in the form of an underground station, Ochanomisu, which takes its name from the once-pure stream flowing nearby – a name that means 'the emperor's tea water'.

India under the Mughals

For hundreds of years groups of Muslims had been drifting into northern India, bringing with them their everyday foods and cooking methods, but when the Muslim empire of the Mughals was established in the sixteenth century a new *haute cuisine* was introduced into India in the form of 'Mughlai' cooking. This style of cooking had been strongly influenced by that of Isfahan in Persia – a place that was as much a symbol of splendour to sixteenth-century Muslims as Versailles to seventeenth-century Frenchmen – which in turn had owed much to the cuisine of Baghdad in the great days of the caliphate.

What was now introduced into India, therefore, included kebabs, pilaf (or pilau) dishes of rice with shredded meat, the trick of mixing fruit into flesh dishes, the use of almonds, almond milk and rose water, and the garnishing of many kinds of food with fragile wafers of tissue beaten out of pure gold and silver. All of these were swiftly absorbed into the cuisine of the Indian princes. Although Muslims did eat beef, their preferred meats were mutton and chicken, so non-

A garden in Kashmir – apples, melons, grapes, watercress, radishes, asparagus, aubergines . . .

vegetarian Hindus could adopt Mughlai-style food without hesitation.

Naturally enough, the new style became most common in the north of India, the heartland of Mughal rule. Even today, the cooking of Kashmir and the Punjab has almost as many links with the Near East as with traditional India. In Kashmir, where Muslims and Hindus shared the landscape for most of the 400 years before 1947 (when what had once been India was partitioned into Hindu India and Muslim Pakistan), it was the minor rather than the major details of the menu that distinguished one cuisine from the other, even if in some ways old habits died hard; Hindus continued to eat far more vegetables than meat, and Muslims more meat than vegetables. Both, however, relied basically on rice and either kohlrabi or a vegetable not unlike spring greens, livened up (after the introductions from America) with red or green chillis. Even so, initiates were always able to tell the Hindu version from the Muslim. Hindus added *hing* (asafoetida), and Muslims, garlic.

The Indian constitution still recognizes thirteen major languages, while there are more than 300 minor ones in everyday use, and since it is probably fair to say that for every language there is an individual version of the Indian cuisine, it is virtually impossible to trace the spread of any culinary influence beyond the obvious.

One very obvious one, however, was a Muslim innovation that spread through the subcontinent with remarkable speed – an addiction to sweetmeats. Just as Spain had learned of marzipan and nougat from the Arabs, so India discovered the delights of sugar candy. (The word 'candy' is derived from the Arabic for sugar.) Confections of all kinds, made from sugar alone, from sugar and almonds, from sugar and rice flour, from sugar and coconut, became immensely popular as did sweet desserts such as *halwa*.* But although Hindus ate candies with enthusiasm, it was the Muslims who were expert at their manufacture. Predominantly Muslim cities like Dacca and Lucknow became, and have remained, the great sweetmeat centres of the sub-continent.

As Muslim power began to falter in the anarchic early decades of the eighteenth century, the traveller from Britain, France, Portugal, Holland or Denmark would have found a number of his compatriots settled comfortably in their trading posts in India, living in semi-Indian style, eating semi-Indian food and begetting semi-Indian children. They had already begun to develop the bogus Hindu-Muslim-European cuisine that has been passed off in the West ever since as 'Indian'. Punjabi-Muslim food suffered least, perhaps, because while the Europeans found it necessary to change the whole character of 'curry' by loading it with meat or poultry, many Punjabi-Muslim dishes were already based on meat and therefore less in need of Europeanization.

Among the favourite European dishes at Surat on the north-west coast of India were two that were characteristically Muslim. One was the enticingly named 'dumpoked fowl' (from the Persian *dampukht*, meaning 'air-cooked'), which was butter-braised chicken stuffed with rice, almonds and raisins. Another was kebabs, 'beef or mutton cut into small pieces, sprinkled with salt and pepper, and dipped with oil and garlic . . . then roasted on a spit, with sweet herbs put between every piece and stuffed in them, and basted with oil and garlic all the while.'[36]

Neither dumpoked fowl nor the kebab was to infiltrate the north European cuisine until well into the twentieth century, but curry made an early appearance in the seventeenth-century Portuguese cookery book *Arte de Cozinha*. In the next century curry recipes appeared in

---

* Mughlai *halwa* probably resembled modern halva – based on puréed vege-tables or grain, enriched with sugar and almonds – more than the Baghdad original, which was more like an almond-spiked fudge.[35]

England, too, along with others for mulligatawny soup (whose name derives from the Tamil for 'pepper water'), a number of chutneys and a few spicy ketchups or catsups. The latter seem to have originated in China, possibly as dipping sauces, and found their way via south-east Asia to India and thence to Britain. The word 'ketchup' comes from the Siamese *kachiap*.[37]

Kebabs cooking over charcoal, the skewers resting on stones.

The visitor from 'Home' would have been – and sometimes was – shocked by the serious and often successful attempts made by Europeans in India to eat and drink themselves to death. Sitting down to dine at one or two in the afternoon, they would spend three hours over an immensely heavy dinner washed down (by the abstemious) with five or six glasses of Madeira. The mortality rates were appalling. Even in the space of a year, between 1756 and 1757, one newly arrived army contingent lost 87 of its 848 men, not from 'epidemical nor malignant disorders' but from irreparable liver damage caused by over-eating and alcoholism.[38]

A century earlier alcoholism would have been to some extent understandable; the water was dangerous and there were few familiar alternatives. But by the mid-eighteenth century chocolate, tea and coffee were well known, and the great centre of coffee production was not very far away from India – at Mocha, near Aden, at the southern tip of the Red Sea.

COFFEE

Coffee originated in Ethiopia, and there are as many myths about who first discovered that it was edible, and then drinkable, as there are about the origins of wine. In fact, the word 'coffee' comes, via the Turkish *kahveh*, from Arabic *qahwah*, which originally meant 'wine'. Coffee became the wine of the Muslims, to whom real wine was forbidden.

Cultivation of the wild *coffea arabica* bush may have begun as early as the sixth century, although the first written reference is attributed to a tenth-century Arab physician. To begin with, the berries seem to have been chewed whole or else crushed to a paste with fat (presumably mutton fat). Later, the entire fruit was infused to make a kind of tisane, but it was only when in the thirteenth century the beans were cleaned and roasted before infusing that modern coffee was invented. It is said to have achieved its first real popularity among Muslims with the religious sect known as dervishes, whose devotions included chanting and whirling continuously until they were reduced to a state of catalepsy. The effect of the caffeine would presumably be to extend the pre-cataleptic period and thus the length of the devotions.

The fashion for coffee reached Aden in the middle of the fifteenth century, travelling from there to Mecca, then to Cairo, Damascus and Aleppo, from which it passed to Constantinople, where the first coffee house was established in 1554.[39]

During the next half-century European travellers sometimes made vague reference to it, but it was left to William Lithgow in 1610 to note down fuller details, remarking that although the people of Constantinople more usually drank cool sherbets 'composed of water, honey and sugar', which were 'exceedingly delectable in the taste', they preferred to honour guests with 'a cup of coffa, made of a kind of seed called coava, and of a blackish colour; which they drink so hot as possible they can'.[40] Pietro della Valle, a few years later, observed that 'it prevents those who consume it from feeling drowsy. For that reason, students who wish to read into the late hours are fond of it.'[41] *Plus ça change . . .* More critically, Sir Thomas Herbert, encountering coffee in Persia in the 1620s, described it as 'a drink imitating that in the Stygian lake, black, thick and bitter'.[42]

When it first arrived in England the merchants made their usual large claims. According to an advertisement in the London *Publick Adviser* of 19 May 1657, coffee was 'a very wholesome and Physical drink' that 'closes the Orifice of the Stomack, fortifies the heat within, helpeth Digestion, quickeneth the Spirits, maketh the heart lightsom, is good against Eye-sores, Coughs, or Colds, Rhumes, Consumption, Head-ach, Dropsie, Gout, Scurvy, King's Evil and many others'.*

Although coffee may have been imported into Italy as early as 1580, the establishment of coffee houses marked the turning point in Europe. The first of them was opened in Oxford in 1650 by a Jew from Turkey. People flocked to it to taste the new, hot, stimulating (but not intoxicating) drink they had read about in travel books, but if it was curiosity that drew them there the first time, it was the congenial company as much as the coffee that persuaded them to go again.

In England the coffee house was to develop into the gentleman's club, but in the rest of Europe it became a café. Marseilles appears to have had the first coffee house on the continent, in 1671, described as a 'coffee liquor' shop. Paris followed a year later with a series of not-very-successful enterprises, and it was 1686 before the Café Procope – welcoming, clean and luxurious – opened up, the first true Paris café. Three years earlier, coffee had come to Vienna ('Mother of Cafés'),

---

* The advertisers left out one ailment that modern research does, in fact, suggest coffee may be good for – asthma. It is also thought to reduce the chance of developing cancer of the colon; on the other hand, some specialists claim that it increases the likelihood of coronary thrombosis.[43] First choose your disease . . .

when the Turks – retreating from the siege – obligingly left some sacks of green coffee beans behind.

The astute peoples of the Near East maintained control over the trade in beans for as long as they could, and it took the English and Dutch East India Companies fifty years of trading at Mocha before they were able to arrange alternative sources of supply. In 1720 the Dutch discovered that coffee could be grown in their territories on Java, and were later responsible for introducing it to Sri Lanka (Ceylon). The English learned to cultivate it in the West Indies, and most of their supplies from the mid-eighteenth until the early nineteenth century came from there. When they afterwards acquired and began to develop Sri Lanka, they imported large numbers of Tamil labourers from South India, an expedient that has had continuing repercussions in Sri Lankan politics ever since.

Coffee provides an excellent illustration of a frequently ignored rule of history. As happens almost without exception when a country's economy is based on a single profitable export crop, the cultivation of coffee during the last 300 years (in Brazil, Colombia and Costa Rica, as in Sri Lanka) has had the most profound effect on social and political conditions, as well as on local land, labour and capital markets.

THE DARK CONTINENT

Tea, coffee and chocolate were the last of the new discoveries brought in to tempt the palate of Europe in the 300 years that followed the voyages of Columbus and da Gama. Coffee, originally from Ethiopia, and chocolate, from America, were to become two of Africa's most important exports in later times.

But in the eighteenth century slaves were still the most profitable trading specie, surviving their journey to the coast in 'great terror' because of their deeply rooted conviction 'that the whites purchase negroes for the purpose of devouring them, or of selling them to others that they may be devoured hereafter'.[44] And after that terror, there was the different terror of the voyage and what came after.

Often those who were sold in slavery were political offenders or prisoners captured during wars in the interior. A few were already the slaves of African masters. And it is now being suggested that many may have been the indirect victims of famine, sold by their 'lineage heads' (or chiefs) so that the rest of the tribal family would have enough food to survive.[45]

The familiar tragedies of Ethiopia and Sudan in the 1980s are only

A coffee house in eighteenth-century Rome, with all comforts including a charcoal brazier and a billiard table.

the most recent in a line stretching far back into history. In many parts of Africa, especially to the north and south of the tropical forest, the climate is notoriously irregular. Where the whole year's rain – in a good year – may fall in a period of two to four months, there may be no rain at all for three or four years in succession, or rain so scattered

that it is useless. And when torrent replaces drought, there are the
locusts, dormant for years but awakened to destructive activity by the
downpour. Modern swarms have been reported covering 500 square
miles and consuming 50,000 tons of vegetation in a day.[46] It is estimated that in drought-prone regions today, 'normal' life and 'normal'

Hunter with prey. Much of Africa in the eighteenth century was still the
haunt of pre- or early neolithic hunters.

agriculture may be possible in only five years out of ten, and there is nothing to suggest that things were any better in the historical past.

Until the very last years of the eighteenth century Europe knew almost nothing about Africa beyond the coastal fringes, and Africa even less about Europe. The intrepid Grand Tourist might well have starved to death for, as Mungo Park reported during his journey to the Niger in 1796, the white man 'was regarded with astonishment and fear, and was obliged to sit all day without victuals, in the shade of a tree'. When food came, it was probably a fish 'half-boiled upon some embers' or a dish 'made of sour milk and meal, called *sinkatoo*'.[47]

Far away to the south an expedition to the lands of the Orange River in 1801 found a city of more than 10,000 inhabitants in the territory that is now Botswana. Surrounded by barren deserts, the people relied heavily on their cattle, 'whose flesh, however, they eat but very sparingly; milk is mostly used in a curdled state, which they keep . . . in leathern bags and clay pots'.[48] Grain food consisted mainly of millet, and there was also a legume not unlike the pigeon pea, and a small, spotted kind of bean. The people had their own unique way of dealing with these foods. All kinds of grain and pulses, reported the expedition, 'appear to be sown promiscuously and, when reaped, to be thrown indiscriminately into their earthen granaries; from whence they are taken and used without selection, sometimes by [making into flatbread and] broiling, but more generally boiling in milk'.[49]

Ending his Grand Tour on the borders of unknown Africa, the travelling gastronome of the eighteenth century would have learned more about people and nations than if he had gone to study their philosophy or their politics. He would also have had one salutary lesson driven home to him – that while cooking may be an art where food is plentiful, when shortages are the currency of everyday life, filling the stomach is the only art.

—— PART SIX ——

THE MODERN WORLD
1789 UNTIL THE PRESENT DAY

The Industrial Revolution was to change the face of the earth for a second time. Between 1800 and 1901 the population of Europe is estimated to have increased from 180 million to 390 million, and most of the new multitudes were crammed into towns and cities, producing machines, not food. One result was an unprecedented expansion of food production on other continents, an expansion made purposeful by railways, fast ships, and developments in canning, freezing and chilling. It was now possible for huge quantities of wheat from the United States and, later, Canada to be carried half across the world to feed the factory labourers of Europe; for tea to be transported in bulk from China, beef from America, and mutton from Australia. Despite regular scandals over adulteration, most governments thought they were feeding their poor quite well and only discovered they were not when conscription was introduced during the First World War. In Britain 41 per cent of the 2.5 million men medically examined in 1917–18 were rejected as unfit. But by then the existence of vitamins had been discovered and in the next half century the science of nutrition developed in parallel with other new sciences. It seemed, for a while, as if all knowledge would soon be within humanity's grasp. But the end of the story is not yet. The last twenty years have shown that the science of today is in many ways as fallible, as open to error, as all the proto-science of our yesterdays.

19

THE INDUSTRIAL REVOLUTION

'The people was all roaring out *Voilà le boulanger et la boulangère et le petit mitron*, saying that now they should have bread as they now had got the baker and his wife and boy.'[1] The year was 1789, the place Paris, the 'baker', Louis XVI and the 'baker's wife', Marie Antoinette.

The French Revolution had not, as it happened, been sparked off by hunger or high prices, and Marie Antoinette's relentlessly mistranslated remark that if there was no bread, the people should eat 'cake'* was no more than one of those minor but eminently quotable political gaffes that their perpetrators are never allowed to forget. Bread shortages had always been a fact of Parisian life, productive of nothing more serious than an occasional riot. It was only after the middle classes made the first breach in the defences of the privileged élite that the ordinary people of France began to take a hand in the game. While the Constituent Assembly discussed the Declaration of the Rights of Man and the abolition of aristocratic privileges, the market women of Paris took the opportunity of demonstrating their disapproval of the fact that, after a series of disastrous harvests, a four pound loaf now cost 14½ sous. The effective daily wage of a builder's labourer at the time was 18 sous.

Throughout the 1790s far more serious food crises and riots were to bedevil the plans of the revolutionaries and their successors – and to sound a warning to the governments of other countries confronted with the problem of expanding towns and an unprecedented increase in population.

The problem was more one of distribution than production since agricultural developments were taking place that promised to make shortages a thing of the past.

---

* *Brioche*, the word she used, does not mean cake, but a kind of yeast bun. Elizabeth David suggests that the eighteenth-century version was similar to a slightly enriched bread.[2]

SCIENTIFIC AGRICULTURE

Many of the new discoveries in farming first saw the light of day in the Low Countries, where small acreages encouraged a system of intensive cultivation. Enrichment of the soil was a primary need, and the regular collection and use of organic fertilizers became a feature of farming there. In the Flemish areas a seven-course system of crop rotation was developed. A specialized dairy industry also came into being (since cattle provided manure as well as milk) and by 1750 butter and cheese were being exported to neighbouring regions.

The rest of Europe learned from this example. When Frederick the Great set his mind to transforming Prussian agriculture, it was Holland he turned to for guidance. The seven-course rotation system was to prove too complex for countries where land hunger was not so intense, but much of Europe compromised on a four-crop variant – wheat and barley for humans; clover to enrich the soil; turnips for the green tops that smothered weeds as well as for the roots that were used for animal fodder.

Even in the eighteenth century, Holland was famous for butter and cheese (Edam and Gouda).

As the early developments of the Industrial Revolution began to mesh together, it became possible for feedstuffs to be mechanically chopped or pulped, then pressed into convenient feedcakes that enabled farmers to keep their cattle alive throughout the winter. Grain yields were greatly increased when Jethro Tull's seed-planting drill came into use, especially when gears were introduced into the distributing machinery in 1782; less seed was now wasted during planting and much more grain harvested because of the evenness of spread. Eighteenth-century improvements in cast iron also made it possible to mass produce traditional farm implements, which reduced not only the price but the farmer's dependence on the blacksmith.

The revolutionary and Napoleonic wars hurried on the progress of 'scientific agriculture', particularly in Britain, where economic blockade made the home production of grain and meat a priority. War, it was said, had to be waged not only against the Corsican monster but the 'unconquered sterility' of unutilized land. 'Let us not be satisfied', declaimed Sir John Sinclair in 1803, 'with the liberation of Egypt, or the subjugation of Malta, but let us subdue Finchley Common; let us conquer Hounslow Heath; let us compel Epping Forest to submit to the yoke of improvement.'[3]

Improvement had been the watchword of many of England's more thoughtful landowners for some time, although one of the results of their meditations had proved highly injurious to the small farmer and the peasant. In the interests of stock management, what had once been open land now had to be hedged or fenced, and many families whose landlords were more interested in livestock than in people found themselves deprived of the little patches of ground where they had been able to grow a few root crops, tether a cow or raise a pig. The Clearances of the early nineteenth century – which emptied the Scottish Highlands and helped to fill Canada – remain as the harshest symbol of this rational new view of farming.

Nevertheless, the experiments were valuable. They showed the path to the future, and it can also be argued that without the improved efficiency that resulted, the lonely British stand against Napoleon might have failed and the subsequent history of Europe and the world would – for better or for worse – have been very different.

THE FACTORY LABOURER

The pace of urbanization and industrialization in Europe might vary, and so might the timing, but new towns and suburbs were thrown up everywhere to accommodate factories and the people who laboured in them. In 1800 Manchester had 75,000 inhabitants; fifty years later, 400,000. Stockholm, a town of only 6,000 people in 1800, grew to

350,000 by 1914. The 10,000 inhabitants of Düsseldorf in 1800 by 1910 became 360,000. The number of people living in London multiplied by four in just over a century; in Vienna by five; in Berlin by nine; in New York – refuge of so many of Europe's hungry and oppressed – by eighty.[4]

The revolutionary McCormick reaper.

For almost the first time in history massive urban poverty could be observed by anyone who cared to see. Conditions in the industrial towns were shocking, not only to early nineteenth-century philanthropists more accustomed to green fields than high-density housing, but to the people who lived in them and paid dearly for the regular wage that had attracted them there. The adult factory labourer rarely died of simple starvation, but bad housing, worse food and non-existent sanitation took an appalling toll.

Both factories and houses were devitalizing and dehumanizing. Bludgeoned at work by the intolerable clamour of the machines, suffocated by the laden air of the weaving shed, the labourer went home to a cellar, an overcrowded slum or a flimsy shack thrown up out of half-bricks by some speculative builder. Cooking facilities were, at best, sketchy. Water, drawn often from rivers and wells contaminated by the seepage from cesspools, had to be collected from street standpipes that might be turned on for no more than five minutes a day.* Sewage systems were a mockery. Florence Nightingale, in one of

* It was hardly surprising that, as one contemporary commentator remarked, 'It is only when the infant enters on breathing existence and when the man has ceased to breathe – at the moment of birth and at the hour of death – that he is really well washed.'[5]

her sanitation reports, pointedly quoted the London woman who, when asked about drains, replied, 'No, thank God, we have none of them foul stinking things here!'[6]

Hundreds of thousands of children died not only from transmittable diseases but from malnutrition. Friedrich Engels described the diet of

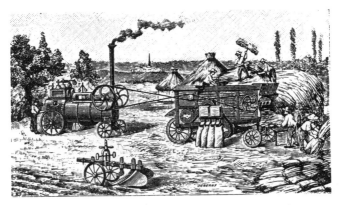

A threshing machine driven by a steam engine.

the poor in the northern manufacturing towns of England in 1844. At the lower end of the poverty scale, 'we find the animal food reduced to a small bit of bacon cut up with the potatoes; lower still, even this disappears, and there remain only bread, cheese, porridge and potatoes, until on the lowest round of the ladder, among the Irish, potatoes form the sole food.'[7] Fifty years later it was reported that 83 per cent of the children in London's Bethnal Green had no solid food other than bread at seventeen out of the twenty-one meals in the week.[8]

Predictably, the people of the Industrial Revolution were chronic sufferers from the scurvy that had formerly been a disease mainly of sailors, while rickets and tuberculosis also sapped their vitality, the first a product of vitamin D deficiency, the second intensified by poor feeding. Lack of vitality, as well as lack of money, perpetuated the diet that helped to cause these diseases in the first place.

In Britain in the 1830s and 1840s a worker might earn anything from five shillings to two pounds a week. In 1841 five shillings bought exactly seven four-pound loaves, just enough to half-fill the stomachs of a typical family of two adults and three children.[9] It left nothing to pay the rent, nothing for tea, nothing for the little piece of bacon that was the poor family's idea of meat.

A 'good meal' consisting of something hot, filling and quickly cooked therefore meant potatoes rather than bread, since potatoes cost only about a shilling for twenty pounds. This left enough in the kitty for tea to go with the potatoes; enabled the man of the house to have a piece of pie or a sausage from a coffee stall at midday; and allowed the whole family to sit down on Sundays to broth, stew and pudding. It was a poverty-line diet, but a great many people lived on it – and a great many others died.

The baked-potato vendor, supplier of the quickest, cheapest hot snack to the town labourer (and predecessor of the fish and chip shop).

A semi-skilled worker on fifteen shillings a week was considerably better off. His household budget might have looked something like this.[10]

	shillings	pence
5 4-lb loaves	3	6½
5 lb meat	2	1
7 pints porter*	1	2
Coal		9½
40 lb potatoes	1	4
3 oz tea, 1 lb sugar	1	6
1 lb butter		9
½ lb soap, ½ lb candles		6½
Rent	2	6
Schooling		4
Miscellaneous		5½
	15s	0d

In bad years the first items to be cut would be meat, porter and butter.

THE POTATO FAMINE

There were several bad years in the 1840s, just as there had been earlier in the century, but the climax came with the first failures of the potato crop in 1845. All the way across Europe, from Ireland to Scotland, to France, Germany and Poland, potatoes began to rot in the fields. In most countries the diet of the poor was seriously affected, especially with the inevitable rise in bread and grain prices, but in Ireland, and to a lesser extent in Scotland, the result was famine.

The potato had been introduced into Ireland in the 1580s and proved its value in the politically stormy centuries that followed. It was not ruined, as grain was, when battle raged over the ground in which it grew; it remained safely hidden throughout the winter, even when the peasant's home and stores were raided or fired by English soldiers; and a tiny cottage plot could produce enough to feed man and wife, six children, even a cow and a pig.

One eighteenth-century observer described the Irish peasant's supper during a period of relative plenty. 'Mark', he said, 'the Irishman's potatoe bowl placed on the floor, the whole family upon

* A dark, heavily hopped beer with a high alcohol content.

their hams around it, devouring a quantity almost incredible, the beggar seating himself to it with a hearty welcome, the pig taking his share as readily as the wife, the cocks, hens, turkies, geese, the cur, the cat, and perhaps the cow – and all partaking of the same dish. No man can often have been a witness of it without being convinced of the plenty, and I will add the cheerfulness that attends it.'[11]

Despite occasional failures and minor famines, nothing occurred to wean the Irish from the potato until in one catastrophic month in 1845 plants all over Europe began first to wilt and then to rot. Tiny, egg-shaped disease spores carried on the winds, beaten down onto the leaves by the rains of a cold, wet summer, devoured the sap and killed the plants. Blight had struck in an acute form.

Potatoes were the staple of the country, as of the town.

It meant more than mere scarcity for the Irish. It meant no seed potatoes from which to grow the next year's crop. It meant that the pig or cow, which might otherwise have been sold to pay the rent, had to be slaughtered because there was nothing for it to fatten on. And no rent paid usually meant eviction by the landlord, either because he was heartless or because he himself was a victim of the shortage.

Hunger was soon compounded by scurvy, brought on by lack of the vitamin C potatoes had supplied, and, later, by failing eyesight and acute nervous debility resulting from shortage of the vitamins A and B₇ that the slaughtered cow's milk would have provided.

One sequel of the Irish potato famine was that Parliament repealed the heavy import duty on grain – an early move towards the free trade that was to have such repercussions on the economy of later nineteenth-century Europe. Another was that many Irish who survived the famine left Ireland forever, some for the growing towns of industrial England, others for the United States. Before 1845 Ireland's annual emigration figure had been approximately 60,000. In 1847 it reached more than 200,000. There was a pause in 1848, when things began to improve, but by 1851 the annual exodus had reached 250,000.

Statistically, the proportion of Irish among immigrants to the United States (44 per cent) was no higher in the five years following the famine than in those preceding it.[12] But that was because there was a great upsurge in emigration from other parts of Europe at the same time, brought on partly by food shortages and partly by severe economic crises and extreme political unrest. In Europe 1848 was 'the year of revolutions'.

BREAD AND MEAT

In industrial Britain in the first half of the nineteenth century, the food of rich and poor alike still came from traditional sources.

Grain was still ground, as it had been for five centuries, in small water- or windmills scattered around the countryside. According to the adjustment of the stones and the fineness of the sifter, different grades of flour could be produced, but none of it was very clean and the oils left in it by the stone-grinding process turned it rancid in a few weeks. Many women still made their own bread, but there was an increasing tendency, particularly in the industrial towns, to buy from the baker. People who held advanced views on hygiene were scandalized to see how commercial bread was made – the perspiration dripping into the dough from the half-naked and far from clean bodies of the kneaders.[13]

The city's meat supply, in most of the world, still arrived on the hoof and was slaughtered in the shambles. London's Smithfield in 1845 was 'an irregular space bounded by dirty houses and the ragged party walls of demolished habitations',[14] and it was estimated that 4,100 cattle and 30,000 sheep, as well as unnumbered pigs and calves, could be crammed into this space ready for slaughter and distribution to retailers and restaurants, as well as to the 'triperies, bone-boiling houses, gut-scraperies' and other marginal trades located nearby.

Slaughterhouses were much the same the world over. The butchers moved placidly about their business, 'wading in blood and covered with it all over. Between them lay the skulls and bones, strewed about in wild confusion; the entrails, which were afterwards loaded upon waggons and carried off; and beyond . . . the unborn calves were lying, in a heap of perhaps thirty or forty; near which, boys standing up to their shoulders in blood, were engaged in stripping off the skin of the largest and most mature ones.'[15]

The day of the 'humane killer' had not yet arrived, though it seems that a skilful slaughterman of the old school was no less humane.[16] However, since the keeping quality of meat depends largely on there being no blood in the carcass, and since the only way to drain a carcass thoroughly is to utilize the pumping action of the victim's own heart, the animal destined for the table has to be stunned first and then bled before it dies. The slaughterhouse is no place for the soft-hearted meat-eater.

It was no place for a lady, either, but that did not prevent gently-bred Victorians from paying it a regular visit in order to partake of a strengthening glass of blood.

Blood was thought of as a specific against consumption (tuberculosis).

ADULTERATION

One of the first subjects to find itself under the new and improved microscope of the nineteenth-century scientist was adulteration.

Ingenious retailers had always practised it on a limited and local scale whenever they had the chance, but the growth of towns and the expansion of roads and railways brought into being, rather too quickly, an organized food industry that was not equipped to cope with problems of handling, transport, availability of raw materials, storage life and marketing. If a particular product was scarce and expensive, wholesalers and retailers had no hesitation in looking for ways to increase the quantity and reduce the selling price.

The simplest way was to bulk out the genuine article with a cheap additive, which might, or might not, be harmful. Pepper had always been adulterated with comparatively innocuous materials like mustard husks, pea flour, juniper berries, and a commodity known as 'pepper dust', which appears to have consisted of the sweepings of the store-room floor.*

Tea had also been counterfeited on a grand scale in the early days, when it was subject to heavy excise duty. There was a flourishing trade in 'smouch', a substance made from ash leaves dried and curled on copper plates, which was sold to tea merchants at a few pence per pound to be mixed with the real stuff. This trick became so common in the last decades of the eighteenth century that Parliament passed an Act condemning it, not only because it cheated the revenue and con-tributed to the 'ruin of fair trade and the encouragement of idleness', but because it resulted in the 'destruction of great quantities of timber, woods and underwoods'.[18]

China tea was green, and fake varieties were often produced from thorn leaves by drying them and then colouring them with verdigris, which was, of course, poisonous. But with the introduction of black Indian tea, easier, cheaper and generally less dangerous alternatives presented themselves. The usual thing was for merchants simply to buy up used tea leaves from hotels, coffee houses and the servants of the rich, stiffen them with a gum solution and re-tint them with black lead. Even after treatment with verdigris or lead, however, tea was still a healthier drink than some of the 'gin' that had been sold a century earlier – compounded, according to one recipe, from in-gredients that included sulphuric acid and oil of turpentine.

Just as there had always been adulteration, so there had always been customers who complained about it. But it was only when the German-born scientist Frederick Accum set the matter out in the scientific terms so dear to the nineteenth-century heart that the public really began to understand how widespread and dangerous the practice had become.

* The preferred adulterant today is papaya seed.[17]

Accum's book *A Treatise on Adulterations of Food, and Culinary Poisons* (1820) revealed to all what was already known in legal and governmental circles: that 'crusted old port' was new port crusted with supertartrate of potash; that pickles owed their appetizing green colour to copper; that many table wines gained their 'nutty' flavour from bitter almonds, which contain prussic acid; that the rainbow hues of London's boiled sweets were produced by the highly poisonous salts of copper and lead; that most commercial bread was loaded with alum; and that the rich orange rind of Gloucester cheese came from ordinary red lead.

The storm that broke over Accum's head when his book was published ultimately drove him from the country, but although the enraged adulterators of food and drink were temporarily victorious, the public had been alerted and listened with attention when later reformers gathered enough courage to reopen the question.

In England this time came in 1850 when the *Lancet*, the medical journal, announced the appointment of an Analytical and Sanitary Commission. Between 1851 and 1854 the two commissioners – Dr Arthur Hill Hassall, a chemist, and Dr Henry Lethaby, a dietician – published a long series of articles reporting on the extraneous matter to be found in samples of staple foods bought at random in London shops. Hassall analysed forty-nine loaves from various sources, not one of which proved to be free from alum, the mineral-salt whitening agent,* and reported that coffee was almost invariably diluted with chicory, acorns or mangelwurzel (a kind of beet). Other researchers also discovered that publicans put the froth on their beer by doctoring it with green vitriol or sulphate of iron, and that cocoa powder often contained a large admixture of brick dust. In 1860, as a direct result of the *Lancet*'s investigations, the first British Food and Drugs Act was passed. It was drastically revised and strengthened in 1872.

Despite subsequent regulations on food purity in almost every country, however, independent venturers have continued to sidestep the law. Among the more disarming twentieth-century cases was that of an Italian gentleman who was charged in 1969 with selling a product described as grated Parmesan cheese – which turned out, on analysis, to consist of grated umbrella handles (Malacca, presumably). Another was the firm selling salami that not only looked like plastic and tasted like plastic, but *was* plastic.[19]

---

* Commercial bread flour today is bleached with chlorine dioxide, which is said to be harmless.

However, adulterated products sometimes have their uses. Austria is reported to have found a way to dispose of the millions of litres of wine withdrawn from the market in 1985 when it was found to be spiked with the anti-freeze component diethylene glycol. Mixed with road salt, the adulterated wine melts ice on the highways much more effectively than salt alone, while doing less environmental damage to trees, plants and the water table.[20]

THE RICH AND THE MIDDLE CLASSES

During the nineteenth century there was something of a population explosion among the middle classes, not because of increased fertility* but because factory owners needed the services of lawyers, bankers and insurers, shippers and carriers, engineers and architects, managers

The kitchens of the Royal Pavilion, as they were in Carême's day.

and clerks, while growing towns needed more shops, more schools, more doctors and more clergymen. Demand created supply, and a great many bright, ambitious young men were ready and waiting for the opportunity to move up in the world.

* Although that came too in the latter decades of the century.

Some of the new middle classes were very little richer than the factory labourer, others not much poorer than the great hereditary landowners, but all had a margin, however slight, of income over expenditure. They were not forced to eat what was cheapest but were able to exercise some choice, and their choice when they entertained (if not every day) was governed by the Jones factor; the middle-class dinner menu was an economy-conscious reflection of what people ate on the next level up on the social scale.

The somewhat haphazard medieval menu had survived in England and America until well into the eighteenth century. The two-course dinner for an ordinary household suggested in *The Compleat House-wife* in 1727 was still markedly similar in style to the fourteenth-century French menu given on p. 185.

FIRST COURSE	SECOND COURSE
Soup	Four partridges and two quails
Ragoût of breast of veal	Lobsters
Roast venison	Almond cheesecake and custards
Broiled leg of lamb with cauliflower	
	With smaller dishes of
	Four pocket and lamb stones
With smaller dishes of	[otherwise known as *animelles*
Jugged hare	or 'lamb's fry', i.e. testicles]
A marrow pudding	Apricot fritters
Stewed eels	Sturgeon
Stewed carp	Fried sole
A palpatoon or	Green peas
˙pupton of pigeons	Potted pigeons
[a kind of hot pâté]	
A roast pig	

By the early nineteenth century, however, partly under the influence of chefs who had fled from revolutionary France, things were beginning to change. French menus by that time had become not so much rationalized as codified. A number of dishes still appeared on the table simultaneously, but they appeared in fairly logical groups, each with a special name.* There were now three courses, the first embracing appetizers and main dishes, the second 'afters' (in the general sense of puddings and savouries), and the third being supplied not from the meat kitchen but by the pastrycook. The serving routine went like this:

FIRST COURSE

The Appetizers

Four tureens of different soups were placed at the corners of the table, while the *entrées* – light 'made dishes' intended to serve as an introduction to the more substantial meats that came later – were ranged tidily along the sides (hence 'side dishes').

When the soups had been disposed of, the tureens were removed and replaced with four dishes of fish (hence the name *relevé*, or 'remove', for this second instalment of the first course).

This was not all, however. The peaceful consumption of soup, fish and *entrées* was constantly interrupted by servants offering platters of salted or preserved meats, or hot dishes of kidneys, liver and the like. These, which were in effect *hors-d'oeuvre* ('extras') designed to stimulate the gastric juices, were known as *assiettes volantes* or *entrées volantes* ('flying dishes' or 'flying entrées') partly because they were light, but mainly because they were passed round instead of being placed on the table. In later times the term *assiette volante* came to be applied to things like soufflés that could not be left standing but had to be served immediately.

Main Dishes

These, consisting of game birds, poultry and large joints of meat, were the *pièces de résistance*, the 'substantial food' or backbone of the meal. Usually, they were garnished with vegetables, and salads were also served.

SECOND COURSE

'Afters'

This was a motley assortment in the old tradition, consisting of cold meats, savouries, aspics, vegetable dishes and sweet dishes, collectively

---

* For a time each group seems to have been elevated into a course, but the inconvenience of having the table cleared and reset six or eight times during the progress of a meal must have proved unacceptable.

known as *entremets*, or 'between-courses', since they came between the meats and the concluding pastries and ices. (*Entremets* in medieval times had not meant food but the entertainment offered to guests while one course was being cleared away and another set.)

This was the system followed in France, but not when the British and others began to adopt the new style of menu planning. The British had always been scornful of French kickshaws – which covered almost everything that came under the headings of *hors-d'oeuvre*, *entrée* or *entremets* – and therefore felt it necessary to make a few adjustments. As one well-travelled diner remarked, kickshaws in England usually consisted of 'very mild but abortive attempts at Continental cooking, and I have always observed that they met with the neglect and contempt that they merited'.[21]

The main change during the Anglicization process involved splitting the courses not after the *pièces de résistance* but in the middle of them, so that the first course consisted of soup, fish, *entrées* and roast or boiled meats, and the second of roast poultry, game birds and *entremets*. It was an ingenious way of ensuring that British diners could find something 'plain and wholesome' in both courses, and so avoid eating kickshaws altogether.

Other changes grew out of the chefs' attempts to bridge the gap between the French language and British taste, and ultimately made nonsense of a culinary jargon that had originally been precise. When soup and fish were served together and taken away together, the *pièces de résistance* that replaced them became, in effect, 'the remove'. *Entrées*, as tastes changed and people began to look down on the plain old-fashioned roast, ceased to be introductory dishes and sometimes came to replace the *pièces de résistance*. And when pastrycooks (and the third course for which they had been responsible) disappeared from all but the grandest houses, pastries and ices were served simultaneously with the *entremets*, which thus, instead of being the 'between-courses', became the last course.

A truly magnificent version of the partly Anglicized French dinner was given by the Prince Regent at the Brighton Pavilion on 15 January 1817, his kitchens at that time being presided over by Antonin Carême, the first of the great nineteenth-century chefs.

It began with four soups:

Le potage à la Monglas	Creamy brown soup made with *foie gras*, truffles, mushrooms and Madeira

La garbure aux choux	Country-style vegetable broth with shredded cabbage
Le potage d'orge perlée à la Crécy	A delicate pink purée of pearl barley and carrots
Le potage de poissons à la russe	'Russian-style' fish soup, probably made from sturgeon

The soups were 'removed' with four fish dishes:

La matelote au vin de Bordeaux	A light stew of freshwater fish cooked in wine from Bordeaux
Les truites au bleu à la provençale	Lightly-cooked trout with a tomato and garlic sauce
Le turbot à l'anglaise, sauce aux homards	Poached turbot with lobster sauce
La grosse anguille à la régence	A large fat eel, richly sauced, garnished with quenelles, truffles and cocks' combs

The fish dishes were followed (the trout and turbot remaining on the table, the *matelote* and eels being taken away) by four *grosses pièces* or *pièces de résistance*:

Le jambon à la broche au Madère	Spit roasted ham with Madeira sauce
L'oie braisée aux racines glacées	Braised goose with glazed root vegetables
Les poulardes à la Perigueux	Truffled roast chickens
Le rond de veau à la royale	Round of veal, enrobed in a creamy sauce, finished with truffle purée and various garnishes

These *grosses pièces* (*and* the turbot *and* the trout) were flanked by no less than thirty-six *entrées*, of which those below form a representative selection:

Les filets de volaille à la maréchale	Boned chicken breasts, egged, crumbed, and fried in butter
Le sauté de merlans aux fines herbes	Sautéd whiting with herbs
La timbale de macaroni à la napolitaine	Macaroni and grated cheese, layered with forcemeat and steamed in a mould
La noix de veau à la jardinière	Rump of veal with fresh vegetables
La darne de saumon au beurre de Montpellier	Middle-cut salmon steak with a sauce of creamed butter blended with green herbs, egg yolks, capers, anchovies etc.
Le sauté de faisans aux truffes	Sautéd pieces of pheasant with truffles
Le turban de filets de lapereaux	A ring of fillets from the breasts of young wild rabbits
Les boudins de volaille à la béchamel	Stuffed chicken quenelles with béchamel sauce
Le sauté de ris de veau à la provençale	Sautéd calves' sweetbreads with tomatoes and garlic
Les galantines de perdreaux à la gelée	Boned, stuffed partridges in aspic
Les petites croustades de mauviettes au gratin	Roast larks, each in a pastry or crisp bread case lined with creamed chicken livers
La côte de boeuf aux oignons glacés	Beef sirloin with glazed onions
La salade de filets de brochets aux huîtres	Salad of pike fillets with oysters
Le pain de carpe au beurre d'anchois	Carp forcemeat steamed in a mould and served with anchovy butter

In addition, there were five *assiettes volantes* of fillets of sole, and five of fillets of hazel grouse covered with a béchamel sauce blended with soured cream and browned in the oven.

All this was only the first course.

Afterwards, eight majestic set pieces were brought in, some of them – made of sugar icing moulded into representations of 'The Chinese hermitage' or 'The ruin of the Turkish mosque' – designed to be looked at, others, like the cheese brioche, French nougat, and orange biscuit, to be nibbled. Then there were four roasts of game and poultry; cockerels, wild duck, chickens and hazel grouse. And thirty-two *entremets*, including ember-roasted truffles, lobster au gratin, pineapple cream, cucumbers in white sauce, liqueur-flavoured jelly, oysters, stuffed lettuce, potatoes in Hollandaise sauce, scrambled eggs with truffles,* spongy Genoese cakes with coffee filling, and so on. And another ten *assiettes volantes*, five containing miniature potato soufflés, and five chocolate soufflés.

Whether the side dishes were superb, as at the tables supplied by Carême, or, as more often, heavy and uninspired, no diner was expected to try them all. Digestively, it would have been difficult enough, but the mechanics of table service made it almost impossible.

What happened with *service à la française* (a style of serving whose days, in the early nineteenth century, were already numbered) was that, once the soup had been taken away and the covers removed from the fish and entrée dishes, 'every man helps the dish before him, and offers some of it to his neighbour . . . If he wishes for anything else, he must ask across the table, or send a servant for it – a very troublesome custom.'[22] It was a custom that was more than troublesome; it also required a degree of self-assertion. The shy or ignorant guest limited not only his own menu but also that of everyone else at the table. Indeed, one young divinity student ruined his future prospects when, invited to dine by an archbishop who was due to examine him in the scriptures, he found before him a dish of ruffs and reeves, wild birds that (although he was too inexperienced to know it) were a rare delicacy.

'Out of sheer modesty the clerical tyro confined himself exclusively to the dish before him, and persevered in his indiscriminating attentions to it till one of the resident dignitaries (all of whom were waiting only the proper moment to participate) observed him, and called the attention of the company by a loud exclamation of alarm. But the warning came too late: the ruffs and reeves had vanished to a bird, and with them . . . all the candidate's chances of preferment.'[23]

Service *à la française* also played havoc with conversation. Oliver

---

* To judge by the menu, there must have been a superlative truffle harvest that year.

Goldsmith had already found it matter for satire in the 1760s, when he wrote of a gentleman embarking at dinner on a good story about 'a farmer of my parish, who used to sup upon wild ducks and flummery; so this farmer – "Doctor Marrowfat", cries his lordship, interrupting him, "give me leave to drink your health" – so being fond of wild ducks and flummery – "Doctor", adds a gentleman who sate next him, "let me advise to a wing of this turkey" – so this farmer being fond – "Hob, nob, Doctor, which do you choose, white or red?" – so being fond of wild ducks and flummery – "Take care of your hand, Sir, it may dip in the gravy."' Later, it was, 'Excellent, the very thing; let me recommend the pig, do but taste the bacon; never eat a better thing in my life . . .'[24]

By the 1830s some of the work entailed in service *à la française* was being delegated to servants, but this proved just as much of a trial to the sensitive gourmet. 'Meaning to be very polite, [they] dodge about to offer each *entrée* to ladies in the first instance; confusion arises, and whilst the same dishes are offered two or three times over to some guests, the same unhappy wights have no option of others.'[25]

It may have been the middle classes who hastened the changeover from service *à la française* to service *à la russe*, since regular and competitive entertaining was part of the new ethos. The nobility in their stately homes had capable staff and experienced butlers and stewards to oversee every detail, but the middle-class Victorian lady had only herself and a handful of untrained, sometimes profoundly ignorant beginners. It must have been a great strain to be actively involved in serving a twenty-five-dish dinner to eighteen people while trying to meet all the other conversational and supervisory responsibilities of the good hostess. Service *a la russe* eased some of the burdens. Here the serving dishes were laid out on the sideboard and the servants handed them round to guests in strict rotation. The first servant would come, offering meat, then another with a dish of potatoes, then a third with a platter of vegetables and a fourth with the sauce boat. No exercise of judgement was required on the servants' part and even the rawest recruit could be expected to grasp the routine. The lady of the house was able to breathe at last and dinners ceased to resemble feeding time at the zoo.

The new system did not please everyone, however. Even with the most efficient attendance, the dishes were 'provokingly lagging, one thing after another, so that contentment is out of the question'.[26] It is a sensation not unknown at formal dinners today.

One immediate effect of the new style was to reduce the total number of dishes served. Clearly, it was impossible – without extending the meal to inordinate length – for servants to offer four soups, four fish dishes, three dozen *entrées*, ten *assiettes volantes*, four *pièces de résistance*, and so on. But the end result was not, as might be thought, that people began to eat less. When service *à la russe* replaced the three buffet-display courses of the old French style, the menu expanded to take in six or eight *obligatory* courses that, in effect, forced more food on the diner than he necessarily wanted, while giving him less in the way of choice.

Great changes were wrought in less than a hundred years. Escoffier's 1911 menu celebrating the coronation of George V was a world away from that presented by Carême at the Royal Pavilion in 1817.

Caviar
Cantaloupe melon

Clear turtle soup
Cold chicken velouté soup

Roast chicken George V

Saddle of Welsh lamb
Peas *à l'anglaise*

Duckling breasts in port-wine aspic

Quail with grapes

Salade orientale
Artichoke hearts Grand Duc

Peaches Queen Mary
Petits fours
Fruit

SCHMALTZ, BAGELS AND PASTRAMI-ON-RYE

For the rich in America, food was not very different, but the same was not true on other levels of society.

At the beginning of the nineteenth century Thomas Jefferson had said, 'In Europe, the object is to make the most of their land, labor being abundant; here, it is to make the most of our labor, land being abundant.'[27]

The great immigrations, particularly the waves that followed 1848 and 1885, changed all that. Until after the Civil War most of America's gross national product was still attributable to the processing of agricultural output by flour mills, tanneries, meat-packing plants and breweries,[28] but as peasants and artisans flooded in from all the countries of Europe – so that, at times, America began to look like a nation of ethnic minorities – industry began to rival agriculture in importance.

Many of the incomers, illiterate even in their own language, found it necessary to cling together in urban enclaves (some of which persist even today). Others, by no means illiterate, gravitated towards particular areas for the more comfortable reason that there they could find familiar foodstuffs – the most reassuring thing on earth for people severed from their roots. For Jews, needing everything kosher, it was not just reassuring; it was essential.

One of the minor but more intriguing mysteries of history is how so many foods that are now thought of as all-American (or perhaps all-New-York would be more accurate) came to be adopted from a cuisine designed more than 3,000 years ago to be exclusive, rather than shared. Other groups of immigrants introduced their own specialities into America, their cookies, their chowders and their slaws, and these became naturalized over a period of centuries. But bagels and lox managed the same trick in a matter of decades.

Perhaps most of it can be put down to the delicatessen,* but a surprising number of fragments of the Yiddish tongue have infiltrated Gentile speech and thought by way of the cuisine. *Schmaltz*, that extreme sentimentalism characteristic of mid-period Hollywood, literally means chicken fat. And when the Pentagon talked of 'the bagel strategy' in the context of bombing patterns during the Vietnam War, no American needed to be told anything more; it meant dropping bombs in rings around the target.†

In the United States today many Jews who have long since abandoned the rituals of Jewishness still sit down to a Friday night meal of noodle soup and roast chicken. They eat plaited loaves, hot salt beef

---

* The delicatessen is so familiar in Britain, too, nowadays, that it is easy to forget how rare it was, even in London, only forty years ago.
† In Britain, the army usually takes the credit for inventing the word *nosh*, but it is in fact Yiddish for snack or titbit.

sandwiches, *gefüllte* fish and *chrayn*, bortsch, matzo balls, and all the festival dishes they brought with them (sometimes the only things they were able to bring with them) from the Old World to the New – stuffed cabbage, stuffed chicken neck, cheesecake and potato pancakes. Many housewives, even the most liberated, still find it impossible to use the same pans and implements for meat cookery as they do for dairy products. Thousands of years of history are not to be shrugged off in a few decades.

20

The Food-supply Revolution

By the 1850s two things had become clear about the food needs and demands of expanding industrial societies. An increasing number of labourers had to be furnished with more food more cheaply. And the new middle classes, possessing no landed estates to supply them with the materials for their *entrées* and *entremets*, were in the market for as wide a variety of socially acceptable foods as the world could provide. It was a situation first defined in Victorian England, but its workings were soon to be observed in the industrializing nations of Europe and the United States of America.

Once the scale of the challenge had been recognized and then, sometimes reluctantly, accepted, many resources were mobilized to meet it. Always throughout history new discoveries and new developments had given rise to further discoveries and developments, but the process had generally been slow. What was so startling about the industrial era was the speed of change, the way in which a specialized and often minor technological improvement in one field of development set off an unforeseen avalanche of progress in others. As an example, improvements in the quality of glass coupled with advances in the science of optics made it possible to manufacture more accurate microscopes, which in turn stimulated biological and chemical research and helped to found the science of bacteriology. The repercussions in medicine, public health, food hygiene and preservation were to be almost incalculable.

It was the railway, however, that had the first and most radical influence on both the quality and quantity of the food available in the cities of the Industrial Revolution. Previously, supplies had been limited by practical factors such as the size of the load that could be hauled by horses or oxen over narrow, pitted roads. Bulky goods had to go by sea, river or canal, which meant that in countries lacking a system of waterways both trade and communications were seriously hampered. But the railway, whose very name in the 1840s was synonymous with profit, changed everything.

In terms of nineteenth-century needs, its bulk carrying capacity was the railway's most immediate recommendation, but its speed was also to prove of benefit.

As was the case with most great cities, London's meat had always been brought in on the hoof, often from many miles' distance, and weary beasts meant poor meat. By the 1850s, however, ready-dressed carcasses were being transported to the capital from as far as Aberdeen, 515 miles away. One contemporary chronicler described Aberdeen as 'a London abattoir. The style in which the butchers of that place dress and pack the carcasses leaves nothing to be desired, and in the course of the year mountains of beef, mutton, pork and veal arrive the night after it is slaughtered in perfect condition.'[1]

The capital's inhabitants were also able to buy better milk than ever before. Until the 1860s town milk was supplied by local cowmen, who had originally kept their animals in the parks and open spaces but had been forced, as the buildings closed in, to resort to dank and insanitary sheds opening off the streets. Many and hideous were the tales told of the thin and watery fluid that was all they could squeeze from their poor, sickly cows, a fluid they sold round the city from buckets topped up with hot water ('Warm from the cow, ma'am!') and open to all the dirt and germs of the air, all the mud and mess of the gutters.

London, 1825; the milk still went straight from cow to customer.

The city cowman's udder-to-doorstep milk at least had no time to turn, unlike the first fresh milk brought in by rail from the countryside. Transported on open trailers, slowly cooling in its traditional pots and jars, it arrived more like dirty cheese. By the end of the 1860s, however, a special kind of mechanical cooler had been developed and metal churns full of quick-cooled milk soon brought a marked improvement in the city's milk supplies.

As well as improving food supplies within the country, railways stimulated trans-oceanic trade by establishing links between farm and seaport. As a result, bulky foods like tea and grain became increasingly important in the world economy. By the last decades of the nineteenth century tea from the new plantations in India and wheat from the new farmlands of North America were flooding into Europe, and the factory worker was able to buy the staples of his diet far more cheaply than ever before.

AMERICAN WHEAT

By the late 1870s the complex of developments set in train by the American Civil War had turned vast expanses of the continent into a granary. Between 1860 and 1900 more than 400 million acres of virgin soil were put under the plough.[2]

Americans had never had to concern themselves with soil conservation systems or scientific crop rotation. They had always had land in excess in relation to the number of people to work it, so that, even when population figures surged as a result of immigration, agriculture still remained oriented towards labour-saving devices such as the McCormick reaper (patented in 1834), the Pitts mechanical thresher (introduced in 1837), the Marsh harvester (1858) and the Appleby binder and knotter for grain sheaves twenty years later. Ploughs were fitted with steel mouldboards, to which prairie soil did not cling. Special cultivators were designed to deal with maize. Combine harvesters were developed to sweep huge fields clean of their crops – machines eventually drawn by as many as thirty horses in harness.

In 1860, at the beginning of the era of expansion, there were 6.2 million draught horses in the United States; forty years later there were 15.5 million. The total value of tools and machinery on American farms multiplied by fourteen in the decades between 1860 and 1920. In 1840 it had taken 233 man-hours to grow a hundred bushels of wheat; by 1920 it took only 87.[3]

The transcontinental railways that opened up the country after the Civil War helped to carry farmers and tools west to the new lands, and grain back to the ports of the eastern seaboard. Here it was loaded into the last of the clippers and the first of the steamships just in time to save the Europe of the 1870s from the results of a series of pitiful harvests.

The overworked soil of Europe was in a sad state. German farming had improved thanks to Liebig's pioneer researches into soil chemistry, but Italian agriculture was actively in decline, and in France, torn for many decades by war and revolution, only one farmholding in fifteen had even as much as a horse-drawn hoe in 1892, only one in 150 a mechanical reaper.[4]

Cheap grain from America – and from a Russia that had finally colonized the rich black soil of its south and south-east and desperately needed exports to finance industrialization – had much the same effect on the European economy as cheap grain from the Balkans had had in the thirteenth century. It supplied an increasingly urgent demand while at the same time throwing the agriculture of other countries into disarray.

In Norway profitability already rested on such a knife-edge that when cheap American cereals began to flood into Europe a great many Norwegians were forced to make the same journey in the opposite direction. In England between 1870 and 1900 the land devoted to grain shrank by more than a quarter, while dairy farming and fruit and vegetable growing increased accordingly (to the benefit of the consumer, if not the farmer). In Denmark farmers turned their attention to bacon production. For some time they had recognized a large potential market in Britain's industrial towns and had succeeded in breeding a pig with stable reproduction and growth features that allowed them to produce bacon of consistent quality, cured just as the English liked it. The Danish butter industry also gained in importance when, in 1877, Gustav de Laval invented a mechanical cream separator that greatly reduced production costs. Of all the countries in Western Europe, Holland was perhaps least changed by the American wheat influx; agriculture there had always been predominantly a matter of cattle, dairy products and vegetables.

By the end of the century social and economic conditions in America led to a slackening off in grain exports, but for Europe the gap was filled by increasing supplies from Canada, the Ukraine and Australia. Except under the special circumstances of total war, the industrial nations of Europe were never again to go short of the materials for their daily bread.

CANNING

What grain and tea from the other side of the world did for industrial Britain was maintain the status quo by ensuring that an increase in population did not mean less food for all. Even the poorest factory worker could afford enough bread to fill his stomach and enough tea to warm it. The less poor had a small budget surplus for bacon or meat.

Bacon, salted and smoked, had a long storage life and had been an international trading commodity for some time, but most of the other preserved foods of earlier times were irrelevant to the nineteenth-century situation. It was not only that really large-scale processing was difficult and frequently uneconomic; it was also that the majority of potential customers in the new industrial towns had neither the time, the space nor the equipment to deal with the special problems they presented.

There had been a hiatus of several centuries in the evolution of preserving techniques, and all that had really been added to the total of medieval experience by the 1790s was the knowledge of how to conserve cooked meats for a limited time by covering them with a thick layer of fat, which excluded air. This discovery seems to have been made in the mid-seventeenth century. A hundred years later good housewives in Europe were potting their fruit syrups and conserves in 'viall glasses',* and at the end of the century, in France, Nicholas Appert combined the two ideas by enclosing meat, fruit, vegetables and even milk in glass bottles that were corked and heated in a bain-marie; the theory was that the heat drove all air from the bottle.

The essential second step, from breakable glass bottle to unbreakable 'tin' cans, was taken by Brian Donkin in England. Donkin had an interest in an iron works and was quick to realize that if Appert's method could be used with tinned iron containers, the prosperity of his business would be assured. By 1812 he had set up a canning factory, and six years later it was turning out satisfactory cured beef, boiled beef, carrots, mutton and vegetable stew, veal and soup.

Canned foods were more expensive than fresh, and for some time were bought mainly by travellers and explorers, who had a continuing need for good, convenient preserved foods. A number of special delicacies, some canned and some in glass, were also dispatched to out-

---

* Ancestors of the Mason jars and Kilner jars of the 1850s.

posts of the empire. As early as the 1830s truffled hare pâté from the Périgord was to be had in Simla and truffled woodcock in Mussoorie, in the foothills of the Himalayas.[5]

Among the most ardent advocates of the new product were seafaring men. It was a well-established custom for passenger ships on long voyages to carry a few live pigs and hens on board, as well as a milk cow or two, and the trials of caring for them were clearly reflected in the enthusiasm with which a former naval captain described, in 1841, the virtues of canned meat. 'Meat thus preserved,' he said, '*eats* nothing, nor *drinks* – it is not apt to die – does not tumble overboard or get its legs broken or its flesh worn off its bones by tumbling about the ship in bad weather . . .'[6]

The size of the potential market soon attracted new manufacturers and trouble began in Britain when one of them, who had a contract to supply the Admiralty, began using larger cans than before – 9 to 14 pounds, instead of the usual 2- to 6-pound sizes. At this time the method was to leave a small hole in the top of the filled cans, to heat them 'in order to drive out the air', and then to close the hole with solder. Everyone thought it was the expulsion of air from the cans that had the preservative effect. But in reality it was the heating that was more important, killing off harmful bacteria, and a level of heat that was adequate for a 6-pound can was not enough to sterilize the contents of the 14-pound size. Nests of bacteria remained in the centre,

Passengers, like livestock, were apt to tumble about in a storm.

which caused the meat to putrefy. In 1850 at one naval victualling yard 111,108 pounds of meat in large-size cans were condemned as unfit for human consumption.

The attendant publicity did nothing for the reputation of canned meat in Britain, and neither did the quality of the mutton that came in from Australia during the next two decades. The meat was coarse and stringy, each can containing an unappetizing lump of overdone and tasteless flesh flanked on one side by a wad of fat and surrounded by a great deal of watery gravy.[7] The experienced cook learned to discard the fat, make the gravy into soup, and cut the meat into neat pieces that, egged, crumbed and browned in the oven or over the fire, made an acceptable dish, especially when there was onion sauce to go with it.[8] The poorer urban housewife served the meat straight from the can, with bread or potatoes on the side.

With all their faults, Australian canned mutton and beef had the great advantage of costing less than half as much as fresh meat in Britain, especially after the disastrous epidemic of cattle disease that raged from 1863 until 1867 and sent the price of home meat soaring. Between 1866 and 1871 imports of Australian meat rose from 16,000 pounds to 22 million.[9]

Australia maintained its lead in the canned-meat export market only until the United States had put the Civil War firmly behind it. Canning factories had been established there as early as 1817 and had soon begun handling not only meat but fish,* and then the fruit and vegetables that were very much an American speciality in the early days of the business. During the Civil War, Union army sutlers carried stocks of American canned meat, oysters and vegetables (even if their customers preferred imported French sardines, salmon and green peas).[11]

After 1868 handmade cans were superseded by machine-cut, and giant canning concerns grew up, especially in Chicago, where assembly lines helped to cut costs and improve standards. Mass production brought a chain reaction. For as long as peas had to be harvested and podded by hand, canning was uneconomic; a mechanical gathering and shelling device soon took care of that. Fish, too, were a problem at first. In the salmon canneries of California Chinese workers were employed to clean and fillet them until the day in 1882 when free

---

* The 'herring boxes without topses' that 'slippers were for Clementine' seem to have been the oval cans in which fish were supplied to the miners of the 1849 Gold Rush.[10]

Chinese immigration into the United States was banned; the invention of the 'iron Chink' swiftly followed.

The flavour of canned food remained open to criticism for many years. Canned peas bore only a distant resemblance to fresh, and salmon was said to taste 'rather of oil than fish, with a palpable touch of tin'.[12] On the other hand, customers on the prairies of the mid-West or in the urban slums of Manchester had no access to, and had probably never even tasted, the fresh product, and so were ready enough to welcome the canned versions, which added much-needed variety to the diet.

Canned foods were convenient and, since the combines established themselves where production costs were lowest, they were also cheap. Their quality began to improve, too, towards the end of the 1870s, by which time manufacturers had learned the lesson of Pasteur's discoveries about the part played by micro-organisms in the 'spoiling' of food. And when, at the end of the century, the Massachusetts Institute of Technology charted the most satisfactory pasteurization times and temperatures for a whole list of foodstuffs, canned foods became not only convenient and cheap, but reliably safe as well.

FREEZING AND CHILLING

In the long run it was to be the canning of fruit and vegetables rather than of meat that did most for the diet of the world's industrial workers, because a more satisfactory method of meat preservation came into use little more than a decade after the first bulk shipments of the canned product in the mid 1860s.

As a preservation process, refrigeration had always been practicable only where there were supplies of hard natural ice. The Chinese had discovered how to keep winter ice for summer use as early as the eighth century BC by building ice houses kept cool by evaporation. By Tang times they had learned to collect huge blocks of ice from the mountains or from frozen rivers and ponds and to bury them in caves or underground pits that acted as giant refrigerators. Insulated by the surrounding soil, the ice did not begin to melt until the heat of the sun penetrated the earth to a depth of several feet. In the sixteenth century ice-packed fresh plums, loquats, the fruit of the strawberry tree, fresh bamboo shoots, and shad were being transported by water to the palace at Peking; on such journeys, the imperial Directorate of Foodstuffs took priority over almost all the other shipping on the Grand Canal.[13] A few decades later the Mughal emperors of India were sending relays of horsemen to bring ice and snow back to Delhi from the Hindu Kush, although this appears to have been intended for immediate use in fruit sorbets rather than for preservation.*

Ice in British India. Where night temperatures were low, the sahibs' servants could ladle water into shallow pans in the evenings, and then, somewhere around 3 a.m., chip it out as ice and rush it to heavily insulated ice houses.

Ice houses were becoming a common feature in Europe's stately homes by the eighteenth century and had been known for longer in the United States, where the Shakers were the acknowledged experts on the subject. Shaker ice houses had heavy-timbered double walls, the gap packed with sawdust; triple roofs insulated in the same way; and stone floors carpeted with sawdust on top of straw. By 1833 the Americans had even mastered the technique of shipping blocks of 'fine clear ice' from Massachusetts to faraway Calcutta. But all these were, so to speak, custom-designed enterprises, dependent on climate and the availability of natural ice.

Then, in the 1830s, ice-making machines began to be patented. These made use either of the expansion of compressed air or the much older technique of evaporation, applied now not to water but to highly volatile substances like liquid ammonia. By the 1850s James Harrison, a Glasgow man who had emigrated to Australia, had

---

* The same, of course, was true of the ice the Italians (or Sicilians) collected from the mountains for the ice cream that is believed to have been their sixteenth- or early seventeenth-century invention.

designed not only an improved ether-compressor which made it possible to operate an ice factory, but (which made him considerably more popular) a refrigerating machine that enabled Australian brewers

For a subscription of $15 the season (May to September), a New York family in 1806 could take delivery of eight pounds of ice per day.

to make beer even in hot weather. In 1873 a public banquet was held at which guests ate meat, poultry and fish that had been frozen for six months.

But freezing plants that were effective on land were not suitable for long sea voyages. Attempts to ship frozen meat from Australia to England were unsuccessful until ammonia-compression replaced ether-compression. In 1877 the SS *Paraguay* successfully carried a cargo of frozen meat from the Argentine to France, and three years later the first load of frozen beef and mutton was shipped from Australia to the United Kingdom. Frozen mutton and lamb followed from New Zealand a few months later.

Chilling, or cool storage, was being developed at much the same time. The first method was to surround the food with a mixture of ice and salt; later, a compressed-air refrigerating machine was used. Since chilling had a less detrimental effect on the quality of meat than freezing and was also quite adequate for relatively short voyages like that from America, beef from the Americas dominated the British market from the 1880s until well after the turn of the century.

Eggs, dairy products, and delicate fruits and vegetables also responded well to chilling once the packers and shippers had discovered the best conditions for each type. Bananas from the West Indies were among the fruits that began to arrive in Europe, in quantity, from the late nineteenth century onwards.

Manufactured ice played a major role in restoring the fortunes of the fishing industry. Pickled herring had been almost the only fish available to the factory labourer during the first half of the century, and it was a fish with limited appeal. In the 1860s and 1870s, however, there appeared the steam trawler, which could travel far and reasonably fast carrying good stocks of ice in the hold. Fish packed in ice immediately after the catch could be kept chilled throughout its journey back to port and then to the city fishmonger.

One coincidental result was the growth of that British institution the fish-and-chip shop. Who first had the idea of marrying batter-coated, deep-fried cod or haddock with fingers of deep-fried potatoes remains a matter of sometimes acrimonious debate. There are claimants from Lancashire, London and Dundee, and the dates put forward range from 1864 to 1874. But the hot-pie shop was well-established in Victorian England, and it seems likely that the fried-fish shop, if not the fish-and-chip shop itself may have been a direct development.

Whatever the truth of its origins, however, the fish-and-chip shop made a valuable contribution to the protein and vitamin C intake of the urban labourer from the latter decades of the nineteenth century until the middle of the twentieth.

Meat for the Millions

With a vast and expanding market for the meats of commerce, it was not surprising that there should have been an international boom in livestock farming. The decades between 1870 and 1890, the heyday of imperialism, were years of land-grabbing and utilization on a majestic scale. In the temperate parts of the British Empire and on the North American plains – the scene of America's own imperial expansion – the stockmen became a force to be reckoned with. The enmity between stockmen and other settlers was to have a powerful influence on politics in almost all the new territories and so, too, was the economic chaos that eventually resulted from over-production. There is nothing new about the beef mountain.

The opening up of the American plains transformed cattle farming in the United States. Until the early 1870s Texas ranchers had held great cattle drives of hundreds of thousands of lanky longhorns, urging them along the 700-mile Chisholm Trail from San Antonio direct to the stockyards of Abilene, at a rate of about a dozen miles a day.[14] From Abilene they were taken by rail to the new meat processing plants in Chicago and Kansas City. But when the Great Plains were cleared of bison and the Indians who had depended on them, the new land was opened to range cattle. What happened then was that the Texans sent their cattle to the plains on the hoof to rest and fatten up before the last, easy journey to the stockyards, while new ranchers went into business on a massive scale, financed by the capital poured into the industry by American and foreign investors. The profits were substantial. In 1881 the Prairie Cattle Company of Edinburgh (Scotland) was able to declare a dividend of 28 per cent.[15]

In 1880 Kansas had sixteen times as many cattle as twenty years earlier; Nebraska thirty times as many. In 1886 in Wyoming alone there were 9 million head.[16] And the cattle were fatter and of finer quality than the old Texas longhorns because much care had been spent on improving the breeds.

The cattlemen were too successful. The meat was there in plenty, but although the industrial towns of America and Europe were desperate for it, the price – because of packing and transport overheads – could not be brought down far enough to stimulate the really steep increase in consumption the ranchers needed. And then, as if they did not have troubles enough, there was a series of climatic disasters between 1885 and 1887 that killed off many thousand head and sent the massive livestock corporations tumbling into liquidation. A great many ranchers and cattle hands lost their livelihood, too, because the margin between success and failure in large-scale stock-rearing was just as narrow as in unambitious small-scale farming. Cattle men and grain growers, anxious to improve their lot, quickly turned to politics and became involved in the Granger and Greenback movements, in the Farmers' Alliances and in Populism – whose agitators in the 1890s urged the movement's members to 'raise less corn and more Hell!'

It was not only in the United States that the farmers moved into politics. Much of Australia's history in the second half of the nineteenth century was shaped by the animosity between diggers (gold miners) and squatters (sheep farmers), while in New Zealand at the turn of the century the 'cow cockies' (dairy farmers) dominated the Farmers' Union and turned their dislike of industrial 'townies' into a red-hot political issue.[17]

In Argentina for many decades cattle and the economy were

indivisible (as, in many ways, they still are). From as early as the 1840s meat was so plentiful that even the chickens and turkeys were fattened on it, while sheeps' skulls were used to fill up quagmires so that roads could be built.[18] By the early years of the twentieth century the ranchers had begun to specialize – some as *criadores* (breeders), others as *invernadores*, who fattened the beasts for export. Both groups had great political power, but the economic power was in the hands of the mainly foreign corporations who operated the *frigorificos*, or packing and shipping houses. Not until the 1930s did the conflict between ranching and packing interests cease to dominate the political scene.

During the first half of the nineteenth century the Industrial Revolution had demonstrated the need for a vast increase in cheap food supplies, and in the process of meeting that need farmers and stock breeders everywhere – once the backbone of the community – began to see themselves, for the first time in history, as a separate group with separate and specialized interests. The pressure they exerted to have those interests satisfied, reinforced in most of the advanced countries by governmental appeasement, was to lead in the second half of the twentieth century (particularly in the West) to a 'system' of agricultural economics of a complexity so complete as to be anarchic.

FILLET OF PEGASUS

There was one kind of animal protein that the urban labourer might have had quite readily during the nineteenth century if he had not had such a prejudice against it.

In Britain eating horsemeat was considered almost on a par with cannibalism, but in France attempts to improve the diet of the poor by popularizing horsemeat were marginally more successful. In 1855 a certain M. Renault, director of a veterinary college, held a comparative tasting of horse versus beef. A 23-year-old horse suffering from incurable paralysis was slaughtered and its meat cooked in the same way as equivalent cuts of beef. The panel of tasters, accredited gourmets all, judged that horse bouillon was superior to beef bouillon and roast fillet of horse appreciably better than the same of beef, while boiled horse, though not quite as good as the best boiled beef, was still superior to beef of ordinary quality.[19] But in England horsemeat found no supporters even when, in 1868, invitations went out for a dinner featuring such poetic delights as lobster with Rosinante-oil mayonnaise, roast fillet of Pegasus, and patties of Bucephalus-marrow.[20]

SUBSTITUTE FOODS

While mass-production techniques were being applied to the foods that had sustained humanity since the beginning of recorded history, a few scientists occupied themselves with looking at substitutes for others. There was no great sense of urgency. Indeed, it was fifty years before anyone took much notice of one of the more important discoveries, sugar beet. It had been known since 1575 that some root plants common in Europe contained a kind of sugar, and in 1747 the German chemist A. S. Marggraf isolated a small, usable percentage from beets. But cane sugar was plentiful enough in relation to demand; in 1788 the French were using only about a kilogram (2.2 pounds) per head per year.*

Then came the Napoleonic Wars, when the British blockade of continental ports cut off supplies of cane sugar coming from the West Indies and south-east Asia. In 1801–2, the world's first sugar-beet factory was built in Silesia, and Napoleon was soon urging similar enterprises on the businessmen of France, Germany and the Low Countries. By the 1840s France had fifty-eight sugar-beet factories producing enough to meet home needs, and Germany and Belgium were also well on the way to becoming self-sufficient. Britain, however, continued to rely on cane sugar from its colonies in the West Indies until well into the twentieth century. Today about 40 per cent of the world's sugar intake is manufactured from beet.

Consumers accepted the new sugar peaceably enough, most of them unaware that it was any different from the old, but it was another matter when scientists began advocating margarine as a better and healthier buy than the rancid and watery butter most city dwellers were accustomed to.

In the late 1860s the food technologist Hippolyte Mège-Mouries had been commissioned by the victualling department of the French navy to find a cheap substitute for butter. Since he had noticed that cow's milk contained fat even when the animals were so undernourished that they were losing weight, he concluded that the milk-fat was actually body-fat. With impeccable logic, he therefore chopped up a quantity of beef suet, minced in some sheep's stomach, steeped the mixture in slightly warm, slightly alkaline water – and found himself with (as he thought) butter.† The flavour was not quite right, but

* In America today consumption is 2.4 pounds per head per *week*; in Britain 1.6 pounds.
† What he had done, of course, was extract the softer fats from the suet.

when he tried again, adding some chopped cow's udder and a little warm milk, the result was gratifyingly successful.

Napoleon III awarded Mège-Mouriès a prize and a factory in which to set up production. This began on a commercial scale in 1873, after some initial opposition from the Paris Council of Hygiene, which first hesitated about allowing the product to be sold for human consumption, and then, even while relenting, forbade the name butter to be used for it.

Other countries were quick to take up the idea. In America, particularly, the manufacture of 'butterine' seemed to offer a prime way of utilizing the byproducts of the stockyards, especially when it was discovered that cows' udders and sheeps' stomachs were superfluous; all that was needed was to melt out the softer elements from the caul fat of oxen and shake them up with milk. By 1876 America was exporting more than a million pounds of butterine to the United Kingdom.[21]

The producers of real butter fought a strong rearguard action (and are still fighting it), and many of the hideous early rumours circulating about the origins of the fats used in margarine, as it finally came to be called, can be traced back to their whispering campaigns. It was to be many years before margarine achieved a really substantial sale, its progress being hindered not only by libellous rumours but by the waxy texture and insipid taste of the early kinds.* Manufacturers had to spend enormous sums on research – on discovering how to 'cream' the artificial product, how to mature it with micro-organisms similar to those involved in the making of butter, how to utilize vegetable oils, and how to add vitamin concentrates (a development of the 1920s) – before they could even begin to persuade the public to accept margarine not as a poor man's substitute for butter, but as a middle-class alternative.

THE QUALITY OF COOKING

When Mark Twain toured Europe in 1878, he loathed the food and tortured himself with visions of what he would have to eat when he arrived safe home again. Buckwheat cakes with maple syrup, hot bread, fried chicken, soft-shell crabs, Boston baked beans, hominy, squash and, of course, 'a mighty porterhouse steak an inch and a half thick, hot and sputtering from the griddle; dusted with fragrant

---

* Even today there are few margarines that could be mistaken for *good* butter.

pepper; enriched with little melting bits of butter of the most un-impeachable freshness and genuineness; the precious juices of the meat trickling out and joining the gravy, archipelagoed with mush-rooms; a township or two of tender, yellowish fat gracing an outlying district of this ample country of beefsteak; the long white bone which divides the sirloin from the tenderloin still in its place.'*²²

While he was prepared to concede that his list might not cover all the gastronomic delights of the known world – 'the Scotchman would shake his head and say, "Where's your haggis?" and the Fijian would sigh and say, "Where's your missionary?"' – he was not prepared to ruin his effect by admitting that buckwheat cakes, fried chicken and mighty steaks were worthy of his rhapsodies only when a really good cook had the handling of them.

Cuisines are like art, architecture, sculpture, literature, music and philosophy – aspects of culture. But whereas architecture is still here to be seen, music to be heard, and poetry to be read, the cooking standards of the past have to be judged at second hand through contemporary reports. It is like knowing Shakespeare only through what his reviewers said of him. More specifically, it means that the images of delight conjured up by a Grimod de la Reynière prove not that the cooking of early nineteenth-century France was wonderful (though it may have been); all they prove is that one eccentric and extremely self-centred gentleman had a high opinion of the best of it and was able to communicate his enthusiasm.

Because of this, only the widest generalizations on the quality of cooking in the past are likely to be valid, and even these have to be drawn from pedestrian sources like recipe books and lists of raw materials. That proviso having been made, however, there were four nineteenth-century developments that may reasonably be supposed to have brought about an increase in the number of good cooks.

COOKING STOVES

First and foremost, there was a revolution in equipment. Until the early years of the nineteenth century most cooking had been done over an open fire or in a primitive, enclosed brick oven heated with coals that had to be raked out before cooking could begin. Although a good many items of ancillary equipment had been evolved to make

* No, Mark Twain did not die young from cholesterol-clogged arteries, but lived to the age of 75, which was well above average for the time.

the cook's task easier, anything other than simple dishes were beyond the scope of the domestic kitchen; more complex food needed large kitchens with large staffs, where undivided attention could be given at every stage of preparation.

In 1795, however, Count Rumford found that it was possible to feed the poor of Munich at a cost of a halfpenny each a day, thanks partly to his special soup and partly to the stove he had invented, which was immensely economical on fuel.[23] Later, bending his powerful mind to the problem of cooking for smaller numbers, he developed a closed-top range that provided adjustable heat from a small fire controlled by a battery of flues, dampers and metal plates.

Flexible heat undoubtedly marked the beginning of a revolution in the kitchen. Sautés, sauces and soufflés (for housewives who knew their ovens) were now within the scope of any household possessing one of the new ranges. The act of cooking itself ceased to be a red-hot torment, and may even, for some, have become a pleasure.

The solid-fuel iron range came into general use in middle-class homes in the 1860s, and the gas version twenty years later. (Gas ovens had in fact been used in the Reform Club as early as the 1830s, but people remained suspicious of gas, especially of its smell, for some time.) Once again the improvement in capability must have seemed magical. Precision adjustment of heat, one of the most important weapons in the cook's armoury, became almost a reality. Although electricity was to infiltrate the world of cooking in the 1890s, the electric range was at first thought to be dangerous so that it was almost three decades before it became popular. Many cooks still look with disfavour on the inflexible electric hob.

COOKERY BOOKS

The second influence on nineteenth-century cooking was the cookery book. There was nothing new about the genre. What was new was that, because of the spread of literacy, far more women were now able to read it.

As the middle classes increasingly required their tables to reflect their status, they also discovered that traditional family recipes were not adequate for the purpose. Nor could they rely on 'cook', who was only too often in need of guidance. Cookery books were the answer, and publishers were only too happy to provide them in ever-growing numbers.

Sometimes the authors were professional chefs, among them Queen

Victoria's Chief Cook in Ordinary Charles Edmé Francatelli, who, in *The Modern Cook* (1845), tried to cater for all tastes by providing recipes for sheeps' jowls, ears and trotters as well as venison and reindeer tongues, but still betrayed his *grande cuisine* instincts in his emphasis on garnishes.

Other authors were surprised amateurs. One of the best of English cookery books, *Modern Cookery for Private Families* by Eliza Acton (1845), was written by a lady who really wanted to be a poet. But her publisher said there was no market for poems by maiden ladies and told her bracingly that what she ought to write was a good sensible cookery book. She did, and the result was an enduring best-seller. The best-*known* English cookery book, however, was written by a young woman journalist with no particular talent in the kitchen. Isabella Beeton's *Book of Household Management* (1861) was encyclopaedic in scope and, although the recipes were pedestrian, Mrs Beeton was the first writer to make a serious attempt to include an estimate of costs, quantities and preparation times.

In Germany, as in England, women had competed on equal terms with men in the writing of cookery books since the early eighteenth century, but in France the men reigned almost supreme and some of their works ran through a remarkable number of editions. One of the most popular, *La Cuisinière de la campagne et de la ville, ou nouvelle cuisine économique*, written by Louis Eustache Audot and intended for the 'modest' household, was first published in 1818 and by 1901 was in its seventy-ninth edition. In 1806, during the reign of Napoleon Bonaparte, Monsieur A. Viard's *Le Cuisinier impérial* was published. When the Bourbons were restored to the throne, it became *Le Cuisinier royal*. By 1853 the Bonapartes were back in business, with Louis Napoleon as president of the Republic. *Le Cuisinier royal* became *Le Cuisinier national*. But not for long. Louis Napoleon translated himself into the Emperor Napoleon III and by 1854 *Le Cuisinier national* was back to being *impérial* again. After the Third Republic was established in 1870, *Le Cuisinier* once more became, and this time remained, *national*.

Some French authors were chefs, but more appear to have been gourmets. The former often reproduced recipes that were beyond the capacity of the average kitchen (and cook), while the latter, influenced by Grimod de la Reynière and Brillat-Savarin, were insufficiently practical, philosophized too much and informed too little.

The same might have been said, if in a rather different sense, of certain American writers, who sternly rebuked the housewife for her ignorance and extravagance and recommended her to look to her morals. In *Christianity in the Kitchen* (1861) Mrs Horace Mann stated categorically, if somewhat obscurely, that 'There is no more prolific cause of bad morals than abuses of diet.' Pork, turtle soup and wedding cake were not only bad for the digestion but, apparently for that very reason, immoral and un-Christian. Fortunately for American cooking, there were other and less dogmatic works available. Catherine Beecher, in *Mrs Beecher's Domestic Receipt Book* (1846), produced one of the first cookery books to include instruction in techniques as well as recipes, and between 1846 and 1896 – a notable year in American cookbook history – several other reliable basic books appeared.

The year 1896 was marked by the publication of *The Boston Cooking-School Cook Book* by Fannie Merritt Farmer. One of the school's founders, Mrs D. A. Lincoln, had begun to rationalize kitchen measurements, having been irritated by instructions to add 'a glass' of this (sherry glass, Burgundy glass or toothglass?) and 'a nut' of that

'Ten minutes for refreshments' before the departure of the train. Nineteenth-century Americans were well used to taking their meals on the run.

(hazelnut, almond or brazil?). When Fannie Farmer published the *Boston Cook Book*, the precise measuring system that became so typical of American cooking was well and truly launched. Despite its obvious usefulness – it more or less guaranteed that an amateur cook attempting an unfamiliar dish for the first time would achieve a result that was at least presentable – it seemed as if it would never catch on in Europe. Even today, distinguished British authors still lapse into measures that may be meaningful to the experienced cook but are less than helpful to the tyro.

In the nineteenth century the great majority of cookery books were designed for middle-class households and must certainly have had some effect on general cooking standards. By the end of the century they were even encouraging better-balanced menus. It was a development long overdue.

The Yankee who, in the 1860s, started the day with 'black tea and toast, scrambled eggs, fresh spring shad, wild pigeon, pigs' feet, two robins* on toast, oysters'[24] may have made no claims to being a gourmet, but Colonel Kenney-Herbert of Madras, mentor in the 1880s and 1890s not only to his regiment but to British wives new to the Indian kitchen, had no hesitation in recommending to them such truly dreadful menus as the following:[25]

Consommé de perdreaux	Clear partridge soup
Matelote d'anguilles	Stewed eels
Poulet à la Villeroy	Chicken pieces sauced, crumbed and deep-fried
Longe de mouton à la Soubise	Loin of mutton with onion sauce
Topinambours au gratin	Creamed Jerusalem artichokes with a coating of melted cheese
Canapés de caviar	Croutons of fried bread coated with caviar and garnished with mayonnaise
Orléans pudding	A chilled custard pudding layered with crushed ratafia biscuits and dried fruits

Although the middle-class cook was the publishers' main target, well-meaning authors also began turning out less ambitious works for the labouring poor. Juliet Corson, who ran one of the first cooking schools in New York, published in the 1870s a string of dull little books with titles like *Fifteen Cent Dinners for Workingmen's Families.*

* The American robin is a member of the thrush family and about twice the size of a European robin.

She may have been encouraged in this by the success of similar works in England. The great chef of the Reform Club, Alexis Soyer – already famous for good works in the shape of soup kitchens for the poor* – had published in 1855 *A Shilling Cookery for the People*, which sold just under a quarter of a million copies. This and similar works, full of recipes for boiled neck of mutton and sheep's head, were probably bought by the wives of small tradesmen and skilled artisans rather than the labouring poor for whom they were nominally intended. It was a sad fact that no cookery book, however economical, could supply the working wife with time, equipment or fuel. Until well into the twentieth century the local tripe shop or pork butcher, the hot dog stand, the street whelk or oyster seller, the muffin man and, above all, the fish-and-chip shop did more for the industrial worker's diet than any cookery book.

RESTAURANTS

At an informed guesstimate, until the middle of the nineteenth century and the spread of the railways, something like 90 per cent of the population of the Western world never, in the whole of their lives, travelled farther than five or ten miles from home.† In culinary terms this meant that despite the availability of cookery books they had no direct experience of any style or quality of cooking other than their own, and therefore no standards of comparison.

Things were different for the rich, of course. They travelled more, went on extended visits to the homes of family and friends, frequently owned houses in both town and country, and employed chefs, cooks or housekeepers who had been trained to a reasonable level of sophistication. The upper-class lady therefore had an educated taste, and her knowledge was expanded (if at second hand) by her husband's reports on eating out at that very British institution, 'the club', as well as at the hotels that had begun to appear in England in the eighteenth century in imitation of the French.

* That usually kindly commentator on the Victorian gastronomic scene, Abraham Hayward, remarked of Soyer that 'his execution is hardly on a par with his conception, and he is more likely to earn his immortality by his soup-kitchen than by his soup.'[26]
† Until 1960s changes in the licensing laws of Scotland, only bona fide travellers were able to buy a drink on a Sunday; a bona fide traveller was legally defined as someone who lived five miles away from the supplier of the drink in question.

The middle-class wife had no such guidelines. When her husband ate out it was likely to be at a chop-house, which was exactly that, a place serving chops, steaks and other small cuts; she herself rarely, if ever, dined out except at the homes of friends or sometimes at a tea shop or tea garden. In France since about 1770 there had been restaurants where respectable women might go with a family party, but the first London restaurants (serving mainly French food) were not established until about 1830 and for another forty years or more it continued to be thought improper for a lady to be seen in a public dining-room.

Paris; a late nineteenth-century *pâtisserie*, spacious and civilized. There was no real British equivalent.

By the last decade of the century, however, things were improving. There was no female equivalent of the American male's free lunch counter, which reached its apogee between 1890 and 1910; a man could walk into almost any saloon in the country and, in return for ordering a drink (or two), help himself from an extensive free buffet. But in both Britain and the United States ladies' tearooms were becoming a little more ambitious, even if luncheons on one side of the Atlantic still consisted of omelette or ham-and-two-veg; and, on the other, of creamed chicken, pineapple salad and waffles. Tearooms rarely, if ever, stayed open after about 6 p.m. but by the 1890s there were quite a few places where a respectable gentleman could take an equally respectable lady to dine of an evening,* even if very few where a lady might dine alone or in the company of another lady.

Even so, woman's culinary horizons were at last widening. Now she was able to judge what other people's food was really like. It added a new dimension to her understanding of cookery books and gave her a much better estimate than before of the meals she produced in her own kitchen.

THE RISE OF THE BRAND NAME

The fourth major new influence on nineteenth-century cooking was the widening range of materials.

After the food adulteration scandals of the mid-century, the quality of basic foodstuffs in Britain and, slightly later, America improved noticeably. More and fresher raw ingredients also became available as the production of grain and meat was taken out of the hands of the small farmer, forcing him to make the changeover to dairy products or fruit and vegetable growing. Milk, cream, butter and eggs began to regain in the towns the important position they had once held in the country. What the British called 'market gardens' and the Americans 'truck farms' came increasingly to supply local centres of population with fruit and vegetables in season, while refrigerated rail and sea transport and improved canning techniques introduced tropical and subtropical foods to places where they had never been seen before. Some of these foods did more than introduce variety to the menu. As their use became more general, they helped to remedy a number of nutritional deficiencies.

Others of them made a very different contribution to the diet by revolutionizing not only America's but the world's breakfasts. In the mid-1850s America had suffered one of its recurring bouts of moral vegetarianism, and the Western Health Reform Institute had been one of the results. Twenty years later the physician in charge there was a certain John H. Kellogg, who, initially for the benefit of his patients, developed a number of 'hygienic comestibles' including the first peanut butter; a kind of double-baked breadcrumb cereal that became known as Granola; and cooked wheat flakes that were intended to be eaten as a dry snack but became much more popular

* The unrespectable lady had always been better served.

taken with milk and sugar or maple syrup as a breakfast dish. At about the same time Henry D. Perky of Denver was busy inventing Shredded Wheat.

In due course Dr Kellogg's brother Will moved into the business and inaugurated a great sales drive for all the early products, as well as a new one, cornflakes. It was the end of an era. No more American breakfasts of littleneck clams, mushroom omelettes, grilled plover,

Canning had the beneficial effect of giving northern peoples access to, and a taste for, many new fruits.

filets mignons or robins-on-toast; no more British breakfasts of kidneys, sausages, scrambled eggs and kedgeree.

Cornflakes were not, of course, wholly or even mainly responsible
for the demise of the traditional breakfast (which had always, in any
case, been very much a minority pleasure), but they and competitive
products such as Grape Nuts and Post Toasties were sold with such
vigour and such claims of healthfulness that they eventually came to
dominate the hurried twentieth-century breakfast table. They still
continue to do so, despite a growing challenge from the soggy end of
the market in the form of commercially debased versions of muesli,
originally developed by another food-reforming pioneer, Dr Max
Bircher-Benner, for the patients at his Zurich clinic.

Brand names and hard sell during the latter part of the nineteenth
century were the prerogative as much of retailers as manufacturers.
The Hartfords' Great American Tea Company of New York and the
grocery empire founded in Glasgow in 1876 by the redoubtable
Tommy Lipton were no less famous in their way than Kellogg, Borden,
Swift and Armour. But the economics of mass production in the field
of canned goods brought more and more manufacturers into the
brand-name field. America, always more hygiene-conscious than other
countries (perhaps because it played host to so many religious sects
that held cleanliness inseparable from godliness), also took readily to
other prepacked goods, although in Britain even in the 1940s local
grocers were still wielding butter-patters for every individual order
and shovelling sugar into thick little blue paper bags.

One direct effect of the mass marketing that went with mass production was that it stimulated customer demand for consistent quality
and stable prices – with two unforeseen and largely undesirable results.
One was that consistency ultimately went too far, when the desire not
to displease (a motive more powerful and more profitable than the
desire to please) led to standardization at a level not of excellence but
of mediocrity. The other result, less apparent but of increasing concern
to many people today, was the multiplication of additives in processed
foods.

There were (and are) two valid reasons for using additives, whether
artificial, synthetic or natural. The first is that all preservation processes, short-term or long-term, have the effect of altering the taste of
the food to a greater or lesser degree. The manufacturer therefore uses
improvers (or 'taste powders') to compensate. Secondly, many prepacked foods lose either quality or visual appeal during transport,
shelf and cupboard life. To overcome this, manufacturers add anti-

caking agents to prevent salt, sugar and powdered milk from coagulating into lumps; emulsifying agents, which help to homogenize, or blend, substances like fat and milk that would otherwise tend to separate; and sequestrants to stop trace minerals from turning fats and oils rancid, and prevent soft drinks from going cloudy.

Right from the beginning, brand-name foods were marketed on the basis of purity, convenience, quality and reliability, and the consumer bought the promises as well as the product. Nothing would have vitiated those promises more quickly than lumpy sugar, curdled sauces and cloudy lemonade. The consumer was, in effect, persuaded to demand an appearance of purity that the manufacturer could only achieve by using additives. And if it was to be a choice between no additives and no sales, the manufacturers' decision was a foregone conclusion. After all, food retailing in Britain in the 1930s absorbed nearly one-third of the national income.[27]

Not until labelling laws began to come into force in the latter part of the twentieth century did the horrified housewife discover what actually went into the cans and packets she had come to rely on – and to discover that her family's favourite instant soup mix consisted solely of 'hydrolized plant protein, salt, yeast hydrolysate, monosodium glutamate, sugar, vegetable fat, caramel colouring, spices, onion powder and calcium silicate'.[28]

— 21 —

THE SCIENTIFIC REVOLUTION

Although it appeared at the time as if the second half of the nineteenth century was well on the way to redressing the food imbalances of the first, among the many new developments were some that had the effect of worsening rather than bettering the diet of the poorest classes. The new milk and the new bread actually helped to increase the incidence of malnutrition instead of decreasing it.

The old methods of milk preservation found little favour with the Victorians, who, rendered wary by recurring adulteration scandals, viewed the sediment in reconstituted dried milk with the deepest suspicion. Condensed milk, however, looked much more attractive.

A British patent had been taken out as early as 1835, but it was the American Gail Borden's improved version that in the 1850s scooped the market. The principles of sterilization not yet being fully understood, it was impossible to produce a satisfactory 'natural' condensed milk in cans, but Borden discovered that if he added sugar (which, in quantity, inhibits bacterial growth) the keeping qualities were very much improved. Borden's milk had a great success with the army in the American Civil War, and the men carried their liking for it back into civilian life. Condensed milk, thick and sweet, had several advantages over fresh – even the genuinely fresh that was now beginning to be carried to the towns by rail – and it was unquestionably more wholesome than the kind supplied by the old-style city cowman.

The cheaper brands of condensed milk, however, were made not from whole milk but from skimmed, and lacked both fats and the as yet unrecognized vitamins A and D. As a result, mothers who fed their infants mainly on the cheaper kind, believing it to be a whole food in a pure and hygienic form, were in fact depriving the children of vital nutrients. In the poorer industrial districts the incidence of rickets and other deficiency diseases began to increase.

Whiter bread, too, was synonymous with less nutritious bread. A new method of milling flour had been introduced in Hungary in the 1840s. Iron rollers processed the grain faster than the old stone mills; the quality was more consistent and the flour kept very much better.

The old mills had pulverized the oily embryo (or 'germ') of the grain at the same time as the starchy endosperm, and it was this that had given the flour its characteristic yellow-brown colour and also turned it rancid within a few weeks. The new roller mills, however, squeezed the grain in such a way that the endosperm popped out of its coating, leaving the germ behind to be sieved off with the bran. As a result, roller-milled flour was whiter than stone-ground and could be stored for months, even years, without deteriorating. This pleased not only the millers, bakers and grocers, but their customers as well, and with the introduction in the 1870s of porcelain rollers – which had no problems of rusting and were easier to clean than iron – roller-milling became the general practice. Unfortunately, the discarded wheat germ contained most of the nutrients of the grain, now lost to the people who needed them most, the industrial poor to whom bread was the mainstay of the diet.

In Asia there had been a similar development, which had an equally swift and destructive effect on the health of the consumer. If white bread was alluring to the peoples of the West, white rice was no less so to Asians. In the last decades of the nineteenth century much rice was having its drab outer sheath polished away by machine, and during this process the germ (like that of wheat) was torn away and discarded. People who lived on a diet based largely on the new polished rice began to contract beri-beri, a deficiency disease that attacks the nerves, heart and digestive system. So concerned did the Dutch become over the death rate in their colonies in the East Indies that in 1886 they sent out a medical team to investigate.

THE DISCOVERY OF VITAMINS

The researches of the Dutch team led to one of the great discoveries in the history of nutrition, the identification of the accessory food factors known as vitamins. (The name comes from *vita*, 'life', and *amine*, the term for any chemical compound containing nitrogen; the terminal 'e' was dropped when it was discovered that all vitamins did not in fact, contain nitrogen.)

It had been obvious to the human race since the very earliest times that different foods had good or bad influences on health, but it was only at the very end of the eighteenth century, when Lavoisier succeeded in proving that humans and animals were heat engines fuelled by food, that science finally succeeded in demolishing the age-old nutritional theory of the four humours. In 1846 Justus von Liebig, in his report *Chemistry and Its Applications to Agriculture and Physiology*, laid the foundations of modern nutrition by demonstrating that living tissues (including foodstuffs) were composed of carbohydrates, fats and 'albuminoids', or proteins. Although minerals were added to this list later in the century and it was discovered that different kinds of protein had different biological values, there was still a large and obviously critical gap in scientific knowledge. If the known food elements were the only ones that existed, then a diet of bread and fatty meat should have been enough to guarantee good health. But this was demonstrably untrue.

The fifth and vital element was isolated as a result of the Dutch team's researches into beri-beri. After three years, a member of the team happened to notice that hens fed on polished rice developed symptoms of beri-beri; when they were given brown rice, or even just bran left from the polishing, they quickly recovered. Abandoning the experiments that had been initiated in the belief that beri-beri was an infectious disease, the doctor, Christian Eijkman, devoted his attention to the constituents of rice polishings.

Not until 1901 did he identify the importance of the germ, and even then it did not immediately occur to anyone that what he had discovered was, in fact, an entire new class of food components, some essential in themselves, others as catalysts without which the body was unable to convert carbohydrate into energy or utilize particular minerals.

In 1905, however, Professor Pekelharing of Utrecht published his belief that some such 'unrecognized substances' did indeed exist, and four years later a German biochemist, Dr Stepp, succeeded (without fully realizing it at the time) in proving the existence of the fat-soluble group of vitamins. Just before the First World War vitamin A was effectively isolated, although for more than a dozen years the new knowledge scarcely filtered beyond the walls of a few laboratories.

During those years much essential work was done, particularly in Britain, and the need for it became all too apparent in 1917–18 when 2.5 million men, theoretically in their physical prime and from all classes of society, were given a medical examination prior to military conscription. Forty-one per cent of them turned out to be not only in poor health but unfit for service,[1] and it was clear that undernourishment was at the root of the problem in most cases. Nutrition became a political issue.

Soon after the war the Accessory Food Factors Committee that had been set up in 1918 sent a team of scientists to Vienna, where the population was suffering from acute malnutrition. When the British team arrived, it found that scurvy was common among the children and that rickets had seriously increased in both incidence and severity. Since Austrian doctors knew very little about vitamins, Dr Harriette Chick and her colleagues had virgin territory on which to put their own experimental knowledge to work and they proved its practical value beyond any shadow of doubt. They succeeded 'in maintaining a large number of artificially fed babies free from [rickets], and ... were invariably successful in healing children admitted with rickets already developed'.[2]

When war broke out again in 1939 nutritionists in many countries were able to advise their governments on workable rationing systems. In Britain bread and potatoes were unrestricted, and the consumer had freedom of choice with restricted foods, even if the choice often boiled down to corned beef or 'luncheon meat'. The Ministry of Food also worked hard at publicizing economical and nourishing dishes, many of them – like oatmeal-and-cheese soup – of a peculiarly revolting kind. On their restricted regimen, however, most British civilians remained not only healthy, but healthier than ever before or (according to some nutritionists) since. The armed forces were also better fed than in any previous war, with cans of American bacon and legs of New Zealand lamb being floated down by parachute even to isolated units in the jungles of Burma.

Many subsequent advances in food technology had their origin in the exigencies of war, although in some cases – as with dried milk* and dehydrated vegetables – there was to be a gap of over twenty years before people who had seen too much of them in the 1940s were able to contemplate them again, even in an improved form, with any equanimity

The general picture of food values as they are known today had been established by the 1950s, although it took many more years of research and discovery to show that the early five-vitamin pattern was highly simplistic, and that a multitude of other 'accessory factors' was also involved. But although the science of nutrition has advanced so much over the last half century that some experts talk as if today's knowledge is as absolute and unquestionable as revealed truth, the more responsible members of the profession acknowledge that many mysteries remain. And it is, of course, one of the lessons of history

---

* This was, of course, 'new' only in the sense that the Central Asian nomads had failed to patent the formula a thousand years before.

that every generation always rests secure in its convictions for just as long as it takes for a new generation and new knowledge to come along.

THE FIRST GREEN REVOLUTION

The Third World in the 1950s was called upon to pay the price for the West's Industrial Revolution of a century earlier. When Europe and America moved into the machine age, they depended for their survival on selling the products of their machines, and the nineteenth-century quest for empire was therefore in large part a quest for overseas markets. As time passed, the colonial powers maintained the viability of those markets by retarding the development of industrialization in their non-white overseas possessions – not by legislating against it (indeed, they often made a show of encouraging it), but by making it difficult for their subjects to learn the managerial skills on which industry depends.

It was not surprising, therefore, that when in the mid-twentieth century independence was returned to the colonial territories, they should have placed excessive emphasis on industry at the expense of agriculture. The 'five-year plans' that abounded in the period after 1947 were only too prone to come to grief because the new nations' economy was distorted by the direct or indirect borrowing necessary to guarantee the food supply.

By the late 1960s, however, it had begun to look as if salvation was at hand. Twenty years earlier the Rockefeller Foundation in cooperation with the Mexican government had embarked on a wheat development programme that, in the intervening period, had increased Mexico's per-acre wheat yields by 250 per cent.

One of the great barriers to increased grain production in hot countries is that when traditional plants are heavily fertilized, they shoot up to an unnatural height and then collapse. If they are grown closely enough together to prevent this, one plant shades the other and the yield is reduced. During the Mexican experiments, however, and after tests involving 40,000 different crossbreeds of plant, it was found that if a short-stemmed grain were thickly sown at the right depth and adequately irrigated, it could take massive doses of fertilizer without becoming lanky, and give spectacularly high yields.

In 1962 the International Rice Research Institute was set up in the Philippines to find a rice as miraculous as the Pitic 62 and Penjamo 62 wheats, rice at that time being the main item of diet for six out of every ten people in the world. Success came quickly, although it was to prove only a qualified success. By 1968 a new crossbred variety, IR8, was being grown on millions of acres in eight countries, yielding on average three times as much grain as traditional varieties and sometimes considerably more.

But IR8 turned out to have disadvantages. Like the new wheats, it needed a great deal of water and fertilizer, and also proved a magnet to the destructive stem-borer insect. Furthermore, although pests liked IR8, many consumers did not; the cooked grain was too sticky and lumpy for people who ate with their fingers. As a result, IR8 was soon succeeded by IR20 and IR22, miracle plants with more acceptable grain quality, high yields and an in-bred resistance to some of the more destructive pests.

Advances like these led some participants in the ecological crystal-ball game of the early 1970s to prophesy that, despite the anticipated population explosion between then and the early twenty-first century, food surpluses would be more probable than food shortages. They were convinced that even if the world population almost doubled, as forecast, science would ensure that the extra 3,000 (or so) million people would be fed. Admittedly, in 1972 more than forty developing countries in Africa, Asia and South America were producing *less* food per head of population than they had done ten years earlier, before the Green Revolution. Admittedly, 150,000 people had recently starved to death in Bangladesh, and another 100,000 in Ethiopia. Given time, the new food grains would change all that.

Many other concerned agencies, however, lacking the laboratory researcher's faith in the unfailing ability of science to come up with the answer, were not so sure. Scientific advances, they believed, were as much at the mercy of social forces as the reverse.

And, indeed, what happened in the latter years of the 1970s was that since the new seeds performed best on good soils, needed reliable water supplies and were heavily dependent on the petrochemical fertilizers whose price had rocketed in the wake of soaring oil prices, the wealthiest farmers in the poor countries increased their yields, while the poorer farmers were driven out of business. Field labourers, too, found themselves idle as successful employers used their profits to buy machinery, the new status symbol that replaced human beings.

There were other consequences, too. In the Philippines and other parts of Asia, the paddy fields had always been used to grow fish as well as rice, but the lavish fertilizers and pesticides poured on the new miracle plants had the effect of killing the fish in the paddy fields and tributary waterways.[3] More rice resulted in less protein.

In 1980 twenty African countries were on the urgent list of the Food and Agriculture Organization, and the average African, despite steeply rising imports, was eating 10 per cent less than in 1970. Omitting China, for which no figures were available, it was estimated that in the developing countries there were 490 million seriously malnourished people, and another 800 million classified as merely undernourished.

PESTS AND PESTICIDES

Because the new varieties of grain were planted over huge areas, there was an increasingly acute danger of disease, pests and drought. The possibility now existed of a country's entire harvest being destroyed by one of the diseases afflicting the particular variety to which farmers had committed themselves. Just as the bacteria to which humans are susceptible can develop resistance to antibiotics, so plant viruses are capable of adapting to new situations.

As well as diseases, the last two centuries had seen an explosive increase in the world population of crop pests, partly because they, like viruses, were attracted to the huge fields essential to mass production, and partly because, as new crops were taken to new lands during the great period of agricultural exchanges, the pests travelled with them and very often flourished in the absence of the natural predators that helped to control them elsewhere.

Pests and diseases take a huge toll of the world's food output despite heavy use of pesticides and fungicides. In the early 1970s fungus diseases were destroying, annually, as much food as would have supplied 300 million people with 2,500 calories a day;[4] in storage after harvest, rats and spoilage ruined more than the same again.[5] With a world population then approaching 4,000 million, 65 per cent of it subsisting on something like half the 3,060 calories a day enjoyed by the people of the 'have' countries, crop loss figures such as these were far from negligible.

Perspectives differ, however. For a time, the 3,060-calorie-a-day people were more interested in the survival of that graceful bird, the Western grebe, than in their hungry fellow humans.

In the 1950s the pesticide DDD had been used in heavy doses to kill off the black gnats of Clear Lake, California. The plankton in the lake became saturated with DDD, as did the fish that fed on them; so also did the Western grebe, which fed on the fish. The grebe population was reduced from 1,000 to 20 pairs within a year.[6] Much publicity was given to this ecological tragedy, with the result that the chemical treatment of Clear Lake was abandoned in favour of biological controls. But when the small freshwater smelt known as the Mississippi silverside was introduced to keep down the gnats by feeding on them, the smelts proliferated so furiously that it became necessary to introduce game fish to keep down the smelts. There was even a point at which it seemed as if humans with rod and line would have to be introduced to keep down the game fish.[7]

Agricultural pests come in all shapes and sizes; this Australian photograph shows that some, at least, can be controlled without chemicals. The centre fence marks the dividing line between rabbit-infested and rabbit-free land.

What all this showed was that it was much easier to destroy ecological balance than to restore it. In America in the 1960s a vigorous campaign was mounted against chemical insecticides, especially DDT, which was roughly similar to DDD and had worked such miracles since its introduction in the 1940s that it was now being over-used. As a result, residues were being found in the human body, in cow's milk, even in the flesh of Antarctic penguins. The campaign against DDT was successful in the United States, despite warnings from Dr Norman

E. Borlaug (who won the Nobel Peace Prize in 1970 for his work in developing the new wheats) that if chemical pesticides were banned the resulting crop losses could reach 50 per cent.[8]

Manufacturers, however, continued to export DDT to the Third World, where the still debatable risk of long-term poisoning by chlorinated hydrocarbon pesticides had to be set against the certainty of short-term starvation without them.

ADDITIVES OR ADULTERANTS?

That sad little epitaph, 'he meant well', should perhaps be inscribed in letters of fire on the walls of every scientific laboratory. Just as the motives of the chemists who invented DDT were impeccable, so the men and women responsible for developing modern food additives were motivated by a perfectly respectable desire to supply the needs that were becoming increasingly urgent as prepacked foods evolved into a new and highly perishable branch of manufacturing industry.

In the commercial food business some additives are honestly necessary and others actively beneficial. But 'additive' was to become an iniquitous word (even though all the different seasonings that go into the best of home cooking are just as much additives as are chemical preservatives). During the Second World War scientists took the opportunity of – and considerable credit for – putting back into certain foodstuffs what improved manufacturing techniques had taken out. British bread flours were now required to contain, either naturally or by deliberate addition, specified proportions of iron, vitamin B_1 and nicotinic acid, and these regulations still apply today.

Not until the 1960s, when convenience foods came into their own – canned, dehydrated, freeze-dried and frozen – did the panic over additives begin, encouraged rather than diminished by their incomprehensible scientific names.

The first to raise a scare were the taste powder monosodium glutamate (MSG – now listed as Additive 621) and the slimming sweeteners known as cyclamates. MSG had been claimed to raise an allergic reaction in some consumers, which became known as Kwok's disease (after Dr Robert Ho Man Kwok, who tracked down its source) but was often referred to as the Chinese restaurant syndrome, since Chinese cooks sometimes use MSG to excess. Tests in 1969 also led to the announcement that MSG caused brain damage in infant mice. As a result, many baby-food manufacturers stopped adding it to their products and the New York City Department of Health warned all cooks to use it sparingly.*

Consumers were similarly alarmed by the announcement that massive doses of cyclamates led to cancer of the bladder in rats and deformity in embryo chickens. Some scientists argued that the method of injecting test animals was at fault, rather than the substance, but within a week of this report cyclamates were ordered off the market in America and, soon afterwards, in a number of other countries including Finland, Sweden, Canada, Japan and Britain. France had never permitted their use in the first place.†

Not long afterwards suspicion fell on nitrates and nitrites, widely used as preservatives, especially in bacon curing and in sausages. The evidence, however, was indirect and they were not banned because they were so useful, although smaller quantities were recommended.

In 1977 the US Food and Drug Administration placed a ban on saccharin, the synthetic sweetener that had been in use since 1879, because in massive doses it could cause cancer in rats. On this occasion, to everyone's astonishment, Americans rose up in wrath. Given the choice between becoming obese because their saccharin was being taken from them (which meant they would have to use sugar instead) or continuing to use saccharin and running the risk of cancer, they went to court and argued that they had the constitutional right to use saccharin and contract cancer if they wanted to, and that attempts to prevent them from doing so were infringements of their liberties. They lost the case.

Throughout the 1970s the intensified marketing of processed foods was matched by an increase in the number and variety of additives

---

* Just for the record – in 1986 the existence of Kwok's disease was persuasively disproved. MSG, even in large doses, does no more than lower the blood pressure slightly, and in after-dinner tests there were no demonstrable biological differences between the allegedly allergic and those who were not. People who claimed to be affected were ten times more likely to suffer symptoms if they had heard of the Chinese restaurant syndrome than if they had not. It seemed that, suggestibility aside, poor hygiene in the kitchen was more likely to cause a reaction than MSG.[9]

† Half a dozen years later a committee of the US National Cancer Institute announced that present evidence did *not* establish that cyclamates caused cancer, though they could not be ruled out as a possible weak, cancer-causing agent.[10]

used, and by a rising tide of public awareness. Artificial colourings, whose presence was easily recognizable and served no more than a cosmetic function, came particularly under attack. 'Red no. 2', ama-

1970s customers were not the first to know about nitrites and nitrates. In 1925, the firm of Spear's boasted that its sausages were entirely free from preservatives.

ranth, was banned in America after tests (of doubtful validity) in 1976, and tartrazine, which belongs to the same group of azo, or coal-tar dyes, became a target ten years later, not for its reputedly cancer-causing properties but because it was believed to be connected with hyperactive behaviour in children.

Today permitted additives run into hundreds – all of them safe, in theory, but some of them potential sources of allergic reaction in people who happen to be sensitive to them. Whether the genuinely useful ones should be banned because one person in 10,000 is allergic remains an open question. No one who is allergic to shellfish or strawberries or chocolate would expect the rest of the world to give up eating them for that reason.

It may seem a pity that recent labelling regulations should make it necessary to buy a book on nutrition and another on E numbers in order to discover, firstly, what the labels mean and, secondly, whether or not to worry about them, but, even so, it should now be possible for consumers to identify, and reject, processed foods containing substances to which they are allergic.

Allergies apart, great gaps remain in biochemical knowledge. Separately and individually, tartrazine and pentasodium triphosphate and stearyl tartrate may be neither more nor less dangerous than the polymers and gases that keep apples fresh in their packs or the assorted residues of radioactivity, mercury and organochloride pesticides that are already present in the human body. The new technique of irradiating food by bombarding it with gamma rays that kill insects and bacteria may, as its adherents claim, be a great and beneficial leap forward from traditional fumigants and preservatives. But the cocktail effect, the way all these chemicals and processes interact with one another, remains a matter for debate.

In view, however, of the extravagant publicity given to artificial additives, this is perhaps the place for a reminder that quite a number of 'natural', 'healthy', 'real' foods would not be on the market today if they were subjected to the kind of tests that have to be undergone by the additives of commerce.

Caffeine, the natural stimulant in coffee, is fatal to humans at a dose of about one-third of an ounce. Nutmeg is hallucinogenic. Two pounds of onions a day are enough to cause anaemia. Rhubarb and spinach contain oxalic acid, which builds kidney stones. Carotene, which puts the colour in egg yolks, sweet potatoes, mangoes and carrots, can result in jaundice. Cabbage in excess can help to cause goitre. Bran, promoted in the high-fibre diet thought to help prevent coronary and colon diseases, can in excess prevent absorption of iron and calcium. Red kidney beans, inadequately boiled, can be toxic. Watermelon seeds are claimed to damage the liver and kidneys. People have been poisoned by the solanin in green potatoes, the prussic acid in bitter almonds, the cyanide in lima beans.

With so many natural hazards, it seems less than intelligent to add artificial ones, but the sad truth is that most customers not only want convenience foods, but want them to appear 'fresh', 'healthy', and 'appetizing'. And that is an impossible combination without additives. The future may show that convenience, over the long term, comes at too high a price.

THE GREEN REVOLUTION MARK 2

What thirty years of chemical involvement in food production and manufacture had done by the mid-1970s was demonstrate that science was still ignorant of many of the forces involved in the 'balance of nature'. The sometimes extremist views of the critics served as a valuable reminder of that ignorance, and one result was that agricultural scientists began at last to look more carefully at the potential side effects of their next crop of miracle cures.

By 1980 the Maize and Wheat Improvement Centre of Texcoco in Mexico, which had developed the miracle wheats of the 1960s, was at the final testing stage with new strains developed for use by poor farmers on poor soil. These varieties, known as the 'multiline' wheats, promised to diminish the risks associated with vast acreages of a uniform crop, since they had a degree of in-built protection against the assaults of nature. Although they looked very much like the first miracle wheats, encapsulated in their genes were several small variations that meant that even quite serious outbreaks of wheat disease would kill only a proportion of the crop instead of the whole.

But although this was a major achievement, other research designed to produce crops that would flourish without either fertilizers or pesticides looked unpromising. The hope of developing grains that generated their own fertilizer, as beans do, began to fade, while plants bred to be unpalatable to insect pests simply encouraged the pests to move on, *en masse*, to tastier fields nearby.

By 1981 nearly every country whose agriculture had been revolutionized by the Green Revolution Mark 1 was once more reduced to importing grain from the world's half dozen grain exporters, notably the United States, where water was in increasingly short supply, where exotic new pests were multiplying and where 3 million acres of land a year were being lost to cultivation by erosion and urban development.

It was clear that traditional plant-breeding methods were not working fast enough, and a number of America's giant corporations saw the possibilities. Molecular biologists who had formerly worked on medicines and drugs were directed to turn their attention to plants. As one leading policy spokesman said, 'There'll be a $50 billion to $100 billion annual market for agribusiness applications of genetic engineering by 1996 – ten times the potential of medical-pharmaceutical applications.'[11]

Genetic engineering in the case of plants means adjusting their heritable characteristics so as to make them more 'efficient' by human standards. This generally entails transferring into the chromosome of one near-perfect type of plant a single gene from another type – the two can be as different as sunflowers and French beans – in order to convert the first into a wholly perfect plant for the purpose the biotechnologist (or genetic engineer) has in mind. Barley could be made salt-tolerant, which would reinstate over-irrigated soil and allow new lands to be opened up; short-stemmed wheats could be made to grow tall without benefit of fertilizers because growing tall would be in their nature; potatoes could be (and are being) crossed with carnivorous plants so that insects landing on them will be destroyed on contact.

The new methods have run into problems, of course. Most of the early genetic research involving plants was directed towards increasing the number that could take nitrogen from the air and convert it into usable ammonia, thus generating their own fertilizer, but nitrogen-fixing proved to be a complex process governed by at least seventeen genes. The sheer intricacy of some plant systems came as a surprise, too. Plant physiology is still imperfectly understood; some of the more highly cultivated plants are just as complicated as humans. Then there was the need to go for genetic raw materials to 'unimproved' stock, where it could still be found; thousands of wild cousins of the major food plants have become extinct during the last twenty or thirty years, accidentally wiped out by the competition from a few high-yield crops. And finally, although new breakthroughs are reported with some regularity, many of the genetic tricks that can be played with broad-leaved plants cannot yet be played with the monocotyledons – the wheat, rice, maize and millet on which the second Green Revolution will depend.

Despite all this, it seems likely that the essential discoveries will be made in the not too distant future. Then, there will be plants that will go from spring to summer to harvest with very little aid from chemicals or, indeed, from humans.

The unasked and unanswered question is, what will the humans do then? Even if the Green Revolution Mark 2 proves less imperfect than the first, social problems will grow and ripen with the new grains. Microtechnology has led to massive unemployment in cities and towns throughout the world; biotechnology will inevitably do the same in the countryside.

CONFUSED NEW WORLD

If some ill-directed time machine had decanted Brillat-Savarin into the 1960s, he might have thought twice before he said, 'Tell me what you eat: I will tell you what you are.'[1] Certainly, he would have qualified it, for no sane analyst of gastronomic history could have deduced a Liverpool pop singer from yoghurt and unpolished rice, or a Manhattan millionaire from black-eyed peas and chitterlings; identified a Frenchman from Scotch whisky, or a Japanese from French bread.

These wild deviations from the logic of the table had very little to do with food. They were political or social gestures, and those who made the gestures knew exactly what they were doing.

But other attitudes towards food were born in the 1960s that over the next twenty years were to introduce genuine confusion not only into the logic of the table but also the minds of the people who sat at it.

The first, conceived and nurtured in America (like so many twentieth-century obsessions), was concerned with appearances. The slim, leggy teenage look was in and, with the ardent encouragement of a new breed of experts and advisers, every woman who was not a slim, leggy teenager either embarked on, or contemplated embarking on, a craze for dieting that has scarcely faltered since. It was to change in only one important respect over the years. When men joined in, vanity became inadmissible as a motive for so much concentrated effort, and dieting for health became the motto.

The second 1960s strand in today's food stemmed from the flower children's deliberate adoption of poverty, reflected in and symbolized by lentils and brown rice, foods endowed with an aura of spirituality through association with the Asian gurus – many of them Buddhist – to whom so many of the sixties generation attributed great and disinterested wisdom. Even when, later, most of the flower children rejoined the sinful human race and gave up their communes for houses and their freedom for wages, they continued to eat 'health foods' as if to reassure themselves that, despite appearances, they had not abandoned their ideals.

The third strand was very different and far less obvious. Before the

1960s there were many among the silent majority in the Western world who canalized their ordinary human need to feel superior into what had for centuries been a socially acceptable (if less than admirable) intolerance of homosexuals, Jews, people who ate garlic or dyed their hair, Catholics, blacks, old clothes, four-letter words, promiscuity, pacifism . . . and so on. Then, at one blow, all these faithful old prejudices became unrespectable, and those who had held them were deprived of an outlet for their need to disapprove.

The next generation, however, with the same need and no traditional focus for it, was saved by the American evangelical tradition and the new obsession with diet and health. Those who might easily have been the bigots of the 1960s became the health evangelists of the 1980s, reborn on the side of the angels. Sometimes, proclaiming the anti-fat, anti-sugar, anti-meat, anti-salt gospel, the new evangelists sound very much like Mrs Horace Mann in *Christianity in the Kitchen*. 'There is no more prolific cause of bad morals than abuses of diet . . .'

ECONOMIC FACTORS

While these social attitudes to food were settling into their new mould, other and weightier events were taking place.

The fiscal and social chaos that afflicted the whole of the Western world as it entered the 1980s was generally attributed to the long-term effects of the trebling of oil prices in the autumn of 1973, but that had been only the final blow in a series that had begun more than a year earlier when Russia, its harvest ruined by frost and drought, went to the United States to make up the deficiencies.

To the American administration, pursuing a policy of détente, this was good news until it emerged that the Russians, promised a fixed price and left to make their own deals with the grain companies, had done so to the tune of almost a quarter of the whole American wheat crop. The administration had no choice but to allow the price on the world market to float upwards, so that late-comers had to pay high. Europe and Japan were among the buyers, and so were India, struck by drought, and Pakistan, with hundreds of thousands of acres ruined by floods. Russia and China were also interested in soy beans, which were already under pressure from the increased home demand for animal feedstuffs that had resulted, in part, from the American government's ban on the use of sex hormones for fattening cattle.

Between April 1972 and August 1973 the wholesale price of American wheat rose from $1.69 to $4 a bushel. Between January and June

1973 soy beans went up from $4 to $12, and when the administration slashed exports by half, the European price shot up to twice the American.

As if all that were not enough, Peru's anchovy fisheries failed, leading to a serious shortage of fishmeal that meant scarcity and escalating prices for both chickens and eggs. The Brazilian wheat crop was flooded and the groundnuts failed. Turkey suffered an epidemic of foot-and-mouth disease. And just to round off the equation, beef production fell in both America and Europe. The American farmer was tempted by high grain prices to switch from cattle to standing crops, while the EEC's guaranteed milk prices made it more attractive to milk cows than to slaughter them.*

Rocketing food prices led to increased wage demands in the rich countries and increased hunger in the poor. The world economy was already creaking badly when the oil crisis tossed the final spanner in the works.

By mid-1974 the Third World faced freight costs that had risen five-fold; was unable to pay the new high import prices of staple foods; and could scarcely afford the fuel for its farm machinery or the essential fertilizers that, like oil, had trebled in price. There was a fertilizer shortage in the developed world, too,† grain stocks were low, the American harvest was poor and, despite a theoretical shortage of beef, the West had its first modern experience of beef mountains when consumers in Europe and America either refused or were unable to pay for an exorbitantly expensive product.

In 1975, 1978-9 and 1981, however, the United States had record harvests, and everything looked brighter again. Those were the harvests governments were subsequently to regard as 'normal' when they were planning – if that is the word – their agricultural policies. It was famine relief workers who remembered, instead, the harvests of 1974 and 1980.

THE POLITICS OF FARMING

Under Europe's Common Agricultural Policy (CAP) surplus butter is sold back to the farmers so that they can feed it to cows, which will

---

* The days are past when beef meant beef; an undisclosed proportion of the beef on sale nowadays is actually cow.
† Assisted by the American habit of spreading 1.3 million tons of it a year on lawns, golf courses and cemeteries.[2]

produce more surplus butter.* America's Payment in Kind (PIK) system gives to farmers who take their grain fields out of production vouchers that entitle them to draw, free of charge from government stocks, 95 per cent of the wheat they would have grown – if they had grown it.

Although this is not the place for a history of these strange games of musical chairs, a word of explanation may be in order. Both CAP and PIK have their roots in history. When the Treaty of Rome was signed in 1957 and the Common Agricultural Policy inaugurated, all Europe still remembered with dreadful clarity the hunger of the war years and after. Britain had succeeded in feeding itself with American aid, but in occupied Europe millions had come near to starving, and the post-war leaders were determined that this would never happen again. The principle of the CAP was admirable; the practice was to prove less so.

In America agricultural support policies emerged from a different background. Until the Industrial Revolution, self-sufficiency was built into the social fabric. Then, in the nineteenth century, the whole economy of a suddenly expanding nation came to depend on farm exports. Farmers in America, as in Australia, New Zealand and, a little later, Canada, became very important people indeed, a political lobby that no administration could afford to ignore. They remain important today, not only to America but also to the world, because – as its critics often forget – it is to America that all nations turn when their own harvests fail.

THE WORLD OF THE UNDERFED

In November 1974 a World Food Conference was held in Rome under the auspices of the United Nations. Its eleven days were distinguished by the expression of many high-flown sentiments, an unedifying search for compromises, some blatant jockeying for position by the United States and the oil-producing nations, and a number of final recommendations amounting to little more than a statement of virtuous intentions. The conference's pledge that 'within a decade no child will go to bed hungry, that no family will fear for its daily bread' had a hollow ring even at the time.

Three-quarters of the way through that decade, no fewer than eighteen African nations were facing serious food shortages, while in

* The new surplus is, of course, a year or two fresher than the old.

Bangladesh the United States alone distributed food aid to 7 million starving people. At the very end of the decade, another 7 million in Ethiopia were in even more desperate need.

In October 1985 pop singer Bob Geldof said to the European Parliament in Strasbourg what half the world was thinking. 'It makes no political sense, little emotional sense and nil moral sense that Europe should wallow in food while millions of people in Africa are dying of starvation.'[3]

The world had rarely seemed a more paradoxical place, with vast quantities of unwanted food stockpiled in the warehouses of the developed countries while a famine of appalling proportions raged in Africa. Especially when, just a year before, a meeting of the United Nations World Food Council – held in Ethiopia itself – had discussed the proposition that 'the potential for mass famine has been largely eliminated.'

This thesis was, in fact, less unsound than it appeared. There was no world shortage of food, and experts were by this time able to identify the symptoms of a forthcoming famine well in advance of the actuality.[4] In theory, it should have been perfectly possible to forestall the kind of disaster that occurred in Ethiopia and, soon after, Sudan and Mozambique.

But theory only too often falls foul of human frailty. If no one is there to observe the symptoms; if for political reasons a government chooses to suppress them; if the life-saving food therefore arrives too late and its distribution is wilfully hindered – then people die. For hunger to be conquered it needs more than grain and goodwill. It needs agricultural education in the danger areas, technology of a kind manageable by the poorest peasant, instruction in the art of self-sufficiency and – hardest of all to achieve – enough democracy for the first warnings of shortage to be not only reported by the peasants, but heeded by those who govern them.

There had been warnings enough, from Western observers, of the growing famine in Ethiopia. But it took a television news programme to activate the strength of public feeling that in turn activates governments.

In the few months covering late 1984 and early 1985 Western nations pledged something like £400 million in food for Ethiopia. On paper, there was more than enough to feed the 8 million of the starving for over half a year. But by April 1985 neither food nor medicine had reached two-thirds of them, and the Ethiopian government was refusing to allow relief aid into the rural areas of the province of Tigre, where there were 2 million of the most desperately afflicted.[5] In February 1988, with a new Ethiopian famine clearly foreseen for more than six months, only 300,000 tonnes of the 700,000 tonnes pledged by donor nations and organizations had actually arrived.

One heart-warming lesson of the Ethiopian famines was that ordinary people in the spoilt and selfish West were still, despite everything, possessed of an enormous fund of private kindliness and generosity. The other, harsher lesson was that, whatever the availability of grain and money, famine relief can still be sabotaged by inefficiency on the part of the donors as well as by lack of the shipping tonnage, rail transport, packing and, above all, local cooperation and distribution that are needed to ensure that the last handful of food actually reaches the mouth of the last starving child, instead of being wasted, lost or stolen along the way.

THE WORLD OF THE OVERFED

Although hunger in a world of plenty is a tale as old as time, the contrast has seldom been demonstrated more graphically than it was in 1985. While the American administration sent $500 million to help save the lives of the wasted skeletons of Ethiopia, Americans themselves spent $5,000 million on trying to lose weight.*[6]

Diet guides, diet drugs, low-calorie foods, health clubs and health farms – all these profited in all Western countries (with the honourable exception of France) from the obsession with image and self. Said one failed dieter, 'To most people, being overweight is a judgement. It says you're weak, self-destructive.' But a nutritionist put it less emotively. 'If you're overweight, all it says is that you eat too much.'[7]

Curiously – or perhaps not so curiously, human nature being what it is – in the health-mad mid-80s even the *haute*st of American *haute cuisine* was noticeably more fattening than the European. Despite an occasional flirtation with the new, abstemious French styles, the kind of New York restaurant that boasted a four-week wait for reservations in 1986 was more likely to specialize in duck and lamb dishes, corn cakes with caviar and crème fraîche, apple desserts with caramel sauce, and chocolate bread pudding. In California it was pizza with

---

* America is the land of statistics and has to pay the price for it by having them quoted. If figures for other countries were available they would probably show the same general picture, if not on such an extreme scale.

wild mushrooms, red pepper fettucine, fried oysters with smoked ham, spicy sausages with fennel and whisky, ham hock and lentil salad, and – of course – chocolate cake.

Massachusetts tried to decide whether the Official State Muffin should be cranberry or apple filled. Gourmet popcorn was introduced. The search for the better bagel continued. The chocolate-covered potato crisp was invented.

Yuppy influence, however, ensured that beer and spirits were out. To get fit, get successful and get rich it was necessary to feel in control of the situation. Since alcohol addles the brain, the liquor manufacturers found themselves facing their toughest time since Prohibition. Not so the producers of tonic water. The whole American continent broke out in a rash of little green bottles. 'Coolers' were in, too, flavoured white-wine-and-soda spritzers like the Wineberry Sausalito Sling, which had a taste 'suggestive of ginger ale and bubble gum'.[8] The ideal accompaniment, no doubt, to the smoked duck garnished with pecans and braised red cabbage.

In Europe, despite a growing number of specialist magazines and television programmes, the most-to-be-dreaded words in the American language ('My husband is a gourmet cook') raised a mercifully faint echo. Things were different in other ways, too. *Cuisine minceur* and *nouvelle cuisine* ensured that, in the most fashionable restaurants, diners lost rather than gained weight. So also did their credit cards, since the overheads of such establishments were high. A typical dish consisting of three slices of breast of pheasant, mirrored in a pool of raspberry sauce and flanked by three black olives, five criss-crossed French beans and a single frond of some out-of-season herb required the services of one master chef, three sous-chefs, a full kitchen brigade and a fourth sous-chef with a background in the art of ikebana.

These demanding cuisines were to find no real place in the domestic kitchen, but inferior restaurants became adept at imitating their tricks of presentation and pricing while ignoring their finesse, and it became necessary for the more highly-exposed chefs (and diners) to change direction. The most favoured new cooking style became *cuisine naturelle*, the most favoured new art style, Dutch still life.

Nouvelle cuisine, at its peak, had been revolutionary in more than the obvious sense. A style for people with expense accounts, it completely reversed the historical tradition that a laden table and a stout figure are evidence of riches and success.

First Catch Your Expert...

History moved slowly for thousands of years until the Industrial Revolution hastened things along. Improved standards of literacy came next, which hastened things further by allowing knowledge and information to be spread more widely and more quickly. Then there were radio, television and the silicon chip.

Where once there had been an interval for thought between the dissemination of theory and counter-theory, by the 1980s the world found itself in the uneasy position of having theory, counter-theory and counter-counter-theory follow so closely on one another's heels that they appeared to be almost simultaneous.

In the matter of dietary principles so much was going on that the average person had little opportunity of finding out what *was* going on, and so fell into the way of accepting, without conscious thought, what was initially presented as the new, scientific certainty of the 1970s and 1980s.

This, expounded with the combination of repetition and passionate conviction that – as all good politicians and evangelists know – suffices to transform even the most dubious proposition into something approaching revealed truth, maintained that sugar, salt and saturated fats* were dangerous to health and should be banned from the diet.

The real truth, however, was not quite like that.

SUGAR

In 1968 the Biological Research Association at Carshalton, Surrey, announced that a positive link between sugar and heart disease had been found.[9] Other studies followed, some – though not all – reaching a similar conclusion.

In 1983 the Royal College of Physicians in London recommended halving the national intake of sugar (which provides calories but has no other dietary value) so as to encourage people to take their calories in a medically more desirable form.† One expert, sounding like a

* Briefly, saturated fats are animal fats, and remain solid at room temperature. Unsaturated fats (or polyunsaturates) are structurally different; they are found in fish, vegetable and seed oils, and remain liquid at room temperature except when incorporated into products such as margarine, when additives are used to solidify them.

† This extraordinarily silly pronouncement reinforced the suspicion that doctors and nutritionists were not only weak on psychology but unable to think of food as anything other than the sum of its nutrient parts.

reverse echo of a seventeenth-century tea or coffee merchant, announced that eating large quantities of refined sugar was directly related to gallstones, diabetes, heart disease, hernia, varicose veins, appendicitis, ulcers, diverticular disease and cancers of the lower gut.[10]

In 1986 the results were published of the most comprehensive study of sugar ever undertaken. The responsible body was the US Food and Drug Administration (FDA), which is bound by extremely strict laws designed to ensure the widest possible margin of safety. The FDA's medical task force found that sugar's only danger was in its contribution to tooth decay. An FDA official announced, 'We can now state categorically that there is no evidence at all to link sugar with obesity, diabetes, high blood pressure, hyperactivity or heart disease.'[11]

SALT

In 1972–5 a study was conducted in two Californian towns, measured against a control town. The published results reported that the subjects had cut their consumption of salt by 30 per cent and that their blood pressure (a major factor in heart disease) had dropped by 6.5 per cent.[12]

In 1982 hypertension (high blood pressure) was estimated to be involved in half the deaths in the United States every year.[13] Japan, with a very high salt intake, was claimed to have the highest rates of hypertension in the world.[14]

In 1986, according to a World Health Organization survey, Japan had the lowest rate of heart disease in the world, 45 per 100,000 as compared with 74 in France, 230 in the United States, 243 in England and Wales, and 298 in Scotland and Northern Ireland.[15]

In 1986, on behalf of the Royal Society of Medicine, six heart disease specialists weighed the evidence of more than 250 studies over the previous ten years. Although investigation of families with a history of high blood pressure showed no heightened sensitivity to salt, the specialists concluded that salt might *perhaps* exert a small influence on blood pressure, but that the effect was tiny compared with being overweight or drinking too much.[16]

SATURATED FATS

The human body manufactures cholesterol – a significant ingredient in the mushy deposits that clog the coronary arteries – from a number of raw materials. Various research studies during the 1960s and 1970s contributed to a belief that consumption of saturated fats dangerously increases the cholesterol level.

In 1970 heart disease was found to be commoner in soft-water areas, which suggested that a deficiency of minerals might contribute to coronary disease.[17]

In 1981 it was discovered that although breast cancer was widely thought to be associated with a diet rich in meat and fats, constipation was a more serious factor.[18]

In 1985 France, with the highest consumption of fat in the EEC, had one of the lowest incidences of heart disease.[19]

In 1987 the results were published of an unusually wide-ranging study of coronary disease carried out at Edinburgh with the support of the British Heart Foundation. Six thousand patients were involved and the research team concluded that inadequate intake or poor absorption of linoleic acid, which is found in fish, wheatgerm, soy beans, avocados, nuts etc., appeared to be of more importance in the development of heart attacks than saturated fats.[20] (Linoleic acid helps to prevent blood cells from clumping together and also helps to break down cholesterol and fatty deposits. Raw garlic, which has roughly similar properties,[21] may well turn out to be relevant to the low French incidence of heart disease.)

THE DANGERS OF DOGMA

In an increasingly intricate world even simplification that is perfectly well intended can deteriorate into over-simplification that is not only misleading but occasionally dangerous.

Where diet is concerned, some people have been persuaded not merely to cut back, but to cut too far back on foods that are essential to health. At a hospital in New York state in 1986, for example, one in four children under the age of two who were brought in because they were failing to gain weight turned out to have been kept by over-anxious parents on a low-cholesterol diet that was denying them the nutrients they needed for normal growth.[22]

On quite another level, the reputed link between specific foods and diseases gave rise in Britain in 1986 to demands for a 'government policy towards food and health' – demands that came not only from evangelists intent on improving the public's diet whether the public liked it or not, but also from distinguished bodies such as the British Medical Association, which suggested that government pricing policies could be used to 'promote a shift away from potentially harmful food products'.

The only interpretation that could be placed on this was that the BMA wanted the government to increase the price of foods of which the BMA disapproved – an invitation, in effect, to doctrinaire legislation of a kind that many people believe is already plentiful enough.

What the BMA in 1986 meant by 'potentially harmful foods' included (of course) sugar, salt and saturated fats – and whether or not these ultimately prove to have a role in bad health, the latter two are undoubtedly important to good health.

Sugar is the exception. It came late into the Western diet and has no nutritional value except as a source of transient energy. It is, however, an essential ingredient in many useful foods, and especially foods relied on by people who are not overburdened with money. While everyone would like to see pensioners, for example, eating something more nourishing for their evening meal than the tea, bread and jam that is all so many of them can afford (or in some cases want), it would be entirely irresponsible to increase the price of jam without *absolute* proof that sugar is harmful. (Honey, it may be added, has little more nutritional value than sugar, and contains traces of pollen to which some people are allergic.)

Salt is another matter. Sodium chloride is essential to all living things. Virtually all the vital functions in the human body, including nerve impulses and heart action, depend on the correct balance between salt and water, and the great majority of people are perfectly able to utilize what they need from their food and excrete the surplus without harm. The fact that salt has been of such importance all the way through history is, of course, an indication that the human race is by now genetically programmed to need it.

Saturated fats take the blame for high serum cholesterol in the body, and cholesterol has become a fearsome word in the last twenty years. But, like salt, it is essential to the system, as a building block of cell membranes, in the sheath that insulates nerves, in the digestive juices and in sex hormones. Fat itself protects the kidneys and nerves from shock, facilitates the absorption of vitamins A, D, E and K, and makes food more palatable. The calcium in milk (including skimmed milk) is believed to protect against cancer of the large intestine.*

* President Reagan having made this disease fashionable in 1985, Americans began to add extravagant quantities of calcium to their diet – thus inviting the formation of kidney stones. According to the director of the American Institute for Biosocial Research, there is also a positive link between excessive milk-drinking and chronic delinquency[23] (though not, presumably, in a septuagenarian president).

Where general health is concerned, the reality is that Western society in the late twentieth century has become prone to what many experts regard as the rags-to-riches diseases of hypertension, coronary heart ailments and a variety of cancers, and has fallen into the easy habit of blaming these on certain foods or groups of foods. Innumerable research studies have been carried out; some of them have been inadequately monitored, others overvalued, and their findings have in all cases been over-simplified. Perhaps the most striking thing about the picture as a whole is its multiplicity of contradictions. In effect, however convinced (and convincing) the health educators may appear to be, the evidence to date is very far from conclusive.

WHAT WE REALLY EAT

The reformers often speak, with pride, of the influence their campaigns have had on the general public and of the health benefits that have accrued.

Certainly, a United Kingdom survey of 2,000 consumers in 1986 reflected a strong interest in 'healthy' eating.[24] Many of those interviewed had changed to wholemeal bread instead of white. They were also eating less butter. This was supported by the statistics; butter consumption had dropped over the previous two years by all of three-quarters of an ounce per head per week.

Pork and beans were the mainstay of the Middle Ages. In colonial America, the Bostonians' Saturday supper was beans simmered with pork and molasses, and eaten with ketchup. In the 1980s, tinned baked beans (usually on toast, and often with pork sausages added) remain a perennial favourite. *Plus ça change* . . .

Then . . . 63 per cent of the people interviewed said they had increased their fruit and vegetable intake. Mysteriously, market statistics showed that fruit and vegetable consumption had actually fallen by 10 per cent over the previous five years. Thirty-three per cent of interviewees said they were eating more fish. Real fish consumption rose by only 9 per cent in 1985–6. Most of the interviewees also said they were eating more fibre, more fresh produce and less meat. But market statistics showed that in 1985 the nation was eating more meat than it had done for ten years – something like two pounds per head per week (not counting poultry) – and in 1986 this figure went up another 10 per cent.

As one American professor engagingly remarked of another survey, 'Sift through dustbins if you want to know what people eat; they're more truthful than people.' Pursuing this policy, a group of 'garbologists' in Green Valley, Arizona, discovered that residents ate twenty times more chocolate and fifteen times more pastries than they admitted in a consumer study. In Tucson, 85 per cent of people questioned said they did not drink beer – but 75 per cent of all dustbins inspected had beer cans in them.[25]

Where 'healthy' food is concerned, the wish, it seems, is not so much father to the deed as substitute for it. The main effect of the campaigns of the last dozen years may only have been to make people feel guiltier as they tuck into what a Gallup poll of 1986 discovered to be the Briton's perfect, expense-no-object meal – vegetable soup, prawn or shrimp cocktail, steak with chips, peas, carrots and salad, gâteau, cheese and biscuits, coffee and wine.

It showed a reassuring consistency of taste. Thirty-nine years earlier the answer to the same question had been tomato soup, sole, roast chicken with roast potatoes, peas and sprouts, trifle and cream, cheese and biscuits, coffee and wine.[26]

EPILOGUE

Epilogue

The history of food is a history of thousands of years of human choice set in the context of an almost Darwinian process of natural selection.

The diet that, over the millennia, ultimately predominated in different parts of the world was the diet best fitted not only to cultivation potential (though that was always a major factor) but also to the specific requirements of the inhabitants, requirements originally shaped more by work and living conditions than by any considerations of pleasure or satisfaction.

People who lived in cold damp climates found that rich, fatty foods were comforting and warming, helping to build up a layer of flesh that acted as insulation against the weather. In milder climates what the field labourer wanted was not so much warming food as energy-giving food to fuel the digging, ploughing and hoeing that made up the pattern of his day. In tropical countries perspiration evaporating from the skin helped to cool the body; strong spices encouraged that perspiration and at the same time stimulated a thirst for the liquid necessary to replace it.

Observations such as these – the product of experience, not scientific analysis – laid the foundations of many food traditions, but over the last 200 or 300 years the basic logic of food habits has become increasingly complicated by shortages, surpluses and the introduction or development of new foods and attitudes. Even the common human desire to catch up with the Joneses has helped to alter traditional diets sometimes for better, sometimes for worse.

Nowadays people who live in cold damp climates have little need for rich, fatty foods; central heating is an excellent substitute. The field labourer who once burned up calories reaping and binding grain now drives a combine harvester. Air conditioning is a pleasanter means of cooling the body than perspiration.

But old habits die hard, and the result is that the contemporary diet has in some ways become divorced from contemporary needs. The sedentary worker of the late twentieth century is eating half as much again in the way of energy-giving foods as his more active predecessor ate at the end of the nineteenth.[1] The sad fact is that the stomachs of rich and poor alike very often have more fuel, and more of the wrong fuel, pumped into them than they need or can contend with.

There is a case, it seems, for education, and two groups of educators are already at work.

THE ANTI EDUCATORS

The object of this group, which includes many members of the medical profession, is to persuade the public to abstain from foods that are claimed to be injurious to health: what else but sugar, salt and saturated fats?

As yet, and despite a good deal of self-congratulation, their influence over the food producers has been greater than over the population at large. To this influence, however, the nation owes bread without salt, croissants without butter, bacon without fat, meat without flavour; any consumer whose tongue papillae contain the requisite 245 taste buds in reasonable working order should be able to extend the list indefinitely.

But the ruin of good food is only the tip of the iceberg. By demanding the near-impossible with a sublime disregard for how it is to be achieved, the Anti campaigners have also been responsible for a number of developments that many people see as actively dangerous.

For example, their insistence on lean meat has led to much metabolic tinkering with food animals in the last fifteen years. Initially, the law permitted steroids, and hormones were used to reduce the body fat of the animal and increase the protein content of its meat, but these were banned in 1987–8. They are still being used – smuggled in – and so are other drugs, not all of them legal.

There is, of course, no way for the consumer to tell whether the meat on the butcher's counter comes from an ordinary, conventionally raised animal or one that has been de-fatted with the aid of chemicals, or intensively reared on antibiotics.*

Identification is easier in the case of most kinds of low-fat, ready-

---

* Or, indeed, on newspaper and old carrier bags. One owner of a feed company (in America) 'fed out three head of cattle to slaughter size on ground cardboard and grapefruit peel, and I want to tell you they dressed out real good. The taste on those guys was terrific. They were lean, but they made the best burgers I ever ate.'[2]

prepared meat dishes. If the meat is unnaturally tender, it may mean that the manufacturer has selected all the less fatty parts of the carcass, then minced and reassembled them with a quantity of cereal or potato

To make margarine, take 100 per cent natural ingredients. And then...

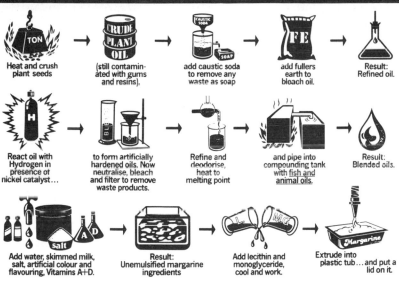

Heat and crush plant seeds → (still contaminated with gums and resins), → add caustic soda to remove any waste as soap → add fullers earth to bleach oil. → Result: Refined oil.

React oil with Hydrogen in presence of nickel catalyst... → to form artificially hardened oils. Now neutralise, bleach and filter to remove waste products. → Refine and deodorise, heat to melting point → and pipe into compounding tank with fish and animal oils. → Result: Blended oils.

Add water, skimmed milk, salt, artificial colour and flavouring, Vitamins A+D. → Result: Unemulsified margarine ingredients → Add lecithin and monoglyceride, cool and work. → Extrude into plastic tub... and put a lid on it.

Above is shown the typical manufacturing process for margarine.
Butter, on the other hand, can be made simply by churning cream.

No buts, it's got to be butter.

If you would like to know more, write for free booklets to BIC, FREEPOST, PO Box 101A, Surbiton, Surrey KT16 5AZ.

Name

Address

The Butter Information Council Ltd

starch, textured vegetable protein (usually soy), a good quantity of water and moisture-repairing polyphosphates, assorted flavourings and edible glue. The resulting paste is usually shaped into patties for frying, or cubes destined for low-fat pies, pasties and stews. Among the parts that can legally be used in such 'meat constructions' are those that the average consumer might reasonably regard as the waste of the slaughterhouse – rectum, testicles, udder, intestine, lips, snouts and lungs.

The campaign against saturated fats is, of course, concerned not only with meat. Low-cholesterol eggs and 'fat-free fat' are being produced in the United States. Polyunsaturate margarines are energetically recommended as a substitute for butter (the illustration on the previous page shows how these are made) and pure vegetable oils are claimed to be very much healthier for cooking than butter, lard or olive oil.* Here is the description given by Jane Grigson (not an enthusiast) of how these 'pure' oils are manufactured.

'First, the oils have to be degummed and neutralized. Phosphoric acid is injected into the oil and mixed under pressure to precipitate the gums.

'Then it is mixed with caustic soda, which forms a soap containing gums and colour which can be separated easily from the oil.

'Next stage is to wash the oil, dry it, bleach with fuller's earth and filter it. At this point it's a fully refined oil but the original taste and smell still remain, making it unacceptable for consumption.

'The final stage, therefore, is deodorization to ensure a bland, odourless oil that won't tinge the flavour of what's cooked in it.'[3]

THE PRO EDUCATORS

The second group of educators – who often confuse themselves and others by failing to realize that they and the Anti group are actually on opposing sides – appear to take a more constructive approach, by advocating 'healthy' foods rather than condemning 'unhealthy' foods.

On the principle that twentieth-century diseases are largely a product of the twentieth-century diet, they recommend a return to the

* Olive oil is a fruit rather than a vegetable oil. After some years of doubt over its cholesterol rating, the experts have now admitted it to the ranks of comparative respectability by declaring it 'neutral', i.e. not actively harmful.

food of 'our ancestors' (dates unspecified), who did not die – as so many people do today – of coronary thrombosis, strokes or cancer.

This is perfectly true. Our ancestors died, instead, of malnutrition, diabetes, yaws, rickets, parasites, leprosy, plague, skin infections, gynaecological disorders, tuberculosis and bladder stones, and they usually died in their 30s. Most modern diseases do not develop until the victims are in their late 40s or 50s. If our ancestors had lived ten years longer, coronary thrombosis, strokes and cancer might have been their fate, too.*

Might or might not. Although a good deal of work has been done on the history of diet, the evidence is inadequate and the results often run counter to nutritional logic. For example . . . In the eighth century the desert Arabs, nourished on dates and mutton, brought down with apparent ease the sophisticated empire of the Persians, whose diet in nutritional terms was infinitely superior. In the early 1500s the Aztecs of Mexico and the Inca of Peru should (if an abundance of vitamins is indeed a formula for health and vigour) have made mincemeat of the ship's-biscuit and salt-meat-eating Spaniards, but they failed dismally. And there have been many exceptions over the centuries to the general rule that amply fed warriors are more effective than hungry ones. In the 1740s the British Navy was winning battles on 5,500 calories a day; during the Napoleonic Wars it was still winning battles on 2,900 calories a day.[5]

On a rather different level, recent research suggests that until the nineteenth century mortality and quality of nutrition may have been less closely linked than is generally supposed. Several studies imply that whether a man was rich and lavishly fed or poor and hungry, he was doomed to die at much the same age.[6]

By claiming historical justification for their theories, the Pro educators are, in effect, merely confusing the issue. They would perhaps be wiser to make an honest, contemporary statement of what their campaign is really all about – which *appears* to be (it is not always easy to judge) an abstemious diet based on materials that are free from additives, adulterants and manufacturing contaminants. Not so

---

* It is sometimes argued that when the average lifespan was short, the diseases of middle age must have appeared earlier. However, it seems that, even in very early times, humanity's life cycle – youth to maturity to natural death – was shorter than that of modern man by less than three years.[4]

much 'healthy' foods (the list of which is apt to change without notice*) as natural foods.

The only problem is that, in the context of received wisdom today, 'natural' is an awkward word. If 'natural' and 'unnatural' are measured according to a scale based on the amount of human intervention in the process of their production (and there seems to be no other way of measuring them), then milk, butter, salt and conventionally farmed meat are just as 'natural' as rice, lentils and whole wheat flour. By conceding the Antis' claim that some of the most important natural foods are actively *un*healthy, the Pro group has painted itself into a corner.

THE MODERATE SOLUTION

In the overall historical context the case for blaming 'the diseases of civilization' on particular foods remains unproved, but the nutritionists' concentration on it has had the effect of diverting attention from other possible causes.

One of the original pointers to diet as the source of twentieth-century diseases was the observation that when people accustomed to a spartan regimen (such as the Japanese) changed to rich, Westernized food, they also fell heir to all the maladies of modern times. It seems possible, however, that the process of change rather than the food itself may have been the stimulant.

Although human biochemistry is still inadequately understood, the human system can be compared to an extremely intricate, delicately lubricated mechanism. All experience of other, similar kinds of mechanism – industrial, technological and scientific – shows that they can be damaged by sudden shocks, and the dietary changes of the twentieth century have (in general terms) been very sudden indeed. For thousands of years most people have had either too little to eat or just enough. Now, in a matter of decades, the peoples of the developed countries have begun to eat far more, and far more richly, than their grandparents; they also expend far less of the physical energy that would help to use up the surplus. It is not unreasonable to suppose that the visible results of the more ample diet (increased stature and

* Until a decade or so ago milk and eggs were excellent, potatoes and bread an evil indulgence. One nutritionist even advocated a slimming diet based on fats. All that has changed, but few observers would deny the possibility – indeed, the extreme probability – of a new dietary bandwagon beginning to roll at any time.

The roast on the plate . . .

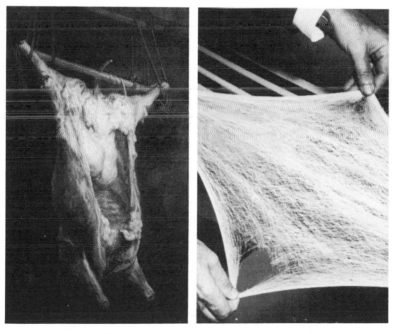

Animal?   Or vegetable?

increased weight) may have been paralleled by *in*visible biochemical stresses.

History has nothing to say about the ideal diet, but if excessive input and abrupt change are indeed integral to the twentieth-century dilemma, the logical conclusion is that moderation in all things is the wisest course. Eating less is likely to be beneficial, but the sudden cutting out (or adopting) of particular foods may be harmful. In the case of salt, fats and other foods that have been consumer-tested for something like 10,000 years, cutting out is by no means better than cutting down, and although most people probably eat too little fibre, a sudden increase in the intake of bran is an invitation to digestive upsets, while a regular high intake can result in anaemia and calcium deficiency. Twice as much (or little) does not mean twice as good when it comes to fuelling a body that works on the most complex system of checks and balances. A sense of proportion – noticeably lacking among the ranks of the health educators – is likely to be one of the safer formulae for health.

PROBLEMS OF A DIFFERENT KIND

When the first edition of *Food in History* was published in 1973, there was a general climate of surplus that encouraged administrative complacency about food and agricultural policies. In the decade that followed, nothing happened to dent that complacency. On the credit side, the failures of the first Green Revolution seemed on the way to being rectified. Substitute foods made from soy protein, leaf protein and a variety of other readily available substances became a reality. The world birth rate appeared to be dropping and the increase in world population that had been forecast (from 3,706 million in 1971 to 7,000 million in 2007) began to look like a vast over-estimate.

But nothing to do with food or society is ever simple. The decline in the birth rate proved to be misleading. In May 1987 new estimates placed world population figures at 7,000 million in 2010, just three years later than previously forecast; by 2022, it would be 8,000 million. And the probability was that more than 7,000 of those 8,000 million people would be inhabitants of the undernourished, under-capitalized Third World countries.[8]

While British experts argue that it will soon be necessary to take 20 per cent of Europe's agricultural land out of production, and America shows little concern over the increasing sterility of large tracts of its own farmlands, millions of acres in the Third World are being lost to the new, growing mega-cities. Cairo has already expanded over as great an acreage as was brought into cultivation only a few decades ago by the building of the Aswan High Dam, while Mexico City, São Paulo, Rio de Janeiro, Calcutta and Bombay are swallowing up the countryside at almost as great a rate.[9] What is happening is that the peasants – as peasants have done all through the ages – are abandoning rural poverty for the false haven of the city. As human labour becomes ever less relevant to agriculture, the influx will inevitably continue, and at an increasing rate.

In the developed world, population increase in the ordinary sense seems (at the moment) to offer no threat to the food supply. But although overall numbers are relatively static, unless consumption is curbed individual needs could rise significantly in the coming decades. People are becoming larger, and larger people need more food. In Japan in 1986 the average 17-year-old boy was two inches taller than he would have been in 1962,[10] while in 1962 the junior school student was already as tall as an adult had been fifty years earlier.[11] In China, too, over the last thirty years, average height has been increasing at the rate of an inch every ten years.[12] And in 1986 Britain's Civil Aviation Authority had to adjust the notional weight of the average male passenger from the 11st 8lb of 1975 to a substantial 12st 6lb.[13]

There is nothing new in all this. In a different context, on a lesser scale and over a longer time span, it has happened before, many times, in the course of history.

It has happened before and the human race has survived. But the earth is finite and it begins to seem as if the human race is not. Taking agricultural land out of production now, because the West has a supposedly unusable surplus of food, could well be the act that lays the foundations of hunger for millions of people among the generations of the future.

One thing is certain. Complacency is something that neither governments nor scientists can afford, because whatever the shape of the future, the role of food in it will be every bit as decisive as it has been in the past.

Notes on Sources

Where an abbreviated reference is given below, full details of the work referred to will be found in the bibliography.

Part One: The Prehistoric World

1 IN THE BEGINNING

1 R. Leakey, *The Making of Mankind* (1981); D. Johanson and M. Edey, *Lucy, the Beginnings of Humankind* (1981).
2 Brothwell, p. 24.
3 F. Ivanhoe, in *Nature* 227, 8 Aug. 1970; D. J. M. Wright, in *Nature* 229, 5 Feb. 1971.

2 FOOD AND COOKING BEFORE 10,000 BC

1 Coles and Higgs, p. 233.
2 D. Kolakowski and R. Malina, in *Nature* 251, 4 Oct. 1974.
3 F. Hole and K. V. Flannery, in *Proceedings of the Prehistoric Society*, Feb. 1968.
4 Raglan, cited in C. D. Darlington, *The Evolution of Man and Society* (1969), p. 33; report in *Sunday Times*, 16 April 1972.
5 D. McGuinness, in *Perception* 5, Oct. 1976.
6 G. Delibrias and N. Guidon, in *Nature* 321, Aug. 1986.
7 Quoted Brothwell, p. 87.
8 Coon, p. 63.
9 Coles and Higgs, p. 296.
10 Daumas, I p. 43.
11 H. W. Bates, *The Naturalist on the River Amazons* (1863).
12 Vries, p. 29; Chang, p. 131.
13 Herodotus IV 60.
14 Personal observation, R. T.
15 F. Galton, *The Art of Travel* (1860), p. 4.
16 Zeuner, pp. 112–28.

3 CHANGING THE FACE OF THE EARTH

1 Te-Tzu Chang, 'The Rice Cultures', in *Philosophical Transactions of the Royal Society of London* B 275 (1976), p. 143.
2 Flannery, in Ucko and Dimbleby, p. 79.
3 J. R. Harlan, in *Archaeology* XX, (1967), pp. 197–201.
4 Dr S. Katz, in *Expedition* (U. of Penn.), March 1987.
5 Renfrew, in Ucko and Dimbleby, p. 150.
6 W. Wendorf, R. Said and R. Schild, in *Science* CLXIX, 18 Sept. 1970, p. 1161; Reed, in Ucko and Dimbleby, p. 362.
7 M. Martin, *A Description of the Western Isles of Scotland* (1703), p. 244.
8 A. Migot, *Tibetan Marches* (1955), 1957 pb, p. 100.
9 E. S. Higgs and M. R. Jarman, in *Antiquity*, March 1969; Reed, in Ucko and Dimbleby, p. 361.
10 Zeuner, pp. 201–40.
11 E. G. Pulleyblank, 'Chinese and Indo-Europeans', in *Journal of the Royal Asiatic Society*, 1966, p. 10; Deerr, I 7n.
12 Excavations, preliminary report, *The Times*, 11 Dec. 1972.
13 *Ceres. The FAO Review* no. 111, 19 no. 3, Aug. 1986.
14 Pliny the Elder, XVIII xlvii.
15 R. Oliver and J. D. Fage, *A Short History of Africa* (1962), 1968 pb, p. 37.
16 Harrison *et al*, p. 120; G. E. Willey, *Introduction to American Archeology* (1966) I 82; *Science*, 5 Jan. 1973; J. A. Mason, *The Ancient Civilizations of Peru* (1957), 1964 pb, p. 31.
17 Brothwell, pp. 60–1.
18 *Ibid*. p. 72.
19 *Ibid*. pp. 68–9.
20 P. S. Bellwood, in *The Times*, 17 Aug. 1973.
21 Report in *Time*, 9 Feb. 1970; W. G. Solheim II in *Scientific American*, April 1972; Te-Tzu Chang, see note 1 above.
22 Report in *The Times*, 23 Dec. 1985.
23 Needham, 1984.
24 Te-Tzu Chang, see note 1 above.
25 W. Watson, in Ucko and Dimbleby, p. 393.
26 Pan Ku, pp. 434–5.

PART TWO: THE NEAR EAST, EGYPT AND EUROPE
3000 BC – AD 1000

4 THE FIRST CIVILIZATIONS

1 J. D. Bernal, *Science in History* (1954), I 93.
2 Quoted in S. N. Kramer, *The Sumerians, Their History, Culture and Character* (1964), p. 341.

3 G. Posener (ed.), *A Dictionary of Egyptian Civilization* (1961), p. 40.

4 H. W. F. Saggs, *Everyday Life in Babylonia and Assyria* (1965), p. 61.

5 *Ur Excavations* III (1947), p. 248.

6 Kramer, see note 2 above, p. 110; Herodotus III 113; Zeuner, p. 190.

7 Singer [2], I 279.

8 Kramer, see note 2 above, pp. 110–11.

9 Saggs, see note 4 above, p. 137.

10 A. Wiedemann, *Das alte Aegypten* (1920), p. 299.

11 Quoted in Isaac Myer, *Oldest Books in the World* (1900), p. 132.

12 Quoted Ghalioungui, in Darby *et al*, II 236.

13 Xenophon, *Anabasis*, trs. R. Warner as *The Persian Expedition*, 1949 pb, II 3.

14 *Ibid.*

15 Quoted in Athenaeus, XIV 652.

16 *Ibid.* 653

17 Needham [1] IV 2, p. 181.

18 Pliny the Elder, XVIII xxvi.

19 M. A. Ruffer, 'Abnormalities of Ancient Egyptian Teeth', in *Studies in the Paleopathology of Egypt* (1921), pp. 288 f.

20 W. B. Emery, *Archaic Egypt*, pb 1961, p. 243.

21 Herodotus, II 77.

22 Report in *The Times*, 19 Nov. 1985.

23 J. Soler, 'The Semiotics of Food in the Bible' [an original and thought-provoking study], in Forster and Ranum [2], p. 136.

5 CLASSICAL GREECE

1 Athenaeus I 12.

2 Homer, *The Iliad* IX, trs. E. V. Rieu, pb 1950.

3 Hesiod, *Works and Days* 589–94, trs. F. L. Lucas in *Greek Poetry for Everyman* (1951).

4 Quoted in Coon, p. 293.

5 Prakash, p. 265.

6 Lichine, p. 204.

7 *Ibid.* p. 205; Hyams, p. 105.

8 Derry and Williams, p. 61.

9 Quoted in H. D. F. Kitto, *The Greeks*, pb 1957, p. 33.

10 Moritz, p. 150.

11 Pliny the Elder XVIII xiv–xv.

12 P. Devambez, R. Flacelière, P.-M. Schuhl and R. Martin, *A Dictionary of Ancient Greek Civilisation* (1967), p. 397.

13 Suetonius, *The Twelve Caesars*, Vitellius xiii, trs. R. Graves, pb 1957.

14 Athenaeus VI 268.

15 *Ibid.* IV 138 and XII 518.

16 *Ibid.* VII 278.
17 Zeuner, p. 450.
18 Athenaeus IV 132.
19 *Ibid.* II 55.

6 IMPERIAL ROME

1 F. R. Cowell, *The Revolutions of Ancient Rome* (1962), pp. 96–7.
2 J. Carcopino, *Daily Life in Ancient Rome* (1941), pb 1967, p. 29.
3 Levy, p. 96; Mossé, pp. 108–10.
4 Quoted Hyams, p. 342.
5 Carcopino, see note 2 above, pp. 28–9.
6 Mossé, pp. 108–10; Rickman, p. 189.
7 Moritz, pp. 25–7.
8 Athenaeus III 115.
9 *Ibid.*
10 *Ibid.* III 110–14.
11 *Ibid.* IV 131.
12 Juvenal, *The Sixteen Satires*, II 66–74, trs. P. Green, pb 1968.
13 J. P. V. D. Balsdon, *Life and Leisure in Ancient Rome* (1969), p. 37.
14 *The Alice B. Toklas Cook Book* (1954), pb 1961, p. 207.
15 Petronius, *The Satyricon*, trs. W. Arrowsmith (1960), pp. 42–76.
16 Suetonius, see note 13 chapter 5 above.
17 Levy, p. 72.
18 Apicius VII v 4.
19 Petronius, see note 15 above, p. 72.
20 *Geoponica* XX 46, quoted in intr. to Apicius, p. 22.
21 *Ibid.*
22 Bardach, p. 139.
23 Athenaeus III 100.
24 *Ibid.* II 67.
25 Miller, p. 201.
26 *Ibid.* p. 26.
27 Herodotus III 111.
28 *Ibid.* 108–10.
29 Miller, pp. 82–3; Athenaeus III 66.
30 Miller, p. 201.
31 *Silappadikaram*, quoted in Miller, p. 25.
32 Simkin, p. 45; Levy, p. 89.
33 Plutarch, *Lives*.
34 S. C. Gilfillan, speech at Third International Congress of Human Genetics, Chicago, reported in *Time*, 23 Sept. 1966.
35 Dr J. O. Nriagu, in *New England Journal of Medicine*, March 1983.

7 THE SILENT CENTURIES

1 Vicens Vives, p. 84.
2 Postan, in G. Barraclough (ed.), *Eastern and Western Europe in the Middle Ages* (1970), p. 143.
3 Eginhard [Einhard], *Early Lives of Charlemagne*, ed. A. J. Grant (1907), pp. 38–9.
4 Ashley, pp. 16–20; Best, p. 104.
5 Cited in Duby, p. 9.
6 *Ibid.*
7 Fagniez, docs. xxix, xxx.
8 Crisp, I p. 95.
9 Zeuner, p. 412.
10 Carefoot and Sprott, p. 34.
11 *Ibid.*
12 Quoted Simkin, p. 173.
13 J. Gernet, *Daily Life in China on the Eve of the Mongol Invasions 1250– 1276* (1962), p. 135.
14 Tannahill, pb 1976, pp. 116 ff.

PART THREE: ASIA UNTIL THE MIDDLE AGES, AND THE ARAB WORLD

8 INDIA

1 F. F. Darling and M. A. Farvar, in *The Careless Technology. Ecology and International Development*, ed. M. T. Farvar and J. P. Milton (1973).
2 Prakash, pp. 15–16.
3 *Ibid* p. 18
4 *Ibid.* p. 38.
5 D. D. Kosambi, *An Introduction to the Study of Indian History* (1956), p. 230.
6 Prakash, pp. 12–15.
7 *Ibid.* p. 192.
8 R. S. Khare, *The Hindu Hearth and Home* (1977), p. 83.
9 Prakash, pp. 108–9.
10 Kautilya, *Arthasastra*, ed. R. P. Kangle (1960–65), II xxvi 7–12.
11 Abou-Zeyd-Hassan, in M. Reinaud, *Rélation des Voyages faits par les Arabes et les Persans dans l'Inde et à la Chine dans le IXe siècle de l'Ère chrétienne* (1845), p. 152.
12 Prakash, p. 158.
13 *Ibid.* p. 236.
14 Kautilya, see note 10 above, II xv 17.
15 Prakash, p. 213–14.

16 *Ibid.*
17 A. L. Basham, *The Wonder that was India* (1954), pb 1971, p. 505.
18 Kautilya, see note 10 above, II xv 47.

9 CENTRAL ASIA

 1 K. Jettmar, *Art of the Steppes* (1967), pp. 238–9.
 2 Herodotus IV 47.
 3 Cited in T. T. Rice, *The Scythians* (1957), p. 63.
 4 *The Travels of Fa-hsien* [AD 399–414], *or Records of the Buddhistic Kingdoms,* trs. H. A. Giles (1923), p. 2.
 5 Marco Polo, pp. 81–2.
 6 *The Remarkable Travels of William de Rubruquis . . . into Tartary and China,* 1253, in J. Pinkerton, *A General Collection of . . . Voyages and Travels* (1808–14), VII p. 49.
 7 Daumas I p. 350.
 8 *Yu-yang-tsa-tsu,* quoted in B. Davidson, p. 121.
 9 Michael Psellus, *Chronographia* VII 69, trs. E. R. A. Sewter as *Fourteen Byzantine Rulers* (1966).
10 H. M. de Valbourg, M. *Misson's Memoirs and Observations in his Travels over England,* trs. Mr Ozell (1719), p. 154.
11 *Ibid.*
12 Center for Brain Sciences and Metabolism conference at MIT, reported in *Sunday Times,* 19 Dec. 1982.
13 Marco Polo, p. 82.
14 Cranstone, in Ucko and Dimbleby, pp. 250–62.
15 Rubruck, see note 6 above, p. 31.

10 CHINA

 1 Shi-Shung Huang and E. M. Bayless in *Science,* 5 April 1968; research at Chiang Mai University, Cambodia, reported in *Nature,* 22 Feb. 1969; research by Dr A. Ferguson, Edinburgh University, report in *The Times,* 29 Aug. 1986.
 2 G. Flatz and H. W. Rotthauwe, in *Lancet,* 14 July 1973.
 3 Schafer, pp. 151 and 168.
 4 Chao Ju-kua, *Chu-fan-chi,* trs. F. Hirth and W. W. Rockhill (1911), II 19.
 5 Smith and Christian, p. 228.
 6 Schafer, in Chang, p. 123.
 7 Chang, in Chang, p. 11.
 8 *Shih ching,* in C. Birch and D. Keene (eds.) *Anthology of Chinese Literature* (1965), pb 1967 pp. 37–8.
 9 *Ibid.* p. 56.
10 Confucius, *The Analects* X 7–8, trs. A. Waley, 1938.

11 *Li-chi, or Book of Rituals*, trs. J. Legge in *Sacred Books of the East*, ed. F. Max-Müller, vol. XXVII (1885), p. 467.
12 Chang, in Chang, p. 11.
13 In Birch and Keene, see note 8 above, p. 101.
14 Needham [1], IV 2 p. 58.
15 *Ibid*. VI 2 pp. 221–43.
16 Ying-shih Yu, in Chang, pp. 81–2.
17 *Ibid*. p. 57.
18 Report in *Time*, 9 May 1969.
19 Yule [2], p. 858.
20 Reported in *The Times*, 7 January 1987.
21 Schafer, p. 29.
22 *Ibid*.
23 Sei Shonagon, quoted in I. Morris, *The World of the Shining Prince. Court Life in Ancient Japan* (1964), pb 1969, p. 100.
24 I-ching, quoted in Schafer, p. 140.
25 D. Morgan, *The Mongols* (1986).
26 R. Grousset, *The Rise and Splendour of the Chinese Empire*, 1952, p. 171; Schafer, p. 280.
27 Marco Polo, p. 149.
28 Grousset, see note 26 above, p. 236.
29 Gernet, see note 13 chapter 7 above, p. 136.
30 Marco Polo, p. 181.
31 Odoric de Pordenone, in Yule [1], II p. 96.
32 *Ibid*. p. 977.
33 Report by directors of the National Palace Museum, Taipei, Taiwan, in *Free China Review*, Feb. 1969.

11 THE ARAB WORLD

1 Al-Jahiz, 'The Investigation of Commerce', quoted in Lopez and Raymond pp. 28–9.
2 Quoted in Duckett, p. 171.
3 Quoted in Arberry, p. 22.
4 A. J. Chejne, 'The Boon-Companion in Early Abbasid Times', in *Journal of the American Oriental Society* (1965), p. 333.
5 Ibn Ishaq, *Life of Muhammad* [c. AD 770, expanded by Ibn Isham c. AD 820]. MS translation by Edward Rehatsek, in the library of the Royal Asiatic Society, London, fol. 1057.
6 A. M. Watson, *passim*.
7 Quoted in Ashtor, p. 127.
8 Arberry, p. 194.
9 *Ibid*. p. 39.
10 Rodinson, p. 151.

11 Arberry, p. 214.

12 Quoted Needham [2], p. 358.

13 Quoted O'Hara-May, p. 43.

14 MacGowan, p. 238.

15 Bernal, I p. 188; Needham [2], p. 267; Prakash, p. 132.

16 G. M. Carstairs, *The Twice-Born. A Study of a Community of High-Caste Hindus* (1957), p. 84; L. I. and S. H. Rudolf, *The Modernity of Tradition, Political Development in India* (1967), p. 214; Chang, p. 10.

17 *Brhadaranyaka Upanishad*, VI iv 18, trs. in vol. 1 of *Sacred Books of the East*, see note 11 chapter 10 above.

18 F. A. Steel and G. Gardiner, *The Complete Indian Housekeeper and Cook* (1888), 1917 edn., p. 176 n.

19 *Salerno Regimen.*

20 *Ibid.*

PART FOUR: EUROPE AD 1000–1492

12 SUPPLYING THE TOWNS

1 L. White Jr, p. 53.

2 Needham [1], with F. Bray, VI 2 p. 417.

3 Anna Comnena, *Alexiad* X v, trs. E. R. A. Sewter (1969).

4 G. Duby and R. Mandrou, *A History of French Civilization* (1965), pp. 101–2.

5 Derry and Williams, pp. 195 and 202.

6 Riley, 19 Edward III, Letterbook F, ff.cii and ccii.

7 Research by Professor H. von Faber and Dr E. Mueller of the University of Hohenheim, reported in *The Times*, 23 October 1986.

8 P. E. Jones, pp. 47–81 *passim*.

9 Riley, 43 Edward III, Letterbook G, fol.ccxxxiii.

10 Lespinasse, royal edict of August 1416.

11 Athenaeus VI 5.

12 Riley, 22 Edward III, Letterbook F, fol.clii.

13 P. G. Molmenti, *Venice, Its Growth to the Fall of the Republic* (1906–8), II p. 135.

14 Riley, *Assisa Panis* (suppl.), fol.79v.

15 William Fitz Stephen [pre-1183], in F. M. Stenton, *Norman London. An Essay* (1934), p. 28.

16 Riley, 2 Richard II, Letterbook H, fol. xcix.

17 *Madras Athenaeum*, quoted in P. L. Simmonds, *The Curiosities of Food* (1859), p. 108.

18 Singer [2], II p. 532.

19 W. A. Janssen and C. D. Meyers, in *Science*, 2 Feb. 1968.

20 Ménagier, p. 241.

21 Al-Jahiz, see note 1 chapter 11 above.
22 Cited in Burnett [2], p. 29.
23 Duby, p. 66 n. 6.
24 Vicens Vives, pp. 88–9, 131, 252.
25 'The Chronicle of Giovanni Villani', quoted Lopez and Raymond, p. 73.
26 Ménagier, p. 222.
27 Duby, p. 145.
28 *Ibid.* p. 146.
29 Research reported in *The Times*, 30 Nov. 1985.
30 Quoted in Drummond and Wilbraham, p. 29.

13 THE LATE MEDIEVAL TABLE

 1 Burnett [2], p. 30; Bridbury, p. 29.
 2 C. Hibbert, *The Roots of Evil, A Social History of Crime and Punishment* (1966), p. 37.
 3 E. Power and M. M. Postan, *Studies in English Trade in the Fifteenth Century* (1951), p. 172.
 4 Bridbury, p. 8.
 5 Quoted in Hibbert, see note 2 above, p. 43.
 6 Quoted in Molmenti, see note 13 chapter 12 above, I i pp. 14–17.
 7 Lattimore, p. 43.
 8 *Time*, 15 March 1982.
 9 Jawaharlal Nehru, *An Autobiography* (1958 edn.), p. 213.
10 Ménagier, pp. 272–3.
11 Austin, p. 31.
12 Ménagier, *passim*.
13 Taillevent, pp. 32–3.
14 Pegge, p. 66.
15 Austin, p. 43.
16 Ménagier, p. 228.
17 *Ibid.*
18 Epulario, *The Italian Banquet* [1516], English trs. 1598.
19 Gédéon Tallemant, Sieur des Réaux, *Historiettes* [17th century], Paris 1834.
20 H. Havard, *Dictionnaire de l'Ameublement* [Fourchette], 1887–90.
21 Knife and fork as a place setting are shown in the late fourteenth-century Greek icon, 'Hospitality of Abraham', in the Benaki Museum, Athens.
22 *Chy sensuivent les gistes . . .* [de] *m. J. L. S.*, quoted in Havard, see note 20 above.
23 T. Coryat, *Coryat's Crudities: Hastily gobled up in Five Moneth's Travells in France* [1611], 1905 edn. II.
24 J. Morris, *Pax Britannica* (1969), p. 248.
25 Furnas, p. 903.

26 Della Casa, p. 102.
27 Fra Bonvicino, in Furnivall [2].
28 Tannhauser, in *ibid*.
29 Della Casa, in *ibid*.
30 Fra Bonvicino, Tannhauser, in *ibid*.
31 Benvenuto Cellini, *Life*, trs. Miss Macdonell (1907), p. 35.
32 Case reported in the *Sunday Times*, 30 Sept. 1984.
33 'Fart', in Samuel Johnson, *Dictionary* (1755).
34 Kautilya, see note 10 chapter 8 above, V iv 9.
35 Claudius xxxii, in Suetonius, see note 13 chapter 5 above.
36 Quoted in Chejne, see note 4 chapter 11 above, p. 332.
37 *Salerno Regimen*.
38 Furnivall [1], p. 136.
39 Pyke, p. 226.
40 *Sunday Times*, 19 Sept. 1976.
41 *The Times*, 1 Jan. 1987.

PART FIVE: THE EXPANDING WORLD 1492–1789

14 NEW WORLDS

1 T. M. [Thomas Mun], 'A Discourse of Trade, from England unto the East-Indies etc' [1621], in *East Indian Trade, Selected Works, 17th Century* (1967), p. 11.
2 *The Life of the Admiral Christopher Columbus*, by his son Ferdinand, trs. B. Keen (1959), p. 154.
3 Da Gama's log, quoted in B. Davidson, pp. 133–4.
4 Quoted in E. Belfort Bax, *German Society at the Close of the Middle Ages* (1894), appendix A.

15 THE AMERICAS

1 *Time*, 20 Oct. 1986.
2 Columbus, see note 2 chapter 14 above, pp. 78, 80.
3 *Ibid*. p. 87.
4 *Time*, 21 April 1986.
5 *The Times*, 27 Oct. 1981.
6 Columbus, see note 2 chapter 14 above, p. 85.
7 *Ibid*. p. 245.
8 *Ibid*. p. 86.
9 Ping-ti Ho, in *American Anthropologist*, April 1955, pp. 191–201.
10 Quoted A. M. Coats, in 'The Fruit with a Shady Past', *Country Life*, 17 May 1973.
11 Pickersgill, in Ucko and Dimbleby, p. 447.

12 Bernal Díaz, *The True History of the Conquest of New Spain*, trs. J. M. Cohen, pb 1963 p. 232.

13 Columbus, see note 2 chapter 14 above, p. 83.

14 Fr. Bernardino de Sahagún, *Historia general de las cosas de Nueva España* [16th century], 1938 edn. II p. 372.

15 G. Powell, 'Jahangir's Turkey-Cock', in *History Today*, Dec. 1970, pp. 857–8.

16 Quoted *ibid.*

17 Tannahill, p. 76.

18 Bernal Díaz, see note 12 above, pp. 198–9.

19 Tannahill, pp. 81–6.

20 Vicens Vives, p. 386.

21 Juan de Castellanos, quoted in Salaman, p. 102.

22 Salaman, p. 143.

23 Jules Charles de l'Écluse, quoted ibid. p. 90.

24 Salaman, pp. 52ff.

25 *Ibid.* p. 104.

26 *Ibid.* p. 106.

27 Rumford, p. 403.

28 Smith and Christian, pp. 280–3.

29 Reynière, 1810 p. 104.

30 Bloch, in Hémardinquer, pp. 234–5.

31 A. Beauvilliers, *L'Art du cuisinier* (1814), 2t, I p. 5 and II p. 213.

32 Vicens Vives, p. 214; Postan, in Barraclough, p. 132.

33 Quoted in H. A. Wyndham, *The Atlantic and Slavery* (1935), p. 221.

34 King Affonso of Congo (Mbemba Nzinga), quoted in Davidson, pp. 194–5.

35 John Ogilby, *America* (1671), pp. 503–5.

36 A. J. R. Russell-Wood, *Fidalgos and Philanthropists: The Santa Casa de Misericordia of Bahia 1550–1755* (1968), pp. 33–4.

37 R. Oliver and J. D. Fage, *A Short History of Africa* (1962), pb 1968, p. 120.

38 Braudel, p. 158.

39 *The Times*, 20 Oct. 1986.

40 Quoted in K. McNaught, *The Pelican History of Canada* (1969), p. 20.

41 Quoted in P. L. Barbour (ed.), *The Jamestown Voyages under the First Charter 1606–9*, (1969) II p. 273.

42 Gabriel Archer, quoted *ibid.* p. 282.

43 Quoted in Furnas, p. 170.

16 FOOD FOR THE TRAVELLER

1 *Cowley's Voyage Round the Globe*, in Captain William Hacke, *A Collection of Original Voyages* (1699), pp. 7 ff.

2 Columbus, see note 2 chapter 14 above, p. 240.

3 Lloyd, p. 256.

4 William Lithgow, *The Totall Discourse of the Rare Adventures and Painefull Peregrinations of long Nineteene Yeares Travayles from Scotland to the most famous Kingdomes in Europe, Asia and Affrica* [1632], 1906 edn. pp. 58–9.

5 Quoted in Drummond and Wilbraham, p. 138.

6 *True and Large Discourse of the Voyage of the whole Fleete of Ships set forth the 20 of Aprill 1601 by the Governours and Assistants of the East Indian Marchants in London, to the East Indies* [1603], reprinted in *East Indian Trade, Selected Works, 17th century,* 1968, p. 6.

7 Pack, p. 7.

8 Sir John Richardson, quoted in Simmonds, see note 17 chapter 12 above, p. 15.

9 Frederick Gerstäcker, *Gerstäcker's Travels* (1854), p. 97.

17 A GASTRONOMIC GRAND TOUR: I

1 Peter Beckford, *Familiar Letters from Italy to a Friend in England* [pre-1787] (1805), letter XXV.

2 Scappi, pp. 392 ff.

3 Prakash, p. 204; Arberry, p. 45.

4 E. N. and M. L. Anderson, in Chang, p. 338.

5 Pegge, p. 46.

6 Quoted in E. H. Wilkins, *A History of Italian Literature* (1954), p. 205.

7 Girolamo Lippomano, *Viaggio* [1577] in M. N. Tommaseo, *Relations des Ambassadeurs Vénitiens sur les Affaires de France au XVIe Siècle* (1838), II pp. 569 and 487.

8 Pliny the Elder, XIX xi.

9 Francesco Carletti, *Ragionamenti* [1594–1606], trs. H. Weinstock as *My Voyage Around the World* (1964), p. 53.

10 Antonio Colmenero, quoted in Franklin, XIII pp. 161–2.

11 Marie de Rabutin-Chantal, Marquise de Sévigné, *Lettres*, ed. Monmerque et Meynard (1862–1875), letter of 25 Oct. 1671.

12 Younger, pp. 273–4.

13 Della Casa, in Furnivall [2].

14 Schafer, in Chang, p. 122.

15 Patrick Lamb, *Royal Cookery: or, the Compleat Court-Cook* (1710), p. 41.

16 Joachim von Sandrart, *Der Teutschen Academie* (1675–9), II p. 313.

17 Misson, see note 10 chapter 9 above, p. 314.

18 Pehr Kalm, *Kalm's account of his visit to England on his way to America in 1748* (1892), p. 15.

19 George Turberville, quoted in Smith and Christian, p. 101.

20 Smith and Christian, pp. 88–9.

21 J. Parkinson, *A Tour of Russia, Siberia, and the Crimea*, ed. S. I. Kotkov 1978, p. 68.
22 Smith and Christian, p. 142.
23 Quoted *ibid.*, p. 155.
24 Reitenfels, quoted *ibid.*, p. 167.
25 Smith and Christian, p. 227.
26 *Ibid.* pp. 217–18.
27 Peyerle, quoted *ibid.*, pp. 114–15.
28 Smith and Christian, p. 125.
29 Pokhlebkin, quoted *ibid.*, p. 173.
30 Just Juel, quoted *ibid.*, p. 174.
31 Elizabeth Justice, *A Voyage to Russia* (1745), p. 18.

18 A GASTRONOMIC GRAND TOUR: 2

1 S. Sewall, *Samuel Sewall's Diary*, ed. Mark Van Doren 1927, p. 179.
2 Furnas, pp. 26–7.
3 E. A. Ellis (ed.) *Northern Cookbook* (1967), p. 48.
4 Quoted in *American Heritage Cookbook* (1964), p. 58.
5 'Applejack', in Lichine.
6 Lichine, p. 459.
7 Lord, p. 45.
8 Lichine, p. 397.
9 Carletti, see note 9 chapter 17 above, p. 46.
10 *American Anthropologist*, 78 iii 1977.
11 Thomas Winterbottom, quoted in Davidson, p. 244.
12 *New England Journal of Medicine*, 313 21, Nov. 1985.
13 Vicens Vives, p. 395.
14 Gerstacker, see note 9 chapter 16 above, p. 78.
15 *Assoc. of Pacific Coast Geographers: Yearbook*, 32 99, 1970.
16 Beckett, p. 131.
17 *Ibid.* p. 16.
18 An Emigrant Mechanic [Alexander Harris], *Settlers and Convicts* (1847).
19 Spence, in Chang, p. 263.
20 Anon. in *Melbourne Punch*, 10 Dec. 1925.
21 Anon. [W. C. Hunter], *The 'Fan Kwae' at Canton, before Treaty days, 1825–1844, By An Old Resident*, 1911 edn., pp. 41–2.
22 W. C. Hunter, *Bits of Old China* (1885), pp. 38–9.
23 *Sunday Times*, 29 Sept. 1974.
24 MacGowan, pp. 237–40.
25 *Ibid.*
26 Eliza Smith, *The Compleat Housewife* (London 1727), the same text being publ. in Virginia (1742) under the name of 'William Parks'; B. C. A. Turner, *The Pan Book of Wine Making* (1965), p. 113.

27 Chang, pp. 34–45.
28 Carletti, see note 9 chapter 17 above, pp. 110–11.
29 Quoted in Yule [1], II.
30 T. Volker, *Porcelain and the Dutch East India Company* ... *1602–1682* (1954), p. 48; Th. H. L. Scheurleer, 'The Dutch at the Tea-Table', in *The Connoisseur*, Oct. 1976.
31 S. Pepys, *The Diary and Correspondence of Samuel Pepys Esq. FRS* [1659–1703], ed. Lord Braybrooke (1825), entry for 25 Oct. 1660.
32 Baikov, in A. and J. Churchill, *A Collection of Voyages and Travels* (1704–32), II p. 50.
33 John Bell, *A Journey from St Petersburg to Pekin 1719–22*, ed. J. L. Stevenson 1965, p. 86.
34 Smith and Christian, p. 234.
35 Arberry, p. 210.
36 Ovington, quoted in Hilton Brown (ed.), *The Sahibs. The Life and Ways of the British in India as Recorded by Themselves* (1948), p. 50.
37 T. de L., pp. 284–6 and 71–2.
38 John Corneille, *Journal of My Service in India* [1754–57], 1966 edn., p. 84.
39 Yule [1], p. 232.
40 Lithgow, see note 4 chapter 16 above, p. 136.
41 Pietro della Valle, *Viaggi* [1614–26], 1843 edn., I pp. 51, 74–6.
42 Thomas Herbert, *Some Yeares Travels into Africa and Asia the Great. Especially Describing the Famous Empires of Persia and Industant* (1638), p. 241.
43 *New England Journal of Medicine*, 22 March 1984; *British Medical Journal*, 9 Jan. 1987.
44 Mungo Park, quoted in Davidson, p. 316.
45 P. D. Curtin, 'Nutrition in African History', in Rotberg and Rabb, pp. 181–2.
46 *Ibid.* p. 176.
47 Mungo Park, quoted in Davidson, pp. 315 and 312.
48 John Barrow, quoted *ibid.*, pp. 276–7.
49 *Ibid.*

PART SIX: THE MODERN WORLD
1789 UNTIL THE PRESENT DAY

19 THE INDUSTRIAL REVOLUTION

1 Thomas Blaikie, *The Diary of a Scotch Gardener at the French Court at the end of the eighteenth century*, ed. F. Birrell (1931), p. 74.
2 E. David, *English Bread and Yeast Cookery* (1977), p. 497.

3 Quoted in E. Halevy, *A History of the English People in 1815*, 1937 pb edn, II pp. 45–6.
4 F. Bédarida in Asa Briggs (ed.), *The Nineteenth Century: The Contradictions of Progress* (1970), p. 119.
5 Quoted in J. L. and B. Hammond, *The Bleak Age* (1947), p. 67.
6 Florence Nightingale, 'Observations by Miss Nightingale on the Evidence contained in the Stational Returns etc', in The Royal Commission on the Sanitary State of the Army in India: *Report of the Commissioners* (1863), preface to vol. 1.
7 Friedrich Engels, *The Condition of the Working Class in England in 1844* (1845).
8 Drummond and Wilbraham, p. 331.
9 Burnett [1], p. 52.
10 S. R. Bosanquet, *The Rights of the Poor and Christian Almsgiving Vindicated* (1841), p. 91.
11 Arthur Young, *A Tour in Ireland 1776–1779* (1780), II p. 237.
12 Furnas, p. 384.
13 Burnett [1], p. 141.
14 Andrew Wynter, quoted in E. R. Pike, *Human Documents of the Victorian Golden Age, 1850–1875* (1967), p. 58.
15 Gerstäcker, see note 9 chapter 16 above, p. 61.
16 B. Walker, 'The Flesher's Trade in Eighteenth and Nineteenth-century Scotland', in Fenton and Kisban, pp. 128–9.
17 *The Times*, 27 March 1984.
18 Quoted in F. P. Robinson, p. 129.
19 T. Stobart, *The Cook's Encyclopaedia* (1980), pb 1982, p. 12.
20 *The Times*, 22 Dec. 1986.
21 R. H. Gronow, *Reminiscences and Recollections* (1892), I p. 51.
22 Pückler-Muskau, *Tour in England, Ireland, and France . . . in 1829 . . . by a German Prince* (1832), III pp. 83–7.
23 Hayward, p. 105.
24 Oliver Goldsmith, *The Citizen of the World* (1762), letter LVIII.
25 Hayward, pp. 90–1.
26 Thomas Walker, quoted in Hayward, p. 87.
27 P. d'A. Jones, *The Consumer Society. A History of American Capitalism* (1963), pb 1967, p. 74.
28 *Ibid.* p. 91.

20 THE FOOD-SUPPLY REVOLUTION

1 Andrew Wynter, quoted in Pike, see note 14 chapter 19 above, p. 59.
2 Derry and Williams, p. 680.
3 W. M. Hurst and L. M. Church, in US Dept of Agriculture Misc. Pub. 157 (1933); Jones, see note 27 chapter 19 above, p. 186.

4 Derry and Williams, p. 686.
5 Victor Jacquemont, cited in P. Woodruff, *The Men Who Ruled India: The Founders* (1953), pp. 234–5; Anon. [Mrs Fanny Parkes], *Wanderings of a Pilgrim in Search of the Picturesque* (1852), II p. 230.
6 Captain Basil Hall, 'Food', in *Encyclopaedia Britannica* (1841).
7 Drummond and Wilbraham, p. 322.
8 Wyvern [A. H. C. Kenney-Herbert], *Culinary Jottings*, 1891 edn. p. 340.
9 Drummond and Wilbraham, p. 322.
10 Furnas, p. 690.
11 Lord, p. 43.
12 Aliph Cheem [Walter Yeldham], 'The Police-Wallah's Little Dinner', in *Lays of Ind* (1875).
13 Mote, in Chang, p. 215.
14 D. Lavender, *The American West*, pb 1969, p. 407.
15 Jones, see note 27 chapter 19 above, p. 170.
16 *Ibid.* p. 169.
17 K. Sinclair, *A History of New Zealand* (1959), pp. 189–212.
18 Gerstäcker, see note 9 chapter 16 above, p. 48.
19 Simmonds, see note 17 chapter 12 above, p. 100.
20 *Ibid.*
21 Drummond and Wilbraham, p. 306.
22 Mark Twain, *A Tramp Abroad* (1894), pp. 572–5.
23 Rumford, p. 404.
24 W. H. Russell, *My Diary North and South* (1863), I p. 48.
25 'Wyvern', see note 8 above, p. 457.
26 Hayward, p. 77.
27 Colin Clark, quoted in Sir W. Crawford and H. Broadley, *The People's Food* (1938), p. 8.
28 Since the manufacturers of this 1960s packet soup have now either mended their ways or gone out of business, they can remain anonymous.

21 THE SCIENTIFIC REVOLUTION

1 Burnett [1], p. 283.
2 Quoted in Drummond and Wilbraham, pp. 441–2.
3 *Time*, 22 Nov. 1971.
4 Carefoot and Sprott, p. 10.
5 US President's Science Advisory Committee report, *World Food Problem*, II p. 554.
6 Carson, pp. 56–9.
7 *Time*, 5 Dec. 1969.
8 Dr N. Borlaug, reported in *The Times*, 9 Nov. 1971.
9 Dr R. A. Kenny, in *Pulse*, October 1986.
10 *Sunday Times*, 25 Jan. 1976.

11 James Murray of Chicago's Policy Research Corpn, quoted in *Time*, 19 Oct. 1981.

22 CONFUSED NEW WORLD

1 Brillat-Savarin, *Aphorisms*, IV.
2 *Time*, 11 Nov. 1974.
3 Quoted in *Sunday Times*, 27 Oct. 1985.
4 Report for the Independent Commission on International Humanitarian Issues, *Famine: A Man-Made Disaster?* (1985).
5 Various sources, incl; *Sunday Times*, 9 June 1985; *The Times*, 6 Feb. 1988.
6 *Time*, 20 Jan. 1986.
7 *Ibid.*
8 *Time*, 18 Aug. 1986.
9 *Sunday Times*, 21 July 1968.
10 Geoffrey Cannon, in *Sunday Telegraph* magazine, March 1983.
11 *The Times*, 20 Oct. 1986.
12 Research by Dr J. Farquhar of Stanford University, report in *Time*, 15 March 1982.
13 *Time*, 15 March 1982.
14 *The Observer*, 30 Aug. 1981.
15 WHO report, 7 Jan. 1987, summarized in *The Times*, 8 Jan. 1987.
16 Report in *The Times*, 2 Oct. 1986.
17 Geol. Survey Prof. Paper 574-C, US Public Health Service, April 1970.
18 Drs N. Petrakis and F. King, University of California, San Francisco, in the *Lancet*, 28 Nov. 1981.
19 Dr B. Pickard, University of Leeds, *Sunday Times*, 11 Aug. 1985.
20 Report in the *Lancet*, 23 Jan. 1987.
21 Dr L. Beeley, in the *British Medical Journal*, 27 Oct. 1986.
22 *Time*, 14 July 1986.
23 Research by Dr M Lipkin and H. Newmark reported in the *New England Journal of Medicine*, 2 Dec. 1985; A. Schauss, director of the American Institute for Biosocial Research, in 'Nutrition and Behavior Complex Interdisciplinary Research', *Nutrition and Health*, 3 no. 1/2, Jan. 1985.
24 Euromonitor report, in *The Independent*, 27 Oct. 1986.
25 Professor W. Rathje, University of Arizona, in *The Grocer*; report in *The Times*, 28 April 1986.
26 Gallup, for Market Research Society, May 1986.

EPILOGUE

1 *Time*, 18 Dec. 1972.
2 Quoted in Orville Schell, *Modern Meat*, New York 1984.

3 *Jane Grigson's Fruit Book* (1982), pb 1983, p. 156.
4 Dr M. C. Dean and T. Bromage, in *Nature*, 317, 6037, Oct. 1985.
5 Drummond and Wilbraham, pp. 465–7.
6 Massimo Livi-Bacci, 'The Nutrition–Mortality Link in Past Times: A Comment', in Rotberg and Rabb, pp. 95–100.
7 Report in *The Times*, 15 May 1987.
8 *Time*, 6 Aug. 1984.
9 *The Times*, 4 July 1986.
10 *The Times*, 10 Jan. 1986.
11 Hiroshi Takeuchi, 'Taller and Broader', in *Japan Quarterly*, IX 1, Jan.–March 1962.
12 *The Times*, 16 Aug. 1984.
13 *The Times*, 16 Dec. 1986.

ILLUSTRATIONS AND SOURCES

The present location or source of each illustration, where appropriate, is shown in italics, followed by the relevant departmental or publication reference. Author and publishers gratefully acknowledge the permission to reproduce granted by the galleries, collections and photographers concerned.

69 Tuna-fish seller. Detail from a krater (fourth century BC), from Lipari. *Mandralisca Museum*, Cefalu, Sicily. Photo Leonard von Matt, Buochs, Switzerland.

72 Cattle and horses threshing grain. Mosaic (*c.* AD 200) from the Roman villa at Zlitzen, Tripolitania. *Castello Museum*, Tripoli. Photo Roger Wood, London.

73 Fresco showing Roman merchant vessel loading cargo. *Vatican Library*, Rome. Photo Mansell/Anderson, London.

74 The slave girl Ishat grinding grain on a saddle quern. Painted limestone figure from Saqqara, Fifth Dynasty (2560–2420 BC). *Cairo Museum*.

75 1. Hopper rubber and lever-operated hopper rubber, after Joseph Needham, *Science and Civilization in China* IV 2 (1954).
   2. Rotary quern in use in nineteenth-century India, from Mrs Fanny Parkes, *Wanderings of a Pilgrim in Search of the Picturesque* (1852).

76 Roman donkey-mill, after relief on a Roman sarcophagus (second century AD) in the Vatican Museum, Rome.

77 Ship mills in fourteenth-century Paris. MS illumination from the *Légende de St Denis* (1317). *Bibliothèque Nationale*, Paris, MS fr. 2090–92, t. 3 fol. 37v.

85 King Arcesilas supervising the weighing and storing of silphium, from a Laconian cup (*c.* 560 BC). *Bibliothèque Nationale*, Paris, C 2866.

95 Trapping hares, from an eleventh-century Byzantine MS of the *Cynegetics* of Oppian. *Bibliothèque Nationale*, Paris.

97 Detail from the Bayeux Tapestry. *Bibliothèque Municipale de Bayeux*. Photo Giraudon, Paris.

100 Monastery with *vivarium*, from a MS of *c.* AD 1000. *Staatliche Bibliothek*, Bamberg, MS Patr. 61.

106 Steatite seals (late third or early second mill. BC) from Mohenjo-Daro, Indus Valley, showing humped bull and primigenius bull. *By courtesy of the Trustees of the British Museum*, Oriental Antiquities.

112 Detail from a MS (1650) of the *Ramayana*. *By permission of the British Library*, Oriental MSS Add. 15 296 fol. 71r.

116 Making chapatis, from a mid-nineteenth-century volume of drawings, 'Illustrations of the Various Trades in Kashmir'. *Foreign and Commonwealth Office*, London, India Office Library Add. Or. 1681.

119 Scroll drawing of sheep and goat by the Song artist Chao Meng-fu (1254–1322), who joined the Mongol court *c.* 1286. *Courtesy of the Smithsonian Institution, Freer Gallery of Art*, Washington DC. Freer Gallery 31.4.

128 Hunting and farming, after a rubbing from a tomb tile of the later Han dynasty (AD 25–220) found at Chengdu in Sichuan and now in a private collection at Chengdu.

134 Cooking over a brazier, from a MS of Chao Lin; fourteenth-century copy of a seventh-century painting. *Collection C. A. Drenowatz*, Zürich. Photo Hinz SWB, Basel.

139 The sweetmeat vendor, by the twelfth-century artist Su Han-ch'en. *By courtesy of the Museum of Fine Arts, Boston. Bequest of Charles B. Hoyt.*

145 Arab tavern, from a MS of al-Hariri. *Bibliothèque Nationale*, Paris, MS ar. 2964 fol. 22.

147 Fat-tailed sheep, after an engraving in Rudolf the Elder, *New History of Ethiopia* (1682).

155 Scratch plough, from a copy (*c.* AD 1000) of the ninth-century Utrecht Psalter. *By permission of the British Library*, Harley MS 603 fol. 54v.

156 Mouldboard plough, from the Luttrell Psalter (*c.* 1340). *By permission of the British Library*, Add. MS 42130 fol. 170r.

160 Grace Churche Market, line and wash drawing from Hugh Alley, 'A Caveat for the City of London, or a Forewarning of Offences against Penal Laws' (1598). *Folger Shakespeare Library*, Washington DC.

164 Marginal drawing from the *Assisa Panis* (1266) showing the punishment of a defaulting baker. *By courtesy of the Corporation of London.*

165 'Intestina vel busecha', from a *Tacuinum sanitatis* illuminated in Lombardy 1350–1400. *Österreichisches Nationalbibliothek*, Vienna. Cod. ser. nov. 2.644 fol. 81.

172 Sheepfold, from the Luttrell Psalter (*c.* 1340). *By permission of the British Library*, Add. MS 42130 fol. 163v.

175 1. Autumn slaughter, detail from a fifteenth-century German/Alsatian altar cloth. *Victoria and Albert Museum*, Tapestries 6–1867.
2. Kitchen scene from a Flemish MS of 1300–50. *Bodleian Library*, Oxford, Western MSS, MS Douce 5 fol. 7.

178 Extraction of brine salt in China. After a rubbing from a stamped brick of the Han period found in Sichuan.

186 Detail from David Teniers the Younger, 'The kitchen of the Archduke Leopold William'. *Foundation Johan Maurits van Nassau, Mauritshuis, The Hague*. Photo A. Dingjan, The Hague.

189 A queen at table, from a fifteenth-century Flemish MS. *Bodleian Library*, Oxford, Western MSS, MS Douce 374 fol. 17.

191 End of a meal, from Christoforo de Messi Sbugo, *Banchetti compositioni de vivande, et apparecchio generale* (1549). *By permission of the British Library*, RR G 2369 fol. 7v.

193 'Scientific researches . . .' Colour aquatint by James Gillray, published 23 May 1802. *By permission of the British Library*, PR 9923–1802.

204 Giuseppe Arcimboldo, 'Summer'. *Kunsthistorisches Museum*, Vienna, no. 1589.

208 Making tortillas, from the *Codex Mendoza* fol. 60, Mexico *c.* 1550. *Bodleian Library*, Oxford.

212 'Comment les sauvages rotissent leurs ennemis', from André Thevet, *La Cosmographie Universelle* (1575), t. 2. *By permission of the British Library*, RR 568 h 4.

215 Potato cultivation, from a Peruvian codex illustrated in F. G. Poma de Ayala, *Nueva coronica y buen gobierno* (1936).

221 The Amerindian town of Secoton in the 1580s. Contemporary watercolour by John White. *By permission of the British Library*, PR 1906.5.9.1 (7).

233 Pierre Paul Sevin. 'The banquet which Clement IX gave to the queen of Sweden, at Monte Cavallo 1667'. *Kungliga Biblioteket*, Stockholm.

235 Cauldron, and cooking tools, from the *Opera di M. Bartolomeo Scappi: Cuoco Secreto di Papa Pio Quinto* (1570). *By permission of the British Library*, RR 1037 h 4.

236 Anonymous seventeenth-century portrait of a spaghetti merchant. *Museo Storico degli Spaghetti*, Pontedassio.

240 Velasquez, 'An old woman cooking eggs'. *By courtesy of the National Gallery of Scotland*, Edinburgh, no. 2180.

245 Jan Davidsz de Heem, 'Still Life'. *By courtesy of the Trustees of the Wallace Collection*, London, P 76.

255 Rum punch. Wall panel from Moses Marcy House, Southbridge. *Photo: Old Sturbridge Village*, Massachusetts.

257 Betel quids being offered to the god Krishna. Painting (Basohli style) *c.* 1710. *By permission of the British Library*, PR Oriental 1955.10.8.069.

263 Australian aboriginals from the Watling Drawings. *British Museum*, (*Natural History*), London. Photo BBC Hulton Picture Library, London.

268 Tea tasting, Chinese watercolour. *Victoria and Albert Museum*, London, D. 1090–1898.

271 A garden in Kashmir, from a nineteenth-century Kashmiri MS book of trades. *Foreign and Commonwealth Office*, London, India Office Library.

273 Detail from a MS (1650) of the *Ramayana*. *By permission of the British Library*, Oriental MSS Add. 15 296 fol. 71r.

277 David Allan, pen and watercolour sketch, 'Roman Coffee House', late eighteenth century. *The National Galleries of Scotland*, Edinburgh.

278 Hunter carrying an antelope; bronze, probably Yoruba work though found at Benin. *By courtesy of the Trustees of the British Museum*, E 22.

284 Map vignette, *c.* 1730, from Gerard van Keulen's 'Die Nieuwe Groote Lichtende Zee-Fakkel'. *By permission of the British Library*, Maps c. 8 d. 6, map 5.

286 The McCormick reaper. From the *Official Descriptive and Illustrated Catalogue of the Great Exhibition*, London 1851.

287 Steam threshing in France at the end of the nineteenth century. Standard motif from the specimen book of the Parisian type founders Deberny & Cie.

288 The baked-potato vendor, daguerreotype by Beard from Henry Mayhew, *London Labour and the London Poor* (1861).

290 Jozef Israëls (1824–1911), 'The Frugal Meal'. *Glasgow Art Gallery and Museum*, no. 737.

292 The abattoir of La Villette, from *Le Monde Illustré*, 1890.

295 Kitchens of the Royal Pavilion, from John Nash, *The Royal Pavilion at Brighton* (1827). *By permission of the British Library*, RR 577 h 19.

307 Cow keeper, watercolour by George Scharf the Elder. *By permission of the British Library*, PR 1862.6.14.120.

311 The captain's table aboard the East Indiaman *Clyde* in a heavy sea, early nineteenth-century aquatint. *National Maritime Museum*, Greenwich, A 302.

314 The ice-making pits at Allahabad, 1828, from Mrs Fanny Parkes, *Wanderings of a Pilgrim in Search of the Picturesque* (1852).

315 Watercolour of an ice cart by Nicolino Calyo, *c.* 1840. *The Museum of the City of New York*, Gift of Mrs Francis P. Garvan in memory of Francis P. Garvan, 555.6.13.

324 'Ten Minutes for Refreshments', lithographed poster for The Great Atlantic and Pacific Tea Company 1886. *Courtesy of the New York Historical Society*, New York City.

327 Jean Béraud, 'La Pâtisserie'. *Musée Carnavalet*, Paris.

329 Display card by Edgar Wright for 'My Lady' Fruits, *c.* 1925. *Angus Watson & Co. Ltd.*

339 Rabbit-proof fencing. *Australian News and Information Bureau*, London, P63/326.

342 Showcard *c.* 1925 for Spear's sausages. *Robert Opie Collection, Museum of Advertising and Packaging*, Gloucester.

358 Oil painting (trade sign for 'Ye Boston Baked Beans'), 1886, by H. Covill. *Courtesy of the New York Historical Society, New York City*, 1937.459.

365 Butter advertisement 1981. *Butter Information Council Ltd.*

369 1. Soy protein, beef-flavoured, in the form of a meat loaf. *General Mills Inc.*, Minneapolis.

   2. Rembrandt, 'The Carcase of an Ox', *c.* 1640. *Glasgow Art Gallery and Museum*, no. 600.

   3. Spun soybean protein analogue. *General Mills Inc.*, Minneapolis.

BIBLIOGRAPHY

In order to accommodate a representative selection of titles published since 1973 (the full list would take up a small volume), I have deleted most of the background works on history, sociology and anthropology listed in the first edition of *Food in History* and limited new entries to publications in English, with a few in French. Except for one or two key historical titles, cookery books are omitted. By slightly abbreviating the bibliographical details – as, for example, by omitting place of publication when it is within the United Kingdom, and reducing all first names to initials – I have made space for a few extra titles. Works of particularly limited scope have been confined to the source notes, although a few that are not directly noted or quoted remain in the bibliography.

Where I have quoted from an edition other than the first, the relevant date is shown at the end of the entry. Pb means paperback.

ACCUM, F. *A Treatise on Adulterations of Food, and Culinary Poisons.* 1820.

ALLEN, E. E. *British Tastes: An Enquiry into the Likes and Dislikes of the Regional Consumer.* 1968.

ALLEN, H. W. *A History of Wine.* 1961.

ANDRÉ, J. *L'Alimentation et la cuisine à Rome. Paris 1961*

Annales: Économies, sociétés, civilisations Paris 1961 continuing. [Frequent, detailed studies of historical aspects of food and nutrition]

APICIUS *De re coquinaria/culinaria.* Trs. Barbara Flower and Elisabeth Rosenbaum as *The Roman Cookery Book*, 1958.

ARBER, A. *Herbals: Their Origin and Evolution. A Chapter in the History of Botany 1470–1670* [1912]. 1938.

ARBERRY, A. J. 'A Baghdad Cookery-Book', in *Islamic Culture*, 13, 1939.

ARON, J.-P. *The Art of Eating in France.* 1975. [Nineteenth century developments]

ASHLEY, W. *The Bread of Our Forefathers: An Inquiry in Economic History.* 1928.

ASHTOR, E. 'An Essay on the Diet of the Various Classes in the Medieval Levant', in Forster and Ranum (eds.) *Biology of Man in History: Selections from the Annales.* Baltimore 1975.

ATHENAEUS *The Deipnosophists.* Trs. Charles Burton Gulik, 1927.

AUBERT, C. *Les aliments fermentés traditionnels: Une richesse méconnue.* Paris 1985.

AULT, W. O. *Open-Field Farming in Medieval England.* 1972.

AUSTIN, T. (ed.) *Two Fifteenth-century Cookery Books.* Early English Text Society, 91, 1888.

AVINON, J. DE *Sevillana Medicina* [1418]. Society of Andalusian Bibliophiles, 1885. [Chapter 14, vegetables; chapter 17, meat preservation]

BARDACH, J. *Harvest of the Sea.* London 1969.

BARNETT, L. M. *British Food Policy During the First World War.* 1985.

BARON, S. *The Desert Locust.* 1971.

BARRACLOUGH, G. (ed.) *Eastern and Western Europe in the Middle Ages.* 1970.

BARRAU, J. [1] 'Plant Introduction in the Tropical Pacific', in *Pacific Viewpoint*, I, 1960.

[2] *Les hommes et leurs aliments. Esquisse d'une histoire écologique et ethnologique de l'alimentation humaine.* Paris 1983.

BECKETT, R. *Convicted Tastes: Food in Australia.* Sydney 1984.

BERGAD, L. W. *Coffee and the Growth of Agrarian Capitalism in Nineteenth-Century Puerto Rico.* Princeton 1983.

BERGIER, J. F. *Une Histoire du Sel.* Paris 1983.

BERNAL, J. D. *Science in History.* London 1954, pb 4 vols, 1969.

BERRIEDALE-JOHNSON, M. *The British Museum Cookbook.* 1987 [Ancient Egyptian and other recipes re-created]

BEST, H. *Rural Economy in Yorkshire, being the farming and account books of Henry Best* [1641]. Surtees Society, 33, 1857.

BHATIA, B. M. *Famines in India 1860–1965.* Bombay 1967.

BITTING, A. W. *Appertizing or the Art of Canning: Its History and Development.* San Francisco 1937.

BITTING, K. G. *Gastronomic Bibliography.* San Francisco 1939.

BODENHEIMER, F. S. *Insects as Human Food.* The Hague 1951.

BOORDE, A. *A Compendyous Regyment or a Dyetary of Helth.* 1542.

BOYD ORR, J. *Collected papers of the Rowett Research Institute*, I. 1925. [Nutritional knowledge in the 1920s]

BRAUDEL, F. *Capitalism and Material Life 1400–1800.* 1973, pb 1974.

BRIDBURY, A. R. *England and the Salt Trade in the Later Middle Ages.* 1955.

BRILLAT-SAVARIN, J.-A. *La Physiologie du Goût*, 1825. Trs. A. Drayton as *The Philosopher in the Kitchen*, pb 1970.

BRODRICK, A. H. (ed.) *Animals in Archaeology.* 1972.

BROOKS, C. E. P. *Climate through the Ages.* 1926.

BROTHWELL, D. and P. *Food in Antiquity: A Survey of the Diet of Early Peoples.* 1969.

BROWN, DR H. M. *The Allergy and Asthma Reference Book.* 1985.

BRUNETON-GOVERNATORI, A. *Le Pain des Bois: Ethnohistoire de la Châtaigne et du Châtaignier.* Toulouse 1984.

BUHRER, E. M. and ZIEHR, W. *Le Pain à travers les âges*. Paris 1985.

BURKILL, I. H. 'The Rise and Decline of the Yam in the Service of Man', in *Advances in Science*, 7, 1951.

BURNETT, J. [1] *Plenty and Want: A Social History of Diet in England from 1815 to the Present Day*. 1966, pb 1968.

[2] *A History of the Cost of Living*. pb 1969.

BUSHKOVITCH, P. *The Merchants of Moscow, 1580–1650*. 1980.

CAMBEL, H. and BRAIDWOOD, R. J. 'An Early Farming Village in Turkey', in *Scientific American*, 222, March 1970.

CAREFOOT, G. L. and SPROTT, E. R. *Famine on the Wind: Plant Diseases and Human History*. 1969.

CARPENTER, K. J. *The History of Scurvy and Vitamin C*. 1986.

CARSON, R. *Silent Spring*. 1962, pb 1968.

CASPALL, J. *Making Fire and Light in the Home pre-1820*. 1986.

CASSON, L. 'Grain Trade in the Hellenistic World', in *Transactions and Proceedings of the American Philological Association*, 1954.

CERRUTI, trs. J. Spencer, *The Four Seasons of the House of Cerruti*. 1985. [Daily life and diet in the fourteenth century]

CHANG, K. C. (ed.) *Food in Chinese Culture: Anthropological and Historical Perspectives*. Yale 1977.

CHAPLIN, R. E. 'Animals in Archaeology', in *Antiquity* vol. XXXIX, 1965.

CHAUDHURI, K. N. *The Trading World of Asia and the English East-India Company 1660–1760*. 1978.

CHEVALLIER, A. *Du Café, son historique, son usage, son utilité, ses altérations, ses succédanés et ses falsifications*. Paris 1862.

CLARK, C. *Population Growth and Land Use*. 1967.

CLARK, J. D. 'The Spread of Food Production in Sub-Saharan Africa', in *Journal of African History*, 3, 1962.

CLUTTON-BROCK, J. *Domesticated Animals from Early Times*. 1982.

COBB, R. C. *The Police and the People: French Popular Protest 1789–1820*. 1970.

COCKRILL, W. R. 'The Water Buffalo', in *Scientific American*, 217, 1967.

COHEN, M. N. *The Food Crisis in Prehistory. Over-population and the Origins of Agriculture*. Yale 1977.

COLAS, A. *Le Sel*. Paris 1985.

COLES, J. M. and HIGGS, E. S. *The Archaeology of Early Man*. 1969.

COLLINS, J. L. 'Antiquity of the Pineapple in America', in *Southwestern Journal of Anthropology*, VII, 1951.

COLUMELLA *De re rustica*. Trs. H. B. Ash, E. S. Forster, and E. H. Heffner as *On Agriculture*, 3 vols, 1941.

CONNOR, R. D. and MASON, J. *The Weights and Measures of England*. 1986.

COON, C. S. *The History of Man: From the First Human to Primitive Culture and Beyond*. 1955, pb 1967.

CORDIER, H. 'L'Alimentation en Chine', in *Journal des Débats*, 19 Nov. 1879.

COST, B. *Ginger East to West: A Cook's Tour, with Recipes, Techniques and Lore.* 1984.

COUFFIGNAL, H. *La Cuisine des Pauvres.* Paris 1972.

COURSEY, D. G. *Yams.* 1967.

CRANE, E. *The Archaeology of Beekeeping.* 1983.

CRISP, F. *Medieval Gardens.* 2 vols, 1924.

CRITCHELL, J. T. and RAYMOND, J. *A History of the Frozen Meat Trade.* 1912.

CURTIS-BENNETT, Sir N. *The Food of the People, being the History of Industrial Feeding.* 1949.

CURWEN, E. C. and HATT, G. *Plough and Pasture: The Early History of Farming.* New York 1953.

Curye on Inglysch: English Culinary Manuscripts of the Fourteenth Century, ed. C. Hieatt and S. Butler. 1985.

CUTTING, C. L. *Fish Saving: A History of Fish Processing from Ancient to Modern Times.* New York 1956.

DARBY, W. J., GHALIOUNGUI, P., and GRIVETTI, L. (eds.) *Food: The Gift of Osiris.* 2 vols, 1977.

DARENNE, E. *Histoire des métiers de l'alimentation.* Meulan 1904.

DAUMAS, M. (ed.) *Histoire Générale des Techniques.* 3 t, Paris 1962–1969.

DAVIDSON, B. (ed.) *The African Past: Chronicles from Antiquity to Modern Times.* 1964, pb 1966.

DAVIS, S.J.H. *The Archaeology of Animals.* 1987.

DE BACH, P. (ed.) *Biological Control of Insect Pests and Weeds.* 1964.

DEERR, N. *The History of Sugar.* 2 vols, 1949.

DELLA CASA, G. *Galateo, or the Book of Manners* [1558]. Trs. R. S. Pine-Coffin, pb 1958.

DENCE, C. *Season to Taste.* 1986. [History]

DERRY, T. K. and WILLIAMS, T. I. *A Short History of Technology from the Earliest Times to AD 1900.* 1960, pb 1970.

DIMBLEBY, G. *Plants and Archaeology.* 1967.

DIOSCORIDES *Materia Medica.* Various trs. [Book II for dietetics, etc.]

DODGE, B. S. *Plants That Changed the World.* 1962.

DOLLINGER, P. *The German Hansa.* Trs. and ed. D. S. Ault and S. H. Steinberg, 1971.

DRUMMOND, J. C. and WILBRAHAM, A. *The Englishman's Food: A History of Five Centuries of English Diet.* 1939. [The original edition is preferable to the 1964 edn. revised by D. F. Hollingsworth.]

DUBY, G. *Rural Economy and Country Life in the Medieval West.* 1968.

DUCKETT, E. *Death and Life in the Tenth Century.* Ann Arbor 1967.

DUFOUR, P. S. *Traités nouveaux et curieux du café, du thé et du chocolat.* Lyon 1685.

DUPAIGNE, B. and MARQUIS, J. *Le Pain.* Paris 1979. [History]

DURBEC, J. A. 'La Grande Boucherie de Paris: Notes historiques d'après des archives privées (XIIe–XVIIe siècles)', in *Bulletin philologique et historique*, 1955–6.

EDLIN, H. *Atlas of Plant Life.* 1973.

ERNLE, Lord [PROTHERO, R. E.] *English Farming Past and Present.* 1912.

FAGNIEZ, G. (ed.) *Documents relatifs à l'histoire de l'industrie et du commerce en France.* 2 t, Paris 1898–1900.

FEI, H.-T. *Peasant Life in China: A Field Study of Country Life in the Yangtse Valley.* 1939.

FENTON, A. and KISBAN, E. (eds.) *Food in Change: Eating Habits from the Middle Ages to the Present Day.* 1986. [Conference papers]

FERNIOT, J. and LE GOFF, J. (eds.) 'La Cuisine et la table: 5,000 ans de gastronomie', in *L'Histoire*, special issue, 1986.

FILBY, F. A. *A History of Food Adulteration and Analysis.* 1934.

FILDES, V. *Breasts, Bottles and Babies.* 1986.

FILLIOZAT, J. *La Doctrine classique de la médecine indienne.* Paris 1949.

FLETCHER, W. W. *The Pest War.* 1974.

FLON, C. (ed.) *The World Atlas of Archaeology.* 1986.

FORBES, R. J. *Studies in Ancient Technology.* 6 vols, Leiden 1955–8. [Vols 2 and 3 are concerned with food and drink.]

Forme of Cury, The, see PEGGE, S., also *Curye on Inglysch.*

FORREST, D. *Tea for the British.* 1973.

FORSTER, E. and FORSTER, R. (eds.) *European Diet from Pre-Industrial to Modern Times.* New York 1976.

FORSTER, R. and RANUM, O. (eds.) *Food and Drink in History: Selections from the Annales,* 5. Baltimore 1979.

FRANCIS, C. A. *A History of Food and Its Preservation.* Princeton 1937.

FRANKLIN, A. *Vie privée des français, 12e à 18e siècles.* 27 t, Paris 1887–1902. [Vol. III *La cuisine*, VI *Les Repas*, VIII *Variétés gastronomiques*, XIII *Le Café, le thé, et le chocolat*]

FRENCH, R. K. *The History and Virtues of Cyder.* 1982.

FURET, L. 'Le Chien comestible chinois', in *Bulletin de la Société Nationale d'Acclimatation*, 1890.

FURNAS, J. C. *The Americans: A Social History of the United States, 1587–1914.* 1970.

FURNIVALL, F. J. (ed.) [1] *The Babees Book.* Early English Text Society, 32, 1868. [Includes John Russell's *Boke of Nurture* and Wynkyn de Worde's *Boke of Kervyng*]

[2] *A Book of Precedence* [c. 1570] by Sir Humphrey Gilbert. Early English Text Society, Extra Series 8, 1869. [Also includes extracts from Latini, Fra Bonvicino, Pandolfini, Della Casa, Thomasin of Zerklaere, and the Knight of Winsbeke]

FUSSELL, G. E. *The English Dairy Farmer, 1500–1900.* 1966.

GHOZLAND, F. *Un siècle de réclames alimentaires.* Paris 1986.

GIRARD, A. R. 'Le triomphe de "La cuisinière bourgeoise": Livres culinaires, cuisine et société en France aux XVIIe et XVIIIe siècles', in *Revue d'histoire moderne et contemporaine*, 24, 1977.

GLAMANN, K. *Dutch-Asiatic trade, 1620–1740*. Copenhagen 1958.

GODECKEN, H. *Le Caviar*. Paris 1986. [History, production, etc.]

GOTTSCHALK, A. *Histoire de l'alimentation et de la gastronomie depuis la préhistoire jusqu'à nos jours*. 2 t, Paris 1948.

GOURRIER, Z. *Les Français et la table*. Paris 1985. [Exhibition catalogue, *Musée National des Arts et Traditions Populaires*]

GRAND-CARTERET, J. *Raphael et Gambrinus, ou l'Art dans la brasserie*. Paris 1886.

GRAY, W. D. *The Relation of Fungi to Human Affairs*. New York 1959.

GRIFFITHS, P. *The History of the Indian Tea Industry*. 1967.

GRIGG, D. *The World Food Problem 1950–80*. 1985.

HANSSEN, M. *E for Additives: The Complete 'E' Number Guide*. 1984.

HARDING, A. (ed.) *Climatic Change in Later Prehistory*. 1982.

HARRIS, M. *Good to Eat: Riddles of Food and Culture*. 1986.

HARRISON, B. *Drink and the Victorians: The Temperance Question in England 1815–1872*. 1971.

HARRISON, S. G., MASEFIELD G. B. and WALLIS, M. *The Oxford Book of Food Plants*. 1969.

HARTLEY, D. [1] *Food in England*. 1954.

[2] *Water in England*. 1978.

HATTOX, R. S. *Coffee and Coffeehouses: The Origins of a Social Beverage in the Medieval Near East*. 1985.

HAYWARD, A. *The Art of Dining, or, Gastronomy and Gastronomers*. 1852.

HELBAEK, H. 'The Domestication of Food Plants in the Old World', in *Science*, 130, 1959.

HEMARDINQUER, J.-J. (ed.) *Pour une histoire de l'alimentation*. Paris 1972. [Articles from the *Annales*]

HERKLOTS, G. A. C. *Vegetable cultivation in South-East Asia*. 1973.

HERODOTUS *The Histories* [c. 446 BC]. Trs. Aubrey de Selincourt, pb 1954.

HIGGS, E. S. (ed.) [1] *Papers in Economic Prehistory. Studies by Members and Associates of the British Academy Major Research Project in the Early History of Agriculture*. 1972.

[2] With J. P. WHITE 'Autumn Killing', in *Antiquity*, 37, 1963.

HIRTH, F. 'Notes on the Early History of the Salt Monopoly in China', in *Journal of the [North] China Branch of the Royal Asiatic Society*, New Series vol. XXII, 1 and 2, 1887.

HOCQUET, J. *Le Roi, le Marchand et le Sel*. Paris 1987.

HOWE, G. M. *Man, Environment and Disease in Britain: A Medical Geography of Britain through the Ages*. 1972.

HUBERT, A. *Le Pain et l'olive: Aspects de l'alimentation en Tunisie*. Paris 1985.

HUTCHINSON, Sir J. B. (ed.) *Essays in Crop Plant Evolution*. 1965.

HUXLEY, E. *Brave New Victuals: An Inquiry into Modern Food Production.* 1965.

HYAMS, E. *Dionysus: A Social History of the Wine Vine.* 1965.

INAMA-STERNEGG, C. T. VON *Deutsche Wirtschaftgeschichte.* 3 vols in 4, Leipzig, 1879–1901. [German housekeeping prior to 1400]

INNIS, H. A. *The Cod Fisheries.* New Haven 1940.

International Action to Avert the Impending Protein Crisis. United Nations Publication E 68 XIII 2, 1969.

ISAAC, E. 'The Influence of Religion on the Spread of Citrus', in *Science*, 129, 1959.

JAMES, M. K. *Studies in the Medieval Wine Trade.* 1971.

JARMAN, M. R., BAILEY, G. N. and JARMAN, H. N. (eds.) *Early European Agriculture: Its Foundations and Development.* 1982.

JEFFERYS, J. B. *Retail Trading in Britain, 1850–1950.* 1954.

JENKINS, J. T. *The Herring and the Herring Fisheries.* 1927.

JENSEN, L. B. *Man's Foods: Nutrition and Environments in Food Gathering Times and Food Producing Times.* 1953.

JONES, E. L. and WOOLF, S. J. (eds.) *Agrarian Change and Economic Development: The Historical Problems.* 1969.

JONES, P. E. *The Butchers of London.* 1976.

KAHAN, A. 'Natural Calamities and their Effect upon the Food Supply in Russia', in *Jahrbücher für Geschichte Osteuropas*, XVI, 1968.

KAPLAN, S. L. [1] *Bread, Politics and Political Economy in the Reign of Louis XV.* 2 vols, The Hague 1977.

[2] *Provisioning Paris: Merchants and Millers in the grain and flour trade during the eighteenth century.* Cornell 1985.

KERLING, N. J. M. *Commercial Relations of Holland and Zeeland with England from the Late Thirteenth Century to the Close of the Middle Ages.* Leiden 1954.

LAMB, H. H. *Climate: Present, Past and Future. Vol. 1: Fundamentals and Climate Now.* 1972.

LANG, G. *The Cuisine of Hungary.* New York 1982.

LATTIMORE, O. *Inner Asian Frontiers of China*, no. 21 in American Geographical Society Research Series. 1940.

LAUWERYS, J. R. *Man's Impact on Nature.* 1969.

LA VARENNE, F. P. DE *Le Vray Cuisinier François.* Paris 1651.

LEE, R. B and DEVORE, I. (eds.) *Man the Hunter.* Chicago 1968.

LEE, T'AO 'Historical Notes on Some Vitamin Deficiency Diseases in China', in *Chinese Medical Journal*, 58, 1940.

LEMNIS, M. and VITRY, H. *Old Polish Traditions in the Kitchen and at the Table.* Warsaw 1979.

LESPINASSE, R. DE *Les Métiers et Corporations de la Ville de Paris.* 3 t, Paris 1886–97.

LEVI-STRAUSS, C. *The Raw and the Cooked.* 1970. Also *Du Miel aux cendres,*

L'Origine des manières de table, and *L'Homme nu*. Paris 1967, 1968, 1971. [Anthropology]

LEVY, J.-P. *The Economic Life of the Ancient World*. Chicago 1967.

LEWIS, A. R. [1] *Naval Power and Trade in the Mediterranean AD 500–1100*. Princeton 1951.

[2] *The Northern Seas: Shipping and Commerce in Northern Europe AD 300–1100*. Princeton 1958.

LICHINE, A. *Encyclopedia of Wines and Spirits*. 1967.

LILLYWHITE, B. *London Coffee Houses: A Reference Book of Coffee Houses of the 17th, 18th and 19th Centuries*. 1963.

LITTLE, E. C. S. (ed.) *Handbook of Utilization of Aquatic Plants*. FAO publication, 1968.

LLOYD, C. *The British Seaman 1200–1860: A Social Survey*. 1968.

LONGMATE, N. *The Waterdrinkers: A History of Temperance*. 1968.

LOPEZ, R. S. and RAYMOND, I. W. *Medieval Trade in the Mediterranean World*. 1955.

LORD, F. A. *Civil War Sutlers and Their Wares*. New York 1969.

LOWENSTEIN, E. *Bibliography of American Cookery Books 1742–1860*. New York 1972.

LUTZ, H. F. *Viticulture and Brewing in the Ancient Orient*. Leipzig and New York 1922.

MACADAMS, R. *Land behind Baghdad*. 1965.

MCCOLLUM, E. V. *A History of Nutrition: The Sequence of Ideas in Nutrition Investigations*. Boston 1957.

MCGEE, H. *On Food and Cooking: The Science and Lore of the Kitchen*. 1984. [Scientific whys and wherefores]

MACGOWAN, Dr 'On the Mutton Wine of the Mongols and Analogous Preparations of the Chinese', in *Journal of the North China Branch of the Royal Asiatic Society*, New Series VII, 1871–2.

MACLEOD, M. J. *Spanish Central America: A Socioeconomic History 1520–1720*. Berkeley 1973.

MAHIAS, M.-C. *Délivrance et Convivialité: le système culinaire des Jaina*. Paris 1985.

MANGELSDORF, P. C. [1] *Plants and Human Affairs*. Bloomington, 1952.

[2] With R. S. MACNEISH and W. C. GALINAT 'The Domestication of Corn', in *Science*, 143, 1964.

Manger et Boire au Moyen Age: Centre d'Études Médiévales de Nice, Actes du Colloque, Octobre 1982. T. 1, *Aliments et Société*, Nice 1984. T. 2, *Cuisines, manières de table et régimes alimentaires*, Nice 1986. [Conference papers]

MARCO POLO *Travels*. Trs. Ronald Latham, pb 1958.

MARGOLIN, J.-C. and SAUZET, R. (eds.) *Pratiques et discours alimentaires à la Renaissance*. Paris 1982.

MARLE, R. VAN *Iconographie de l'Art profane au Moyen-Âge et à la Renaissance*. T. 1, *La Vie Quotidienne*. The Hague 1931.

MAURIZIO, A. *Histoire de l'alimentation végétale depuis la préhistoire jusqu'à nos jours.* Paris 1932.

MAY, R. J. *Kaikai Aniani. A Guide to Bush Foods, Markets and Culinary Arts of Papua New Guinea.* 1984.

MEDICAL RESEARCH COUNCIL *Vitamins: A Survey of Present Knowledge.* 1932.

MEGAW, J. V. S. (ed.) *Hunters, Gatherers and First Farmers beyond Europe.* 1977. [Symposium papers]

MELLANBY, K. *Pesticides and Pollution.* London 1967.

Mémoires concernant l'histoire, les sciences, les arts, les moeurs, les usages etc des Chinois, par les missionaires de Pé-kin. 16t, Paris 1776–1814.

MENAGIER DE PARIS [*c.* 1393] Ed. and trs. Eileen Power, as *The Goodman of Paris,* 1928.

MENNELL, S. *All Manners of Food: Eating and Taste in England and France from the Middle Ages to the Present.* 1985.

MERCER, R. (ed.) *Farming Practice in British Prehistory.* 1982.

MERVYN, L. *The Dictionary of Vitamins.* 1984.

MILLER, J. I. *The Spice Trade of the Roman Empire, 29 BC to AD 641.* 1969.

MINNS, R. *Bombers and Mash: The Domestic Front 1939–45.* 1985.

MINTZ, S. W. *Sweetness and Power: The Political, Social and Economic Effects of Sugar on the Modern World.* 1985.

MONCKTON, H. A. [1] *A History of English Ale and Beer.* 1966.
[2] *A History of the English Public House.* 1970.

MORETTINI, A. *Olivicultura.* Rome 1950.

MORITZ, L. A. *Grain-mills and Flour in Classical Antiquity.* 1958.

MOSSE, C. *The Ancient World at Work.* 1969.

MOURANT, A. E. and ZEUNER, F. E. (eds.) *Man and Cattle.* 1963.

MUKERJEE, R. *Races, Lands and Food.* New York 1946.

MULTHAUF, R. P. *Neptune's Gift: A History of Common Salt.* Baltimore 1978.

[NAVY] *Handbook of Cookery for Use in H.M. Navy.* 1914.

NEEDHAM, J. [1] *Science and Civilization in China.* 6 vols. 1954–continuing.
[2] *Clerks and Craftsmen in China and the West: Lectures and Addresses on the History of Science and Technology.* 1970.

NENQUIN, J. A. E. *Salt, a Study in Economic Prehistory.* Bruges 1961.

NEWALL, V. *An Egg at Easter.* 1971. [Folklore and symbolism]

O'HARA-MAY, J. *The Elizabethan Dyetary of Health.* Lawrence, Kansas, 1977.

O'MALLEY, L. S. *Indian Caste Customs.* 1932.

OPPENHEIM, L. 'On Beer and Brewing Techniques in Ancient Mesopotamia', in *Journal of the American Oriental Society,* Suppl. 1950.

ORDISH, G. *The Great Wine Blight.* 1972.

OSTOYA, P. 'La Préhistoire révéle l'origine du maïs', in *Science Progrès 3353,* 1964.

OXFORD SYMPOSIUM ON FOOD AND COOKERY *Food in Motion: The Migration of Foodstuffs and Cookery Techniques,* 1983. *Cookery: Science, Lore, and Books,* 1986. [Conference papers]

PACK, J. *Nelson's Blood: The story of naval rum*. 1982.

PAGNOL, J. *La truffe*. Paris 1983.

PALLADIUS, *De Re Rustica* [4th century]. Ed. the Rev. Barton Lodge, as *On Husbondrie: From the unique MS of about 1420 AD in Colchester Castle*. Early English Text Society, 52, 72, 1873 and 1879.

PALMER, A. *Movable Feasts: A Reconnaissance of the Origins and Consequences of Fluctuations in Meal-times etc*. 1952.

PAN KU *Han Shu*. Trs. and ed. N. L. Swann in *Food and Money in Ancient China: The Earliest Economic History of China to AD 25. Han Shu 24 with related texts Han Shu 19 and Shih-chi 129*. Princeton 1950.

PARMENTIER, A. A. *Traité sur la culture et les usages des pommes de terre*. Paris 1789.

PARTRIDGE, M. *Farm Tools through the Ages*. 1973.

PEGGE, S. (ed.) *The Forme of Cury: A Roll of Ancient English Cookery, Compiled about AD 1390 by the Master-cooks of King Richard II*. 1780.

PELLAT, C. (trs. and ed.) *Calendrier de Cordoue*. Leyden 1961.

PING-TI HO 'The Introduction of American Food Plants into China', in *American Anthropologist*, 57 2 i, April 1955.

PINTO, E. H. *Treen, and Other Wooden Bygones*. 1969.

PIRIE, N. W. [1] 'Leaf Protein as a Human Food', in *Science* 152, 1966. [2] *Food Resources Conventional and Novel*. pb 1969.

PLATINA [Sacchi, Bartolomeo de'] *De Honesta Voluptate*. Venice 1475.

PLINY THE ELDER *Natural History* [First century AD]. Trs. H. Rackham, 1950. [Book XIV 5-16 wines, 22 drunkards. XVIII 27–28 bread. XXII plants and fruits]

POLLARD, S. and HOLMES, C. *The Process of Industrialization 1750–1870*. 1968.

POSTAN, M. M. *The Trade of Medieval Europe: The North*, in *The Cambridge Economic History*, II. 1952.

POSTGATE, J. *Microbes and Man*. pb 1969.

PRAKASH, OM *Food and Drinks in Ancient India*. Delhi 1961.

The Production of Protein Foods and Concentrates from Oilseeds. Tropical Products Institute publication, 1967.

PRIESTLAND, G. *Frying Tonight: The Saga of Fish and Chips*. 1972.

PYKE, M. *Man and Food*. 1970.

RENFREW, J. M. *Palaeoethnobotany: The Prehistoric Food Plants of the Near East and Europe*. 1973.

RENNER, H. D. *The Origin of Food Habits*. 1944.

REVEL, J.-F. *Culture et Cuisine: Un Festin en Paroles*. Paris 1981.

REYNIERE, GRIMOD DE LA [Laurent, Alexandre-Balthazar] *Almanach des gourmands, ou calendrier nutritif*. Paris 1803–12.

RICH, E. E. and WILSON, C. H. (eds.) *The Economy of Expanding Europe in the Sixteenth and Seventeenth Centuries*, in *The Cambridge Economic History*, IV, 1967.

RICHARDS, D. S. (ed.) *Islam and the Trade of Asia: A Colloquium*. 1970.

RICKMAN, G. *Roman Granaries and Store Buildings*. 1971.

RILEY, H. T. (ed.) *Memorials of London and London Life 1276–1419*. 1868.

RINJING DORJE *Food in Tibetan Life*. New Delhi 1985.

ROACH, F. A. *Cultivated Fruits of Britain: Their Origin and History*. 1985.

ROBINSON, E. F. *The Early History of Coffee Houses in England*. 1893.

ROBINSON, F. P. *The Trade of the East India Company from 1709–1813*. 1912.

ROBSON, J. R. K. (ed.) *Food, Ecology and Culture: Readings in the Anthropology of Dietary Practices*. 1980.

RODINSON, M. 'Recherches sur les documents arabes rélatifs à la cuisine', in *Revue des études islamiques*, 17–18, 1949.

ROHDE, E. S. *The Old English Herbals*. 1972.

ROOT, W. *The Food of France*. 1958.

ROTBERG, R. I. and RABB, T. K. (eds.) *Hunger and History: The Impact of Changing Food Production and Consumption Patterns on Society*. 1985.

ROWNTREE, B. S. *Poverty: A Study of Town Life*. 1901.

RUMFORD, BENJAMIN THOMPSON, Count 'Of Food: And Particularly of Feeding the Poor' [1795], in *Works*, V, 1876.

RYDER, M. L. *Sheep and Man*. 1983.

SALAMAN, R. N. *The History and Social Influence of the Potato*. 1949.

Salerno Regimen. Rhymed version, as *The Englishman's Doctor*, by Sir John Harington, 1608.

SALVETTI, F. *Rue des Bouchers: les métiers de la viande à travers les âges*. Paris 1986.

SCAPPI, BARTOLOMEO 'Cuoco Secreto di Papa Pio Quinto', in *Opera di M. B. Scappi*. Venice 1570.

SCHAFER, E. H. *The Golden Peaches of Samarkand. A Study of T'ang Exotics*. Berkeley and Los Angeles 1963.

SCOTT, J. M, *The Tea Story*. 1964.

SHIH SHENG-HAN *On 'Fan Sheng-Chih Shu', an Agriculturalistic Book of China Written by Fan Sheng-Chih in the First Century BC*. Peking 1959.

SIGERIST, H. E. *Primitive and Archaic Medicine*. New York 1951, pb 1967.

SIMKIN, C. G. F. *The Traditional Trade of Asia*. 1968.

SIMMONDS, F. J. 'The Economics of Biological Control', in *Journal of the Royal Society of Arts*, CXV, 1967.

SIMMONDS, N. W. *The Evolution of the Banana*. 1962.

SIMON, A. L. [1] *Bottlescrew Days: Wine Drinking in England during the Eighteenth Century*. 1926.

[2] *Bibliotheca Gastronomica*. 1953.

SINGER, C. [1] *A Short History of Medicine*. 1928.

[2] With E. J. HOLMYARD, A. R. HALL and T. I. WILLIAMS. *A History of Technology*. 5 vols, 1954–8.

SKINNER, G. *The Cuisine of the South Pacific*. 1983.

SMITH, E. 'On the Food of the Poorer Labouring Classes in England'. Appendix 6 to the *Sixth report of the Medical Officer of the Privy Council*. 1863.

SMITH, P. and DANIEL, C. *The Chicken Book*. Berkeley 1982.

SMITH, P. H. *Politics and Beef in Argentina: Patterns of Conflict and Change*. New York 1969.

SMITH, R. E. F. and CHRISTIAN, D. *Bread and salt: A social and economic history of food and drink in Russia*. 1984.

SOLHEIM II, W. G. 'An Earlier Agricultural Revolution', in *Scientific American*, 226, April 1972.

SOURDEL, D. and J. *La Civilisation de l'Islam classique*. Paris 1968.

STAMP, L. D. (ed.) *A History of Land Use in Arid Regions*. Arid Zone Research XVII, UNESCO publication, 1961.

STEINKRAUS, K. H. *Handbook of Indigenous Fermented Foods*. New York 1983.

STOBART, T. *Herbs, Spices and Flavourings*. 1970.

STORCK, J. and TEAGUE, W. D. *Flour for Man's Bread: A History of Milling*. St Paul, Minnesota, 1952.

STOUFF, L. *Ravitaillement et alimentation en Provence aux XIVe et XVe siècles*. Paris 1970.

STUYVENBERG, J. H. VAN (ed.) *Margarine. An Economic, Social and Scientific History, 1869–1969*. 1969.

Table et le partage, La: Colloque de l'École du Louvre. Paris 1986. [Exhibition-related symposium papers]

T. DE L. [Terrien de Lacouperie] 'Ketchup, Catchup, Catsup', in the *Babylonian and Oriental Record*, III 12, November 1889; and 'The Etymology of Ketchup' in IV 3, February 1890.

TAILLEVENT [Tirel, Guillaume] *Le Viandier* [c. 1375]. Ed. J. Pichon and G. Vicaire, Paris 1892.

TANAKA, SEN'O *The Tea Ceremony*. Tokyo 1973.

TANNAHILL, R. *Flesh and Blood: A History of the Cannibal Complex*. 1975.

THEOPHRASTUS, *History of Plants*. Ed. A. F. Hort, 2 vols, 1916.

THOMAS, W. J. (ed.) *Man's Role in Changing the Face of the Earth*. Chicago 1956.

UCKO, P. J. and DIMBLEBY, G. W. (eds.) *The Domestication and Exploitation of Plants and Animals*. 1969.

UKERS, W. H. *All about Coffee*. 2nd edn. New York 1935.

VALLENTINE, H. R. *Water in the Service of Man*. pb 1967.

VANDENBROEKE, C. 'Cultivation and Consumption of the Potato in the 17th and 18th century', in *Acta Historica Nederlandica*, 5, 1971.

VAVILOV, N. I. 'Studies on the Origin of Cultivated Plants', in *Bulletin of Applied Botany*, XVI, 2, 1926.

VEEN, J. VAN *Dredge, Drain, Reclaim. The Art of a Nation*. The Hague 1962.

VICAIRE, G. *Bibliographie gastronomique*. Paris 1890.

VICENS VIVES, J. *An Economic History of Spain*. Princeton 1969.

VILLENA, Don ENRIQUE DE *Arte Cisoria* [1423]. Madrid 1967.

VRIES, A. DE *Primitive Man and His Food*. Chicago 1962.

WALFORD, C. *The Famines of the World. Past and Present*. 1879.

WARD, B. and DUBOS, R. *Only One Earth: The Care and Maintenance of a Small Planet*. 1972.

WARNER, R. *Antiquitates Culinariae*. 1791.

WATSON, A. M. *Agricultural Innovation in the Early Islamic World: The Diffusion of Crops and Farming Techniques: 700–1100*. 1984.

WATTEVILLE, H. DE *The British Soldier: His Daily Life from Tudor to Modern Times*. 1954.

WEATHERWAX, P. 'History and Origin of Corn', in *Corn and Corn Improvement*. New York 1955.

WEISS, H. B. *The History of Applejack or Apple Brandy in New Jersey from Colonial Times to the Present*. Trenton NJ 1954.

WHEATON, B. K. *Savouring the Past: The French Kitchen and Table from 1300 to 1789*. 1983.

WHITE, K. D. *Roman Farming*. 1970.

WHITE JR, L. *Medieval Technology and Social Change*. 1962.

WHITEAKER, S. *The Compleat Strawberry*. 1985.

WILLETT, F. 'The Introduction of Maize into West Africa: An Assessment of Recent Evidence', in *Africa*, XXXII, 1962.

WILSON, C. A. *Food and Drink in Britain from the Stone Age to Recent Times*. 1973.

WISEMAN, J. *A History of the British Pig*. 1986.

WOODFORDE, J. *The Strange Story of False Teeth*. 1968.

WOODHAM-SMITH, C. *The Great Hunger, Ireland 1845–49*. 1962.

WRIGHT, L. *Home Fires Burning: The History of Domestic Heating and Cooking*. 1964.

WRIGLEY, G. *Tropical Agriculture*. 1961, rev. edn. 1971.

YOUNGER, W. *Gods, Men, and Wine*. 1966.

YULE, Sir H. [1] Trs. and ed. *Cathay and the Way Thither*. Hakluyt Society Second Series, 33, 37, 38, 41, 1913–16.

[2] With A. C. BURRELL. *Hobson-Jobson: A Glossary of Colloquial Anglo-Indian Words and Phrases, and of Kindred Terms, Etymological, Historical, Geographical and Discursive*. 1886.

ZEUNER, F. E. *A History of Domesticated Animals*. 1963.

INDEX

About the Author

Although she would much have preferred to go to art school, Reay Tannahill attended the University of Glasgow, where she gained an M.A. in history and economics, and a post-graduate diploma in social science. She spent some years as an advertising and publishing executive before turning to full-time historical research and writing.

Her first two books, *Regency England* (1964) and *Paris in the Revolution* (1966), were followed by *The Fine Art of Food* (1968). While she was working on this, she discovered that, although histories of gastronomy abounded, no one had ever attempted a serious overview of food as a catalyst of social and historical development throughout the world and across the ages. The result was *Food in History* (1973), and its success led her American publisher to suggest a companion volume on the second great human imperative. *Sex in History* was published in 1980, and has been translated into nine languages, including Turkish, Japanese and Serbo-Croat.

Since then, Reay Tannahill has written two best-selling historical novels, *A Dark and Distant Shore* (1983) and *The World, the Flesh and the Devil* (Crown, 1987).